50% OFF Online SAT Prep Cour

MW00667286

Dear Customer,

We consider it an honor and a privilege that you chose our SAT Study Guide. As a way of showing our appreciation and to help us better serve you, we are offering **50% off their online SAT Prep Course.** Many SAT courses are needlessly expensive and don't deliver enough value. With their course, you get access to the best SAT prep material, and **you only pay half price**.

Mometrix has structured their online course to perfectly complement your printed study guide. The SAT Prep Course contains **in-depth lessons** that cover all the most important topics, **240+ video reviews** that explain difficult concepts, over **1,250 practice questions** to ensure you feel prepared, and more than **500 digital flashcards**, so you can study while you're on the go.

Online SAT Prep Course

Topics Covered:

- Reading
  - Information and Ideas
  - Denotative vs. Connotative Meaning & Context Clues
  - Rhetoric
- Writing and Language
  - Expression of Ideas
  - Writing an Essay
  - Common Sentence Errors
- Mathematics
  - Foundational Math Concepts
  - Algebra
  - Problem Solving and Data Analysis

Course Features:

- SAT Study Guide
  - Get content that complements our best-selling study guide.
- Full-Length Practice Tests
  - With over 1,250 practice questions, you can test yourself again and again.
- Mobile Friendly
  - If you need to study on the go, the course is easily accessible from your mobile device.
- SAT Flashcards
  - Their course includes a flashcards mode with over 500 content cards for you to study.

To receive this discount, visit their website: mometrix.com/university/sat or simply scan this QR code with your smartphone. At the checkout page, enter the discount code: **TPBSAT50**

SCAN HERE

If you have any questions or concerns, please contact Mometrix at support@mometrix.com.

Sincerely,

Test Prep Books in partnership with Mometrix TEST PREPARATION

FREE Test Taking Tips Video/DVD Offer

To better serve you, we created videos covering test taking tips that we want to give you for FREE. **These videos cover world-class tips that will help you succeed on your test.**

We just ask that you send us feedback about this product. Please let us know what you thought about it—whether good, bad, or indifferent.

To get your **FREE videos**, you can use the QR code below or email freevideos@studyguideteam.com with "Free Videos" in the subject line and the following information in the body of the email:

a. The title of your product

b. Your product rating on a scale of 1-5, with 5 being the highest

c. Your feedback about the product

If you have any questions or concerns, please don't hesitate to contact us at info@studyguideteam.com.

Thank you!

SCAN HERE

SAT Prep Book 2023-2024 with 7 Practice Tests

SAT Study Guide Review for Math, Reading, and Writing on the College Board Exam [8th Edition]

Joshua Rueda

Written and edited by TPB Publishing.

ISBN 13: 9781637753385
ISBN 10: 1637753381

Welcome

Dear Reader,

Welcome to your new Test Prep Books study guide! We are pleased that you chose us to help you prepare for your exam. There are many study options to choose from, and we appreciate you choosing us. Studying can be a daunting task, but we have designed a smart, effective study guide to help prepare you for what lies ahead.

Whether you're a parent helping your child learn and grow, a high school student working hard to get into your dream college, or a nursing student studying for a complex exam, we want to help give you the tools you need to succeed. We hope this study guide gives you the skills and the confidence to thrive, and we can't thank you enough for allowing us to be part of your journey.

In an effort to continue to improve our products, we welcome feedback from our customers. We look forward to hearing from you. Suggestions, success stories, and criticisms can all be communicated by emailing us at info@studyguideteam.com.

Sincerely,
Test Prep Books Team

FREE Videos/DVD OFFER

Doing well on your exam requires both knowing the test content and understanding how to use that knowledge to do well on the test. We offer completely FREE test taking tip videos. **These videos cover world-class tips that you can use to succeed on your test.**

To get your **FREE videos**, you can use the QR code below or email freevideos@studyguideteam.com with "Free Videos" in the subject line and the following information in the body of the email:

a. The title of your product
b. Your product rating on a scale of 1-5, with 5 being the highest
c. Your feedback about the product

If you have any questions or concerns, please don't hesitate to contact us at info@studyguideteam.com.

SCAN HERE

Quick Overview

As you draw closer to taking your exam, effective preparation becomes more and more important. Thankfully, you have this study guide to help you get ready. Use this guide to help keep your studying on track and refer to it often.

This study guide contains several key sections that will help you be successful on your exam. The guide contains tips for what you should do the night before and the day of the test. Also included are test-taking tips. Knowing the right information is not always enough. Many well-prepared test takers struggle with exams. These tips will help equip you to accurately read, assess, and answer test questions.

A large part of the guide is devoted to showing you what content to expect on the exam and to helping you better understand that content. In this guide are practice test questions so that you can see how well you have grasped the content. Then, answer explanations are provided so that you can understand why you missed certain questions.

Don't try to cram the night before you take your exam. This is not a wise strategy for a few reasons. First, your retention of the information will be low. Your time would be better used by reviewing information you already know rather than trying to learn a lot of new information. Second, you will likely become stressed as you try to gain a large amount of knowledge in a short amount of time. Third, you will be depriving yourself of sleep. So be sure to go to bed at a reasonable time the night before. Being well-rested helps you focus and remain calm.

Be sure to eat a substantial breakfast the morning of the exam. If you are taking the exam in the afternoon, be sure to have a good lunch as well. Being hungry is distracting and can make it difficult to focus. You have hopefully spent lots of time preparing for the exam. Don't let an empty stomach get in the way of success!

When travelling to the testing center, leave earlier than needed. That way, you have a buffer in case you experience any delays. This will help you remain calm and will keep you from missing your appointment time at the testing center.

Be sure to pace yourself during the exam. Don't try to rush through the exam. There is no need to risk performing poorly on the exam just so you can leave the testing center early. Allow yourself to use all of the allotted time if needed.

Remain positive while taking the exam even if you feel like you are performing poorly. Thinking about the content you should have mastered will not help you perform better on the exam.

Once the exam is complete, take some time to relax. Even if you feel that you need to take the exam again, you will be well served by some down time before you begin studying again. It's often easier to convince yourself to study if you know that it will come with a reward!

Test-Taking Strategies

1. Predicting the Answer

When you feel confident in your preparation for a multiple-choice test, try predicting the answer before reading the answer choices. This is especially useful on questions that test objective factual knowledge. By predicting the answer before reading the available choices, you eliminate the possibility that you will be distracted or led astray by an incorrect answer choice. You will feel more confident in your selection if you read the question, predict the answer, and then find your prediction among the answer choices. After using this strategy, be sure to still read all of the answer choices carefully and completely. If you feel unprepared, you should not attempt to predict the answers. This would be a waste of time and an opportunity for your mind to wander in the wrong direction.

2. Reading the Whole Question

Too often, test takers scan a multiple-choice question, recognize a few familiar words, and immediately jump to the answer choices. Test authors are aware of this common impatience, and they will sometimes prey upon it. For instance, a test author might subtly turn the question into a negative, or he or she might redirect the focus of the question right at the end. The only way to avoid falling into these traps is to read the entirety of the question carefully before reading the answer choices.

3. Looking for Wrong Answers

Long and complicated multiple-choice questions can be intimidating. One way to simplify a difficult multiple-choice question is to eliminate all of the answer choices that are clearly wrong. In most sets of answers, there will be at least one selection that can be dismissed right away. If the test is administered on paper, the test taker could draw a line through it to indicate that it may be ignored; otherwise, the test taker will have to perform this operation mentally or on scratch paper. In either case, once the obviously incorrect answers have been eliminated, the remaining choices may be considered. Sometimes identifying the clearly wrong answers will give the test taker some information about the correct answer. For instance, if one of the remaining answer choices is a direct opposite of one of the eliminated answer choices, it may well be the correct answer. The opposite of obviously wrong is obviously right! Of course, this is not always the case. Some answers are obviously incorrect simply because they are irrelevant to the question being asked. Still, identifying and eliminating some incorrect answer choices is a good way to simplify a multiple-choice question.

4. Don't Overanalyze

Anxious test takers often overanalyze questions. When you are nervous, your brain will often run wild, causing you to make associations and discover clues that don't actually exist. If you feel that this may be a problem for you, do whatever you can to slow down during the test. Try taking a deep breath or counting to ten. As you read and consider the question, restrict yourself to the particular words used by the author. Avoid thought tangents about what the author *really* meant, or what he or she was *trying* to say. The only things that matter on a multiple-choice test are the words that are actually in the question. You must avoid reading too much into a multiple-choice question, or supposing that the writer meant something other than what he or she wrote.

5. No Need for Panic

It is wise to learn as many strategies as possible before taking a multiple-choice test, but it is likely that you will come across a few questions for which you simply don't know the answer. In this situation, avoid panicking. Because most multiple-choice tests include dozens of questions, the relative value of a single wrong answer is small. As much as possible, you should compartmentalize each question on a multiple-choice test. In other words, you should not allow your feelings about one question to affect your success on the others. When you find a question that you either don't understand or don't know how to answer, just take a deep breath and do your best. Read the entire question slowly and carefully. Try rephrasing the question a couple of different ways. Then, read all of the answer choices carefully. After eliminating obviously wrong answers, make a selection and move on to the next question.

6. Confusing Answer Choices

When working on a difficult multiple-choice question, there may be a tendency to focus on the answer choices that are the easiest to understand. Many people, whether consciously or not, gravitate to the answer choices that require the least concentration, knowledge, and memory. This is a mistake. When you come across an answer choice that is confusing, you should give it extra attention. A question might be confusing because you do not know the subject matter to which it refers. If this is the case, don't eliminate the answer before you have affirmatively settled on another. When you come across an answer choice of this type, set it aside as you look at the remaining choices. If you can confidently assert that one of the other choices is correct, you can leave the confusing answer aside. Otherwise, you will need to take a moment to try to better understand the confusing answer choice. Rephrasing is one way to tease out the sense of a confusing answer choice.

7. Your First Instinct

Many people struggle with multiple-choice tests because they overthink the questions. If you have studied sufficiently for the test, you should be prepared to trust your first instinct once you have carefully and completely read the question and all of the answer choices. There is a great deal of research suggesting that the mind can come to the correct conclusion very quickly once it has obtained all of the relevant information. At times, it may seem to you as if your intuition is working faster even than your reasoning mind. This may in fact be true. The knowledge you obtain while studying may be retrieved from your subconscious before you have a chance to work out the associations that support it. Verify your instinct by working out the reasons that it should be trusted.

8. Key Words

Many test takers struggle with multiple-choice questions because they have poor reading comprehension skills. Quickly reading and understanding a multiple-choice question requires a mixture of skill and experience. To help with this, try jotting down a few key words and phrases on a piece of scrap paper. Doing this concentrates the process of reading and forces the mind to weigh the relative importance of the question's parts. In selecting words and phrases to write down, the test taker thinks about the question more deeply and carefully. This is especially true for multiple-choice questions that are preceded by a long prompt.

9. Subtle Negatives

One of the oldest tricks in the multiple-choice test writer's book is to subtly reverse the meaning of a question with a word like *not* or *except*. If you are not paying attention to each word in the question, you can easily be led astray by this trick. For instance, a common question format is, "Which of the following is...?" Obviously, if the question instead is, "Which of the following is not...?," then the answer will be quite different. Even worse, the test makers are aware of the potential for this mistake and will include one answer choice that would be correct if the question were not negated or reversed. A test taker who misses the reversal will find what he or she believes to be a correct answer and will be so confident that he or she will fail to reread the question and discover the original error. The only way to avoid this is to practice a wide variety of multiple-choice questions and to pay close attention to each and every word.

10. Reading Every Answer Choice

It may seem obvious, but you should always read every one of the answer choices! Too many test takers fall into the habit of scanning the question and assuming that they understand the question because they recognize a few key words. From there, they pick the first answer choice that answers the question they believe they have read. Test takers who read all of the answer choices might discover that one of the latter answer choices is actually *more* correct. Moreover, reading all of the answer choices can remind you of facts related to the question that can help you arrive at the correct answer. Sometimes, a misstatement or incorrect detail in one of the latter answer choices will trigger your memory of the subject and will enable you to find the right answer. Failing to read all of the answer choices is like not reading all of the items on a restaurant menu: you might miss out on the perfect choice.

11. Spot the Hedges

One of the keys to success on multiple-choice tests is paying close attention to every word. This is never truer than with words like *almost*, *most*, *some*, and *sometimes*. These words are called "hedges" because they indicate that a statement is not totally true or not true in every place and time. An absolute statement will contain no hedges, but in many subjects, the answers are not always straightforward or absolute. There are always exceptions to the rules in these subjects. For this reason, you should favor those multiple-choice questions that contain hedging language. The presence of qualifying words indicates that the author is taking special care with his or her words, which is certainly important when composing the right answer. After all, there are many ways to be wrong, but there is only one way to be right! For this reason, it is wise to avoid answers that are absolute when taking a multiple-choice test. An absolute answer is one that says things are either all one way or all another. They often include words like *every*, *always*, *best*, and *never*. If you are taking a multiple-choice test in a subject that doesn't lend itself to absolute answers, be on your guard if you see any of these words.

12. Long Answers

In many subject areas, the answers are not simple. As already mentioned, the right answer often requires hedges. Another common feature of the answers to a complex or subjective question are qualifying clauses, which are groups of words that subtly modify the meaning of the sentence. If the question or answer choice describes a rule to which there are exceptions or the subject matter is complicated, ambiguous, or confusing, the correct answer will require many words in order to be expressed clearly and accurately. In essence, you should not be deterred by answer choices that seem excessively long. Oftentimes, the author of the text will not be able to write the correct answer without offering some qualifications and modifications. Your job is to read the answer choices thoroughly and completely and to select the one that most accurately and precisely answers the question.

13. Restating to Understand

Sometimes, a question on a multiple-choice test is difficult not because of what it asks but because of how it is written. If this is the case, restate the question or answer choice in different words. This process serves a couple of important purposes. First, it forces you to concentrate on the core of the question. In order to rephrase the question accurately, you have to understand it well. Rephrasing the question will concentrate your mind on the key words and ideas. Second, it will present the information to your mind in a fresh way. This process may trigger your memory and render some useful scrap of information picked up while studying.

14. True Statements

Sometimes an answer choice will be true in itself, but it does not answer the question. This is one of the main reasons why it is essential to read the question carefully and completely before proceeding to the answer choices. Too often, test takers skip ahead to the answer choices and look for true statements. Having found one of these, they are content to select it without reference to the question above. The savvy test taker will always read the entire question before turning to the answer choices. Then, having settled on a correct answer choice, he or she will refer to the original question and ensure that the selected answer is relevant. The mistake of choosing a correct-but-irrelevant answer choice is especially common on questions related to specific pieces of objective knowledge.

15. No Patterns

One of the more dangerous ideas that circulates about multiple-choice tests is that the correct answers tend to fall into patterns. These erroneous ideas range from a belief that B and C are the most common right answers, to the idea that an unprepared test-taker should answer "A-B-A-C-A-D-A-B-A." It cannot be emphasized enough that pattern-seeking of this type is exactly the WRONG way to approach a multiple-choice test. To begin with, it is highly unlikely that the test maker will plot the correct answers according to some predetermined pattern. The questions are scrambled and delivered in a random order. Furthermore, even if the test maker was following a pattern in the assignation of correct answers, there is no reason why the test taker would know which pattern he or she was using. Any attempt to discern a pattern in the answer choices is a waste of time and a distraction from the real work of taking the test. A test taker would be much better served by extra preparation before the test than by reliance on a pattern in the answers.

Bonus Content

We host multiple bonus items online, including all seven practice tests in digital format. Scan the QR code or go to this link to access this content:

testprepbooks.com/bonus/sat

SCAN ME

The first time you access the tests, you will need to register as a "new user" and verify your email address.

If you have any issues, please email support@testprepbooks.com.

Introduction to the SAT

Function of the Test

The SAT is a standardized test taken by high school students across the United States and given internationally for college placement. It is designed to measure problem solving ability, communication, and understanding complex relationships. The SAT also serves as a qualifying measure to identify students for college scholarships, depending on the college being applied to. All colleges in the U.S. accept the SAT, and, in addition to admissions and scholarships, use SAT scores for course placement as well as academic counseling.

Most of the high school students who take the SAT are seniors. In 2016, the number of students who took the SAT was just under 1.7 million. It's important to note that since many updates have been implemented during the 2016 year, the data points cannot be compared to those in previous years. In 2014, 42.6 percent of students met the College Board's "college and career readiness" benchmark, and in 2015, 41.9 percent met this benchmark.

Test Administration

The SAT is offered on seven days throughout the year at schools throughout the United States. Internationally, the SAT is offered on five days throughout the year. There are thousands of testing centers worldwide. Test-takers can view the test centers in their area when they register for the test, or they can view testing locations at the College Board website, a not-for-profit that owns and publishes the SAT.

The SAT registration fee is $46, and the SAT with Essay registration fee is $60, although both of these have fee waivers available. Also note that students outside the U.S. may have to pay an extra processing fee. Additional fees include registering by phone, changing fee, late registration fee, or a waitlist fee. Test-takers may register four score reports for free up to nine days after the test. Any additional score reports cost $12, although fee waivers are available for this as well.

Test Format

The SAT gauges a student's proficiency in three areas: Reading, Mathematics, and Writing and Language. The reading portion of the SAT measures comprehension, requiring candidates to read multi-paragraph fiction and non-fiction segments including informational visuals, such as charts, tables and graphs, and answer questions based on this content. Fluency in problem solving, conceptual understanding of equations, and real-world applications are characteristics of the math test. The writing and language portion requires students to evaluate and edit writing and graphics to obtain an answer that correctly conveys the information given in the passage.

The SAT contains 154 multiple-choice questions, with each section comprising over 40 questions. A different length of time is given for each section, for a total of three hours, plus fifty minutes for the essay (optional).

Section	**Time (In Minutes)**	**Number of Questions**
Reading	65	52
Writing and Language	35	44
Mathematics	80	58
Essay (optional)	50 (optional)	1 (optional)
Total	**180**	**154 + optional essay**

Scoring

Scores for the new SAT are based on a scale from 400 to 1600. Scores range from 200 to 800 for Evidence-Based Reading and Writing, and 200 to 800 for Math. The optional essay is scored from 2 to 8. The SAT also no longer penalizes for incorrect answers. Therefore, a student's raw score is the number of correctly answered questions.

On the College Board website, there are indicators to determine what the benchmark scores are. The scores are divided up into green, yellow, or red. Green meets or exceeds the benchmark, and shows a 480 to 800 in Evidence-Based Reading and Writing, and a 530 to 800 in Math.

Recent/Future Developments

Starting June 2021, the optional SAT essay will be discontinued in most states. In schools where the students take the SAT as part of SAT School Day administrations, the optional SAT may still be available, but students should check with their school first. For students who take the SAT on a Saturday, the optional essay will not be available.

Study Prep Plan for the SAT

1 **Schedule** - Use one of our study schedules below or come up with one of your own.

2 **Relax** - Test anxiety can hurt even the best students. There are many ways to reduce stress. Find the one that works best for you.

3 **Execute** - Once you have a good plan in place, be sure to stick to it.

One Week Study Schedule

Day 1	Reading
Day 2	Writing and Language
Day 3	Mathematics
Day 4	Additional Topics in Math
Day 5	SAT Practice Tests #1, #2, & #3
Day 6	SAT Practice Tests #4, #5, #6, & #7
Day 7	Take Your Exam!

Two Week Study Schedule

Day 1	Reading	Day 8	SAT Practice Test #2
Day 2	Writing and Language	Day 9	SAT Practice Test #3
Day 3	Capitalization Rules	Day 10	SAT Practice Test #4
Day 4	Problem Solving and Data Analysis	Day 11	SAT Practice Test #5
Day 5	Passport to Advanced Math	Day 12	SAT Practice Test #6
Day 6	Additional Topics in Math	Day 13	SAT Practice Test #7
Day 7	SAT Practice Test #1	Day 14	Take Your Exam!

One Month Study Schedule

Day 1	Reading	Day 11	Creating Equivalent Forms of Expressions	Day 21	Answer Explanations #3
Day 2	Words in Context	Day 12	Rewriting Simple Rational Expressions	Day 22	SAT Practice Test #4
Day 3	Interpreting Data and Considering Implications	Day 13	Additional Topics in Math	Day 23	Answer Explanations #4
Day 4	Writing and Language	Day 14	Congruence and Similarity	Day 24	SAT Practice Test #5
Day 5	Standard English Conventions	Day 15	Essay	Day 25	Answer Explanations #5
Day 6	Capitalization Rules	Day 16	SAT Practice Test #1	Day 26	SAT Practice Test #6
Day 7	Sentence Fragments	Day 17	Answer Explanations #1	Day 27	Answer Explanations #6
Day 8	Mathematics	Day 18	SAT Practice Test #2	Day 28	SAT Practice Test #7
Day 9	Problem Solving and Data Analysis	Day 19	Answer Explanations #2	Day 29	Answer Explanations #7
Day 10	Comparing Linear and Exponential Growth	Day 20	SAT Practice Test #3	Day 30	Take Your Exam!

Build your own prep plan by visiting:
testprepbooks.com/prep

Math Reference Sheet

Symbol	Phrase
+	added to, increased by, sum of, more than
-	decreased by, difference between, less than, take away
×	multiplied by, 3 (4, 5 . . .) times as large, product of
÷	divided by, quotient of, half (third, etc.) of
=	is, the same as, results in, as much as
x, t, n, etc.	a variable which is an unknown value or quantity
<	is under, is below, smaller than, beneath
>	is above, is over, bigger than, exceeds
≤	no more than, at most, maximum; less than or equal to
≥	no less than, at least, minimum; greater than or equal to
√	square root of, exponent divided by 2

Geometry	Description
$P = 2l + 2w$	for perimeter of a rectangle
$P = 4 \times s$	for perimeter of a square
$P = a + b + c$	for perimeter of a triangle
$A = \frac{1}{2} \times b \times h = \frac{bh}{2}$	for area of a triangle
$A = b \times h$	for area of a parallelogram
$A = \frac{1}{2} \times h(b_1 + b_2)$	for area of a trapezoid
$A = \frac{1}{2} \times a \times P$	for area of a regular polygon
$C = 2 \times \pi \times r$	for circumference (perimeter) of a circle
$A = \pi \times r^2$	for area of a circle
$c^2 = a^2 + b^2; c = \sqrt{a^2 + b^2}$	for finding the hypotenuse of a right triangle
$SA = 2xy + 2yz + 2xz$	for finding surface area
$V = \frac{1}{3}xyh$	for finding volume of a rectangular pyramid
$V = \frac{4}{3}\pi r^3;\ \frac{1}{3}\pi r^2 h;\ \pi r^2 h$	for volume of a sphere; a cone; and a cylinder

Radical Expressions	Description
$\sqrt[n]{a} = a^{\frac{1}{n}}; \sqrt[n]{a^m} = (\sqrt[n]{a})^m = a^{\frac{m}{n}}$	a is the radicand, n is the index, m is the exponent
$\sqrt{x^2} = (x^2)^{\frac{1}{2}} = x$	to convert square root to exponent
$a^m \times a^n = a^{m+n}$	multiplying radicands with exponents
$(a^m)^n = a^{m \times n}$	multiplying exponents
$(a \times b)^m = a^m \times b^m$	parentheses with exponents

Property	Addition	Multiplication
Commutative	$a + b = b + a$	$a \times b = b \times a$
Associative	$(a + b) + c = a + (b + c)$	$(a \times b) \times c = a \times (b \times c)$
Identity	$a + 0 = a;\ 0 + a = a$	$a \times 1 = a;\ 1 \times a = a$
Inverse	$a + (-a) = 0$	$a \times \frac{1}{a} = 1;\ a \neq 0$
Distributive	$a(b + c) = ab + ac$	

Data	Description
Mean	equal to the total of the values of a data set, divided by the number of elements in the data set
Median	middle value in an odd number of ordered values of a data set, or the mean of the two middle values in an even number of ordered values in a data set
Mode	the value that appears most often
Range	the difference between the highest and the lowest values in the set

Graphing	Description
(x, y)	ordered pair, plot points in a graph
$y = mx + b$	slope-intercept form; m represents the slope of the line and b represents the y-intercept
$f(x)$	read as f of x, which means it is a function of x
(x_2, y_2) and (x_2, y_2)	two ordered pairs used to determine the slope of a line
$m = \frac{y_2 - y_1}{x_2 - x_1}$	to find the slope of the line, m, for ordered pairs
$Ax + By = C$	standard form of an equation, also for solving a system of equations through the elimination method
$M = (\frac{x_1 + x_2}{2}, \frac{y_1 + y_2}{2})$	for finding the midpoint of an ordered pair
$y = ax^2 + bx + c$	quadratic function for a parabola
$y = a(x - h)^2 + k$	quadratic function for a parabola with vertex
$y = ab^x; y = a \times b^x$	function for exponential curve
$y = ax^2 + bx + c$	standard form of a quadratic function
$x = \frac{-b}{2a}$	for finding axis of symmetry in a parabola; given quadratic formula in standard form
$f = \sqrt{\frac{\Sigma(x - \bar{x})^2}{n - 1}}$	function for standard deviation of the sample; where $\bar{x}$ = sample mean and n = sample size

Proportions and Percentage	Description
$\frac{\text{gallons}}{\text{cost}} = \frac{\text{gallons}}{\text{cost}} : \frac{7 \text{ gallons}}{\$14.70} = \frac{x}{\$20}$	written as equal ratios with a variable representing the missing quantity
$\frac{y_1}{x_1} = \frac{y_2}{x_2}$	for direct proportions
$(y_1)(x_1) = (y_2)(x_2)$	for indirect proportions
$\frac{\text{change}}{\text{original value}} \times 100 = \text{percent change}$	for finding percentage change in value
$\frac{\text{new quantity} - \text{old quantity}}{\text{old quantity}} \times 100$	for calculating the increase or decrease in percentage

Reading

The Reading section of the SAT measures test takers' ability to read, understand, and interpret the types of texts they will encounter in higher education and their vocational pursuits. The passages included in this section are drawn from previously-published literary or informational texts. Some passages include graphics such as charts, graphs, and tables, which the test taker must interpret alongside the written text to correctly answer the questions. Other questions will follow two passages that are purposely paired for the test taker to compare and contrast.

The Reading section contains 52 questions, which must be answered in the allotted 65 minutes. The majority of the passages in this section are pulled from informational or nonfiction works, covering topics pertaining to history, humanities, science, and social studies. At least one single passage or a pair of passages to be considered together will be drawn from the seminal founding U.S. documents or the *Great Global Conversation,* which is an umbrella term used to describe works from countries around the world and spanning several centuries that address universal topics like justice, freedom, and human dignity. Test takers will encounter only one literary passage in the Reading Section. This except is drawn from an American or international fictional piece, such as a published novel or short story.

In addition to encountering a variety of topics in the passages, test takers will need to employ their comprehension skills pertaining to understanding texts written for different purposes. Some texts may tell a story or describe a process. Others will present an argument and support for an opinion, while still other passages may delineate the purpose of a study or experiment. The text complexity or reading level of each passage also varies; passages may span the gamut from a ninth-grade reading level to that expected of a first-year university student or post-secondary scholar.

Questions on the Reading section will generally fall into one of three principal categories: information and ideas, rhetoric, and synthesis. As the name implies, **information and ideas** questions focus on the direct or indirect ideas or facts that the passage presents. The answers to some of these questions will not necessarily be explicitly revealed in the passage; rather, test takers must use their inferential skills to uncover the author's implied meaning. **Rhetoric** questions require test takers to consider the method or manner in which the author conveys their intended message. Lastly, **synthesis** questions ask test takers to draw conclusions from a passage or make connections between a pair of passages or between passages and an accompanying graphic.

While the vast majority of questions in the Reading section address the test taker's ability to understand written language and ideas in each passage, a small number of questions will also assess the test taker's ability to interpret graph, tables, and charts. For this reason, in addition to studying reading comprehension techniques and honing skills related to synthesis and inference, test takers should practice reading and interpreting tables, graphs, and charts. Test takers should review the material in this section pertaining to critical reading skills and refer to the information in the Writing and Language section about specific comprehension skills pertinent to history and the sciences texts, as well as graphic-interpreting techniques.

Command of Evidence

Command of evidence, or the ability to use contextual clues, factual statements, and corroborative phrases to support an author's message or intent, is an important part of the Reading section of the SAT.

A test taker's ability to parse out factual information and draw conclusions based on evidence is important to critical reading comprehension. The test will ask students to read text passages, and then answer questions based on information contained in them. These types of questions may ask test takers to identify stated facts. They may also require test takers to draw logical conclusions, identify data based on graphs, make inferences, and to generally display analytical thinking skills.

Finding Evidence in a Passage

The basic tenet of reading comprehension is the ability to read and understand a text. One way to understand a text is to look for information that supports the author's main idea, topic, or position statement. This information may be factual, or it may be based on the author's opinion. This section will focus on the test taker's ability to identify factual information, as opposed to opinionated bias. The Reading section will ask test takers to read passages containing factual information, and then logically relate those passages by drawing conclusions based on evidence.

In order to identify factual information within a text passage, test takers should begin by looking for statements of fact. **Factual statements** can be either true or false. Identifying factual statements as opposed to opinion statements is important in demonstrating full command of evidence in reading. For example, the statement *The temperature outside was unbearably hot* may seem like a fact; however, it's not. While anyone can point to a temperature gauge as factual evidence, the statement itself reflects only an opinion. Some people may find the temperature unbearably hot. Others may find it comfortably warm. Thus, the sentence, *The temperature outside was unbearably hot,* reflects the opinion of the author who found it unbearable. If the text passage followed up the sentence with atmospheric conditions indicating heat indices above 140 degrees Fahrenheit, then the reader knows there is factual information that supports the author's assertion of *unbearably hot*.

In looking for information that can be proven or disproven, it's helpful to scan for dates, numbers, timelines, equations, statistics, and other similar data within any given text passage. These types of indicators will point to proven particulars. For example, the statement, *The temperature outside was unbearably hot on that summer day, July 10, 1913,* most likely indicates factual information, even if the reader is unaware that this is the hottest day on record in the United States. Be careful when reading biased words from an author. Biased words indicate opinion, as opposed to fact. The following list contains a sampling of common biased words:

Remember, most of what is written is actually opinion or carefully worded information that seems like fact when it isn't. To say, *duplicating DNA results is not cost-effective* sounds like it could be a scientific fact, but it isn't. Factual information can be verified through independent sources.

The simplest type of test question may provide a text passage, then ask the test taker to distinguish the correct factual supporting statement that best answers the corresponding question on the test. However, be aware that most questions may ask the test taker to read more than one text passage and identify which answer best supports an author's topic. While the ability to identify factual information is critical, these types of questions require the test taker to identify chunks of details, and then relate them to one another.

Displaying Analytical Thinking Skills

Analytical thinking involves being able to break down visual information into manageable portions in order to solve complex problems or process difficult concepts. This skill encompasses all aspects of command of evidence in reading comprehension.

A reader can approach analytical thinking in a series of steps. First, when approaching visual material, a reader should identify an author's thought process. Is the line of reasoning clear from the presented passage, or does it require inference and coming to a conclusion independent of the author? Next, a reader should evaluate the author's line of reasoning to determine if the logic is sound. Look for evidentiary clues and cited sources. Do these hold up under the author's argument? Third, look for bias. Bias includes generalized, emotional statements that will not hold up under scrutiny, as they are not based on fact. From there, a reader should ask if the presented evidence is trustworthy. Are the facts cited from reliable sources? Are they current? Is there any new factual information that has come to light since the passage was written that renders the argument useless? Next, a reader should carefully think about information that opposes the author's view. Do the author's arguments guide the reader to identical thoughts, or is there room for sound arguments? Finally, a reader should always be able to identify an author's conclusion and be able to weigh its effectiveness.

The ability to display analytical thinking skills while reading is key in any standardized testing situation. Test takers should be able to critically evaluate the information provided, and then answer questions related to content by using the steps above.

Making Inferences

Simply put, an **inference** is an educated guess drawn from evidence, logic, and reasoning. The key to making inferences is identifying clues within a passage, and then using common sense to arrive at a reasonable conclusion. Consider it "reading between the lines."

One way to make an inference is to look for main topics. When doing so, pay particular attention to any titles, headlines, or opening statements made by the author. Topic sentences or repetitive ideas can be clues in gleaning inferred ideas. For example, if a passage contains the phrase *While some consider DNA testing to be infallible, it is an inherently flawed technique,* the test taker can infer the rest of the passage will contain information that points to problems with DNA testing.

The test taker may be asked to make an inference based on prior knowledge but may also be asked to make predictions based on new ideas. For example, the test taker may have no prior knowledge of DNA other than its genetic property to replicate. However, if the reader is given passages on the flaws of DNA testing with enough factual evidence, the test taker may arrive at the inferred conclusion that the author does not support the infallibility of DNA testing in all identification cases.

When making inferences, it is important to remember that the critical thinking process involved must be fluid and open to change. While a reader may infer an idea from a main topic, general statement, or other clues, they must be open to receiving new information within a particular passage. New ideas presented by an author may require the test taker to alter an inference. Similarly, when asked questions that require making an inference, it's important to read the entire test passage and all of the answer options. Often, a test taker will need to refine a general inference based on new ideas that may be presented within the test itself.

Author's Use of Evidence to Support Claims

Authors utilize a wide range of techniques to tell a story or communicate information. Readers should be familiar with the most common of these techniques. Techniques of writing are also commonly known as rhetorical devices, and they are some of the evidence that authors use to support claims.

In nonfiction writing, authors employ argumentative techniques to present their opinion to readers in the most convincing way. Persuasive writing usually includes at least one type of appeal: an appeal to logic (**logos**), emotion (**pathos**), or credibility and trustworthiness (**ethos**). When a writer appeals to logic, they are asking readers to agree with them based on research, evidence, and an established line of reasoning. An author's argument might also appeal to readers' emotions, perhaps by including personal stories and **anecdotes** (a short narrative of a specific event). A final type of appeal, appeal to authority, asks the reader to agree with the author's argument on the basis of their expertise or credentials. Consider three different approaches to arguing the same opinion:

Logic (Logos)

Below is an example of an appeal to logic. The author uses evidence to disprove the logic of the school's rule (the rule was supposed to reduce discipline problems, but the number of problems has not been reduced; therefore, the rule is not working) and call for its repeal.

> Our school should abolish its current ban on cell phone use on campus. This rule was adopted last year as an attempt to reduce class disruptions and help students focus more on their lessons. However, since the rule was enacted, there has been no change in the number of disciplinary problems in class. Therefore, the rule is ineffective and should be done away with.

Emotion (Pathos)

An author's argument might also appeal to readers' emotions, perhaps by including personal stories and anecdotes.

The next example presents an appeal to emotion. By sharing the personal anecdote of one student and speaking about emotional topics like family relationships, the author invokes the reader's empathy in asking them to reconsider the school rule.

> Our school should abolish its current ban on cell phone use on campus. If they aren't able to use their phones during the school day, many students feel isolated from their loved ones. For example, last semester, one student's grandmother had a heart attack in the morning. However, because he couldn't use his cell phone, the student didn't know about his grandmother's accident until the end of the day—when she had already passed away, and it was too late to say goodbye. By preventing students from contacting their friends and family, our school is placing undue stress and anxiety on students.

All three examples begin from the same opinion—the school's phone ban needs to change—but rely on different argumentative styles to persuade the reader.

Credibility (Ethos)

Finally, an appeal to authority includes a statement from a relevant expert. In this case, the author uses a doctor in the field of education to support the argument.

> Our school should abolish its current ban on cell phone use on campus. According to Dr. Bartholomew Everett, a leading educational expert, "Research studies show that cell phone usage has no real impact on student attentiveness. Rather, phones provide a valuable technological resource for learning. Schools need to learn how to integrate this new technology into their curriculum." Rather than banning phones altogether, our school should follow the advice of experts and allow students to use phones as part of their learning.

Informational Graphics

A test taker's ability to draw conclusions from an informational graphic is a sub-skill in displaying one's command of reading evidence. Drawing **conclusions** requires the reader to consider all information provided in the passage, then to use logic to piece it together to form a reasonably correct resolution. In this case, a test taker must look for facts as well as opinionated statements. Both should be considered in order to arrive at a conclusion. These types of questions test one's ability to conduct logical and analytical thinking.

Identifying data-driven evidence in informational graphics is very similar to analyzing factual information. However, it often involves the use of graphics in order to do so. In these types of questions, the test taker will be presented with a graph, or organizational tool, and asked questions regarding the information it contains. On the following page, review the pie chart organizing percentages of primary occupations of public transportation passengers in US cities.

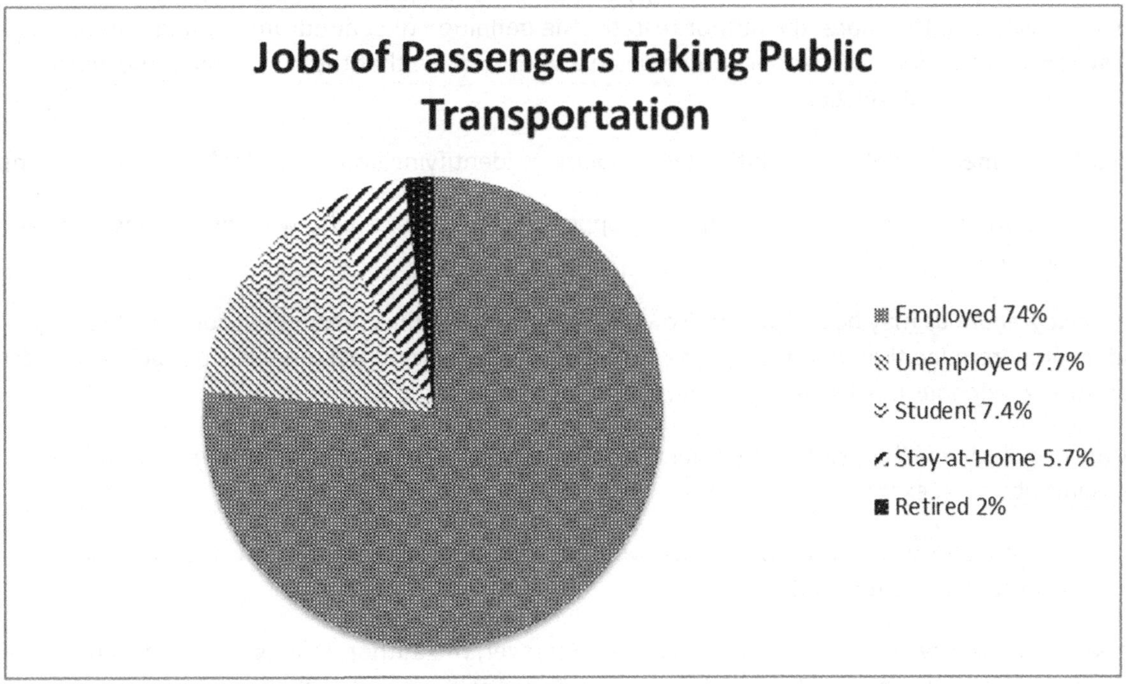

This figure depicts the jobs of passengers taking public transportation in U.S. cities. A corresponding SAT question may have the test taker study the chart, then answer a question regarding the values. For example, is the number of students relying on public transportation greater or less than the number of the unemployed? Similarly, the test may ask if people employed outside the home are less likely to use public transportation than homemakers. Note that the phrase *less likely* may weigh into the reader's choice of optional answers and that the test taker should look for additional passage data to arrive at a conclusion one way or another.

Words in Context

In order to successfully complete the Reading section of the SAT, the test taker should be able to identify the meaning of words in context. This involves a set of skills that requires the test taker to answer questions about unfamiliar words within a particular text passage. Additionally, the test taker may be asked to answer critical thinking questions based on unfamiliar word meanings. Identifying the meaning of different words in context is very much like solving a puzzle. By using a variety of techniques, a test taker should be able to correctly identify the meaning of unfamiliar words and concepts with ease.

Using Context Clues

A context clue is a hint that an author provides to the reader in order to help define difficult or unique words. When reading a passage, a test taker should take note of any unfamiliar words, and then examine the sentence around them to look for clues to the word meanings. Let's look at an example:

> He faced a *conundrum* in making this decision. He felt as if he had come to a crossroads. This was truly a puzzle, and what he did next would determine the course of his future.

The word *conundrum* may be unfamiliar to the reader. By looking at context clues, the reader should be able to determine its meaning. In this passage, context clues include the idea of making a decision and of being unsure. Furthermore, the author restates the definition of conundrum in using the word *puzzle* as a synonym. Therefore, the reader should be able to determine that the definition of the word *conundrum* is a difficult puzzle.

Similarly, a reader can determine difficult vocabulary by identifying antonyms. Let's look at an example:

> Her *gregarious* nature was completely opposite of her twin's, who was shy, retiring, and socially nervous.

The word *gregarious* may be unfamiliar. However, by looking at the surrounding context clues, the reader can determine that *gregarious* does not mean shy. The twins' personalities are being contrasted. Therefore, *gregarious* must mean sociable, or something similar to it.

At times, an author will provide contextual clues through a cause and effect relationship. Look at the next sentence as an example:

> The athletes were *elated* when they won the tournament; unfortunately, their off-court antics caused them to forfeit the win.

The word *elated* may be unfamiliar to the reader. However, the author defines the word by presenting a cause and effect relationship. The athletes were so elated at the win that their behavior went overboard, and they had to forfeit. In this instance, *elated* must mean something akin to overjoyed, happy, and overexcited.

Cause and effect is one technique authors use to demonstrate relationships. A **cause** is why something happens. The **effect** is what happens as a result. For example, a reader may encounter text such as *Because he was unable to sleep, he was often restless and irritable during the day.* The cause is insomnia due to lack of sleep. The effect is being restless and irritable. When reading for a cause and effect relationship, look for words such as "if", "then", "such", and "because." By using cause and effect, an author can describe direct relationships, and convey an overall theme, particularly when taking a stance on their topic.

An author can also provide contextual clues through **comparison and contrast**. Let's look at an example:

> Her torpid state caused her parents, and her physician, to worry about her seemingly sluggish well-being.

The word *torpid* is probably unfamiliar to the reader. However, the author has compared *torpid* to a state of being and, moreover, one that's worrisome. Therefore, the reader should be able to determine that *torpid* is not a positive, healthy state of being. In fact, through the use of comparison, it means sluggish. Similarly, an author may contrast an unfamiliar word with an idea. In the sentence *Her torpid state was completely opposite of her usual, bubbly self,* the meaning of *torpid*, or sluggish, is contrasted with the words *bubbly self.*

A test taker should be able to critically assess and determine unfamiliar word meanings through the use of an author's context clues in order to fully comprehend difficult text passages.

Relating Unfamiliar Words to Familiar Words

The Reading section of the SAT will test a reader's ability to use context clues, and then relate unfamiliar words to more familiar ones. Using the word *torpid* as an example, the test may ask the test taker to relate the meaning of the word to a list of vocabulary options and choose the more familiar word as closest in meaning. In this case, the test may say something like the following:

> Which of the following words means the same as the word *torpid* in the above passage?

Then they will provide the test taker with a list of familiar options such as happy, disgruntled, sluggish, and animated. By using context clues, the reader has already determined the meaning of *torpid* as slow or sluggish, so the reader should be able to correctly identify the word *sluggish* as the correct answer.

One effective way to relate unfamiliar word meanings to more familiar ones is to substitute the provided word in each answer option for the unfamiliar word in question. Although this will not always lead to a correct answer every time, this strategy will help the test taker narrow answer options. Be careful when utilizing this strategy. Pay close attention to the meaning of sentences and answer choices because it's easy to mistake answer choices as correct when they are easily substituted, especially when they are the same part of speech. Does the sentence mean the same thing with the substituted word option in place or does it change entirely? Does the substituted word make sense? Does it possibly mean the same as the unfamiliar word in question?

How an Author's Word Choice Shapes Meaning, Style, and Tone

Authors choose their words carefully in order to artfully depict meaning, style, and tone, which is most commonly inferred through the use of adjectives and verbs. The **tone** is the predominant emotion present in the text, and represents the attitude or feelings that an author has towards a character or event.

To review, an **adjective** is a word used to describe something, and usually precedes the noun, a person, place, or object. A **verb** is a word describing an action. For example, the sentence "The scary woodpecker ate the spider" includes the adjective "scary," the noun "woodpecker," and the verb "ate." Reading this sentence may rouse some negative feelings, as the word "scary" carries a negative charge. The **charge** is the emotional connotation that can be derived from the adjectives and verbs and is either positive or negative. Recognizing the charge of a particular sentence or passage is an effective way to understand the meaning and tone the author is trying to convey.

Many authors have conflicting charges within the same text, but a definitive tone can be inferred by understanding the meaning of the charges relative to each other. It's important to recognize key conjunctions, or words that link sentences or clauses together. There are several types and subtypes of conjunctions. Three are most important for reading comprehension:

1. **Cumulative conjunctions** add one statement to another.
   Examples: and, both, also, as well as, not only
   e.g. The juice is sweet *and* sour.
2. **Adversative conjunctions** are used to contrast two clauses.
   Examples: but, while, still, yet, nevertheless
   e.g. She was tired, *but* she was happy.
3. **Alternative conjunctions** express two alternatives.
   Examples: or, either, neither, nor, else, otherwise
   e.g. He must eat, *or* he will die.

Identifying the meaning and tone of a text can be accomplished with the following steps:

- Identify the adjectives and verbs.
- Recognize any important conjunctions.
- Label the adjectives and verbs as positive or negative.
- Understand what the charge means about the text.

To demonstrate these steps, examine the following passage from the classic children's poem, "The Sheep":

> Lazy sheep, pray tell me why
>
> In the pleasant fields you lie,
>
> Eating grass, and daisies white,
>
> From the morning till the night?
>
> Everything can something do,
>
> But what kind of use are you?

–Taylor, Jane and Ann. "The Sheep."

This selection is a good example of conflicting charges that work together to express an overall tone. Following the first two steps, identify the adjectives, verbs, and conjunctions within the passage. For this example, the adjectives are underlined, the verbs are in **bold**, and the conjunctions *italicized*:

> Lazy sheep, pray **tell** me why
>
> In the pleasant fields you **lie**,
>
> **Eating** grass, and daisies white,
>
> From the morning till the night?
>
> Everything can something do,
>
> *But* what kind of use are you?

For step three, read the passage and judge whether feelings of positivity or negativity arose. Then assign a charge to each of the words that were outlined. This can be done in a table format, or simply by writing a + or – next to the word.

The word lazy carries a negative connotation; it usually denotes somebody unwilling to work. To **tell** someone something has an exclusively neutral connotation, as it depends on what's being told, which has not yet been revealed at this point, so a charge can be assigned later. The word pleasant is an inherently positive word. To **lie** could be positive or negative depending on the context, but as the subject (the sheep) is lying in a pleasant field, then this is a positive experience. **Eating** is also generally positive.

After labeling the charges for each word, it might be inferred that the tone of this poem is happy and maybe even admiring or innocuously envious. However, notice the adversative conjunction, "but" and what follows. The author has listed all the pleasant things this sheep gets to do all day, but the tone changes when the author asks, "What kind of use are you?" Asking someone to prove their value is a rather hurtful thing to do, as it implies that the person asking the question doesn't believe the subject has any value, so this could be listed under negative charges. Referring back to the verb **tell**, after reading the whole passage, it can be deduced that the author is asking the sheep to tell what use the sheep is, so this has a negative charge.

+	–
Pleasant • Lie in fields • From morning to night	• Lazy • Tell me • What kind of use are you

Upon examining the charges, it might seem like there's an even amount of positive and negative emotion in this selection, and that's where the conjunction "but" becomes crucial to identifying the tone. The conjunction "but" indicates there's a contrasting view to the pleasantness of the sheep's daily life, and this view is that the sheep is lazy and useless, which is also indicated by the first line, "lazy sheep, pray tell me why."

It might be helpful to look at questions pertaining to tone. For this selection, consider the following question:

The author of the poem regards the sheep with a feeling of what?
a. Respect
b. Disgust
c. Apprehension
d. Intrigue

Considering the author views the sheep as lazy with nothing to offer, Choice *A* appears to reflect the opposite of what the author is feeling.

Choice *B* seems to mirror the author's feelings towards the sheep, as laziness is considered a disreputable trait, and people (or personified animals, in this case) with unfavorable traits might be viewed with disgust.

Choice *C* doesn't make sense within context, as laziness isn't usually feared.

Choice *D* is tricky, as it may be tempting to argue that the author is intrigued with the sheep because they ask, "pray tell me why." This is another out-of-scope answer choice as it doesn't *quite* describe the feelings the author experiences and there's also a much better fit in Choice *B*.

Analysis in History/Social Studies and in Science

The Reading section of the SAT will include one passage from social sciences such as history, economics, psychology, or sociology. For these types of passages and questions, the test taker will need to utilize all their reading comprehension skills, but mastery of further skills will help. This section addresses those skills.

Comprehending Test Questions Prior to Reading

While preparing for a historical passage on a standardized test, first read the test questions, and then quickly scan the test answers prior to reading the passage itself. Notice there is a difference between the terms **read** and **scan**. **Reading** involves full concentration while addressing every word. **Scanning** involves quickly glancing at text in chunks, noting important dates, words, and ideas along the way. Reading the test questions will help the test taker know what information to focus on in the historical passage. Scanning answers will help the test taker focus on possible answer options while reading the passage.

When reading standardized test questions that address historical passages, be sure to clearly understand what each question is asking. Is a question asking about vocabulary? Is another asking for the test taker to find a specific historical fact? Do any of the questions require the test taker to draw conclusions, identify an author's topic, tone, or position? Knowing what content to address will help the test taker focus on the information they will be asked about later. However, the test taker should approach this reading comprehension technique with some caution. It is tempting to only look for the right answers within any given passage. However, do not put on "reading blinders" and ignore all other information presented in a passage. It is important to fully read every passage and not just scan it. Strictly looking for what may be the right answers to test questions can cause the test taker to ignore important contextual clues that actually require critical thinking in order to identify correct answers. Scanning a passage for what appears to be wrong answers can have a similar result.

When reading the test questions prior to tackling a historical passage, be sure to understand what skills the test is assessing, and then fully read the related passage with those skills in mind. Focus on every word in both the test questions and the passage itself. Read with a critical eye and a logical mind.

Reading for Factual Information

Standardized test questions that ask for factual information are usually straightforward. These types of questions will either ask the test taker to confirm a fact by choosing a correct answer, or to select a correct answer based on a negative fact question.

For example, the test taker may encounter a passage from Lincoln's Gettysburg Address. A corresponding test question may ask the following:

> Which war is Abraham Lincoln referring to in the following sentence?
>
> > Now we are engaged in a great civil war, testing whether that nation, or any nation so conceived and so dedicated, can long endure.

This type of question is asking the test taker to confirm a simple fact. Given options such as World War I, the War of Spanish Succession, World War II, and the American Civil War, the test taker should be able to correctly identify the American Civil War based on the words "civil war" within the passage itself, and, hopefully, through general knowledge. In this case, reading the test question and scanning answer options ahead of reading the Gettysburg Address would help quickly identify the correct answer. Similarly, a test taker may be asked to confirm a historical fact based on a negative fact question. For example, a passage's corresponding test question may ask the following:

> Which option is incorrect based on the above passage?

Given a variety of choices speaking about which war Abraham Lincoln was addressing, the test taker would need to eliminate all correct answers pertaining to the American Civil War and choose the answer choice referencing a different war. In other words, the correct answer is the one that contradicts the information in the passage.

It is important to remember that reading for factual information is straightforward. The test taker must distinguish fact from bias. **Factual statements** can be proven or disproven independent of the author and from a variety of other sources. Remember, successfully answering questions regarding factual information may require the test taker to re-read the passage, as these types of questions test for attention to detail.

Reading for Tone, Message, and Effect

The SAT does not just address a test taker's ability to find facts within a historical reading passage; it also evaluates a reader's ability to determine an author's viewpoint through the use of tone, message, and overall effect. This type of reading comprehension requires inference skills, deductive reasoning skills, the ability to draw logical conclusions, and overall critical thinking skills. Reading for factual information is straightforward. Reading for an author's tone, message, and overall effect is not. It's key to read carefully when asked test questions that address a test taker's ability to identify and analyze these writing devices. These are not questions that can be easily answered by quickly scanning for the right information.

Tone

An author's **tone** is the use of particular words, phrases, and writing style to convey an overall meaning. Tone expresses the author's attitude towards a particular topic. For example, a historical reading passage may begin like the following:

> The presidential election of 1960 ushered in a new era, a new Camelot, a new phase of forward thinking in U.S. politics that embraced brash action and unrest and responded with admirable leadership.

From this opening statement, a reader can draw some conclusions about the author's attitude towards President John F. Kennedy. Furthermore, the reader can make additional, educated guesses about the state of the Union during the 1960 presidential election. By close reading, the test taker can determine that the repeated use of the word *new* and words such as *admirable leadership* indicate the author's tone of admiration regarding the President Kennedy's boldness. In addition, the author assesses that the era during President Kennedy's administration was problematic through the use of the words *brash action* and *unrest.* Therefore, if a test taker encountered a test question asking about the author's use of tone and their assessment of the Kennedy administration, the test taker should be able to identify an answer indicating admiration. Similarly, if asked about the state of the Union during the 1960s, a test taker should be able to correctly identify an answer indicating political unrest.

When identifying an author's tone, the following list of words may be helpful. This is not an inclusive list. Generally, parts of speech that indicate attitude will also indicate tone:

- Comical
- Angry
- Ambivalent
- Scary
- Lyrical
- Matter-of-fact
- Judgmental
- Sarcastic
- Malicious
- Objective
- Pessimistic
- Patronizing
- Gloomy
- Instructional
- Satirical
- Formal
- Casual

Message

An author's **message** is the same as the overall meaning of a passage. It is the main idea, or the main concept the author wishes to convey. An author's message may be stated outright, or it may be implied. Regardless, the test taker will need to use careful reading skills to identify an author's message or purpose.

Often, the message of a particular passage can be determined by thinking about why the author wrote the information. Many historical passages are written to inform and to teach readers established, factual information. However, many historical works are also written to convey biased ideas to readers. Gleaning bias from an author's message in a historical passage can be difficult, especially if the reader is presented with a variety of established facts as well. Readers tend to accept historical writing as factual. This is not always the case. Any discerning reader who has tackled historical information on topics such as United States political party agendas can attest that two or more works on the same topic may have completely different messages supporting or refuting the value of the identical policies.

Therefore, it is important to critically assess an author's message separate from factual information. One author, for example, may point to the rise of unorthodox political candidates in an election year based on the failures of the political party in office while another may point to the rise of the same candidates in the same election year based on the current party's successes. The historical facts of what has occurred leading up to an election year are not in refute. Labeling those facts as a failure or a success is a bias within an author's overall *message*, as is excluding factual information in order to further a particular point. In a standardized testing situation, a reader must be able to critically assess what the author is trying to say separate from the historical facts that surround their message.

Using the example of Lincoln's Gettysburg Address, a test question may ask the following:

> What message is the speaker trying to convey through this address?

Then they will ask the test taker to select an answer that best expresses Lincoln's message to his audience. Based on the options given, a test taker should be able to select the answer expressing the idea that Lincoln's audience should recognize the efforts of those who died in the war as a sacrifice to preserving human equality and self-government.

Effect

An author may want to challenge a reader's intellect, inspire imagination, or spur emotion. An author may present information to appeal to a physical, aesthetic, or transformational sense. Take the following text as an example:

> In 1963, Martin Luther King stated "I have a dream." The gathering at the Lincoln Memorial was the beginning of the Civil Rights movement and, with its reference to the Emancipation Proclamation, Dr. King's words electrified those who wanted freedom and equality while rising from hatred and slavery. It was the beginning of radical change.

The test taker may be asked about the effect this statement might have on King's audience. Through careful reading of the passage, the test taker should be able to choose an answer that best identifies an effect of grabbing the audience's attention. The historical facts are in place: King made the speech in 1963 at the Lincoln Memorial, kicked off the civil rights movement, and referenced the Emancipation Proclamation. The words *electrified* and *radical change* indicate the effect the author wants the reader to understand as a result of King's speech. In this historical passage, facts are facts. However, the author's message goes beyond the facts to indicate the effect the message had on the audience and, in addition, the effect the event should have on the reader.

When reading historical passages, the test taker should perform due diligence in their awareness of the test questions and answers up front. From there, the test taker should carefully, and critically, read all historical excerpts with an eye for detail, tone, message (biased or unbiased), and effect. Being able to synthesize these skills will result in success in a standardized testing situation.

Science Passages

The SAT includes at least two science passages that address the fundamental concepts of Earth science, biology, chemistry, and/or physics. While prior general knowledge of these subjects is helpful in determining correct test answers, the test taker's ability to comprehend the passages is key to success. When reading scientific excerpts, the test taker must be able to examine quantitative information, identify hypotheses, interpret data, and consider implications of the material they are presented with. It is helpful, at this point, to reference the above section on comprehending test questions prior to reading. The same rules apply: read questions and scan questions, along with their answers, prior to fully reading a passage. Be informed prior to approaching a scientific text. A test taker should know what they will be asked and how to apply their reading skills. In this section of the test, it is also likely that a test taker will encounter graphs and charts to assess their ability to interpret scientific data with an appropriate conclusion. This section may use the identification of hypotheses, the reading and examination of data, and the interpretation of data representation passages to determine the skill levels of test takers in the comprehension of scientific data.

Examine Hypotheses

When presented with fundamental, scientific concepts, it is important to read for understanding. The most basic skill in achieving this literacy is to understand the concept of hypothesis and, moreover, to be able to identify it in a particular passage. A **hypothesis** is a proposed idea that needs further investigation in order to be proven true or false. While it can be considered an educated guess, a hypothesis goes more in depth in its attempt to explain something that is not currently accepted within scientific theory. It requires further experimentation and data gathering to test its validity and is subject to change, based on scientifically conducted test results. Being able to read a science passage and understand its main purpose, including any hypotheses, helps the test taker understand data-driven evidence. It helps the test taker to be able to correctly answer questions about the science excerpt they are asked to read.

When reading to identify a hypothesis, a test taker should ask, "What is the passage trying to establish? What is the passage's main idea? What evidence does the passage contain that either supports or refutes this idea?" Asking oneself these questions will help identify a hypothesis. Additionally, hypotheses are logical statements that are testable and use very precise language.

Review the following hypothesis example:

> Consuming excess sugar in the form of beverages has a greater impact on childhood obesity and subsequent weight gain than excessive sugar from food.

While this is likely a true statement, it is still only a conceptual idea in a text passage regarding how sugar consumption affects childhood obesity, unless the passage also contains tested data that either proves or disproves the statement. A test taker could expect the rest of the passage to cite data proving that children who drink empty calories gain more weight and are more likely to be obese than children who eat sugary snacks.

A hypothesis goes further in that, given its ability to be proven or disproven, it may result in further hypotheses that require extended research. For example, the hypothesis regarding sugar consumption in drinks, after undergoing rigorous testing, may lead scientists to state another hypothesis such as the following:

> Consuming excess sugar in the form of beverages as opposed to food items is a habit found in mostly sedentary children.

This new, working hypothesis further focuses not just on the source of an excess of calories, but tries an "educated guess" that empty caloric intake has a direct, subsequent impact on physical behavior.

The data-driven chart below is similar to an illustration a test taker might see in relation to the hypothesis on sugar consumption in children:

Behaviors of Healthy and Unhealthy Kids

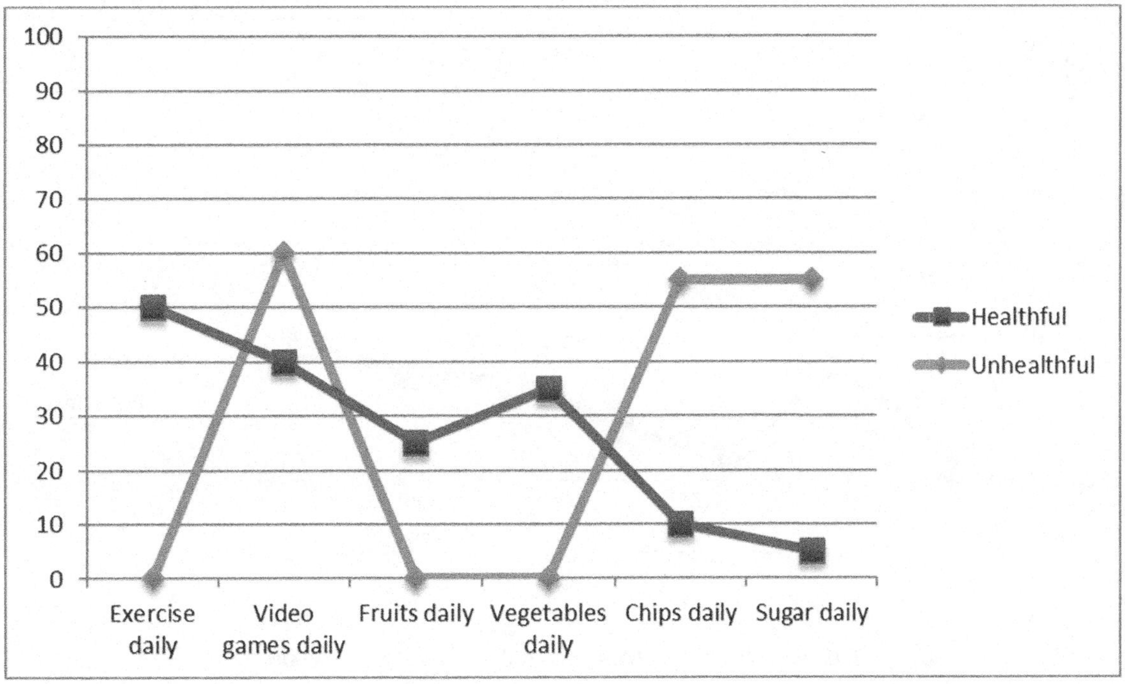

While this guide will address other data-driven passages a test taker could expect to see within a given science excerpt, note that the hypothesis regarding childhood sugar intake and rate of exercise has undergone scientific examination and yielded results that support its truth.

When reading a science passage to determine its hypothesis, a test taker should look for a concept that attempts to explain a phenomenon, is testable, is logical, is precisely worded, and yields data-driven results. The test taker should scan the presented passage for any word or data-driven clues that will help identify the hypothesis, and then be able to correctly answer test questions regarding the hypothesis by using their critical thinking skills.

Interpreting Data and Considering Implications

The Reading section of the SAT will contain one data-driven science passage that requires the test taker to examine evidence within a particular type of graphic. The test taker will then be required to interpret the data and answer questions demonstrating their ability to draw logical conclusions.

In general, there are two types of data: qualitative and quantitative. Science passages may contain both, but simply put, **quantitative** data is reflected numerically and qualitative is not. **Qualitative** data is based on its qualities. In other words, qualitative data tends to present information more in subjective generalities (for example, relating to size or appearance). Quantitative data is based on numerical findings such as percentages. Quantitative data will be described in numerical terms. While both types of data are valid, the test taker will more likely be faced with having to interpret quantitative data through one or more graphic(s), and then be required to answer questions regarding the numerical data. The section of this study guide briefly addresses how data may be displayed in line graphs, bar charts, circle graphs, and scatter plots. A test taker should take the time to learn the skills it takes to interpret quantitative data. An example of a line graph is as follows:

Cell Phone Use in Kiteville, 2000-2006

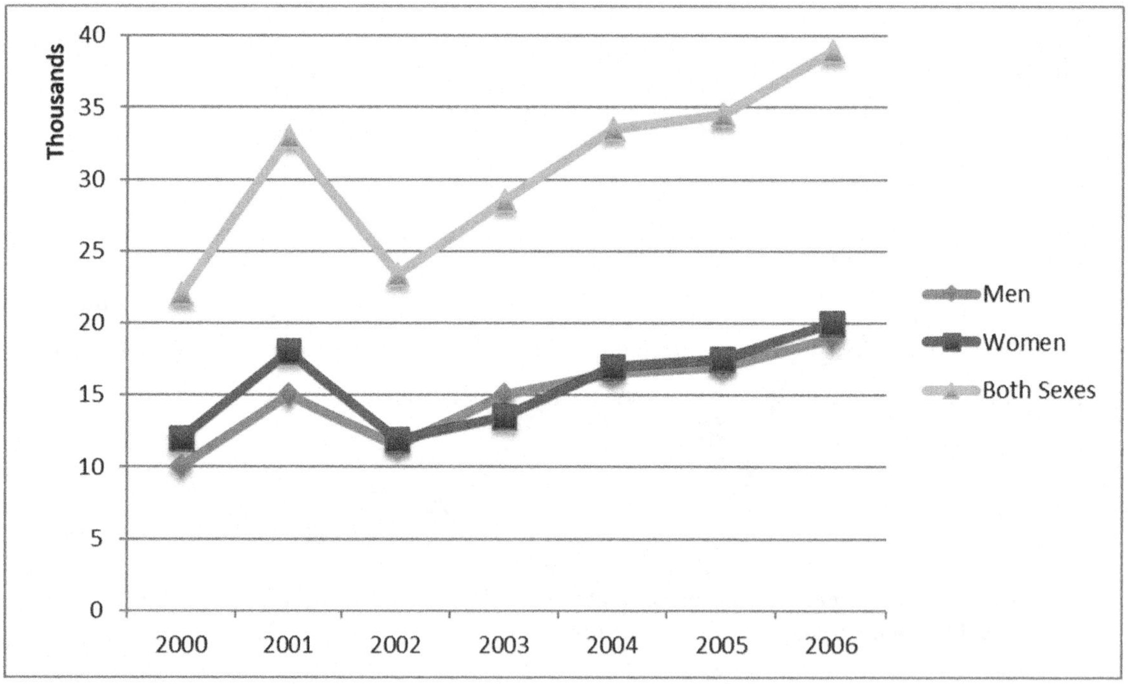

A **line graph** presents quantitative data on both horizontal (side to side) and vertical (up and down) axes. It requires the test taker to examine information across varying data points. When reading a line graph, a test taker should pay attention to any headings, as these indicate a title for the data it contains. In the above example, the test taker can anticipate the line graph contains numerical data regarding the use of cellphones during a certain time period. From there, a test taker should carefully read any outlying words or phrases that will help determine the meaning of data within the horizontal and vertical axes. In this example, the vertical axis displays the total number of people in increments of 5,000. Horizontally, the graph displays yearly markers, and the reader can assume the data presented accounts for a full calendar year. In addition, the line graph also uses different shapes to mark its data points. Some data points represent the number of men. Some data points represent the number of women, and a third type of data point represents the number of both sexes combined.

A test taker may be asked to read and interpret the graph's data, then answer questions about it. For example, the test may ask, *In which year did men seem to decrease cellphone use?* then require the test taker to select the correct answer. Similarly, the test taker may encounter a question such as *Which year yielded the highest number of cellphone users overall?* The test taker should be able to identify the correct answer as 2006.

A **bar graph** presents quantitative data through the use of lines or rectangles. The height and length of these lines or rectangles corresponds to the magnitude of the numerical data for that particular category or attribute. The data presented may represent information over time, showing shaded data over time or over other defined parameters. A bar graph will also utilize horizontal and vertical axes. An example of a bar graph is as follows:

Population Growth in Major U.S. Cities

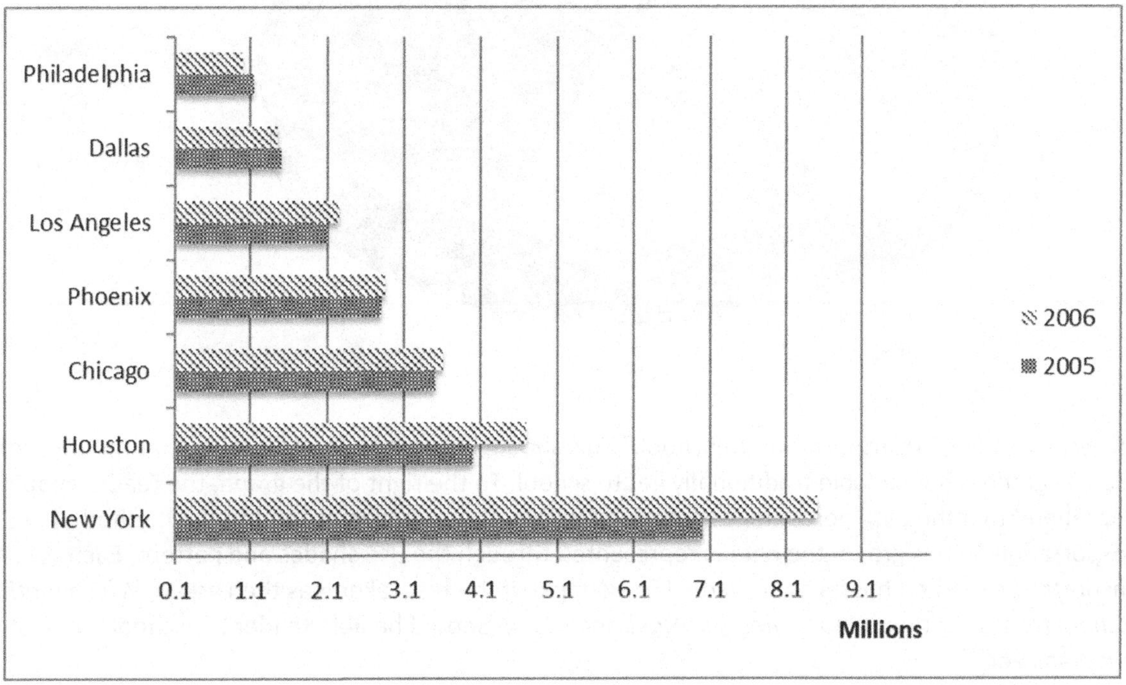

Reading the data in a bar graph is similar to the skills needed to read a line graph. The test taker should read and comprehend all heading information, as well as information provided along the horizontal and vertical axes. Note that the graph pertains to the population of some major U.S. cities. The "values" of these cities can be found along the left side of the graph, along the vertical axis. The population values can be found along the horizontal axes. Notice how the graph uses shaded bars to depict the change in population over time, as the heading indicates. Therefore, when the test taker is asked a question such as, *Which major U.S. city experienced the greatest amount of population growth during the depicted two year cycle,* the reader should be able to determine a correct answer of New York. It is important to pay particular attention to color, length, data points, and both axes, as well as any outlying header information in order to be able to answer graph-like test questions.

A **circle graph** (also sometimes referred to as a **pie chart**) presents quantitative data in the form of a circle. The same principles apply: the test taker should look for numerical data within the confines of the circle itself but also note any outlying information that may be included in a header, footer, or to the side of the circle. A circle graph will not depict horizontal or vertical axis information, but will instead rely on the reader's ability to visually take note of segmented circle pieces and apply information accordingly.

An example of a circle graph is as follows:

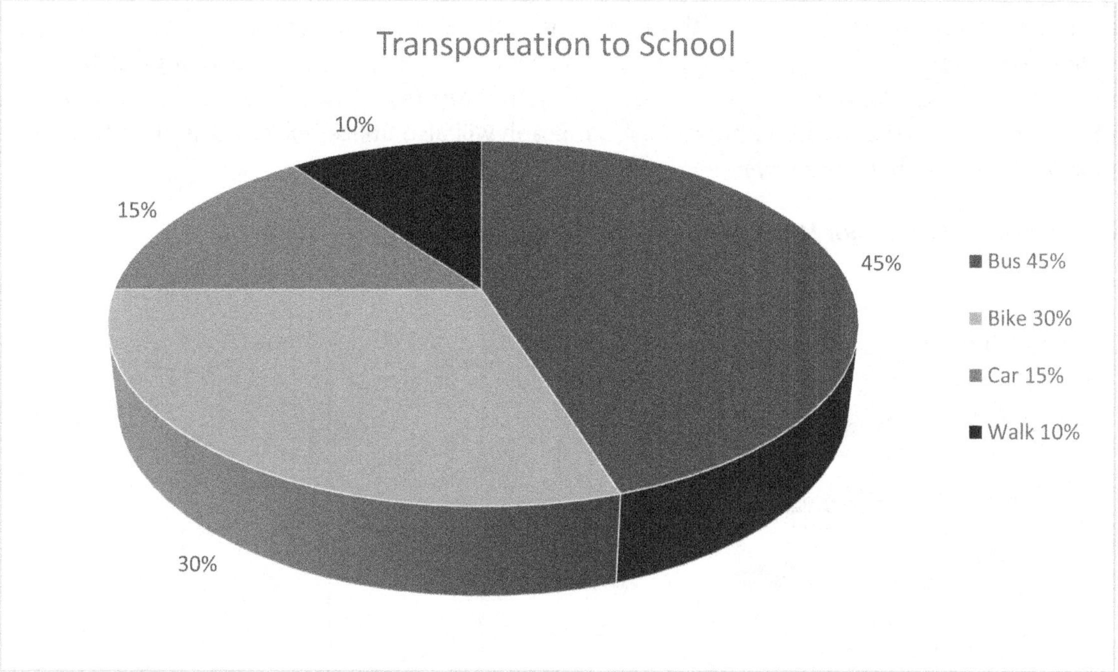

Notice the heading "Transportation to School." This should indicate to the test taker that the topic of the circle graph is how people traditionally get to school. To the right of the graph, the reader should comprehend that the data percentages contained within it directly correspond to the method of transportation. In this graph, the data is represented through the use shades and pattern. Each transportation method has its own shade. For example, if the test taker was then asked, *Which method of school transportation is most widely utilized,* the reader should be able to identify school bus as the correct answer.

Be wary of test questions that ask test takers to draw conclusions based on information that is not present. For example, it is not possible to determine, given the parameters of this circle graph, whether the population presented is of a particular gender or ethnic group. This graph does not represent data from a particular city or school district. It does not distinguish between student grade levels and, although the reader could infer that the typical student must be of driving age if cars are included, this is not necessarily the case. Elementary school students may rely on parents or others to drive them by personal methods. Therefore, do not read too much into data that is not presented. Only rely on the quantitative data that is presented in order to answer questions.

A **scatter plot** or **scatter diagram** is a graph that depicts quantitative data across plotted points. It will involve at least two sets of data. It will also involve horizontal and vertical axes.

An example of a scatter plot is as follows:

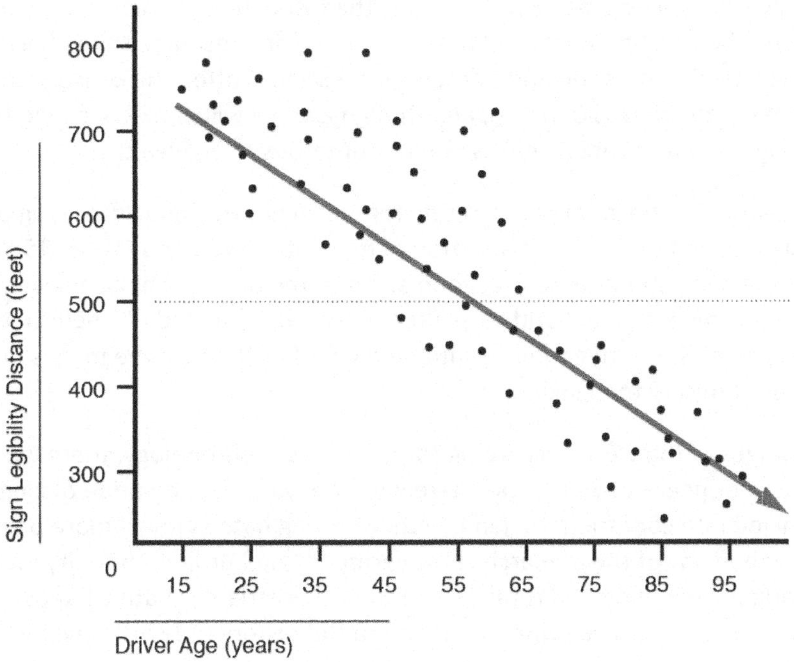

The skills needed to address a scatter plot are essentially the same as in other graph examples. Note any topic headings, as well as horizontal or vertical axis information. In the sample above, the reader can determine the data addresses a driver's ability to correctly and legibly read road signs as related to their age. Again, note the information that is absent. The test taker is not given the data to assess a time period, location, or driver gender. It simply requires the reader to note an approximate age to the ability to correctly identify road signs from a distance measured in feet. Notice that the overall graph also displays a trend. In this case, the data indicates a negative one and possibly supports the hypothesis that as a driver ages, their ability to correctly read a road sign at over 500 feet tends to decline over time. If the test taker were to be asked, *At what approximation in feet does a sixteen-year-old driver correctly see and read a street sign,* the answer would be the option closest to 700 feet.

Reading and examining scientific data in excerpts involves all of a reader's contextual reading, data interpretation, drawing logical conclusions based only on the information presented, and their application of critical thinking skills across a set of interpretive questions. Thorough comprehension and attention to detail is necessary to achieve test success.

Practice Quiz

Questions 1–5 are based on the following passage from Common Sense *by Thomas Paine:*

MANKIND being originally equals in the order of creation, the equality could only be destroyed by some subsequent circumstance; the distinctions of rich, and poor, may in a great measure be accounted for, and that without having recourse to the harsh ill sounding names of oppression and avarice. Oppression is often the consequence, but seldom or never the means of riches; and though avarice will preserve a man from being necessitously poor, it generally makes him too timorous to be wealthy.

But there is another and greater distinction for which no truly natural or religious reason can be assigned, and that is, the distinction of men into KINGS and SUBJECTS. Male and female are the distinctions of nature, good and bad the distinctions of heaven; but how a race of men came into the world so exalted above the rest, and distinguished like some new species, is worth enquiring into, and whether they are the means of happiness or of misery to mankind.

In the early ages of the world, according to the scripture chronology, there were no kings; the consequence of which was there were no wars; it is the pride of kings which throw mankind into confusion. Holland. without a king hath enjoyed more peace for this last century than any of the monarchical governments in Europe. Antiquity favors the same remark; for the quiet and rural lives of the first patriarchs hath a happy something in them, which vanishes away when we come to the history of Jewish royalty.

Government by kings was first introduced into the world by the Heathens, from whom the children of Israel copied the custom. It was the most prosperous invention the Devil ever set on foot for the promotion of idolatry. The Heathens paid divine honors to their deceased kings, and the Christian world hath improved on the plan by doing the same to their living ones. How impious is the title of sacred majesty applied to a worm, who in the midst of his splendor is crumbling into dust!

As the exalting one man so greatly above the rest cannot be justified on the equal rights of nature, so neither can it be defended on the authority of scripture; for the will of the Almighty, as declared by Gideon and the prophet Samuel, expressly disapproves of government by kings. All anti-monarchical parts of scripture have been very smoothly glossed over in monarchical governments, but they undoubtedly merit the attention of countries, which have their governments yet to form. "Render unto Caesar the things which are Caesar's" is the scripture doctrine of courts, yet it is no support of monarchical government, for the Jews at that time were without a king, and in a state of vassalage to the Romans.

Near three thousand years passed away from the Mosaic account of the creation, till the Jews under a national delusion requested a king. Till then their form of government (except in extraordinary cases, where the Almighty interposed) was a kind of republic administered by a judge and the elders of the tribes. Kings they had none, and it was held sinful to acknowledge any being under that title but the Lord of Hosts. And when a man seriously reflects on the idolatrous homage which is paid to the persons of kings, he need not wonder that the Almighty, ever jealous of his honor, should disapprove of a form of government which so impiously invades the prerogative of heaven.

1. According to the passage, what role does avarice, or greed, play in poverty?
   a. a. Avarice makes a man poor.
   b. Avarice is the consequence of wealth.
   c. Avarice prevents a man from being poor, but makes him too fearful to be wealthy.
   d. Avarice is what drives a person to be wealthy.

2. Of these distinctions, which does the author believe to be beyond natural or religious reason?
   a. Good and bad
   b. Male and female
   c. Human and animal
   d. King and subjects

3. According to the passage, what are the Heathens responsible for?
   a. Government by kings
   b. Quiet and rural lives of patriarchs
   c. Paying divine honors to their living kings
   d. Equal rights of nature

4. Which of the following best states Paine's rationale for the denouncement of monarchy?
   a. It is against the laws of nature.
   b. It is against the equal rights of nature and is denounced in scripture.
   c. Despite scripture, a monarchal government is unlawful.
   d. Neither the law nor scripture denounce monarchy.

5. Based on the passage, what is the best definition of the word *idolatrous*?
   a. Worshipping kings
   b. Being deceitful
   c. Sinfulness
   d. Engaging in illegal activities

See answers on next page.

Answer Explanations

1. C: In lines 6 and 7, it is stated that avarice can prevent a man from being necessitously poor, but it also makes him too timorous, or fearful, to be wealthy. Choice *A* is incorrect because avarice prevents a man from being poor. Choice *B* is incorrect because the passage states that oppression, not avarice, is the consequence of wealth. Choice *D* is incorrect because the passage does not state that avarice drives a person's desire to be wealthy.

2. D: Paine believes that the distinction that is beyond a natural or religious reason is between king and subjects. Choice *A* is incorrect because he states that the distinction between good and bad is made in heaven. Choice *B* is incorrect because he states that the distinction between male and female is natural. Choice *C* is incorrect because he does not mention anything about the distinction between humans and animals.

3. A: The passage states that the Heathens were the first to introduce government by kings into the world. Choice *B* is incorrect because the quiet lives of patriarchs came before the Heathens introduced this type of government and Paine puts it in opposition to government by kings. Choice *C* is incorrect because it was Christians, not Heathens, who paid divine honors to living kings. Heathens honored deceased kings. Choice *D* is incorrect because, while equal rights of nature are mentioned in the paragraph, they are not mentioned in relation to the Heathens.

4. B: Paine asserts that a monarchy is against the equal rights of nature and cites several parts of scripture that also denounce it. He doesn't say it is against the laws of nature. Because he uses scripture to further his argument, it is not despite scripture that he denounces the monarchy. Paine addresses the law by saying the courts also do not support a monarchical government.

5. A: To be idolatrous is to worship someone or something other than God, in this case, kings. Choice *B* is incorrect because it is not defined as being deceitful. Choice *C* is incorrect because, while idolatry is considered a sin, it is an example of a sin, not a synonym for it. Choice *D* is incorrect because, while idolatry may have been considered illegal in some cultures, it is not a definition for the term.

Writing and Language

The Writing and Language section of the SAT presents passages with deliberate errors; the section is designed to assess the test taker's command of standard conventions of English Language and their ability to edit errors appropriately. While questions will ask test takers to select more effective alternatives to given sentences and revise and edit errors, they will not require test takers to identify specific grammatical rules.

The section includes four passages, each of approximately 400-450 words in length. There is one passage dedicated to each of the following four categories: careers, science, humanities, and social studies. Careers passages present trends or debates in various industries like technology, communications, or healthcare. Science passages are drawn from topics in earth science, chemistry, biology, or physics. Humanities passages may focus on any number of topics such as arts, literature, dance, or music. Social studies passages may pull topics from a variety of areas including history, sociology, psychology, anthropology, and political science. All of the information needed to answer the questions is provided within the passages and test takers do not need to have prior knowledge of the passages' content to obtain the correct answers.

Test takers are given 35 minutes to read the four passages and then answer a total of 44 multiple-choice questions—eleven per passage. In addition to surveying the test taker's ability to comprehend and revise passages about various topics, the section tests one's skill in understanding various writing styles. The test taker will encounter at least one passage written in one of three different writing styles: narrative, argumentative, and explanatory or informative.

In addition, test takers can expect to interpret graphs, tables, charts, or other graphics that, in some way, support factual content or an opinion presented in the graphic's passage. After reading the passage and reviewing the graphic, test takers may be asked to correct an error in the passage that contradicts information presented in the graphic. Alternatively, they may need to use information gleaned from the graphic to select a more specific description for part or all of the passage in place of the vague description originally provided. Essentially, the passage may misinterpret the graphic or the graphic may otherwise illuminate important data or facts that can strengthen the argument or explanation in the passage; test takers will be required to identify these findings.

Passages and the questions pertaining to them usually appear side by side on the test, with the passage on the left side of the page and the questions on the right. Some or all passages may span multiple pages, so test takers should ensure they have read the entire passage before answering questions that pertain to the passage in its entirety. In contrast, some test takers find it useful to answer questions addressing specific points or details as that information is encountered in the passage; question numbers embedded within the passage should be used to guide the test taker to the section of the passage for which a question pertains. Test takers should then carefully read the underlined text in the passage following the number and determine if errors are present.

The related question will then ask test takers to consider the underlined sentence or section and the provided answer choices. Test takers must select the answer choice that offers that best revision or most effective replacement for the underlined section. If the original sentence seems correct as is, test takers should select Choice *A*—NO CHANGE—which represents that the initial sentence was free from errors and should remain unchanged.

Underlined text will not necessarily follow all of the embedded boxed numbers in the passage. In these situations, test takers should still use the boxed number to guide their attention to the pertinent question, and then the appropriate question will inform them on what to do. Some sentences or paragraphs may be numbered, and test takers will have to decide how that text should be ordered or where a particular sentence or paragraph should be inserted.

There are two principal question types on the Writing and Language Section. For the Expression of Ideas questions, test takers will select answers that improve the text's organization, topic development, and the effectiveness of the language used. The scope of these questions assesses one's understanding of text structure and organization, ability to analyze evidence and arguments and strengthen them with designated improvements, and their specific skills in comprehending passages addressing topics in science, history, and the humanities. Standard English Convention questions address one's skill in identifying and correcting errors in sentence structure, word usage, grammar, and punctuation. These questions evaluate the test taker's skill in determining the correct meaning of words in context, selecting precise words, and revising text to be more concise, coherent, and consistent in tone and style.

While the vast majority of questions in the Writing and Language section are comprised of these two question types in roughly equal proportions, as mentioned, a small number of questions will also assess the test taker's ability to interpret graph, tables, and charts. For this reason, in addition to studying grammatical rules, vocabulary, and word usage and developing writing skills and an eye and ear for issues with organization and flow, test takers should practice reading and interpreting tables, graphs, and charts. As such. the sections that follow provide a review of material pertinent to success in this section, covering topics on English language conventions, text structure and readability, syntax and grammar, analyzing opinions and facts, and interpreting graphics.

Expression of Ideas

This Writing and Language section is about *how* the information is communicated rather than the subject matter itself. The good news is there isn't any writing! Instead, it's like being an editor helping the writer find the best ways to express their ideas. Things to consider include: how well a topic is developed, how accurately facts are presented, whether the writing flows logically and cohesively, and how effectively the writer uses language. This can seem like a lot to remember, but these concepts are the same ones taught way back in elementary school.

One last thing to remember while going through this guide is not to be intimidated by the terminology. Phrases like "pronoun-antecedent agreement" and "possessive determiners" can sound confusing and complicated, but the ideas are often quite simple and easy to understand. Though proper terminology is used to explain the rules and guidelines, the SAT Writing and Language Test is not a technical grammar test.

Organization

Good writing is not merely a random collection of sentences. No matter how well written, sentences must relate and coordinate appropriately to one another. If not, the writing seems random, haphazard, and disorganized. Therefore, good writing must be **organized** (where each sentence fits a larger context and relates to the sentences around it).

Transition Words

The writer should act as a guide, showing the reader how all the sentences fit together. Consider this example:

> Seat belts save more lives than any other automobile safety feature. Many studies show that airbags save lives as well. Not all cars have airbags. Many older cars don't. Air bags aren't entirely reliable. Studies show that in 15% of accidents, airbags don't deploy as designed. Seat belt malfunctions are extremely rare.

There's nothing wrong with any of these sentences individually, but together they're disjointed and difficult to follow. The best way for the writer to communicate information is through the use of **transition words**. Here are examples of transition words and phrases that tie sentences together, enabling a more natural flow:

To show causality: *as a result, therefore*, and *consequently*
To compare and contrast: *however, but,* and *on the other hand*
To introduce examples: *for instance, namely*, and *including*
To show order of importance: *foremost, primarily, secondly*, and *lastly*

The above is not a complete list of transitions. There are many more that can be used; however, most fit into these or similar categories. The important point is that the words should clearly show the relationship between sentences, supporting information, and the main idea.

Here is an update to the previous example using transition words. These changes make it easier to read and bring clarity to the writer's points:

> Seat belts save more lives than any other automobile safety feature. Many studies show that airbags save lives as well. However, not all cars have airbags. For instance, some older cars don't. Furthermore, air bags aren't entirely reliable. For example, studies show that in 15% of accidents, airbags don't deploy as designed. But, on the other hand, seat belt malfunctions are extremely rare.

Also be prepared to analyze whether the writer is using the best transition word or phrase for the situation. Take this sentence for example: "As a result, seat belt malfunctions are extremely rare." This sentence doesn't make sense in the context above because the writer is trying to show the **contrast** between seat belts and airbags, not the causality.

Logical Sequence

Even if the writer includes plenty of information to support their point, the writing is only effective when the information is in a logical order. **Logical sequencing** is really just common sense, but it's also an important writing technique. First, the writer should introduce the main idea, whether for a paragraph, a section, or the entire piece. Second, they should present evidence to support the main idea by using transitional language. This shows the reader how the information relates to the main idea and to the sentences around it. The writer should then take time to interpret the information, making sure necessary connections are obvious to the reader. Finally, the writer can summarize the information in a closing section.

Although most writing follows this pattern, it isn't a set rule. Sometimes writers change the order for effect. For example, the writer can begin with a surprising piece of supporting information to grab the reader's attention, and then transition to the main idea. Thus, if a passage doesn't follow the logical order, don't immediately assume it's wrong. However, most writing usually settles into a logical sequence after a nontraditional beginning.

Focus

Good writing stays **focused** and on topic. During the test, determine the main idea for each passage and then look for times when the writer strays from the point they're trying to make. Let's go back to the seat belt example. If the writer suddenly begins talking about how well airbags, crumple zones, or other safety features work to save lives, they might be losing focus from the topic of "safety belts."

Focus can also refer to individual sentences. Sometimes the writer does address the main topic, but in a confusing way. For example:

> Thanks to seat belt usage, survival in serious car accidents has shown a consistently steady increase since the development of the retractable seat belt in the 1950s.

This statement is definitely on topic, but it's not easy to follow. A simpler, more focused version of this sentence might look like this:

> Seat belts have consistently prevented car fatalities since the 1950s.

Providing **adequate information** is another aspect of focused writing. Statements like "seat belts are important" and "many people drive cars" are true, but they're so general that they don't contribute much to the writer's case. When reading a passage, watch for these kinds of unfocused statements.

Introductions and Conclusions

Examining the writer's strategies for introductions and conclusions puts the reader in the right mindset to interpret the rest of the passage. Look for methods the writer might use for introductions such as:

- Stating the main point immediately, followed by outlining how the rest of the piece supports this claim.
- Establishing important, smaller pieces of the main idea first, and then grouping these points into a case for the main idea.
- Opening with a quotation, anecdote, question, seeming paradox, or other piece of interesting information, and then using it to lead to the main point.

Whatever method the writer chooses, the **introduction** should make their intention clear, establish their voice as a credible one, and encourage a person to continue reading.

Conclusions tend to follow a similar pattern. In them, the writer restates their main idea a final time, often after summarizing the smaller pieces of that idea. If the introduction uses a quote or anecdote to grab the reader's attention, the conclusion often makes reference to it again. Whatever way the writer chooses to arrange the conclusion, the final restatement of the main idea should be clear and simple for the reader to interpret.

Finally, conclusions shouldn't introduce any new information.

Precision

People often think of **precision** in terms of math, but precise word choice is another key to successful writing. Since language itself is imprecise, it's important for the writer to find the exact word or words to convey the full, intended meaning of a given situation. For example:

> The number of deaths has gone down since seat belt laws started.

There are several problems with this sentence. First, the word *deaths* is too general. From the context, it's assumed that the writer is referring only to *deaths* caused by car accidents. However, without clarification, the sentence lacks impact and is probably untrue. The phrase "gone down" might be accurate, but a more precise word could provide more information and greater accuracy. Did the numbers show a slow and steady decrease of highway fatalities or a sudden drop? If the latter is true, the writer is missing a chance to make their point more dramatically. Instead of "gone down" they could substitute *plummeted, fallen drastically*, or *rapidly diminished* to bring the information to life. Also, the phrase "seat belt laws" is unclear. Does it refer to laws requiring cars to include seat belts or to laws requiring drivers and passengers to use them? Finally, *started* is not a strong verb. Words like *enacted* or *adopted* are more direct and make the content more real. When put together, these changes create a far more powerful sentence:

> The number of highway fatalities has plummeted since laws requiring seat belt usage were enacted.

However, it's important to note that precise word choice can sometimes be taken too far. If the writer of the sentence above takes precision to an extreme, it might result in the following:

> The incidence of high-speed, automobile accident related fatalities has decreased 75% and continued to remain at historical lows since the initial set of federal legislations requiring seat belt use were enacted in 1992.

This sentence is extremely precise, but it takes so long to achieve that precision that it suffers from a lack of clarity. Precise writing is about finding the right balance between information and flow. This is also an issue of **conciseness** (discussed in the next section).

The last thing to consider with precision is a word choice that's not only unclear or uninteresting, but also confusing or misleading. For example:

> The number of highway fatalities has become hugely lower since laws requiring seat belt use were enacted.

In this case, the reader might be confused by the word *hugely*. Huge means large, but here the writer uses *hugely* to describe something small. Though most readers can decipher this, doing so disconnects them from the flow of the writing and makes the writer's point less effective.

On the test, there can be questions asking for alternatives to the writer's word choice. In answering these questions, always consider the context and look for a balance between precision and flow.

Conciseness

"Less is more" is a good rule to follow when writing a sentence. Unfortunately, writers often include extra words and phrases that seem necessary at the time, but add nothing to the main idea. This confuses the reader and creates unnecessary repetition. Writing that lacks **conciseness** is usually guilty of excessive wordiness and redundant phrases. Here's an example containing both of these issues:

> When legislators decided to begin creating legislation making it mandatory for automobile drivers and passengers to make use of seat belts while in cars, a large number of them made those laws for reasons that were political reasons.

There are several empty or "fluff" words here that take up too much space. These can be eliminated while still maintaining the writer's meaning. For example:

"decided to begin" could be shortened to "began"
"making it mandatory for" could be shortened to "requiring"
"make use of" could be shortened to "use"
"a large number" could be shortened to "many"

In addition, there are several examples of redundancy that can be eliminated:

"legislators decided to begin creating legislation" and "made those laws"
"automobile drivers and passengers" and "while in cars"
"reasons that were political reasons"

These changes are incorporated as follows:

> When legislators began requiring drivers and passengers to use seat belts, many of them did so for political reasons.

There are many examples of redundant phrases, such as "add an additional," "complete and total," "time schedule," and "transportation vehicle." If asked to identify a redundant phrase on the test, look for words that are close together with the same (or similar) meanings.

Proposition

The **proposition** (also called the **claim** since it can be true or false) is a clear statement of the point or idea the writer is trying to make. The length or format of a proposition can vary, but it often takes the form of a **topic sentence**. A good topic sentence is:

- Clear: does not weave a complicated web of words for the reader to decode or unwrap
- Concise: presents only the information needed to make the claim and doesn't clutter up the statement with unnecessary details
- Precise: clarifies the exact point the writer wants to make and doesn't use broad, overreaching statements

Look at the following example:

> The civil rights movement, from its genesis in the Emancipation Proclamation to its current struggles with de facto discrimination, has changed the face of the United States more than any other factor in its history.

Is the statement clear? Yes, the statement is fairly clear, although other words can be substituted for "genesis" and "de facto" to make it easier to understand.

Is the statement concise? No, the statement is not concise. Details about the Emancipation Proclamation and the current state of the movement are unnecessary for a topic sentence. Those details should be saved for the body of the text.

Is the statement precise? No, the statement is not precise. What exactly does the writer mean by "changed the face of the United States"? The writer should be more specific about the effects of the movement. Also, suggesting that something has a greater impact than anything else in U.S. history is far too ambitious a statement to make.

A better version might look like this:

> The civil rights movement has greatly increased the career opportunities available for Black Americans.

The unnecessary language and details are removed, and the claim can now be measured and supported.

Support

Once the main idea or proposition is stated, the writer attempts to prove or **support** the claim with text evidence and supporting details.

Take for example the sentence, "Seat belts save lives." Though most people can't argue with this statement, its impact on the reader is much greater when supported by additional content. The writer can support this idea by:

- Providing statistics on the rate of highway fatalities alongside statistics for estimated seat belt usage.
- Explaining the science behind a car accident and what happens to a passenger who doesn't use a seat belt.
- Offering anecdotal evidence or true stories from reliable sources about how seat belts prevent fatal injuries in car crashes.

However, using only one form of supporting evidence is not nearly as effective as using a variety to support a claim. Presenting only a list of statistics can be boring to the reader, but providing a true story that's both interesting and humanizing helps. In addition, one example isn't always enough to prove the writer's larger point, so combining it with other examples is extremely effective for the writing. Thus, when reading a passage, don't just look for a single form of supporting evidence.

Another key aspect of supporting evidence is a **reliable source**. Does the writer include the source of the information? If so, is the source well known and trustworthy? Is there a potential for bias? For example, a seat belt study done by a seat belt manufacturer may have its own agenda to promote.

Effective Language Use

Language can be analyzed in a variety of ways. But one of the primary ways is its effectiveness in communicating and especially convincing others.

Rhetoric is a literary technique used to make the writing (or speaking) more effective or persuasive. Rhetoric makes use of other effective language devices such as irony, metaphors, allusion, and repetition. An example of the rhetorical use of repetition would be: "Let go, I say, let go!!!".

Figures of Speech

A **figure of speech** (sometimes called an **idiom**) is a rhetorical device. It's a phrase that's not intended to be taken literally.

When the writer uses a figure of speech, their intention must be clear if it's to be used effectively. Some phrases can be interpreted in a number of ways, causing confusion for the reader. In the SAT Writing and Language Test, questions may ask for an alternative to a problematic word or phrase. Look for clues to the writer's true intention to determine the best replacement. Likewise, some figures of speech may seem out of place in a more formal piece of writing. To show this, here is the previous seat belt example but with one slight change:

> Seat belts save more lives than any other automobile safety feature. Many studies show that airbags save lives as well. However, not all cars have airbags. For instance, some older cars don't. In addition, air bags aren't entirely reliable. For example, studies show that in 15% of accidents, airbags don't deploy as designed. But, on the other hand, seat belt malfunctions happen once in a blue moon.

Most people know that "once in a blue moon" refers to something that rarely happens. However, because the rest of the paragraph is straightforward and direct, using this figurative phrase distracts the reader. In this example, the earlier version is much more effective.

Now it's important to take a moment and review the meaning of the word *literally***.** This is because it's one of the most misunderstood and misused words in the English language. **Literally** means that something is exactly what it says it is, and there can be no interpretation or exaggeration. Unfortunately, *literally* is often used for emphasis as in the following example:

> This morning, I literally couldn't get out of bed.

This sentence meant to say that the person was extremely tired and wasn't able to get up. However, the sentence can't *literally* be true unless that person was tied down to the bed, paralyzed, or affected by a strange situation that the writer (most likely) didn't intend. Here's another example:

> I literally died laughing.

The writer tried to say that something was very funny. However, unless they're writing this from beyond the grave, it can't *literally* be true.

Rhetorical Fallacies

A **rhetorical fallacy** is an argument that doesn't make sense. It usually involves distracting the reader from the issue at hand in some way. There are many kinds of rhetorical fallacies. Here are just a few, along with examples of each:

- **Ad Hominem:** Makes an irrelevant attack against the person making the claim, rather than addressing the claim itself. For example, Senator Wilson opposed the new seat belt legislation, but should we really listen to someone who's been divorced four times?
- **Exaggeration:** Represents an idea or person in an obviously excessive manner. For example, Senator Wilson opposed the new seat belt legislation. Maybe she thinks if more people die in car accidents, it will help with overpopulation.
- **Stereotyping** (or **Categorical Claim**): Claims that all people of a certain group are the same in some way. For example, Senator Wilson still opposes the new seat belt legislation. You know women can never admit when they're wrong.

When examining a possible rhetorical fallacy, carefully consider the point the writer is trying to make and if the argument directly relates to that point. If something feels wrong, there's a good chance that a fallacy is at play. The SAT Writing and Language section doesn't expect the fallacy to be named using specific terms like those above. However, questions can include identifying why something is a fallacy or suggesting a sounder argument.

Style, Tone, and Mood

Style, tone, and mood are often thought to be the same thing. Though they're closely related, there are important differences to keep in mind. The easiest way to do this is to remember that style "creates and affects" tone and mood. More specifically, **style** is *how the writer uses words* to create the desired tone and mood for their writing.

Style

Style can include any number of technical writing choices, and some may have to be analyzed on the test. A few examples of style choices include:

- Sentence Construction: When presenting facts, does the writer use shorter sentences to create a quicker sense of the supporting evidence, or do they use longer sentences to elaborate and explain the information?
- Technical Language: Does the writer use jargon to demonstrate their expertise in the subject, or do they use ordinary language to help the reader understand things in simple terms?
- Formal Language: Does the writer refrain from using contractions such as *won't* or *can't* to create a more formal tone, or do they use a colloquial, conversational style to connect to the reader?
- Formatting: Does the writer use a series of shorter paragraphs to help the reader follow a line of argument, or do they use longer paragraphs to examine an issue in great detail and demonstrate their knowledge of the topic?

On the test, examine the writer's style and how their writing choices affect the way the passage comes across.

Tone

As mentioned, **tone** refers to the writer's attitude toward the subject matter. Tone conveys how the writer feels about characters, situations, events, ideas, etc. Nonfiction writing is sometimes thought to have no tone at all, but this is incorrect.

A lot of nonfiction writing has a neutral tone, which is an extremely important tone for the writer to take. A neutral tone demonstrates that the writer is presenting a topic impartially and letting the information speak for itself. On the other hand, nonfiction writing can be just as effective and appropriate if the tone isn't neutral. For instance, take the previous examples involving seat belt use. In them, the writer mostly chooses to retain a neutral tone when presenting information. If the writer would instead include their own personal experience of losing a friend or family member in a car accident, the tone would change dramatically. The tone would no longer be neutral. Now it would show that the writer has a personal stake in the content, allowing them to interpret the information in a different way. When analyzing tone, consider what the writer is trying to achieve in the passage, and how they *create* the tone using style.

Mood

Mood refers to the feelings and atmosphere that the writer's words create for the reader. Like tone, many nonfiction pieces can have a neutral mood. To return to the previous example, if the writer would choose to include information about a person they know being killed in a car accident, the passage would suddenly carry an emotional component that is absent in the previous examples. Depending on how they present the information, the writer can create a sad, angry, or even hopeful mood. When analyzing the mood, consider what the writer wants to accomplish and whether the best choice was made to achieve that end.

Consistency

Whatever style, tone, and mood the writer uses, good writing should remain **consistent** throughout. If the writer chooses to include the tragic, personal experience above, it would affect the style, tone, and mood of the entire piece. It would seem out of place for such an example to be used in the middle of a neutral, measured, and analytical piece. To adjust the rest of the piece, the writer needs to make additional choices to remain consistent. For example, the writer might decide to use the word *tragedy* in place of the more neutral *fatality*, or they could describe a series of car-related deaths as an *epidemic*. Adverbs and adjectives such as *devastating* or *horribly* could be included to maintain this consistent attitude toward the content. When analyzing writing, look for sudden shifts in style, tone, and mood, and consider whether the writer would be wiser to maintain the prevailing strategy.

Syntax

Syntax is the order of words in a sentence. While most of the writing on the test has proper syntax, there may be questions on ways to vary the syntax for effectiveness. One of the easiest writing mistakes to spot is **repetitive sentence structure**. For example:

> Seat belts are important. They save lives. People don't like to use them. We have to pass seat belt laws. Then more people will wear seat belts. More lives will be saved.

What's the first thing that comes to mind when reading this example? The short, choppy, and repetitive sentences! In fact, most people notice this syntax issue more than the content itself. By combining some sentences and changing the syntax of others, the writer can create a more effective writing passage:

> Seat belts are important because they save lives. Since people don't like to use seat belts, though, more laws requiring their usage need to be passed. Only then will more people wear them and only then will more lives be saved.

Many rhetorical devices can be used to vary syntax (more than can possibly be named here). These often have intimidating names like anadiplosis, metastasis, and paremptosis. The test questions don't ask for definitions of these tricky techniques, but they can ask how the writer plays with the words and what effect that has on the writing. For example, **anadiplosis** is when the last word (or phrase) from a sentence is used to begin the next sentence:

> Cars are driven by people. People cause accidents. Accidents cost taxpayers money.

The test doesn't ask for this technique by name, but be prepared to recognize what the writer is doing and why they're using the technique in this situation. In this example, the writer is probably using anadiplosis to demonstrate causation.

Quantitative Information

As mentioned, some passages in the test contains **infographics** such as charts, tables, or graphs. In these cases, interpret the information presented and determine how well it supports the claims made in the text. For example, if the writer makes a case that seat belts save more lives than other automobile safety measures, they might want to include a graph (like the one below) showing the number of lives saved by seat belts versus those saved by air bags.

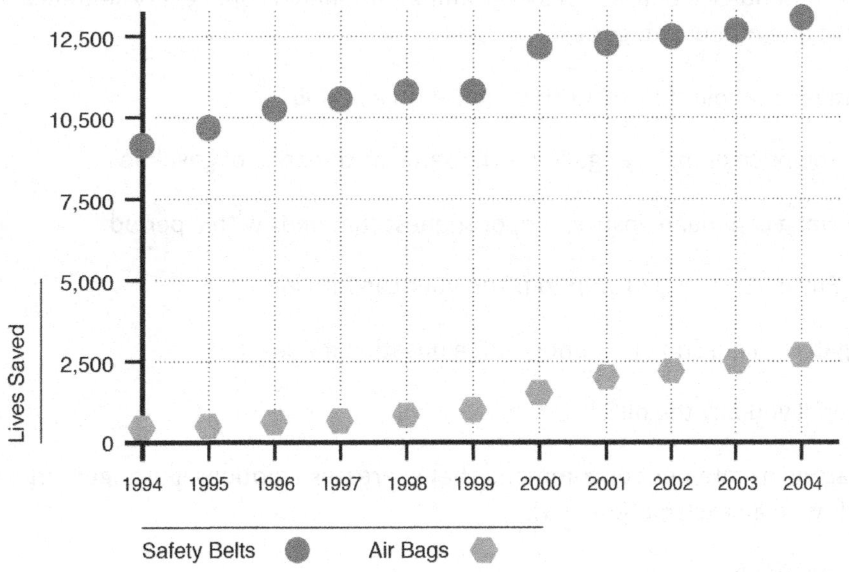

Based on data from the National Highway Traffic Safety Administration

If the graph clearly shows a higher number of lives are saved by seat belts, then it's effective. However, if the graph shows air bags save more lives than seat belts, then it doesn't support the writer's case.

Finally, graphs should be easy to understand. Their information should immediately be clear to the reader at a glance. Here are some basic things to keep in mind when interpreting infographics:

- In a **bar graph**, higher bars represent larger numbers. Lower bars represent smaller numbers.
- **Line graphs** often show trends over time. Points that are higher represent larger numbers than points that are lower. A line that consistently ascends from left to right shows a steady increase over time. A line that consistently descends from left to right shows a steady decrease over time. A line that bounces up and down represents instability or inconsistency in the trend. When interpreting a line graph, determine the point the writer is trying to make, and then see if the graph supports that point.
- **Pie charts** are used to show proportions or percentages of a whole but are less effective in showing change over time.
- **Tables** present information in numerical form, not as graphics. When interpreting a table, make sure to look for patterns in the numbers.

There can also be timelines, illustrations, or maps on the test. When interpreting these, keep in mind the writer's intentions and determine whether or not the graphic supports the case.

Standard English Conventions

Types of Sentences

There isn't an overabundance of absolutes in grammar, but here is one: every sentence in the English language falls into one of four categories.

- **Declarative:** a simple statement that ends with a period

  The price of milk per gallon is the same as the price of gasoline.

- **Imperative:** a command, instruction, or request that ends with a period

  Buy milk when you stop to fill up your car with gas.

- **Interrogative:** a question that ends with a question mark

  Will you buy the milk?

- **Exclamatory:** a statement or command that expresses emotions like anger, urgency, or surprise and ends with an exclamation mark

  Buy the milk now!

Declarative sentences are the most common type, probably because they are comprised of the most general content, without any of the bells and whistles that the other three types contain. They are, simply, declarations or statements of any degree of seriousness, importance, or information.

Imperative sentences often seem to be missing a subject. The subject is there, though; it is just not visible or audible because it is *implied*. Look at the imperative example sentence.

Buy the milk when you fill up your car with gas.

You is the implied subject, the one to whom the command is issued. This is sometimes called **the understood you** because it is understood that *you* is the subject of the sentence.

Interrogative sentences—those that ask questions—are defined as such from the idea of the word **interrogation**, the action of questions being asked of suspects by investigators. Although that is serious business, interrogative sentences apply to all kinds of questions.

To exclaim is at the root of **exclamatory** sentences. These are made with strong emotions behind them. The only technical difference between a declarative or imperative sentence and an exclamatory one is the exclamation mark at the end. The example declarative and imperative sentences can both become an exclamatory one simply by putting an exclamation mark at the end of the sentences.

The price of milk per gallon is the same as the price of gasoline!
Buy milk when you stop to fill up your car with gas!

After all, someone might be really excited by the price of gas or milk, or they could be mad at the person that will be buying the milk! However, as stated before, exclamation marks in abundance defeat their own purpose! After a while, they begin to cause fatigue! When used only for their intended purpose, they can have their expected and desired effect.

Parts of Speech

Nouns

A **noun** is a person, place, thing, or idea. All nouns fit into one of two types, common or proper.

A **common noun** is a word that identifies any of a class of people, places, or things. Examples include numbers, objects, animals, feelings, concepts, qualities, and actions. *A, an,* or *the* usually precedes the common noun. These parts of speech are called *articles*. Here are some examples of sentences using nouns preceded by articles.

A building is under construction.
The girl would like to move to *the* city.

A **proper noun** (also called a **proper name**) is used for the specific name of an individual person, place, or organization. The first letter in a proper noun is capitalized. "My name is *Mary*." "I work for *Walmart*."

Nouns sometimes serve as adjectives (which themselves describe nouns), such as "hockey player" and "state government."

- An **abstract noun** is an idea, state, or quality. It is something that can't be touched, such as happiness, courage, evil, or humor.

A **concrete noun** is something that can be experienced through the senses (touch, taste, hear, smell, see). Examples of concrete nouns are birds, skateboard, pie, and car.

A **collective noun** refers to a collection of people, places, or things that act as one. Examples of collective nouns are as follows: team, class, jury, family, audience, and flock.

Pronouns

A word used in place of a noun is known as a **pronoun.** Pronouns are words like *I, mine, hers,* and *us*.

Pronouns can be split into different classifications (seen below) which make them easier to learn; however, it's not important to memorize the classifications.

- Personal pronouns: refer to people, places, things, etc.
  - First person: we, I, our, mine
  - Second person: you, yours
  - Third person: he, them
- Possessive pronouns: demonstrate ownership (mine, his, hers, its, ours, theirs, yours)
- Interrogative pronouns: ask questions (what, which, who, whom, whose)
- Relative pronouns: include the five interrogative pronouns and others that are relative (whoever, whomever, that, when, where)
- Demonstrative pronouns: replace something specific (this, that, those, these)
- Reciprocal pronouns: indicate something was done or given in return (each other, one another)
- Indefinite pronouns: have a nonspecific status (anybody, whoever, someone, everybody, somebody)

Indefinite pronouns such as *anybody, whoever, someone, everybody*, and *somebody* command a singular verb form, but others such as *all, none,* and *some* could require a singular or plural verb form.

Antecedents

An **antecedent** is the noun to which a pronoun refers; it needs to be written or spoken before the pronoun is used. For many pronouns, antecedents are imperative for clarity. In particular, many of the personal, possessive, and demonstrative pronouns need antecedents. Otherwise, it would be unclear who or what someone is referring to when they use a pronoun like *he* or *this*.

Pronoun reference means that the pronoun should refer clearly to one, clear, unmistakable noun (the antecedent).

Pronoun-antecedent agreement refers to the need for the antecedent and the corresponding pronoun to agree in gender, person, and number. Here are some examples:

- The *kidneys* (plural antecedent) are part of the urinary system. *They* (plural pronoun) serve several roles.

The kidneys are part of the *urinary system* (singular antecedent). *It* (singular pronoun) is also known as the renal system.

Pronoun Cases

The subjective pronouns —*I, you, he/she/it, we, they,* and *who*—are the subjects of the sentence.

Example: *They* have a new house.

The objective pronouns—*me, you* (*singular*), *him/her, us, them,* and *whom*—are used when something is being done for or given to someone; they are objects of the action.

Example: The teacher has an apple for *us*.

The possessive pronouns—*mine, my, your, yours, his, hers, its, their, theirs, our,* and *ours*—are used to denote that something (or someone) belongs to someone (or something).

Example: It's *their* chocolate cake.
Even Better Example: It's *my* chocolate cake!

One of the greatest challenges and worst abuses of pronouns concerns *who* and *whom*. Just knowing the following rule can eliminate confusion. *Who* is a subjective-case pronoun used only as a subject or subject complement. *Whom* is only objective-case and, therefore, the object of the verb or preposition.

Who is going to the concert?

You are going to the concert with *whom*?

Hint: When using *who* or *whom*, think of whether someone would say *he* or *him*. If the answer is *he*, use *who*. If the answer is *him*, use *whom*. This trick is easy to remember because *he* and *who* both end in vowels, and *him* and *whom* both end in the letter *M*.

Verbs

A **verb** is the part of speech that describes an action, state of being, or occurrence.

A verb forms the main part of a predicate of a sentence. This means that the verb explains what the noun (which will be discussed shortly) is doing. A simple example is *time flies*. The verb *flies* explains what the action of the noun, *time*, is doing. This example is a *main* verb.

Helping (auxiliary) verbs are words like *have, do, be, can, may, should, must,* and *will*. "I *should* go to the store." Helping verbs assist main verbs in expressing tense, ability, possibility, permission, or obligation.

Particles are minor function words like *not, in, out, up,* or *down* that become part of the verb itself. "I might *not*."

Participles are words formed from verbs that are often used to modify a noun, noun phrase, verb, or verb phrase.

The *running* teenager collided with the cyclist.

Participles can also create compound verb forms.

He is *speaking*.

Verbs have five basic forms: the **base** form, the **-*s*** form, the **-*ing*** form, the **past** form, and the **past participle** form.

The past forms are either **regular** (*love/loved; hate/hated*) or **irregular** because they don't end by adding the common past tense suffix "-ed" (*go/went; fall/fell; set/set*).

Verb Forms

Shifting verb forms entails **conjugation,** which is used to indicate tense, voice, or mood.

Verb tense is used to show when the action in the sentence took place. There are several different verb tenses, and it is important to know how and when to use them. Some verb tenses can be achieved by changing the form of the verb, while others require the use of helping verbs (e.g., *is, was,* or *has*).

Present tense shows the action is happening currently or is ongoing:

I walk to work every morning.

She is stressed about the deadline.

Past tense shows that the action happened in the past or that the state of being is in the past:

I walked to work yesterday morning.

She was stressed about the deadline.

Future tense shows that the action will happen in the future or is a future state of being:

I will walk to work tomorrow morning.

She will be stressed about the deadline.

Present perfect tense shows action that began in the past, but continues into the present:

I have walked to work all week.

She has been stressed about the deadline.

Past perfect tense shows an action was finished before another took place:

I had walked all week until I sprained my ankle.

She had been stressed about the deadline until we talked about it.

Future perfect tense shows an action that will be completed at some point in the future:

By the time the bus arrives, I will have walked to work already.

Voice

Verbs can be in the active or passive voice. When the subject completes the action, the verb is in **active voice**. When the subject receives the action of the sentence, the verb is in **passive voice**.

Active: Jamie ate the ice cream.

Passive: The ice cream was eaten by Jamie.

In active voice, the subject (*Jamie*) is the "do-er" of the action (*ate*). In passive voice, the subject *ice cream* receives the action of being eaten.

While passive voice can add variety to writing, active voice is the generally preferred sentence structure.

Mood

Mood is used to show the speaker's feelings about the subject matter. In English, there is indicative mood, imperative mood, and subjunctive mood.

Indicative mood is used to state facts, ask questions, or state opinions:

Bob will make the trip next week.

When can Bob make the trip?

Imperative mood is used to state a command or make a request:

Wait in the lobby.

Please call me next week.

Subjunctive mood is used to express a wish, an opinion, or a hope that is contrary to fact:

If I were in charge, none of this would have happened.

Allison wished she could take the exam over again when she saw her score.

Adjectives

Adjectives are words used to modify nouns and pronouns. They can be used alone or in a series and are used to further define or describe the nouns they modify.

Mark made us a delicious, four-course meal.

The words *delicious* and *four-course* are adjectives that describe the kind of meal Mark made.

Articles are also considered adjectives because they help to describe nouns. Articles can be general or specific. The three articles in English are: *a, an*, and *the*.

Indefinite articles *(a, an)* are used to refer to nonspecific nouns. The article *a* proceeds words beginning with consonant sounds, and the article *an* proceeds words beginning with vowel sounds.

A car drove by our house.

An alligator was loose at the zoo.

He has always wanted a ukulele. (The first *u* makes a *y* sound.)

Note that *a* and *an* should only proceed nonspecific nouns that are also singular. If a nonspecific noun is plural, it does not need a preceding article.

Alligators were loose at the zoo.

The **definite article** *(the)* is used to refer to specific nouns:

The car pulled into our driveway.

Note that *the* should proceed all specific nouns regardless of whether they are singular or plural.

The cars pulled into our driveway.

Comparative adjectives are used to compare nouns. When they are used in this way, they take on positive, comparative, or superlative form.

The **positive** form is the normal form of the adjective:

Alicia is tall.

The **comparative** form shows a comparison between two things:

Alicia is taller than Maria.

Superlative form shows comparison between more than two things:

Alicia is the tallest girl in her class.

Usually, the comparative and superlative can be made by adding *–er* and *–est* to the positive form, but some verbs call for the helping verbs *more* or *most*. Other exceptions to the rule include adjectives like *bad*, which uses the comparative *worse* and the superlative *worst*.

An **adjective phrase** is not a bunch of adjectives strung together, but a group of words that describes a noun or pronoun and, thus, functions as an adjective. *Very happy* is an adjective phrase; so are *way too hungry* and *passionate about traveling*.

Adverbs

Adverbs have more functions than adjectives because they modify or qualify verbs, adjectives, or other adverbs as well as word groups that express a relation of place, time, circumstance, or cause. Therefore, adverbs answer any of the following questions: *How, when, where, why, in what way, how often, how much, in what condition,* and/or *to what degree. How good looking is he? He is <u>very</u> handsome.*

Here are some examples of adverbs for different situations:

how: quickly
when: daily
where: there
in what way: easily
how often: often
how much: much
in what condition: badly
what degree: hardly

As one can see, for some reason, many adverbs end in *-ly.*

Adverbs do things like emphasize (*really, simply,* and *so*), amplify (*heartily, completely,* and *positively*), and tone down (*almost, somewhat,* and *mildly*).

Adverbs also come in phrases.

The dog ran as though his life depended on it.

Prepositions

Prepositions are connecting words and, while there are only about 150 of them, they are used more often than any other individual groups of words. They describe relationships between other words. They are placed before a noun or pronoun, forming a phrase that modifies another word in the sentence. **Prepositional phrases** begin with a preposition and end with a noun or pronoun, the **object of the preposition.** *A pristine lake is near the store and behind the bank.*

Some commonly used prepositions are *about, after, anti, around, as, at, behind, beside, by, for, from, in, into, of, off, on, to,* and *with.*

Complex prepositions, which also come before a noun or pronoun, consist of two or three words such as *according to, in regards to,* and *because of.*

Conjunctions

Conjunctions are vital words that connect words, phrases, thoughts, and ideas. Conjunctions show relationships between components. There are two types:

Coordinating conjunctions are the primary class of conjunctions placed between words, phrases, clauses, and sentences that are of equal grammatical rank; the coordinating conjunctions are *for, and, nor, but, or, yet,* and *so.* A useful memorization trick is to remember that the first letter of these conjunctions collectively spell the word *fanboys*.

I need to go shopping, *but* I must be careful to leave enough money in the bank.
She wore a black, red, *and* white shirt.

Subordinating conjunctions are the secondary class of conjunctions. They connect two unequal parts, one **main** (or **independent**) and the other *subordinate* (or *dependent*). I must go to the store *even though* I do not have enough money in the bank.

Because I read the review, I do not want to go to the movie.

Notice that the presence of subordinating conjunctions makes clauses dependent. *I read the review* is an independent clause, but *because* makes the clause dependent. Thus, it needs an independent clause to complete the sentence.

Interjections

Interjections are words used to express emotion. Examples include *wow*, *ouch*, and *hooray*. Interjections are often separate from sentences; in those cases, the interjection is directly followed by an exclamation point. In other cases, the interjection is included in a sentence and followed by a comma. The punctuation plays a big role in the intensity of the emotion that the interjection is expressing. Using a comma or semicolon indicates less excitement than using an exclamation mark.

Capitalization Rules

Here's a non-exhaustive list of things that should be capitalized:

- The first word of every sentence
- The first word of every line of poetry
- The first letter of proper nouns (World War II)
- Holidays (Valentine's Day)
- The days of the week and months of the year (Tuesday, March)
- The first word, last word, and all major words in the titles of books, movies, songs, and other creative works (In the novel, To Kill a Mockingbird, note that a is lowercase since it's not a major word, but to is capitalized since it's the first word of the title.)
- Titles when preceding a proper noun (President Roberto Gonzales, Aunt Judy)

When simply using a word such as president or secretary, though, the word is not capitalized.

> Officers of the new business must include a *president* and *treasurer*.

Seasons—spring, fall, etc.—are not capitalized.

North, *south*, *east*, and *west* are capitalized when referring to regions but are not when being used for directions. In general, if it's preceded by *the* it should be capitalized.

> I'm from the South.
> I drove south.

End Punctuation

Periods (.) are used to end a sentence that is a statement (**declarative**) or a command (**imperative**). They should not be used in a sentence that asks a question or is an exclamation. Periods are also used in abbreviations, which are shortened versions of words.

Declarative: The boys refused to go to sleep.
Imperative: Walk down to the bus stop.
Abbreviations: Joan Roberts, M.D., Apple Inc., Mrs. Adamson
If a sentence ends with an abbreviation, it is inappropriate to use two periods. It should end with a single period after the abbreviation.

The chef gathered the ingredients for the pie, which included apples, flour, sugar, etc.

Question marks *(?)* are used with direct questions (**interrogative**). An **indirect question** can use a period:

Interrogative: When does the next bus arrive?

Indirect Question: I wonder when the next bus arrives.

An **exclamation point** *(!)* is used to show strong emotion or can be used as an interjection. This punctuation should be used sparingly in formal writing situations.

What an amazing shot!

Whoa!

Commas

A **comma** (,) is the punctuation mark that signifies a pause—breath—between parts of a sentence. It denotes a break of flow. Proper comma usage helps readers understand the writer's intended emphasis of ideas.

In a complex sentence—one that contains a **subordinate** (dependent) clause or clauses—the use of a comma is dictated by where the subordinate clause is located. If the subordinate clause is located before the main clause, a comma is needed between the two clauses.

I will not pay for the steak, *because I don't have that much money.*

Generally, if the subordinate clause is placed after the main clause, no punctuation is needed.

I did well on my exam because I studied two hours the night before.

Notice how the last clause is dependent because it requires the earlier independent clauses to make sense.

Use a comma on both sides of an interrupting phrase.

I will pay for the ice cream, *chocolate and vanilla*, and then will eat it all myself.

The words forming the phrase in italics are nonessential (extra) information. To determine if a phrase is nonessential, try reading the sentence without the phrase and see if it's still coherent.

A comma is not necessary in this next sentence because no interruption—nonessential or extra information—has occurred. Read sentences aloud when uncertain.

I will pay for his chocolate and vanilla ice cream and then will eat it all myself.

If the nonessential phrase comes at the beginning of a sentence, a comma should only go at the end of the phrase. If the phrase comes at the end of a sentence, a comma should only go at the beginning of the phrase.

Other types of interruptions include the following:

- interjections: Oh no, I am not going.
- abbreviations: Barry Potter, M.D., specializes in heart disorders.
- direct addresses: Yes, Claudia, I am tired and going to bed.
- parenthetical phrases: His wife, lovely as she was, was not helpful.
- transitional phrases: Also, it is not possible.

The second comma in the following sentence is called an **Oxford comma**.

I will pay for ice cream, syrup, and pop.

It is a comma used after the second-to-last item in a series of three or more items. It comes before the word *or* or *and*. Not everyone uses the Oxford comma; it is optional, but many believe it is needed. The comma functions as a tool to reduce confusion in writing. So, if omitting the Oxford comma would cause confusion, then it's best to include it.

Commas are used in math to mark the place of thousands in numerals, breaking them up so they are easier to read. Other uses for commas are in dates (*March 19, 2016*), letter greetings (*Dear Sally,*), and in between cities and states (*Louisville, KY*).

Semicolons

A **semicolon** *(;)* is used to connect ideas in a sentence in some way. There are three main ways to use semicolons.

Link two independent clauses without the use of a coordinating conjunction:

I was late for work again; I'm definitely going to get fired.

Link two independent clauses with a transitional word:

The songs were all easy to play; therefore, he didn't need to spend too much time practicing.

Between items in a series that are already separated by commas or if necessary to separate lengthy items in a list:

Starbucks has locations in Media, PA; Swarthmore, PA; and Morton, PA.

Several classroom management issues presented in the study: the advent of a poor teacher persona in the context of voice, dress, and style; teacher follow-through from the beginning of the school year to the end; and the depth of administrative support, including ISS and OSS protocol.

Colons

A **colon** (:) is used after an independent clause to present an explanation or draw attention to what comes next in the sentence. There are several uses.

Explanations of ideas:

They soon learned the hardest part about having a new baby: sleep deprivation.

Lists of items:

Shari picked up all the supplies she would need for the party: cups, plates, napkins, balloons, streamers, and party favors.

Time, subtitles, general salutations:

The time is 7:15.

I read a book entitled *Pluto: A Planet No More.*

To whom it may concern:

Parentheses and Dashes

Parentheses are half-round brackets that look like this: *( )*. They set off a word, phrase, or sentence that is an afterthought, explanation, or side note relevant to the surrounding text but not essential. A pair of commas is often used to set off this sort of information, but parentheses are generally used for information that would not fit well within a sentence or that the writer deems not important enough to be structurally part of the sentence.

The picture of the heart (see above) shows the major parts you should memorize.
Mount Everest is one of three mountains in the world that are over 28,000 feet high (K2 and Kanchenjunga are the other two).

See how the sentences above are complete without the parenthetical statements? In the first example, *see above* would not have fit well within the flow of the sentence. The second parenthetical statement could have been a separate sentence, but the writer deemed the information not pertinent to the topic.

The **em-dash** (—) is a mark longer than a hyphen used as a punctuation mark in sentences and to set apart a relevant thought. Even after plucking out the line separated by the dash marks, the sentence will be intact and make sense.

> Looking out the airplane window at the landmarks—Lake Clarke, Thompson Community College, and the bridge—she couldn't help but feel excited to be home.

The dashes use is similar to that of parentheses or a pair of commas. So, what's the difference? Many believe that using dashes makes the clause within them stand out while using parentheses is subtler. It's advised to not use dashes when commas could be used instead.

Ellipses

An **ellipsis** (...) is used to show that there is more to the quoted text than is necessary for the current discussion. Writers use them in place of words, lines, phrases, list content, or paragraphs that might just as easily have been omitted from a passage of writing. This can be done to save space or to focus only on the specifically relevant material.

> Exercise is good for some unexpected reasons. Watkins writes, "Exercise has many benefits such as...reducing cancer risk."

In the example above, the ellipsis takes the place of the other benefits of exercise that are more expected.

The ellipsis may also be used to show a pause in sentence flow.

> "I'm wondering...how this could happen," Dylan said in a soft voice.

Quotation Marks

Double quotation marks are used at the beginning and end of a direct quote. They are also used with certain titles and to indicate that a term being used is slang or referenced in the sentence. Quotation marks should not be used with an indirect quote. Single quotation marks are used to indicate a quote within a quote.

> Direct quote: "The weather is supposed to be beautiful this week," she said.
>
> Indirect quote: One of the customers asked if the sale prices were still in effect.
>
> Quote within a quote: "My little boy just said 'Mama, I want cookie,'" Maria shared.

Titles: Quotation marks should also be used to indicate titles of short works or sections of larger works, such as chapter titles. Other works that use quotation marks include poems, short stories, newspaper articles, magazine articles, web page titles, and songs.

> "The Road Not Taken" is my favorite poem by Robert Frost.
>
> "What a Wonderful World" is one of my favorite songs.

Specific or emphasized terms: Quotation marks can also be used to indicate a technical term or to set off a word that is being discussed in a sentence. Quotation marks can also indicate sarcasm.

> The new step, called "levigation," is a very difficult technique.

> He said he was "hungry" multiple times, but he only ate two bites.

Use with other punctuation: The use of quotation marks with other punctuation varies, depending on the role of the ending or separating punctuation.

In American English, commas and periods go inside quotation marks:

> "This is the last time you are allowed to leave early," his boss stated.

> The newscaster said, "We have some breaking news to report."

Question marks or exclamation points go inside the quotation marks when they are part of a direct quote:

> The doctor shouted, "Get the crash cart!"

When the question mark or exclamation point is part of the sentence, not the quote, it should be placed outside of the quotation marks:

> Was it Jackie that said, "Get some potatoes at the store"?

Apostrophes

This punctuation mark, the **apostrophe** (') is a versatile mark. It has several different functions:

- Quotes: Apostrophes are used when a second quote is needed within a quote.
  - In my letter to my friend, I wrote, "The girl had to get a new purse, and guess what Mary did? She said, 'I'd like to go with you to the store.' I knew Mary would buy it for her."
- Contractions: Another use for an apostrophe in the quote above is a contraction. *I'd is used for I would.*
- Possession: An apostrophe followed by the letter s shows possession (Mary's purse). If the possessive word is plural, the apostrophe generally just follows the word. Not all possessive pronouns require apostrophes.
  - The trees' leaves are all over the ground.

Hyphens

The **hyphen** (-) is a small hash mark that can be used to join words to show that they are linked.

Hyphens can connect two words that work together as a single adjective (a compound adjective).

> honey-covered biscuits

Some words always require hyphens even if not serving as an adjective.

merry-go-round

Hyphens always go after certain prefixes like *anti-* & *all-*.

Hyphens should also be used when the absence of the hyphen would cause a strange vowel combination (*semi-engineer*) or confusion. For example, *re-collect* should be used to describe something being gathered twice rather than being written as *recollect*, which means to remember.

Subjects

Every sentence must include a subject and a verb. The **subject** of a sentence is who or what the sentence is about. It's often directly stated and can be determined by asking "Who?" or "What?" did the action:

Most sentences contain a **direct subject**, in which the subject is mentioned in the sentence.

Kelly mowed the lawn.

Who mowed the lawn? *Kelly*

The air-conditioner ran all night

What ran all night? *the air-conditioner*

The subject of imperative sentences is the implied *you*, because imperative subjects are commands:

Go home after the meeting.

Who should go home after the meeting? *you* (implied)

In **expletive sentences** that start with "there are" or "there is," the subject is found after the predicate. The subject cannot be "there," so it must be another word in the sentence:

There is a cup sitting on the coffee table.

What is sitting on the coffee table? *a cup*

Simple and Complete Subjects

A **complete subject** includes the simple subject and all the words modifying it, including articles and adjectives. A **simple subject** is the single noun without its modifiers.

A warm, chocolate-chip cookie sat on the kitchen table.

Complete subject: *a warm, chocolate-chip cookie*

Simple subject: *cookie*

The words *a, warm, chocolate,* and *chip* all modify the simple subject *cookie*.

There might also be a **compound subject**, which would be two or more nouns without the modifiers.

A little girl and her mother walked into the shop.

Complete subject: *A little girl and her mother*

Compound subject: *girl, mother*

In this case, *the girl and her mother* are both completing the action of walking into the shop, so this is a compound subject.

Predicates

In addition to the subject, a sentence must also have a predicate. The **predicate** contains a verb and tells something about the subject. In addition to the verb, a predicate can also contain a direct or indirect object, object of a preposition, and other phrases.

The cats napped on the front porch.

In this sentence, cats is the subject because the sentence is about cats.

The **complete predicate** is everything else in the sentence: *napped on the front porch.* This phrase is the predicate because it tells us what the cats did.

This sentence can be broken down into a simple subject and predicate:

Cats napped.

In this sentence, *cats* is the simple subject, and *napped* is the **simple predicate**.

Although the sentence is very short and doesn't offer much information, it's still considered a complete sentence because it contains a subject and predicate.

Like a compound subject, a sentence can also have a **compound predicate**. This is when the subject is or does two or more things in the sentence.

This easy chair reclines and swivels.

In this sentence, *this easy chair* is the complete subject. *Reclines and swivels* shows two actions of the chair, so this is the compound predicate.

Subject-Verb Agreement

The subject of a sentence and its verb must agree. The cornerstone rule of subject-verb agreement is that subject and verb must agree in number. Whether the subject is singular or plural, the verb must follow suit.

Incorrect: The houses is new.
Correct: The houses are new.
Also Correct: The house is new.

In other words, a singular subject requires a singular verb; a plural subject requires a plural verb. The words or phrases that come between the subject and verb do not alter this rule.

> Incorrect: The houses built of brick is new.
> Correct: The houses built of brick are new.
>
> Incorrect: The houses with the sturdy porches is new.
> Correct: The houses with the sturdy porches are new.

The subject will always follow the verb when a sentence begins with *here* or *there.* Identify these with care.

> Incorrect: Here *is* the *houses* with sturdy porches.
> Correct: Here *are* the *houses* with sturdy porches.

The subject in the sentences above is not *here*, it is *houses*. Remember, *here* and *there* are never subjects. Be careful that contractions such as *here's* or *there're* do not cause confusion!

Two subjects joined by *and* require a plural verb form, except when the two combine to make one thing:

> Incorrect: Garrett and Jonathan is over there.
> Correct: Garrett and Jonathan are over there.
>
> Incorrect: Spaghetti and meatballs are a delicious meal!
> Correct: Spaghetti and meatballs is a delicious meal!

In the example above, *spaghetti and meatballs* is a compound noun. However, *Garrett and Jonathan* is not a compound noun.

Two singular subjects joined by *or, either/or,* or *neither/nor* call for a singular verb form.

> Incorrect: Butter or syrup are acceptable.
> Correct: Butter or syrup is acceptable.

Plural subjects joined by *or*, *either/or*, or *neither/nor* are, indeed, plural.

> The chairs or the boxes are being moved next.

If one subject is singular and the other is plural, the verb should agree with the closest noun.

> Correct: The chair or the boxes are being moved next.
> Correct: The chairs or the box is being moved next.

Some plurals of money, distance, and time call for a singular verb.

> Incorrect: Three dollars *are* enough to buy that.
> Correct: Three dollars *is* enough to buy that.

For words declaring degrees of quantity such as *many of, some of,* or *most of,* let the noun that follows of be the guide:

Incorrect: Many of the books is in the shelf.
Correct: Many of the books are in the shelf.

Incorrect: Most of the pie *are* on the table.
Correct: Most of the pie *is* on the table.

For indefinite pronouns like *anybody* or *everybody*, use singular verbs.

Everybody *is* going to the store.

However, the pronouns *few, many, several, all, some,* and *both* have their own rules and use plural forms.

Some *are* ready.

Some nouns like *crowd* and *congress* are called **collective nouns** and they require a singular verb form.

Congress *is* in session.
The news *is* over.

Books and movie titles, though, including plural nouns such as *Great Expectations*, also require a singular verb. Remember that only the subject affects the verb. While writing tricky subject-verb arrangements, say them aloud. Listen to them. Once the rules have been learned, one's ear will become sensitive to them, making it easier to pick out what's right and what's wrong.

Direct Objects

The **direct object** is the part of the sentence that receives the action of the verb. It is a noun and can usually be found after the verb. To find the direct object, first find the verb, and then ask the question *who* or *what* after it.

The bear climbed the tree.

What did the bear climb? *the tree*

Indirect Objects

An **indirect object** receives the direct object. It is usually found between the verb and the direct object. A strategy for identifying the indirect object is to find the verb and ask the questions *to whom/for whom* or *to what/for what*.

Jane made her daughter a cake.

For whom did Jane make the cake? *her daughter*

Cake is the direct object because it is what Jane made, and *daughter* is the indirect object because she receives the cake.

Complements

A **complement** completes the meaning of an expression. A complement can be a pronoun, noun, or adjective. A **verb complement** refers to the direct object or indirect object in the sentence. An **object complement** gives more information about the direct object:

The magician got the kids excited.

Kids is the direct object, and *excited* is the object complement.

A **subject complement** comes after a linking verb. It is typically an adjective or noun that gives more information about the subject:

The king was noble and spared the thief's life.

Noble describes the *king* and follows the linking verb *was*.

Predicate Nouns

A **predicate noun** renames the subject:

John is a carpenter.

The subject is *John*, and the predicate noun is *carpenter*.

Predicate Adjectives

A **predicate adjective** describes the subject:

Margaret is beautiful.

The subject is *Margaret*, and the predicate adjective is *beautiful*.

Homonyms

Homonyms are words that sound the same but are spelled differently, and they have different meanings. There are several common homonyms that give writers trouble.

There, *They're*, and *Their*

The word *there* can be used as an adverb, adjective, or pronoun:

There are ten children on the swim team this summer.

I put my book over *there*, but now I can't find it.

The word *they're* is a contraction of the words *they* and *are*:

They're flying in from Texas on Tuesday.

The word *their* is a possessive pronoun:

I store *their* winter clothes in the attic.

Its and *It's*

Its is a possessive pronoun:

The cat licked *its* injured paw.

It's is the contraction for the words *it* and *is*:

It's unbelievable how many people opted not to vote in the last election.

Your and You're

Your is a possessive pronoun:

Can I borrow *your* lawnmower this weekend?

You're is a contraction for the words *you* and *are*:

You're about to embark on a fantastic journey.

To, Too, and *Two*

To is an adverb or a preposition used to show direction, relationship, or purpose:

We are going *to* New York.

They are going *to* see a show.

Too is an adverb that means more than enough, also, and very:

You have had *too* much candy.

We are on vacation that week, *too*.

Two is the written-out form of the numeral 2:

Two of the shirts didn't fit, so I will have to return them.

New and *Knew*

New is an adjective that means recent:

There's a *new* customer on the phone.

Knew is the past tense of the verb *know*:

I *knew* you'd have fun on this ride.

Affect and *Effect*

Affect and *effect* are complicated because they are used as both nouns and verbs, have similar meanings, and are pronounced the same.

	Affect	Effect
Noun Definition	emotional state	result
Noun Example	The patient's affect was flat.	The effects of smoking are well documented.
Verb Definition	to influence	to bring about
Verb Example	The pollen count affects my allergies.	The new candidate hopes to effect change.

Independent and Dependent Clauses

Independent and **dependent** clauses are strings of words that contain both a subject and a verb. An independent clause *can* stand alone as complete thought, but a dependent clause *cannot*. A dependent clause relies on other words to be a complete sentence.

Independent clause: The keys are on the counter.
Dependent clause: If the keys are on the counter

Notice that both clauses have a subject (*keys*) and a verb (*are*). The independent clause expresses a complete thought, but the word *if* at the beginning of the dependent clause makes it *dependent* on other words to be a complete thought.

Independent clause: If the keys are on the counter, please give them to me.

This example constitutes a complete sentence since it includes at least one verb and one subject and is a complete thought. In this case, the independent clause has two subjects (*keys* & an implied *you*) and two verbs (*are* & *give*).

Independent clause: I went to the store.
Dependent clause: Because we are out of milk,

Complete Sentence: Because we are out of milk, I went to the store.
Complete Sentence: I went to the store because we are out of milk.

Phrases

A **phrase** is a group of words that do not make a complete thought or a clause. They are parts of sentences or clauses. Phrases can be used as nouns, adjectives, or adverbs. A phrase does not contain both a subject and a verb.

Prepositional Phrases

A **prepositional phrase** shows the relationship between a word in the sentence and the object of the preposition. The **object of the preposition** is a noun that follows the preposition.

The orange pillows are on the couch.

On is the preposition, and *couch* is the object of the preposition.

She brought her friend with the nice car.

With is the preposition, and *car* is the object of the preposition. Here are some common prepositions:

about	as	at	after
by	for	from	in
of	on	to	with

Verbals and Verbal Phrases

Verbals are forms of verbs that act as other parts of speech. They can be used as nouns, adjectives, or adverbs. Though they are verb forms, they are not to be used as the verb in the sentence. A word group that is based on a verbal is considered a **verbal phrase**. There are three major types of verbals: participles, gerunds, and infinitives.

Participles are verbals that act as adjectives. The present participle ends in *–ing*, and the past participle ends in *–d*, *-ed*, *-n*, or-*t*.

Verb	Present Participle	Past Participle
walk	walking	walked
share	sharing	shared

Participial phrases are made up of the participle and modifiers, complements, or objects.

Crying for most of an hour, the baby didn't seem to want to nap.

Having already taken this course, the student was bored during class.

Crying for most of an hour and *Having already taken this course* are the participial phrases.

Gerunds are verbals that are used as nouns and end in *–ing*. A gerund can be the subject or object of the sentence like a noun. Note that a present participle can also end in *–ing*, so it is important to distinguish between the two. The gerund is used as a noun, while the participle is used as an adjective.

Swimming is my favorite sport.

I wish I were sleeping.

A **gerund phrase** includes the gerund and any modifiers or complements, direct objects, indirect objects, or pronouns.

Cleaning the house is my least favorite weekend activity.

Cleaning the house is the gerund phrase acting as the subject of the sentence.

The most important goal this year is raising money for charity.

Raising money for charity is the gerund phrase acting as the direct object.

The police accused the woman of stealing the car.

The gerund phrase *stealing the car* is the object of the preposition in this sentence.

An **infinitive** is a verbal made up of the word *to* and a verb. Infinitives can be used as nouns, adjectives, or adverbs.

Examples: To eat, to jump, to swim, to lie, to call, to work

An *infinitive phrase* is made up of the infinitive plus any complements or modifiers. The infinitive phrase *to wait* is used as the subject in this sentence:

To wait was not what I had in mind.

The infinitive phrase *to sing* is used as the subject complement in this sentence:

Her dream is to sing.

The infinitive phrase *to grow* is used as an adverb in this sentence:

Children must eat to grow.

Appositive Phrases

An **appositive** is a noun or noun phrase that renames a noun that comes immediately before it in the sentence. An appositive can be a single word or several words. These phrases can be **essential** or **nonessential**. An essential appositive phrase is necessary to the meaning of the sentence and a nonessential appositive phrase is not. It is important to be able to distinguish these for purposes of comma use.

Essential: My sister Christina works at a school.

Naming which sister is essential to the meaning of the sentence, so no commas are needed.

Nonessential: My sister, who is a teacher, is coming over for dinner tonight.

Who is a teacher is not essential to the meaning of the sentence, so commas are required.

Absolute Phrases

An **absolute phrase** modifies a noun without using a conjunction. It is not the subject of the sentence and is not a complete thought on its own. Absolute phrases are set off from the independent clause with a comma.

Arms outstretched, she yelled at the sky.

All things considered, this has been a great day.

The Four Types of Sentence Structures

A **simple sentence** has one independent clause.

I am going to win.

A **compound sentence** has two independent clauses. A conjunction—*for, and, nor, but, or, yet, so*—links them together. Note that each of the independent clauses has a subject and a verb.

I am going to win, but the odds are against me.

A **complex sentence** has one independent clause and one or more dependent clauses.

I am going to win, even though I don't deserve it.

Even though I don't deserve it is a dependent clause. It does not stand on its own. Some conjunctions that link an independent and a dependent clause are *although, because, before, after, that, when, which*, and *while.*

A **compound-complex sentence** has at least three clauses, two of which are independent and at least one that is a dependent clause.

While trying to dance, I tripped over my partner's feet, but I regained my balance quickly.

The dependent clause is *While trying to dance.*

Sentence Fragments

A **sentence fragment** is an incomplete sentence. An independent clause is made up of a subject and a predicate, and both are needed to make a complete sentence.

Sentence fragments often begin with relative pronouns (when, which), subordinating conjunctions (because, although) or gerunds (trying, being, seeing). They might be missing the subject or the predicate.

The most common type of fragment is the isolated dependent clause, which can be corrected by joining it to the independent clause that appears before or after the fragment:

Fragment: While the cookies baked.

Correction: While the cookies baked, we played cards. (We played cards while the cookies baked.)

Run-on Sentences

A **run-on sentence** is created when two independent clauses (complete thoughts) are joined without correct punctuation or a conjunction. Run-on sentences can be corrected in the following ways:

Join the independent clauses with a comma and coordinating conjunction.

Run-on: We forgot to return the library books we had to pay a fine.

Correction: We forgot to return the library books, so we had to pay a fine.

Join the independent clauses with a semicolon, dash, or colon when the clauses are closely related in meaning.

Run-on: I had a salad for lunch every day this week I feel healthier already.

Correction: I had a salad for lunch every day this week; I feel healthier already.

Join the independent clauses with a semicolon and a conjunctive adverb.

Run-on: We arrived at the animal shelter on time however the dog had already been adopted.

Correction: We arrived at the animal shelter on time; however, the dog had already been adopted.

Separate the independent clauses into two sentences with a period.

Run-on: He tapes his favorite television show he never misses an episode.

Correction: He tapes his favorite television show. He never misses an episode.

Rearrange the wording of the sentence to create an independent clause and a dependent clause.

Run-on: My wedding date is coming up I am getting more excited to walk down the aisle.

Correction: As my wedding date approaches, I am getting more excited to walk down the aisle.

Dangling and Misplaced Modifiers

A **modifier** is a phrase that describes, alters, limits, or gives more information about a word in the sentence. The two most common issues are dangling and misplaced modifiers.

A **dangling modifier** is created when the phrase modifies a word that is not clearly stated in the sentence.

Dangling modifier: Having finished dinner, the dishes were cleared from the table.

Correction: Having finished dinner, Amy cleared the dishes from the table.

In the first sentence, *having finished dinner* appears to modify *the dishes*, which obviously can't finish dinner. The second sentence adds the subject *Amy*, to make it clear who has finished dinner.

Dangling modifier: Hoping to improve test scores, all new books were ordered for the school.

Correction: Hoping to improve test scores, administrators ordered all new books for the school.

Without the subject *administrators*, it appears the books are hoping to improve test scores, which doesn't make sense.

Misplaced modifiers are placed incorrectly in the sentence, which can cause confusion. Compare these examples:

Misplaced modifier: Rory purchased a new flat screen television and placed it on the wall above the fireplace, with all the bells and whistles.

Revised: Rory purchased a new flat screen television, with all the bells and whistles, and placed it on the wall above the fireplace.

The bells and whistles should modify the television, not the fireplace.

Misplaced modifier: The delivery driver arrived late with the pizza, who was usually on time.

Revised: The delivery driver, who usually was on time, arrived late with the pizza.

This suggests that the delivery driver was usually on time, instead of the pizza.

Misplaced modifier: We saw a family of ducks on the way to church.

Revised: On the way to church, we saw a family of ducks.

The misplaced modifier, here, suggests the *ducks* were on their way to church, instead of the pronoun *we*.

Split Infinitives

An **infinitive** is made up of the word *to* and a verb, such as: to run, to jump, to ask. A **split infinitive** is created when a word comes between *to* and the verb.

Split infinitive: To quickly run

Correction: To run quickly

Split infinitive: To quietly ask

Correction: To ask quietly

Double Negatives

A **double negative** is a negative statement that includes two negative elements. This is incorrect in Standard English.

Incorrect: She hasn't never come to my house to visit.

Correct: She has never come to my house to visit.

The intended meaning is that she has never come to the house, so the double negative is incorrect. However, it is possible to use two negatives to create a positive statement.

Correct: She was not unhappy with her performance on the quiz.

In this case, the double negative, *was not unhappy*, is intended to show a positive, so it is correct. This means that she was somewhat happy with her performance.

Faulty Parallelism

It is necessary to use parallel construction in sentences that have multiple similar ideas. Using parallel structure provides clarity in writing. **Faulty parallelism** is created when multiple ideas are joined using different sentence structures. Compare these examples:

Incorrect: We start each practice with stretches, a run, and fielding grounders.
Correct: We start each practice with stretching, running, and fielding grounders.

Incorrect: I watched some television, reading my book, and fell asleep.
Correct: I watched some television, read my book, and fell asleep.

Incorrect: Some of the readiness skills for kindergarten are to cut with scissors, to tie shoes, and dressing independently.
Correct: Some of the readiness skills for kindergarten are being able to cut with scissors, to tie shoes, and to dress independently.

Subordination

If multiple pieces of information in a sentence are not equal, they can be joined by creating an independent clause and a dependent clause. The less important information becomes the **subordinate clause:**

Draft: The hotel was acceptable. We wouldn't stay at the hotel again.

Revised: Though the hotel was acceptable, we wouldn't stay there again.

The more important information (*we wouldn't stay there again*) becomes the main clause, and the less important information (*the hotel was acceptable*) becomes the subordinate clause.

Practice Quiz

Questions 1–5 are based on the following passage.

The Middle Ages were a time of great superstition and theological debate. Many beliefs were developed and practiced, while some died out or were listed as heresy. Boethianism is a Medieval theological philosophy that attributes sin to gratification and righteousness with virtue and God's providence. Boethianism holds that sin, greed, and corruption are means to attain temporary pleasure, but that they inherently harm the person's soul as well as other human beings.

In *The Canterbury Tales,* we observe more instances of bad actions punished than goodness being rewarded. This would appear to be some reflection of Boethianism. In the "Pardoner's Tale," all three thieves wind up dead, which is a result of their desire for wealth. Each wrongdoer pays with their life, and they are unable to enjoy the wealth they worked to steal. Within his tales, Chaucer gives reprieve to people undergoing struggle, but also interweaves stories of contemptible individuals being cosmically punished for their wickedness. The thieves idolize physical wealth, which leads to their downfall. This same theme and ideological principle of Boethianism is repeated in the "Friar's Tale," whose summoner character attempts to gain further wealth by partnering with a demon. The summoner's refusal to repent for his avarice and corruption leads to the demon dragging his soul to Hell. Again, we see the theme of the individual who puts faith and morality aside in favor for a physical prize. The result, of course, is that the summoner loses everything.

The examples of the righteous being rewarded tend to appear in a spiritual context within the *Canterbury Tales*. However, there are a few instances where we see goodness resulting in physical reward. In the *Priores's Tale*, we see corporal punishment for barbarism *and* a reward for goodness. The Jews are punished for their murder of the child, giving a sense of law and order (though racist) to the plot. While the boy does die, he is granted a lasting reward by being able to sing even after his death, a miracle that marks that the murdered youth led a pure life. Here, the miracle represents eternal favor with God.

Again, we see the theological philosophy of Boethianism in Chaucer's *The Canterbury Tales* through acts of sin and righteousness and the consequences that follow. When pleasures of the world are sought instead of God's favor, we see characters being punished in tragic ways. However, the absence of worldly lust has its own set of consequences for the characters seeking to obtain God's favor.

1. What would be a potential reward for living a good life, as described in Boethianism?
    a. A long life sustained by the good deeds one has done over a lifetime
    b. Wealth and fertility for oneself and the extension of one's family line
    c. Vengeance for those who have been persecuted by others who have a capacity for committing wrongdoing
    d. God's divine favor for one's righteousness

2. What might be the main reason why the author chose to discuss Boethianism through examining *The Canterbury Tales?*
   a. *The Canterbury Tales* is a well-known text.
   b. *The Canterbury Tales* is the only known fictional text that contains use of Boethianism.
   c. *The Canterbury Tales* presents a manuscript written in the medieval period that can help illustrate Boethianism through stories and show how people of the time might have responded to the idea.
   d. Within each individual tale in *The Canterbury Tales*, the reader can read about different levels of Boethianism and how each level leads to greater enlightenment.

3. What "ideological principle" is the author referring to in the middle of the second paragraph when talking about the "Friar's Tale"?
   a. The principle that the act of ravaging another's possessions is the same as ravaging one's soul
   b. The principle that thieves who idolize physical wealth will be punished in an earthly sense as well as eternally
   c. The principle that fraternization with a demon will result in one losing everything, including their life
   d. The principle that a desire for material goods leads to moral malfeasance punishable by a higher being

4. Which of the following words, if substituted for the word *avarice* in paragraph two, would least change the meaning of the sentence?
   a. Perniciousness
   b. Pithiness
   c. Covetousness
   d. Precariousness

5. Based on the passage, what view does Boethianism take on desire?
   a. Desire does not exist in the context of Boethianism.
   b. Desire is a virtue and should be welcomed.
   c. Having desire is evidence of demonic possession.
   d. Desire for pleasure can lead toward sin.

See answers on next page.

Answer Explanations

1. D: The author explains that Boethianism is a Medieval theological philosophy that attributes sin to temporary pleasure and righteousness with virtue and God's providence. Other than Choice *D*, the choices listed are all physical things. While these could still be divine rewards, Boethianism holds that the true reward for being virtuous is God's favor. It is also stressed in the article that physical pleasures cannot be taken into the afterlife. Therefore, the best choice is *D*, God's favor.

2. C: Choices *A* and *B* are generalized statements, and we have no evidence to support Choice *B*. Choice *D* is very compelling, but it looks at Boethianism in a way that the author does not. The author does not mention "different levels of Boethianism" when discussing the tales, only that the concept appears differently in different tales. Boethianism also doesn't focus on enlightenment.

3. D: Choice *A* is incorrect; while the text does mention thieves ravaging others' possessions, it is only meant as an example and not as the principle itself. Choice *B* is incorrect for the same reason as Choice *A*. Choice *C* is mentioned in the text and is part of the example that proves the principle, but it is not the principle itself. Choice *B* is incorrect for the same reason as *A*. Choice *C* is mentioned in the text and is part of the example that proves the principle, and also not the principle itself.

4. C: The word *avarice* most nearly means *covetousness*, or extremely desirous of money or wealth. Choice *A* means evil or mischief and does not relate to the context of the sentence. Choice *B* is also incorrect, because *pithiness* means shortness or conciseness. Choice *D* is close because *precariousness* means dangerous or instability, which goes well with the context. However, we are told of the summoner's specific characteristic of greed, which makes Choice *C* the best answer.

5. D: Boethianism acknowledges desire as something that leads out of holiness, so Choice *A* is incorrect. Choice *B* is incorrect because in the passage, Boethianism is depicted as being wary of desire and anything that binds people to the physical world. Choice *C* can be eliminated because the author never says that desire indicates demonic possession.

Mathematics

The Math section of the SAT focuses on a variety of math concepts and practices including real world applications of math operations and relations. The test includes a total of 58 questions to be answered in 80 minutes. The test contains multiple choice type questions and grid in questions where the test taker will be asked to fill in the answer rather than selecting from a number of options. The test provides instructions on how to complete the grid in questions. Test takers must be careful to only mark one circle in each column of the grid. Answers written only in the boxes above the circles will not be counted. If a fraction is an answer to a grid in question, they need not be simplified, but they must be converted to improper fractions. The Math Test also includes both a calculator section and a no calculator section. Test takers are not allowed to use calculators on the no calculator section; this is to assess math fluency, use of number operations, and number sense.

The Math section will ask the test taker to demonstrate their abilities in problem solving and modeling that reflect the types of situations that students will encounter in future college courses, careers, and everyday life. The Math section is broken down into three major content sections: Heart of Algebra, Problem Solving and Data Analysis, and Passport to Advanced Math. The test also incorporates additional topics in math that will help prepare students for their college and career.

The Heart of Algebra section encompasses the study of algebra and the major concepts needed to solve and create linear equations and functions. Students must also use analytical and problem-solving skills to solve questions concerning linear inequalities and systems of equations. Questions in this section are presented in a variety of ways including graphical and algebraic representations of problems that require different strategies and processes to complete.

The Problem Solving and Data Analysis section presents questions involving units and quantities that must be manipulated and converted using ratios, rates, and proportional relationships. Test takers will also need to interpret graphs, charts, and other representations of data to identify key features of a data set such as measures of center, patterns, spread, and deviations.

The Passport to Advanced Math section covers topics that will help ready students for more advanced math topics. One of the major topics in this section is knowledge of expressions and how to work with them. Also included in this section are building functions and interpreting complex equations.

The Additional Topics in Math section covers two main areas: geometric and trigonometric concepts. These include, but are not limited to, volume formulas, trigonometric ratios, and equations and theorems related to circles.

Scores for the Math section of the SAT range from 200 to 800. The three main areas of the Math section, heart of algebra, problem solving and data analysis, and passport to advanced math, are also given subscores which range from 1 to 15.

Heart of Algebra

Solving Linear Equations

A function is called **linear** if it can take the form of the equation $f(x) = ax + b$, or $y = ax + b$, for any two numbers a and b. A linear equation forms a straight line when graphed on the coordinate plane. An example of a linear function is shown below on the graph.

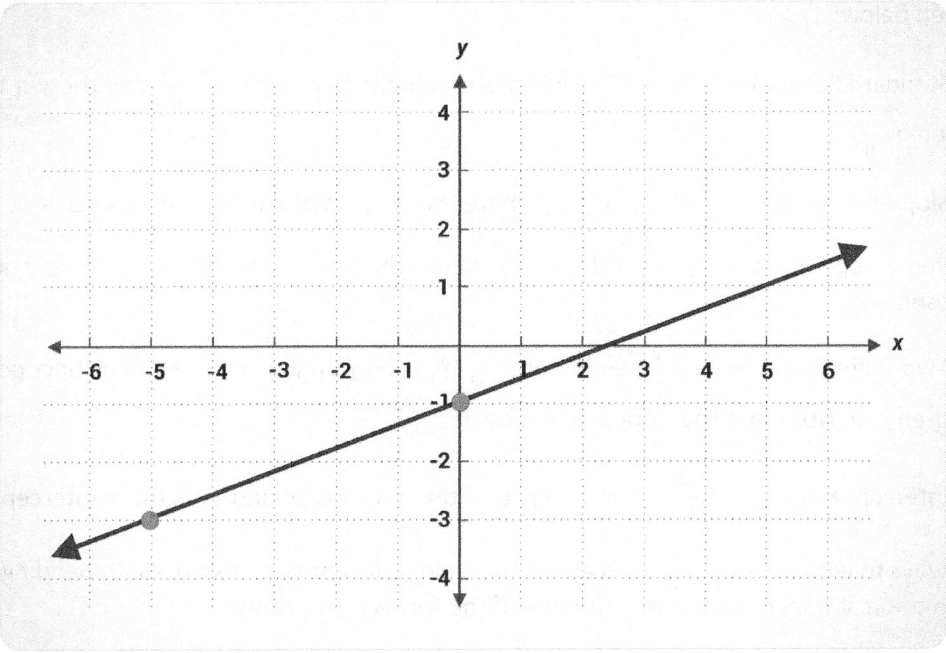

This is a graph of the following function: $y = \frac{2}{5}x - 1$. A table of values that satisfies this function is shown below.

x	y
-5	-3
0	-1
5	1
10	3

These points can be found on the graph using the form (x, y).

When graphing a linear function, note that the ratio of the change of the y-coordinate to the change in the x-coordinate is constant between any two points on the resulting line, no matter which two points are chosen. In other words, in a pair of points on a line, (x_1, y_1) and (x_2, y_2), with $x_1 \neq x_2$ so that the two points are distinct, then the ratio $\frac{y_2 - y_1}{x_2 - x_1}$ will be the same, regardless of which particular pair of points are chosen. This ratio, $\frac{y_2-y_1}{x_2-x_1}$, is called the **slope** of the line and is frequently denoted with the letter m. If slope m is positive, then the line goes upward when moving to the right, while if slope m is negative, then the line goes downward when moving to the right. If the slope is 0, then the line is called **horizontal**, and the y-coordinate is constant along the entire line. In lines where the x-coordinate is constant along the entire line, y is not actually a function of x. For such lines, the slope is not defined. These lines are called **vertical** lines.

Linear functions may take forms other than $y = ax + b$. The most common forms of linear equations are explained below:

1. Standard Form: $Ax + By = C$, in which the slope is given by $m = \frac{-A}{B}$, and the y-intercept is given by $\frac{C}{B}$.

2. Slope-Intercept Form: $y = mx + b$, where the slope is m and the y-intercept is b.

3. Point-Slope Form: $y - y_1 = m(x - x_1)$, where the slope is m and (x_1, y_1) is any point on the chosen line.

4. Two-Point Form: $\frac{y-y_1}{x-x_1} = \frac{y_2-y_1}{x_2-x_1}$, where (x_1, y_1) and (x_2, y_2) are any two distinct points on the chosen line. Note that the slope is given by $m = \frac{y_2-y_1}{x_2-x_1}$.

5. Intercept Form: $\frac{x}{x_1} + \frac{y}{y_1} = 1$, in which x_1 is the x-intercept and y_1 is the y-intercept.

These five ways to write linear equations are all useful in different circumstances. Depending on the given information, it may be easier to write one of the forms over another.

If $y = mx$, y is directly proportional to x. In this case, changing x by a factor changes y by that same factor. If $y = \frac{m}{x}$, y is inversely proportional to x. For example, if x is increased by a factor of 3, then y will be decreased by the same factor, 3.

Sometimes, rather than a situation where there's an equation such as $y = ax + b$ and finding y for some value of x is requested, the result is given and finding x is requested.

The key to solving any equation is to remember that from one true equation, another true equation can be found by adding, subtracting, multiplying, or dividing both sides by the same quantity. In this case, it's necessary to manipulate the equation so that one side only contains x. Then the other side will show what x is equal to.

For example, in solving $3x - 5 = 2$, adding 5 to each side results in $3x = 7$. Next, dividing both sides by 3 results in $x = \frac{7}{3}$. To ensure the calculated results of x is correct, this calculated value can be substituted into the original equation and solved to see if it makes a true statement. For example, $3(\frac{7}{3}) - 5 = 2$ can be simplified by cancelling out the two 3s. This yields $7 - 5 = 2$, which is a true statement.

Sometimes an equation may have more than one x-term. For example, consider the following equation:

$$3x + 2 = x - 4$$

Moving all of the x-terms to one side by subtracting x from both sides results in $2x + 2 = -4$. Next, subtract 2 from both sides so that there is no constant term on the left side. This yields $2x = -6$. Finally, divide both sides by 2, which leaves $x = -3$.

Solving Linear Inequalities

Solving linear inequalities is very similar to solving equations, except for one rule: when multiplying or dividing an inequality by a negative number, the inequality symbol changes direction. Given the following inequality, solve for x: $-2x + 5 < 13$. The first step in solving this equation is to subtract 5 from both sides. This leaves the inequality: $-2x < 8$. The last step is to divide both sides by -2. By using the rule, the answer to the inequality is $x > -4$.

Since solutions to inequalities include more than one value, number lines are often used to model the answer. For the previous example, the answer is modelled on the number line below. It shows that any number greater than -4, not including -4, satisfies the inequality.

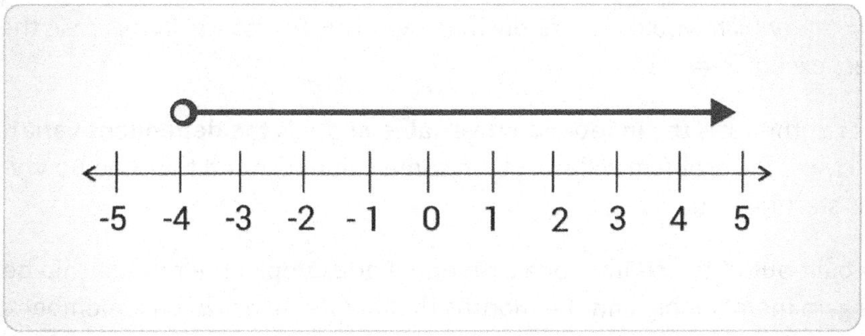

Similar to linear equations, a linear inequality may have a solution set consisting of all real numbers, or can contain no solution. When solved algebraically, a linear inequality in which the variable cancels out and results in a true statement (ex. $7 \geq 2$) has a solution set of all real numbers. A linear inequality in which the variable cancels out and results in a false statement (ex. $7 \leq 2$) has no solution.

Building Linear Functions

A **function** is a special kind of relation where, for each value of x, there is only a single value of y that satisfies the relation. So, $x^2 = y^2$ is *not* a function because in this case, if x is 1, y can be either 1 or -1: the pair $(1, 1)$ and $(1, -1)$ both satisfy the relation. More generally, for this relation, any pair of the form $(a, \pm a)$ will satisfy it. On the other hand, consider the following relation: $y = x^2 + 1$. This is a function because for each value of x, there is a unique value of y that satisfies the relation. Notice, however, there are multiple values of x that give us the same value of y. This is perfectly acceptable for a function. Therefore, y is a function of x.

To determine if a relation is a function, check to see if every x-value has a unique corresponding y-value.

A function can be viewed as an object that has x as its input and outputs a unique y-value. It is sometimes convenient to express this using **function notation**, where the function itself is given a name, often f. To emphasize that f takes x as its input, the function is written as $f(x)$. In the above example, the equation could be rewritten as:

$$f(x) = x^2 + 1$$

To write the value that a function yields for some specific value of x, that value is put in place of x in the function notation. For example, $f(3)$ means the value that the function outputs when the input value is 3. If $f(x) = x^2 + 1$, then:

$$f(3) = 3^2 + 1 = 10$$

A function can also be viewed as a table of pairs (x, y), which lists the value for y for each possible value of x.

The set of all possible values for x in $f(x)$ is called the **domain** of the function, and the set of all possible outputs is called the **range** of the function. Note that usually the domain is assumed to be all real numbers, except those for which the expression for $f(x)$ is not defined, unless the problem specifies otherwise. An example of how a function might not be defined is in the case of $f(x) = \frac{1}{x+1}$, which is not defined when $x = -1$ (which would require dividing by zero). Therefore, in this case the domain would be all real numbers except $x = -1$.

If y is a function of x, then x is the **independent variable** and y is the **dependent variable**. This is because in many cases, the problem will start with some value of x and then see how y changes depending on this starting value.

Functions can be built out of the context of a situation. For example, the relationship between the money paid for a gym membership and the months that someone has been a member can be described through a function. If the one-time membership fee is $40 and the monthly fee is $30, then the function can be written $f(x) = 30x + 40$. The x-value represents the number of months the person has been part of the gym, while the output is the total money paid for the membership. The table below shows this relationship. It is a representation of the function because the initial cost is $40 and the cost increases each month by $30.

x (months)	**y (money paid to gym)**
0	40
1	70
2	100
3	130

Functions can also be built from existing functions. For example, a given function $f(x)$ can be transformed by adding a constant, multiplying by a constant, or changing the input value by a constant. The new function $g(x) = f(x) + k$ represents a vertical shift of the original function. In $f(x) = 3x - 2$, a vertical shift 4 units up would be:

$$g(x) = 3x - 2 + 4 = 3x + 2$$

Multiplying the function times a constant k represents a vertical stretch, based on whether the constant is greater than or less than 1. The function represents a stretch:

$$g(x) = kf(x) = 4(3x - 2) = 12x - 8$$

Changing the input x by a constant, forms the function:

$$g(x) = f(x + k) = 3(x + 4) - 2 = 3x + 12 - 2 = 3x + 10$$

This represents a horizontal shift to the left 4 units. If $(x - 4)$ was plugged into the function, it would represent a vertical shift.

To evaluate functions, plug in the given value everywhere the variable appears in the expression for the function. For example, find $g(-2)$ where $g(x) = 2x^2 - \frac{4}{x}$. To complete the problem, plug in -2 in the following way:

$$g(-2) = 2(-2)^2 - \frac{4}{-2}2 \cdot 4 + 2 = 8 + 2 = 10$$

Solving Systems of Inequalities

A **linear inequality in two variables** is a statement expressing an unequal relationship between those two variables. Typically written in slope-intercept form, the variable y can be greater than, less than, greater than or equal to, or less than or equal to a linear expression that includes the variable $x,$ such as $y > 3x$ and $y \leq \frac{1}{2}x - 3$. Questions may include instructions to model real-world scenarios, such as the following:

You work part time cutting lawns for $15 each and cleaning houses for $25 each. Your goal is to make more than $90 this week. Write an inequality to represent the possible pairs of lawns and houses needed to reach your goal.

This scenario can be expressed as $15x + 25y > 90$ where x is the number of lawns cut and y is the number of houses cleaned.

The graph consists of a boundary line dividing the coordinate plane and shading on one side of the boundary. Graph the boundary line just as a linear equation would be graphed. If the inequality symbol is > or <, use a dashed line to indicate that the line is not part of the solution set. If the inequality symbol is ≥ or ≤, use a solid line to indicate that the boundary line is included in the solution set. Pick an ordered pair (x, y) on either side of the line to test in the inequality statement. If substituting the values for x and y results in a true statement $[15(3) + 25(2) > 90]$, that ordered pair and all others on that side of the boundary line are part of the solution set. To indicate this, shade that region of the graph. If substituting the ordered pair results in a false statement, the ordered pair and all others on that side are not part of the solution set. Therefore, the other region of the graph contains the solutions and should be shaded. The following is an example of the graph of $y \leq x + 2$.

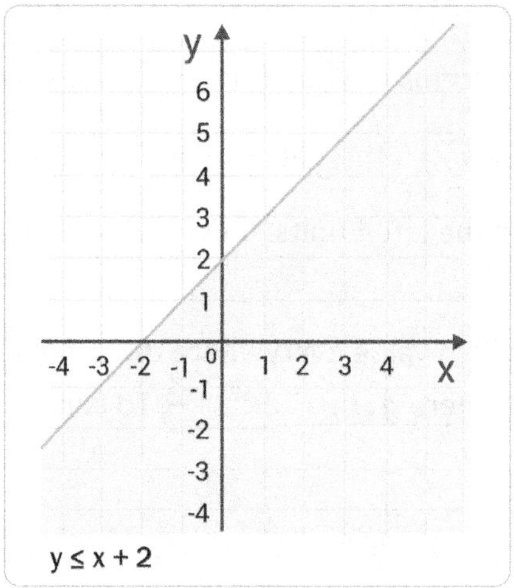

Systems of linear inequalities are like systems of equations, but the solutions are different. Since inequalities have infinitely many solutions, their systems also have infinitely many solutions. Finding the solutions of inequalities involves graphs. A system of two equations and two inequalities is linear; thus, the lines can be graphed using slope-intercept form. A system of linear inequalities consists of two linear inequalities that make comparisons between two variables. The solution set for a system of inequalities is the region of a graph consisting of ordered pairs that make BOTH inequalities true. To graph the solution set, first graph each linear inequality with appropriate shading. Identify the region of the graph where the shading for the two inequalities overlaps. This region contains the solution set for the system. In the example below, the line with the positive slope is solid, meaning the values on that line are included in the solution. The line with the negative slope is dotted, so the coordinates on that line are not included.

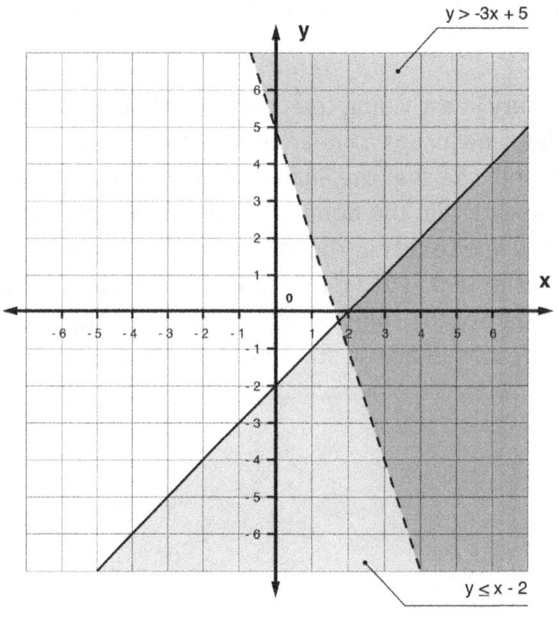

Solving Systems of Linear Equations

A **system of equations** is a group of equations that have the same variables or unknowns. These equations can be linear, but they are not always so. Finding a solution to a system of equations means finding the values of the variables that satisfy each equation. For a linear system of two equations and two variables, there could be a single solution, no solution, or infinitely many solutions.

A single solution occurs when there is one value for x and y that satisfies the system. This would be shown on the graph where the lines cross at exactly one point. When there is no solution, the lines are parallel and do not ever cross. With infinitely many solutions, the equations may look different, but they are the same line. One equation will be a multiple of the other, and on the graph, they lie on top of each other.

The process of **elimination** can be used to solve a system of equations. For example, the following equations make up a system:

$$x + 3y = 10 \text{ and } 2x - 5y = 9$$

Immediately adding these equations does not eliminate a variable, but it is possible to change the first equation by multiplying the whole equation by -2. This changes the first equation to:

$$-2x - 6y = -20$$

The equations can be then added to obtain $-11y = -11$. Solving for y yields $y = 1$. To find the rest of the solution, 1 can be substituted in for y in either original equation to find the value of $x = 7$. The solution to the system is $(7, 1)$ because it makes both equations true, and it is the point in which the lines intersect. If the system is **dependent**—having infinitely many solutions—then both variables will cancel out when the elimination method is used, resulting in an equation that is true for many values of x and y. Since the system is dependent, both equations can be simplified to the same equation or line.

A system can also be solved using **substitution**. This involves solving one equation for a variable and then plugging that solved equation into the other equation in the system. For example, $x - y = -2$ and $3x + 2y = 9$ can be solved using substitution. The first equation can be solved for x, where $x = -2 + y$. Then it can be plugged into the other equation:

$$3(-2 + y) + 2y = 9$$

Solving for y yields:

$$-6 + 3y + 2y = 9$$

That shows that $y = 3$. If $y = 3$, then $x = 1$.

This solution can be checked by plugging in these values for the variables in each equation to see if it makes a true statement.

Finally, a solution to a system of equations can be found graphically. The solution to a linear system is the point or points where the lines cross. The values of x and y represent the coordinates (x, y) where the lines intersect. Using the same system of equations as above, they can be solved for y to put them in slope-intercept form, $y = mx + b$. These equations become $y = x + 2$ and $y = -\frac{3}{2}x + 4.5$. The slope is the coefficient of x, and the y-intercept is the constant value.

This system with the solution is shown below:

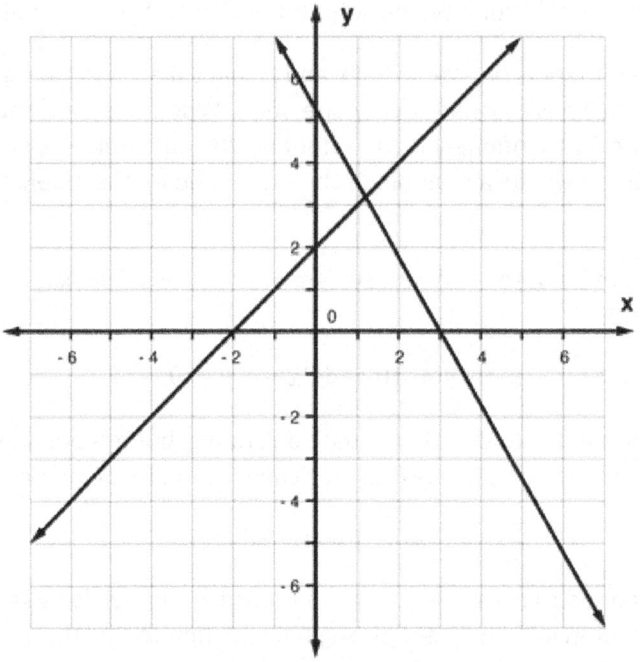

Finding solutions to systems of equations is essentially finding what values of the variables make both equations true. It is finding the input value that yields the same output value in both equations. For functions $g(x)$ and $f(x)$, the equation $g(x) = f(x)$ means the output values are being set equal to each other. Solving for the value of x means finding the x-coordinate that gives the same output in both functions. For example, $f(x) = x + 2$ and $g(x) = -3x + 10$ is a system of equations. Setting $f(x) = g(x)$ yields the equation:

$$x + 2 = -3x + 10$$

Solving for x, gives the x-coordinate $x = 2$ where the two lines cross. This value can also be found by using a table or a graph. On a table, both equations can be given the same inputs, and the outputs can be recorded to find the point(s) where the lines cross. Any method of solving finds the same solution, but some methods are more appropriate for some systems of equations than others.

Interpreting Variables and Constants in Expressions

Algebraic expressions look similar to equations, but they do not include the equal sign. **Algebraic expressions** are comprised of numbers, variables, and mathematical operations. Some examples of algebraic expressions are $8x + 7y - 12z$, $3a^2$, and $5x^3 - 4y^4$.

Algebraic expressions and equations can be used to represent real-life situations and model the behavior of different variables. For example, $2x + 5$ could represent the cost to play games at an arcade. In this case, 5 represents the price of admission to the arcade, and 2 represents the cost of each game played. To calculate the total cost, use the number of games played for x, multiply it by 2, and add 5.

In word problems, multiple quantities are often provided with a request to find some kind of relation between them. This often will mean that one variable (the dependent variable whose value needs to be found) can be written as a function of another variable (the independent variable whose value can be figured from the given information). The usual procedure for solving these problems is to start by giving each quantity in the problem a variable, and then figuring the relationship between these variables.

For example, suppose a car gets 25 miles per gallon. How far will the car travel if it uses 2.4 gallons of fuel? In this case, y would be the distance the car has traveled in miles, and x would be the amount of fuel burned in gallons (2.4). Then the relationship between these variables can be written as an algebraic equation, $y = 25x$. In this case, the equation is $y = 25 \times 2.4 = 60$, so the car has traveled 60 miles.

Some word problems require more than just one simple equation to be written and solved. Consider the following situations and the linear equations used to model them.

Suppose Margaret is 2 miles to the east of John at noon. Margaret walks to the east at 3 miles per hour. How far apart will they be at 3 p.m.? To solve this, x would represent the time in hours past noon, and y would represent the distance between Margaret and John. Now, noon corresponds to the equation where x is 0, so the y-intercept is going to be 2. It's also known that the slope will be the rate at which the distance is changing, which is 3 miles per hour.

This means that the slope will be 3 (be careful at this point: if units were used, other than miles and hours, for x- and y-variables, a conversion of the given information to the appropriate units would be required first). The simplest way to write an equation given the y-intercept, and the slope is the Slope-Intercept form, which is $y = mx + b$. Recall that m here is the slope, and b is the y-intercept. So, $m = 3$ and $b = 2$. Therefore, the equation will be $y = 3x + 2$. The word problem asks how far to the east Margaret will be from John at 3 p.m., which means when x is 3. So, substitute $x = 3$ into this equation to obtain:

$$y = 3 \times 3 + 2 = 9 + 2 = 11$$

Therefore, she will be 11 miles to the east of him at 3 p.m.

For another example, suppose that a box with 4 cans in it weighs 6 lbs., while a box with 8 cans in it weighs 12 lbs. Find out how much a single can weighs. To do this, let x denote the number of cans in the box, and y denote the weight of the box with the cans in lbs. This line touches two pairs: $(4, 6)$ and $(8, 12)$. A formula for this relation could be written using the two-point form, with $x_1 = 4, y_1 = 6, x_2 = 8, y_2 = 12$. This would yield $\frac{y-6}{x-4} = \frac{12-6}{8-4}$, or $\frac{y-6}{x-4} = \frac{6}{4} = \frac{3}{2}$. However, only the slope is needed to solve this problem, since the slope will be the weight of a single can. From the computation, the slope is $\frac{3}{2}$. Therefore, each can weigh $\frac{3}{2}$ lb.

Understanding Connections Between Algebraic and Graphical Representations

To graph relations and functions, the **Cartesian plane** is used. This means to think of the plane as being given a grid of squares, with one direction being the x-axis and the other direction the y-axis. Generally, the independent variable is placed along the horizontal axis, and the dependent variable is placed along the vertical axis. Any point on the plane can be specified by saying how far to go along the x-axis and how far along the y-axis with a pair of numbers (x, y). Specific values for these pairs can be given names such as $C = (-1, 3)$. Negative values mean to move left or down; positive values mean to move right or up. The point where the axes cross one another is called the **origin**. The origin has coordinates $(0, 0)$ and is usually called O when given a specific label.

An illustration of the Cartesian plane, along with the plotted points $(2, 1)$ and $(-1, -1)$, is below.

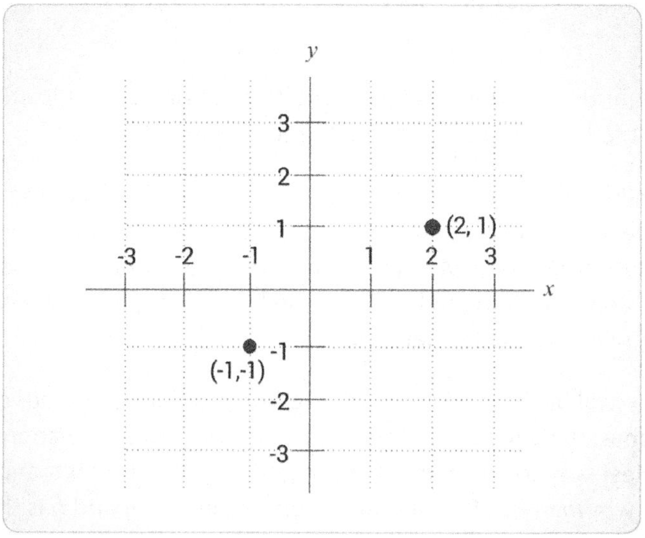

Relations also can be graphed by marking each point whose coordinates satisfy the relation. If the relation is a function, then there is only one value of y for any given value of x. This leads to the **vertical line test**: if a relation is graphed, then the relation is a function if any possible vertical line drawn anywhere along the graph would only touch the graph of the relation in no more than one place. Conversely, when graphing a function, then any possible vertical line drawn will not touch the graph of the function at any point or will touch the function at just one point. This test is made from the definition of a function, where each x-value must be mapped to one and only one y-value.

Equations and inequalities in two variables represent a relationship. Jim owns a car wash and charges \$40 per car. The rent for the facility is \$350 per month. An equation can be written to relate the number of cars Jim cleans to the money he makes per month. Let x represent the number of cars and y represent the profit Jim makes each month from the car wash. The equation $y = 40x - 350$ can be used to show Jim's profit or loss. Since this equation has two variables, the coordinate plane can be used to show the relationship and predict profit or loss for Jim.

The following graph shows that Jim must wash at least nine cars to pay the rent, where $x = 9$. Anything nine cars and above yield a profit shown in the value on the y-axis.

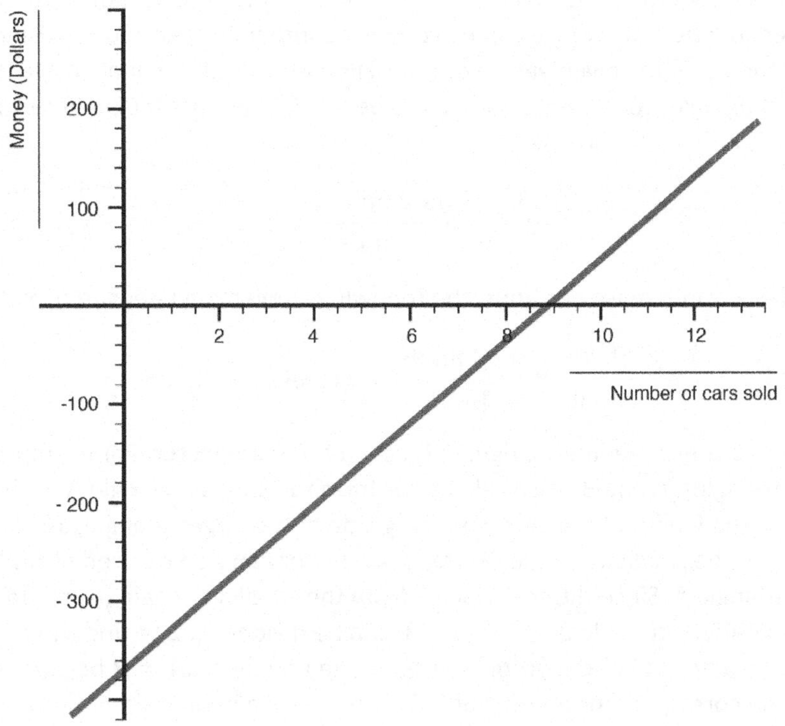

With a single equation in two variables, the solutions are limited only by the situation the equation represents. When two equations or inequalities are used, more constraints are added. For example, in a system of linear equations, there is often—although not always—only one answer. The point of intersection of two lines is the solution. For a system of inequalities, there are infinitely many answers.

Problem Solving and Data Analysis

Ratios, Rates, and Proportions

Ratios are used to show the relationship between two quantities. The ratio of oranges to apples in the grocery store may be 3 to 2. That means that for every 3 oranges, there are 2 apples. This comparison can be expanded to represent the actual number of oranges and apples, such as 36 oranges to 24 apples. Another example may be the number of boys to girls in a math class. If the ratio of boys to girls is given as 2 to 5, that means there are 2 boys to every 5 girls in the class. Ratios can also be compared if the units in each ratio are the same. The ratio of boys to girls in the math class can be compared to the ratio of boys to girls in a science class by stating which ratio is higher and which is lower.

Rates are used to compare two quantities with different units. **Unit rates** are the simplest form of rate. With unit rates, the denominator in the comparison of two units is one. For example, if someone can type at a rate of 1,000 words in 5 minutes, then their unit rate for typing is $\frac{1,000}{5} = 200$ words in one minute or 200 words per minute. Any rate can be converted into a unit rate by dividing to make the denominator one. 1,000 words in 5 minutes has been converted into the unit rate of 200 words per minute.

Ratios and rates can be used together to convert rates into different units. For example, if someone is driving 50 kilometers per hour, that rate can be converted into miles per hour by using a ratio known as the **conversion factor**. Since the given value contains kilometers and the final answer needs to be in miles, the ratio relating miles to kilometers needs to be used. There are 0.62 miles in 1 kilometer. This, written as a ratio and in fraction form, is

$$\frac{0.62 \text{ miles}}{1 \text{ km}}$$

To convert 50 km/hour into miles per hour, the following conversion needs to be set up:

$$\frac{50 \text{ km}}{\text{hour}} \times \frac{0.62 \text{ miles}}{1 \text{ km}} = 31 \text{ miles per hour}$$

The ratio between two similar geometric figures is called the **scale factor**. For example, a problem may depict two similar triangles, A and B. The scale factor from the smaller triangle A to the larger triangle B is given as 2 because the length of the corresponding side of the larger triangle, 16, is twice the corresponding side on the smaller triangle, 8. This scale factor can also be used to find the value of a missing side, x, in triangle A. Since the scale factor from the smaller triangle (A) to larger one (B) is 2, the larger corresponding side in triangle B (given as 25), can be divided by 2 to find the missing side in A ($x = 12.5$). The scale factor can also be represented in the equation $2A = B$ because two times the lengths of A gives the corresponding lengths of B. This is the idea behind similar triangles.

Much like a scale factor can be written using an equation like $2A = B$, a **relationship** is represented by the equation $Y = kX$. X and Y are proportional because as values of X increase, the values of Y also increase. A relationship that is inversely proportional can be represented by the equation $Y = \frac{k}{X}$, where the value of Y decreases as the value of X increases and vice versa.

Proportional reasoning can be used to solve problems involving ratios, percentages, and averages. Ratios can be used in setting up proportions and solving them to find unknowns. For example, if a student completes an average of 10 pages of math homework in 3 nights, how long would it take the student to complete 22 pages? Both ratios can be written as fractions. The second ratio would contain the unknown.

The following proportion represents this problem, where x is the unknown number of nights:

$$\frac{10 \text{ pages}}{3 \text{ nights}} = \frac{22 \text{ pages}}{x \text{ nights}}$$

Solving this proportion entails cross-multiplying and results in the following equation: $10x = 22 \times 3$. Simplifying and solving for x results in the exact solution: $x = 6.6$ nights. The result would be rounded up to 7 because the homework would actually be completed on the seventh night.

The following problem uses ratios involving percentages:

If 20% of the class is girls and 30 students are in the class, how many girls are in the class?

To set up this problem, it is helpful to use the common proportion:

$$\frac{\%}{100} = \frac{is}{of}$$

Within the proportion, % is the percentage of girls, 100 is the total percentage of the class, *is* is the number of girls, and *of* is the total number of students in the class. Most percentage problems can be written using this language. To solve this problem, the proportion should be set up as $\frac{20}{100} = \frac{x}{30}$ and then solved for x. Cross-multiplying results in the equation $20 \times 30 = 100x$, which results in the solution $x = 6$. There are 6 girls in the class.

Ratios can be used to solve problems that concern length, volume, and other units. A problem may ask for the volume of a cone that has a radius, $r = 7m$ and a height, $h = 16m$. Referring to the formulas provided on the test, the volume of a cone is given as:

$$V = \pi r^2 \frac{h}{3}$$

r is the radius, and h is the height. Plugging $r = 7$ and $h = 16$ into the formula, the following is obtained:

$$V = \pi(7^2)\frac{16}{3}$$

Therefore, the volume of the cone is found to be approximately 821m^3. Sometimes, answers in different units are sought. If this problem wanted the answer in liters, 821m^3 would need to be converted.

Using the equivalence statement $1\text{ m}^3 = 1{,}000\text{ L}$, the following ratio would be used to solve for liters:

$$821\text{ m}^3 \times \frac{1{,}000\text{ L}}{1\text{ m}^3}$$

Cubic meters in the numerator and denominator cancel each other out, and the answer is converted to 821,000 liters, or 8.21×10^5 L.

Other conversions can also be made between different given and final units. If the temperature in a pool is 30 °C, what is the temperature of the pool in degrees Fahrenheit? To convert these units, an equation is used relating Celsius to Fahrenheit. The following equation is used:

$$T_{°F} = 1.8T_{°C} + 32$$

Plugging in the given temperature and solving the equation for T yields the result:

$$T_{°F} = 1.8(30) + 32 = 86\text{ °F}$$

Units in both the metric system and U.S. customary system are widely used.

Percentages

The word **percent** comes from the Latin phrase for "per one hundred." A percent is a way of writing out a fraction. It is a fraction with a denominator of 100. Thus, $65\% = \frac{65}{100}$.

To convert a fraction to a percent, the denominator is written as 100. For example:

$$\frac{3}{5} = \frac{60}{100} = 60\%$$

In converting a percent to a fraction, the percent is written with a denominator of 100, and the result is simplified. For example:

$$30\% = \frac{30}{100} = \frac{3}{10}$$

The basic percent equation is the following:

$$\frac{is}{of} = \frac{\%}{100}$$

The placement of numbers in the equation depends on what the question asks.

Example 1
Find 40% of 80.

Basically, the problem is asking, "What is 40% of 80?" The 40% is the percent, and 80 is the number to find the percent "of." The equation is:

$$\frac{x}{80} = \frac{40}{100}$$

After cross-multiplying, the problem becomes 100x = 80(40). Solving for *x* produces the answer: *x* = 32.

Example 2
What percent of 100 is 20?

20 fills in the "is" portion, while 100 fills in the "of." The question asks for the percent, so that will be *x*, the unknown. The following equation is set up:

$$\frac{20}{100} = \frac{x}{100}$$

Cross-multiplying yields the equation $100x = 20(100)$. Solving for x gives the answer: 20%.

Example 3
30% of what number is 30?

The following equation uses the clues and numbers in the problem:

$$\frac{30}{x} = \frac{30}{100}$$

Cross-multiplying results in the equation $30(100) = 30x$. Solving for x gives the answer: $x = 100$.

Unit Rates and Conversions

When rates are expressed as a quantity of one, they are considered **unit rates**. To determine a unit rate, the first quantity is divided by the second. Knowing a unit rate makes calculations easier than simply having a rate. For example, suppose a 3-pound bag of onions costs \$1.77. To calculate the price of 5 pounds of onions, a proportion could show:

$$\frac{3}{1.77} = \frac{5}{x}$$

However, by knowing the unit rate, the value of pounds of onions is multiplied by the unit price. The unit price is calculated:

$$\frac{\$1.77}{3 \text{ lb}} = \$0.59/\text{lb}$$

Multiplying the weight of the onions by the unit price yields:

$$5 \text{ lb} \times \frac{\$0.59}{\text{lb}} = \$2.95$$

The lb units cancel out.

Similar to unit-rate problems, unit conversions appear in real-world scenarios including cooking, measurement, construction, and currency. Given the conversion rate, unit conversions are written as a fraction (ratio) and multiplied by a quantity in one unit to convert it to the corresponding unit. To determine how many minutes are in $3\frac{1}{2}$ hours, the conversion rate of 60 minutes to 1 hour is written as $\frac{60 \text{ min}}{1 \text{ h}}$. Multiplying the quantity by the conversion rate results in:

$$3\frac{1}{2}\text{h} \times \frac{60 \text{ min}}{1\text{h}} = 210 \text{ min}$$

(The h unit is canceled)

To convert a quantity in minutes to hours, the fraction for the conversion rate is flipped to cancel the *min* unit. To convert 195 minutes to hours, $195 \text{ min} \times \frac{1 \text{ h}}{60 \text{ min}}$ is multiplied. The result is $\frac{195 \text{ h}}{60}$ which reduces to $3\frac{1}{4}$ h.

Converting units may require more than one multiplication. The key is to set up conversion rates so that units cancel each other out and the desired unit is left. To convert 3.25 yards to inches, given that 1yd = 3ft and 12in = 1ft, the calculation is performed by multiplying:

$$3.25 \text{ yd} \times \frac{3 \text{ ft}}{1 \text{ yd}} \times \frac{12 \text{ in}}{1 \text{ ft}}$$

The yd and ft units will cancel, resulting in 117 in.

When working with different systems of measurement, conversion from one unit to another may be necessary. The conversion rate must be known to convert units. One method for converting units is to write and solve a proportion. The arrangement of values in a proportion is extremely important. Suppose that a problem requires converting 20 fluid ounces to cups. To do so, a proportion can be written using the conversion rate of $8 \text{ fl oz} = 1 \text{ c}$ with x representing the missing value. The proportion can be written in any of the following ways:

$$\frac{1}{8} = \frac{x}{20} \left(\frac{c\ for\ conversion}{fl\ oz\ for\ conversion} = \frac{unknown\ c}{fl\ oz\ given} \right)$$

$$\frac{8}{1} = \frac{20}{x} \left(\frac{fl\ oz\ for\ conversion}{c\ for\ conversion} = \frac{fl\ oz\ given}{unknown\ c} \right)$$

$$\frac{1}{x} = \frac{8}{20} \left(\frac{c\ for\ conversion}{unknown\ c} = \frac{fl\ oz\ for\ conversion}{fl\ oz\ given} \right)$$

$$\frac{x}{1} = \frac{20}{8} \left(\frac{unknown\ c}{c\ for\ conversion} = \frac{fl\ oz\ given}{fl\ oz\ for\ conversion} \right)$$

To solve a proportion, the ratios are cross-multiplied and the resulting equation is solved. When cross-multiplying, all four proportions above will produce the same equation:

$$(8)(x) = (20)(1) \rightarrow 8x = 20$$

Divide by 8 to isolate the variable x, which yields $x = 2.5$. The variable x represented the unknown number of cups. Therefore, the conclusion is that 20 fluid ounces converts (is equal) to 2.5 cups.

Sometimes converting units requires writing and solving more than one proportion. Suppose an exam question asks to determine how many hours are in 2 weeks. Without knowing the conversion rate between hours and weeks, this can be determined knowing the conversion rates between weeks and days, and between days and hours. First, weeks are converted to days, then days are converted to hours. To convert from weeks to days, the following proportion can be written:

$$\frac{7}{1} = \frac{x}{2} \left(\frac{days\ conversion}{weeks\ conversion} = \frac{days\ unknown}{weeks\ given} \right)$$

Cross-multiplying produces:

$$(7)(2) = (x)(1) \rightarrow 14 = x$$

Therefore, 2 weeks is equal to 14 days. Next, a proportion is written to convert 14 days to hours:

$$\frac{24}{1} = \frac{x}{14} \left(\frac{conversion\ hours}{conversion\ days} = \frac{unknown\ hours}{given\ days} \right)$$

Cross-multiplying produces:

$$(24)(14) = (x)(1) \rightarrow 336 = x$$

Therefore, the answer is that there are 336 hours in 2 weeks.

Scatterplots

A **scatter plot** is a way to visually represent the relationship between two variables. Each variable has its own axis, and usually the independent variable is plotted on the horizontal axis while the dependent variable is plotted on the vertical axis. Data points are plotted in a process that's similar to how ordered pairs are plotted on an xy-plane. Once all points from the data set are plotted, the scatter plot is finished. Below is an example of a scatter plot that's plotting the quality and price of an item. Note that price is the independent variable and quality is the dependent variable:

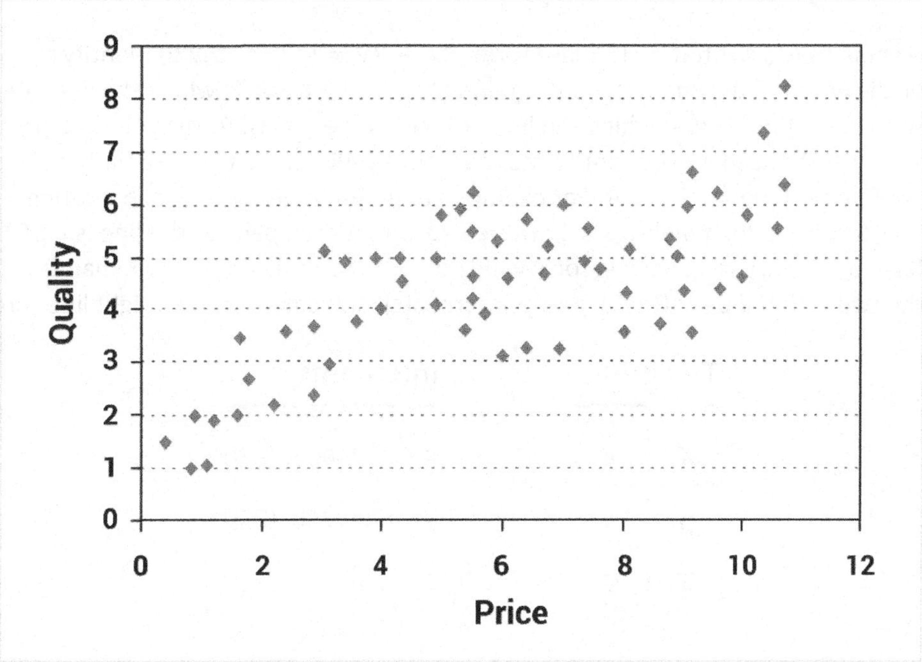

In this example, the quality of the item increases as the price increases.

Regression lines are a way to calculate a relationship between the independent variable and the dependent variable. A straight line means that there's a linear trend in the data. Technology can be used to find the equation of this line (e.g., a graphing calculator or Microsoft Excel®). In either case, all of the data points are entered, and a line is "fit" that best represents the shape of the data. If the line of best-fit has a positive slope (rises from left to right), then the variables have a positive correlation. If the line of best-fit has a negative slope (falls from left to right), then the variables have a negative correlation. If a line of best-fit cannot be drawn, then no correlation exists. A positive or negative correlation can be categorized as strong or weak, depending on how closely the points are graphed around the line of best-fit. Other functions used to model data sets include quadratic and exponential models.

Regression lines can be used to estimate data points not already given. Consider a data set with the average daily temperature at the beach and number of beach visitors. If an equation of a line is found that fits this data set, its input is the average daily temperature and its output is the projected number of visitors. Thus, the number of beach visitors on a 100-degree day can be estimated. The output is a data point on the regression line, and the number of daily visitors is expected to be greater than on a 96-degree day because the regression line has a positive slope.

The formula for a regression line is $y = mx + b$, where m is the slope and b is the y-intercept. Both the slope and y-intercept are found in the **Method of Least Squares**, which is the process of finding the equation of the line through minimizing residuals. The slope represents the rate of change in y as x gets larger. Therefore, because y is the dependent variable, the slope actually provides the predicted values given the independent variable. The y-intercept is the predicted value for when the independent variable equals zero. In the temperature example, the y-intercept is the expected number of beach visitors for a very cold average daily temperature of zero degrees.

Investigating Key Features of a Graph

When a linear equation is written in standard form, $Ax + By = C$, it is easy to identify the x- and y-intercepts for the graph of the line. Just as the y-intercept is the point at which the line intercepts the y-axis, the x-intercept is the point at which the line intercepts the x-axis. At the y-intercept, $x = 0$, and at the x-intercept, $y = 0$. Given an equation in standard form, substitute $x = 0$ to find the y-intercept, and substitute $y = 0$ to find the x-intercept. For example, to graph $3x + 2y = 6$, substituting 0 for y results in $3x + 2(0) = 6$. Solving for x yields $x = 2$; therefore, an ordered pair for the line is $(2, 0)$. Substituting 0 for x results in $3(0) + 2y = 6$. Solving for y yields $y = 3$; therefore, an ordered pair for the line is $(0, 3)$. Plot the two ordered pairs (the x- and y-intercepts), and construct a straight line through them.

T - chart

x	y
0	3
2	0

Intercepts

x - intercept : (2,0)

y - intercept : (0,3)

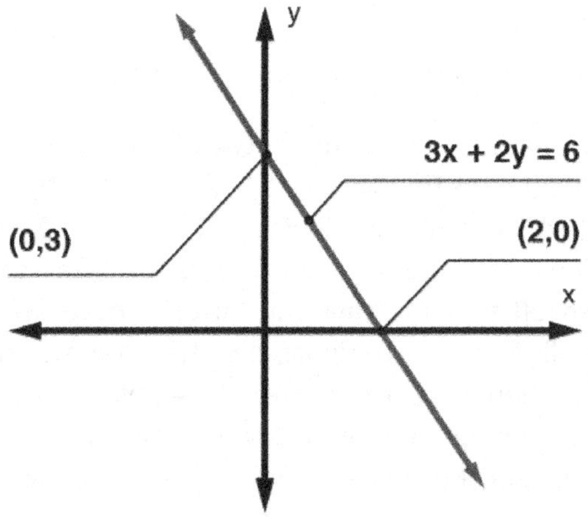

The standard form of a quadratic function is:

$$y = ax^2 + bx + c$$

The graph of a quadratic function is a U-shaped (or upside-down U) curve, called a **parabola**, which is symmetric about a vertical line (axis of symmetry). To graph a parabola, determine its vertex (high or low point for the curve) and at least two points on each side of the axis of symmetry.

Given a quadratic function in standard form, the axis of symmetry for its graph is the line $x = -\frac{b}{2a}$. The vertex for the parabola has an x-coordinate of $-\frac{b}{2a}$. To find the y-coordinate for the vertex, substitute the calculated x-coordinate. To complete the graph, select two different x-values, and substitute them into the quadratic function to obtain the corresponding y-values. This will give two points on the parabola. Use these two points and the axis of symmetry to determine the two points corresponding to these. The corresponding points are the same distance from the axis of symmetry (on the other side) and contain the same y-coordinate.

Plotting the vertex and four other points on the parabola allows for construction of the curve.

Quadratic Function

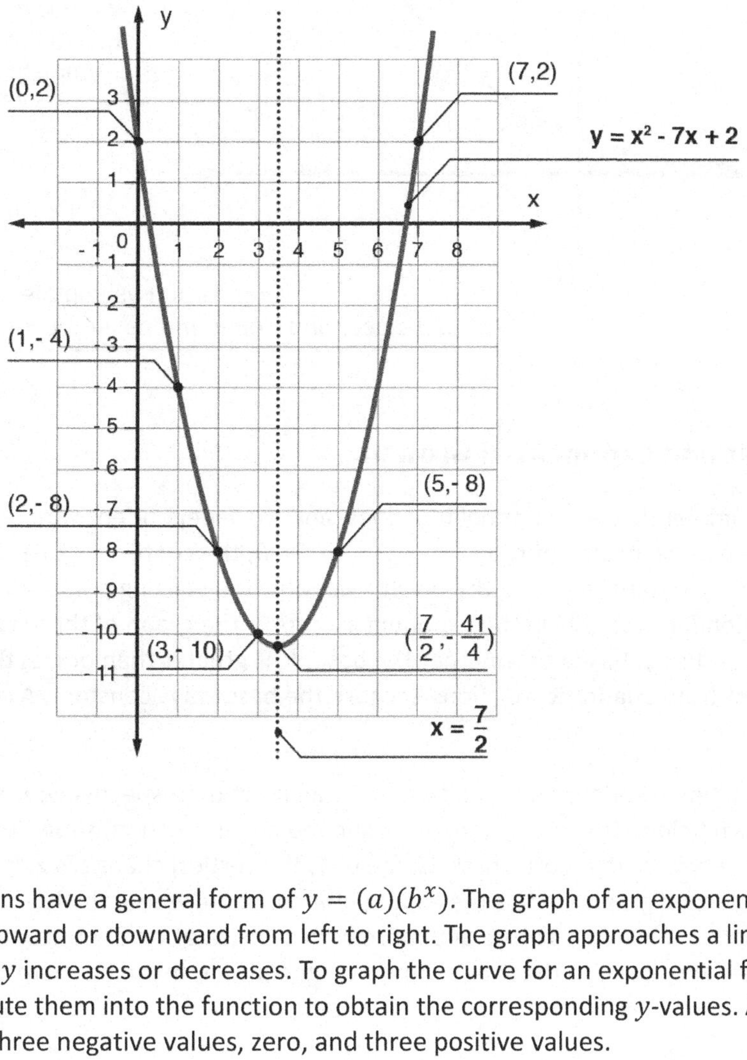

Exponential functions have a general form of $y = (a)(b^x)$. The graph of an exponential function is a curve that slopes upward or downward from left to right. The graph approaches a line, called an **asymptote**, as x or y increases or decreases. To graph the curve for an exponential function, select x-values, and substitute them into the function to obtain the corresponding y-values. A general rule of thumb is to select three negative values, zero, and three positive values.

Plotting the seven points on the graph for an exponential function should allow for the construction of a smooth curve through them.

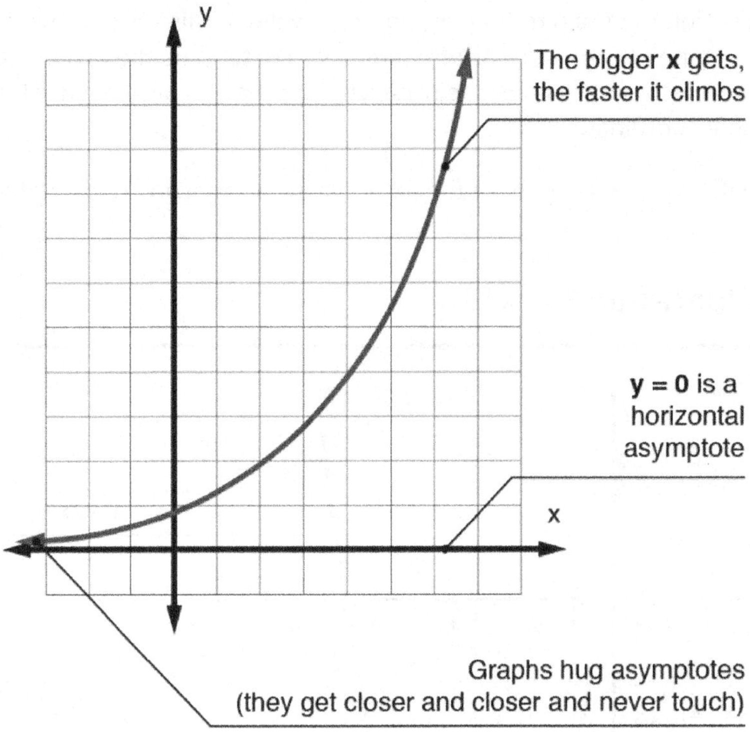

Comparing Linear and Exponential Growth

Linear functions are simpler than exponential functions, and the independent variable x has an exponent of 1. Written in the most common form, $y = mx + b$, the coefficient of x indicates how fast the function grows at a constant rate, and the b-value denotes the starting point. An exponential function has an independent variable in the exponent $y = ab^x$. The graph of these types of functions is described as **growth** or **decay**, based on whether the base, b, is greater than or less than 1. These functions are different from quadratic functions because the base stays constant. A common base is base e.

The following two functions model a linear and exponential function respectively: $y = 2x$ and $y = 2^x$. Their graphs are shown below. The first graph, modeling the linear function, shows that the growth is constant over each interval. With a horizontal change of 1, the vertical change is 2. It models constant positive growth. The second graph models the exponential function, where the horizontal change of 1 yields a vertical change that increases more and more with each iteration of horizontal change. The exponential graph gets very close to the x-axis, but never touches it, meaning there is an asymptote there. The y-value can never be zero because the base of 2 can never be raised to an input value that yields an output of zero.

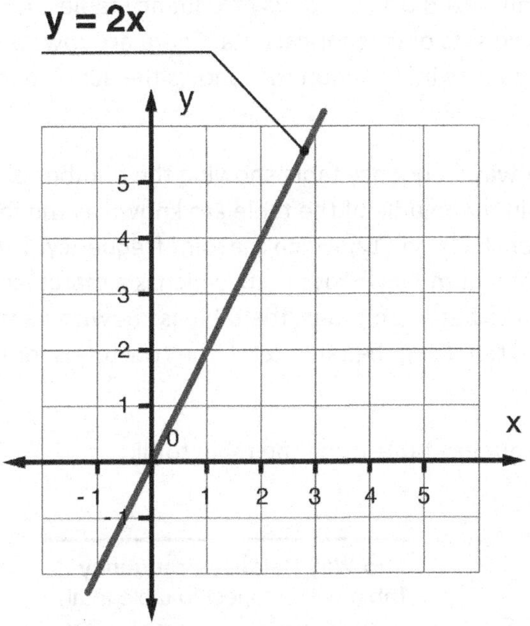

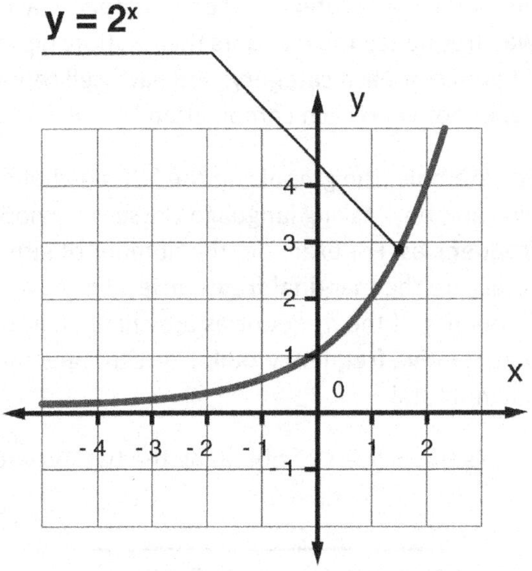

Given a table of values, the type of function can be determined by observing the change in y over equal intervals. For example, the tables below model two functions. The changes in interval for the x-values is 1 for both tables. For the first table, the y-values increase by 5 for each interval. Since the change is constant, the situation can be described as a linear function. The equation would be:

$$y = 5x + 3$$

For the second table, the change for y is 20, 100, and 500, respectively. The increases are multiples of 5, meaning the situation can be modeled by an exponential function. The equation below models this situation:

$$y = 5^x + 3$$

$y = 5x + 3$	
x	y
1	8
2	13
3	18
4	23

$y = 5^x + 3$	
x	y
1	8
2	28
3	128
4	628

Two-Way Tables

Data that isn't described using numbers is known as **categorical data.** For example, age is numerical data but hair color is categorical data. Categorical data is summarized using two-way frequency tables. A **two-way frequency table** counts the relationship between two sets of categorical data. There are rows and columns for each category, and each cell represents frequency information that shows the actual data count between each combination.

For example, the graphic on the left-side below is a two-way frequency table showing the number of girls and boys taking language classes in school. Entries in the middle of the table are known as the **joint frequencies**. For example, the number of girls taking French class is 12, which is a joint frequency. The totals are the **marginal frequencies**. For example, the total number of boys is 20, which is a marginal frequency. If the frequencies are changed into percentages based on totals, the table is known as a **two-way relative frequency table.** Percentages can be calculated using the table total, the row totals, or the column totals.

Here's the process of obtaining the two-way relative frequency table using the table total:

Two-Way Frequency Table

	Spanish	French	German	**Total**
Boys	10	2	8	**20**
Girls	15	12	3	**30**
Total	**25**	**14**	**11**	**50**

Joint frequencies

Marginal frequencies

Divide all tables entries by the table total (50) →

Two-Way Relative Frequency Table (with respect to table total)

	Spanish	French	German	**Total**
Boys	0.2	0.04	0.16	**0.40**
Girls	0.3	0.24	0.06	**0.60**
Total	**0.5**	**0.28**	**0.22**	**1.00**

The middle entries are known as **joint probabilities** and the totals are **marginal probabilities.** In this data set, it appears that more girls than boys take Spanish class. However, that might not be the case because more girls than boys were surveyed, and the results might be misleading. To avoid such errors, **conditional relative frequencies** are used. The relative frequencies are calculated based on a row or column.

Here are the conditional relative frequencies using column totals:

Two-Way Frequency Table

	Spanish	French	German	Total
Boys	10	2	8	**20**
Girls	15	12	3	**30**
Total	**25**	**14**	**11**	**50**

Divide each column entry by that column's total

Two-Way Relative Frequency Table (with respect to table total)

	Spanish	French	German	Total
Boys	0.4	0.14	0.73	**0.4**
Girls	0.6	0.86	0.27	**0.6**
Total	**1.00**	**1.00**	**1.00**	**1.00**

Two-way frequency tables can help in making many conclusions about the data. If either the row or column of conditional relative frequencies differs between each row or column of the table, then an association exists between the two categories. For example, in the above tables, the majority of boys are taking German while the majority of girls are taking French. If the frequencies are equal across the rows, there is no association, and the variables are labelled as independent. It's important to note that the association does exist in the above scenario, though these results may not occur the next semester when students are surveyed.

When measuring event probabilities, two-way frequency tables can be used to report the raw data and then used to calculate probabilities. If the frequency tables are translated into relative frequency tables, the probabilities presented in the table can be plugged directly into the formulas for conditional probabilities. By plugging in the correct frequencies, the data from the table can be used to determine if events are independent or dependent.

Conditional probability is the probability that event A will happen given that event B has already occurred. An example of this is calculating the probability that a person will eat dessert once they have eaten dinner. This is different than calculating the probability of a person just eating dessert.

The formula for the conditional probability of event A occurring given B is:

$$P(A|B) = \frac{P\ (A \text{ and } B)}{P(B)}$$

It's defined as the probability of both A and B occurring divided by the probability of event B occurring. If A and B are independent, then the probability of both A and B occurring is equal to $P(A)P(B)$, so $P(A|B)$ reduces to just $P(A)$. This means that A and B have no relationship, and the probability of A occurring is the same as the conditional probability of A occurring given B. Similarly, $P(B|A) = \frac{P\ (B \text{ and } A)}{P(A)} = P(B)$, if A and B are independent.

Two events aren't always independent. For example, having glasses and having brown hair aren't independent characteristics. There definitely can be overlap because people with brown hair can wear glasses. Also, two events that exist at the same time don't have to have a relationship. For example, even if everyone in a given sample is wearing glasses, the characteristics aren't related. In this case, the probability of a brunette wearing glasses is equal to the probability of a female being a brunette multiplied by the probability of a female wearing glasses. This mathematical test of $P(A \cap B) = P(A)P(B)$ verifies that two events are independent.

Conditional probability is the probability that an event occurs given that another event has happened. If the two events are related, the probability that the second event will occur changes if the other event has happened. However, if the two events aren't related and are therefore independent, the first event to occur won't impact the probability of the second event occurring.

Making Inferences About Population Parameters

Inferential statistics attempts to use data about a subset of some population to make inferences about the rest of the population. An example of this would be taking a collection of students who received tutoring and comparing their results to a collection of students who did not receive tutoring, then using that comparison to try to predict whether the tutoring program in question is beneficial.

To be sure that inferences have a high probability of being true for the whole population, the subset that is analyzed needs to resemble a miniature version of the population as closely as possible. For this reason, statisticians like to choose random samples from the population to study, rather than picking a specific group of people based on some similarity. For example, studying the incomes of people who live in Portland does not tell anything useful about the incomes of people who live in Tallahassee.

A **population** is the entire set of people or things of interest. Suppose a study is intended to determine the number of hours of sleep per night for college females in the United States. The population would consist of EVERY college female in the country. A **sample** is a subset of the population that may be used for the study. It would not be practical to survey every female college student, so a sample might consist of one hundred students per school from twenty different colleges in the country. From the results of the survey, a sample statistic can be calculated. A sample statistic is a numerical characteristic of the sample data, including mean and variance. A sample statistic can be used to estimate a corresponding population parameter. A **population parameter** is a numerical characteristic of the entire population. Suppose our sample data had a mean (average) of 5.5. This sample statistic can be used as an estimate of the population parameter (average hours of sleep for every college female in the United States).

A population parameter is usually unknown and therefore estimated using a sample statistic. This estimate may be very accurate or relatively inaccurate based on errors in sampling. A **confidence interval** indicates a range of values likely to include the true population parameter. These are constructed at a given confidence level, such as 95 percent. This means that if the same population is sampled repeatedly, the true population parameter would occur within the interval for 95 percent of the samples.

The accuracy of a population parameter based on a sample statistic may also be affected by **measurement error**. Measurement error is the difference between a quantity's true value and its measured value. Measurement error can be divided into random error and systematic error. An example of random error for the previous scenario would be a student reporting 8 hours of sleep when she sleeps 7 hours per night. Systematic errors are those attributed to the measurement system. Suppose the sleep survey gave response options of 2, 4, 6, 8, or 10 hours. This would lead to systematic measurement error.

Statistics

The field of **statistics** describes relationships between quantities that are related, but not necessarily in a deterministic manner. For example, a graduating student's salary will often be higher when the student graduates with a higher GPA, but this is not always the case. Likewise, people who smoke tobacco are more likely to develop lung cancer, but, in fact, it is possible for non-smokers to develop the disease as well. Statistics describes these kinds of situations, where the likelihood of some outcome depends on the starting data.

Comparing data sets within statistics can mean many things. The first way to compare data sets is by looking at the center and spread of each set. The center of a data set is measured by mean, median, and mode.

Suppose that X is a set of data points $(x_1, x_2, x_3, \ldots x_n)$ and some description of the general properties of this data need to be found.

The first property that can be defined for this set of data is the **mean**. To find the mean, add up all the data points, then divide by the total number of data points. This can be expressed using **summation notation** as:

$$\bar{X} = \frac{x_1 + x_2 + x_3 + \ldots + x_n}{n} = \frac{1}{n}\sum_{i=1}^{n} x_i$$

For example, suppose that in a class of 10 students, the scores on a test were 50, 60, 65, 65, 75, 80, 85, 85, 90, 100. Therefore, the average test score will be:

$$\frac{1}{10}(50 + 60 + 65 + 65 + 75 + 80 + 85 + 85 + 90 + 100) = 75.5$$

The mean is a useful number if the distribution of data is normal (more on this later), which roughly means that the frequency of different outcomes has a single peak and is roughly equally distributed on both sides of that peak. However, it is less useful in some cases where the data might be split or where there are some **outliers**. Outliers are data points that are far from the rest of the data. For example, suppose there are 90 employees and 10 executives at a company. The executives make $1,000 per hour, and the employees make $10 per hour. Therefore, the average pay rate will be $\frac{1{,}000 \cdot 10 + 10 \cdot 90}{100} = 109$, or $109 per hour. In this case, this average is not very descriptive.

Another useful measurement is the **median**. In a data set X consisting of data points $x_1, x_2, x_3, \ldots x_n$, the median is the point in the middle. The middle refers to the point where half the data comes before it and half comes after, when the data is recorded in numerical order. If *n* is odd, then the median is $x_{\frac{n+1}{2}}$.

If *n* is even, it is defined as $\frac{1}{2}\left(x_{\frac{n}{2}} + x_{\frac{n}{2}+1}\right)$, the mean of the two data points closest to the middle of the data points. In the previous example of test scores, the two middle points are 75 and 80. Since there is no single point, the average of these two scores needs to be found. The average is:

$$\frac{75 + 80}{2} = 77.5$$

The median is generally a good value to use if there are a few outliers in the data. It prevents those outliers from affecting the "middle" value as much as when using the mean.

Since an outlier is a data point that is far from most of the other data points in a data set, this means an outlier also is any point that is far from the median of the data set. The outliers can have a substantial effect on the mean of a data set, but they usually do not change the median or mode, or do not change them by a large quantity. For example, consider the data set (3, 5, 6, 6, 6, 8). This has a median of 6 and a mode of 6, with a mean of $\frac{34}{6} \approx 5.67$. Now, suppose a new data point of 1,000 is added so that the data set is now (3, 5, 6, 6, 6, 8, 1,000). The median and mode, which are both still 6, remain unchanged. However, the average is now $\frac{1{,}034}{7}$, which is approximately 147.7. In this case, the median and mode will be better descriptions for most of the data points.

Outliers in a given data set are sometimes the result of an error by the experimenter, but oftentimes, they are perfectly valid data points that must be taken into consideration.

One additional measure to define for X is the **mode**. This is the data point that appears more frequently. If two or more data points all tie for the most frequent appearance, then each of them is considered a mode. In the case of the test scores, where the numbers were 50, 60, 65, 65, 75, 80, 85, 85, 90, 100, there are two modes: 65 and 85.

The **spread** of a data set refers to how far the data points are from the center (mean or median). The spread can be measured by the range or the quartiles and interquartile range. A data set with all its data points clustered around the center will have a small spread. A data set covering a wide range of values will have a large spread. The **interquartile range** *(IQR)* is the range of the middle 50 percent of the data set. This range can be seen in the large rectangle on a box plot. The **standard deviation** *(σ)* quantifies the amount of variation with respect to the mean. A lower standard deviation shows that the data set doesn't differ greatly from the mean. A larger standard deviation shows that the data set is spread out farther from the mean. The formula used for standard deviation depends on whether it's being used for a population or a sample (a subset of a population). The formula for sample standard deviation is:

$$s = \sqrt{\frac{\sum(x - \bar{x})^2}{n - 1}}$$

In this formula, s represents the standard deviation value, x is each value in the data set, $\bar{x}$ is the sample mean, and n is the total number of data points in the set. Note that sample standard deviations use *one less than the total* in the denominator. The population standard deviation formula is similar:

$$\sigma = \sqrt{\frac{\sum(x - \mu)^2}{N}}$$

For population standard deviations, sigma (σ) represents the standard deviation, x represents each value in the data set, mu (μ) is the population mean, and N is the total number of data points for the population.

The shape of a data set is another way to compare two or more sets of data. If a data set isn't symmetric around its mean, it's said to be **skewed.** If the tail to the left of the mean is longer, it's said to be **skewed**

to the left. In this case, the mean is less than the median. Conversely, if the tail to the right of the mean is longer, it's said to be **skewed to the right** and the mean is greater than the median. When classifying a data set according to its shape, its overall **skewness** is being discussed. If the mean and median are equal, the data set isn't skewed; it is **symmetric**, and is considered normally distributed.

Evaluating Reports

The presentation of statistics can be manipulated to produce a desired outcome. Consider the statement, "Four out of five dentists recommend our toothpaste." This is a vague statement that is obviously biased. (Who are the five dentists this statement references?) This statement is very different from the statement, "Four out of every five dentists recommend our toothpaste." Whether intentional or unintentional, statistics can be misleading. Statistical reports should be examined to verify the validity and significance of the results. The context of the numerical values allows for deciphering the meaning, intent, and significance of the survey or study. Questions on this material will require students to use critical-thinking skills to justify or reject results and conclusions.

When analyzing a report, consider who conducted the study and their intent. Was it performed by a neutral party or by a person or group with a vested interest? A study on health risks of smoking performed by a health insurance company would have a much different intent than one performed by a cigarette company. Consider the sampling method and the data collection method. Was it a true random sample of the population, or was one subgroup overrepresented or underrepresented?

The three most common types of data gathering techniques are sample surveys, experiments, and observational studies. **Sample surveys** involve collecting data from a random sample of people from a desired population. The measurement of the variable is only performed on this set of people. To have accurate data, the sampling must be unbiased and random. For example, surveying students in an advanced calculus class on how much they enjoy math classes is not a useful sample if the population should be all college students based on the research question. An **experiment** is the method in which a hypothesis is tested using a controlled process called the scientific method.

A cause and the effect of that cause are measured, and the hypothesis is accepted or rejected. Experiments are usually completed in a controlled environment where the results of a control population are compared to the results of a test population. The groups are selected using a randomization process in which each group has a representative mix of the population being tested. Finally, an **observational study** is similar to an experiment. However, this design is used when circumstances prevent or do not allow for a designated control group and experimental group (e.g., lack of funding or unrealistic expectations). Instead, existing control and test populations must be used, so this method has a lack of randomization.

Consider the sleep study scenario from the previous section. If all twenty schools included in the study were state colleges, the results may be biased due to a lack of private-school participants. Consider the measurement system used to obtain the data. Was the system accurate and precise, or was it a flawed system? If, for the sleep study, the possible responses were limited to 2, 4, 6, 8, or 10 hours, it could be argued that the measurement system was flawed. Would odd numbers be rounded up or down? Without clarity of the system, the results could vary greatly. What about students who sleep 12 hours per night? The closest option for them would be 10 hours, which is significantly less.

Every scenario involving statistical reports will be different. The key is to examine all aspects of the study before determining whether to accept or reject the results and corresponding conclusions.

Passport to Advanced Math

Creating Quadratic and Exponential Functions

A polynomial of degree 2 is called **quadratic**. Every quadratic function can be written in the form $ax^2 + bx + c$. The graph of a quadratic function, $y = ax^2 + bx + c$, is called a **parabola**. Parabolas are vaguely U-shaped.

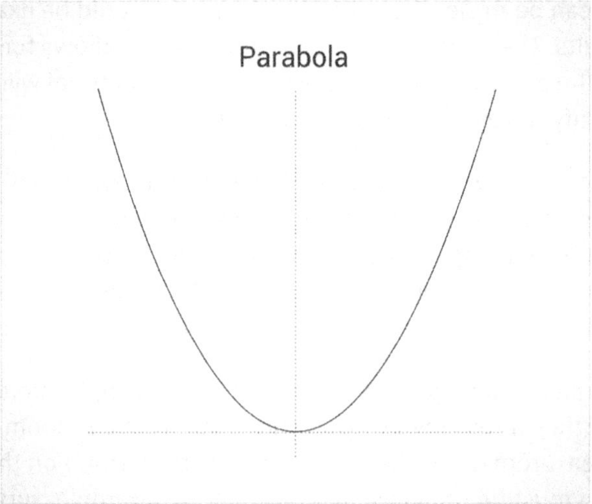

Whether the parabola opens upward or downward depends on the sign of a. If a is positive, then the parabola will open upward. If a is negative, then the parabola will open downward. The value of a will also affect how wide the parabola is. If the absolute value of a is large, then the parabola will be fairly skinny. If the absolute value of a is small, then the parabola will be quite wide.

Changes to the value of b affect the parabola in different ways, depending on the sign of a. For positive values of a, increasing b will move the parabola to the left, and decreasing b will move the parabola to the right. On the other hand, if a is negative, the effects will be the opposite: increasing b will move the parabola to the right, while decreasing b will move the parabola to the left.

Changes to the value of c move the parabola vertically. The larger that c is, the higher the parabola gets. This does not depend on the value of a.

The quantity $D = b^2 - 4ac$ is called the **discriminant** of the parabola. When the discriminant is positive, then the parabola has two real zeros, or x intercepts. However, if the discriminant is negative, then there are no real zeros, and the parabola will not cross the x-axis. The highest or lowest point of the parabola is called the **vertex.** If the discriminant is zero, then the parabola's highest or lowest point is on the x-axis, and it will have a single real zero. The x-coordinate of the vertex can be found using the equation $x = -\frac{b}{2a}$. Plug this x-value into the equation and find the y-coordinate.

A quadratic equation is often used to model the path of an object thrown into the air. The x-value can represent the time in the air, while the y-value can represent the height of the object. In this case, the maximum height of the object would be the y-value found when the x-value is $-\frac{b}{2a}$.

An **exponential function** is a function of the form $f(x) = b^x$, where b is a positive real number other than 1. In such a function, b is called the **base**.

The domain of an exponential function is all real numbers, and the range is all positive real numbers. There will always be a horizontal asymptote of $y = 0$ on one side. If b is greater than 1, then the graph will be increasing moving to the right. If b is less than 1, then the graph will be decreasing moving to the right. Exponential functions are one-to-one. The basic exponential function graph will go through the point $(0, 1)$.

Example
Solve $5^{x+1} = 25$.

Get the x out of the exponent by rewriting the equation $5^{x+1} = 5^2$ so that both sides have a base of 5.

Since the bases are the same, the exponents must be equal to each other.

This leaves $x + 1 = 2$ or $x = 1$.

To check the answer, the x-value of 1 can be substituted back into the original equation.

Determining Forms of Expressions

There is a four-step process in problem-solving that can be used as a guide:

1. Understand the problem and determine the unknown information.
2. Translate the verbal problem into an algebraic equation.
3. Solve the equation by using inverse operations.
4. Check the work and answer the given question.

Example
Three times the sum of a number plus 4 equals the number plus 8. What is the number?

The first step is to determine the unknown, which is the number, or x.

The second step is to translate the problem into the equation, which is $3(x + 4) = x + 8$.

The equation can be solved as follows:

$3x + 12 = x + 8$	Apply the distributive property
$3x = x - 4$	Subtract 12 from both sides of the equation
$2x = -4$	Subtract x from both sides of the equation
$x = -2$	Divide both sides of the equation by 2

The final step is checking the solution. Plugging the value for x back into the equation yields the following problem:

$$3(-2) + 12 = -2 + 8$$

Using the order of operations shows that a true statement is made: $6 = 6$

The four-step process of problem solving can be used with geometric reasoning problems as well. There are many geometric properties and terminology included within geometric reasoning.

For example, the perimeter of a rectangle can be written in the terms of the width, or the width can be written in terms of the length.

Example

The width of a rectangle is 2 centimeters less than the length. If the perimeter of the rectangle is 44 centimeters, then what are the dimensions of a rectangle?

The first step is to determine the unknown, which is in terms of the length, l.

The second step is to translate the problem into the equation using the perimeter of a rectangle, $P = 2l + 2w$. The width is the length minus 2 centimeters. The resulting equation is:

$$2l + 2(l - 2) = 44$$

The equation can be solved as follows:

$2l + 2l - 4 = 44$	Apply the distributive property on the left side of the equation
$4l - 4 = 44$	Combine like terms on the left side of the equation
$4l = 48$	Add 4 to both sides of the equation
$l = 12$	Divide both sides of the equation by 4

The length of the rectangle is 12 centimeters. The width is the length minus 2 centimeters, which is 10 centimeters. Checking the answers for length and width forms the following equation:

$$44 = 2(12) + 2(10)$$

The equation can be solved using the order of operations to form a true statement: $44 = 44$.

Equations can also be created from complementary angles (angles that add up to 90°) and supplementary angles (angles that add up to 180°).

Example

Two angles are complementary. If one angle is four times the other angle, what is the measure of each angle?

The first step is to determine the unknown, which is the measure of the first angle. (It could be the measure of either, but we will choose to solve for the first angle.)

The second step is to translate the problem into the equation using the known statement: the sum of two complementary angles is 90°. The resulting equation is $4x + x = 90$. The equation can be solved as follows:

$5x = 90$	Combine like terms on the left side of the equation
$x = 18$	Divide both sides of the equation by 5

The first angle is 18° and the second angle is 4 times the unknown, which is 4 times 18 or 72°.

Going back to check the answer with the original question, 72 and 18 have a sum of 90, making them complementary angles. Seventy-two degrees is also four times the other angle, 18 degrees.

Creating Equivalent Expressions Involving Exponents and Radicals

An **exponent** is written as a^b. In this expression, a is called the **base** and b is called the **exponent.** It is properly stated that a is raised to the n-th power. Therefore, in the expression 2^3, the exponent is 3, while the base is 2. Such an expression is called an **exponential expression**. Note that when the exponent is 2, it is called **squaring** the base, and when it is 3, it is called **cubing** the base.

When the exponent is a positive integer, this indicates the base is multiplied by itself the number of times written in the exponent. So, in the expression 2^3, multiply 2 by itself with 3 copies of 2:

$$2^3 = 2 \times 2 \times 2 = 8$$

One thing to notice is that, for positive integers n and m, $a^n a^m = a^{n+m}$ is a rule. In order to make this rule be true for an integer of 0, $a^0 = 1$, so that:

$$a^n a^0 = a^{n+0} = a^n$$

And, in order to make this rule be true for negative exponents, $a^{-n} = \frac{1}{a^n}$.

Another rule for simplifying expressions with exponents is shown by the following equation: $(a^m)^n = a^{mn}$. This is true for fractional exponents as well. So, for a positive integer, define $a^{\frac{1}{n}}$ to be the number that, when raised to the n-th power, provides a. In other words, $(a^{\frac{1}{n}})^n = a$ is the desired equation. It should be noted that $a^{\frac{1}{n}}$ is the n-th root of a. This also can be written as $a^{\frac{1}{n}} = \sqrt[n]{a}$. The symbol on the right-hand side of this equation is called a **radical.** If the root is left out, assume that the 2nd root should be taken, also called the **square** root:

$$a^{\frac{1}{2}} = \sqrt[2]{a} = \sqrt{a}$$

Additionally, $\sqrt[3]{a}$ is also called the **cube** root.

Note that when multiple roots exist, $a^{\frac{1}{n}}$ is defined to be the **positive** root. So, $4^{\frac{1}{2}} = 2$. Also note that negative numbers do not have even roots in the real numbers.

This also enables finding exponents for any rational number:

$$a^{\frac{m}{n}} = (a^{\frac{1}{n}})^m = (a^m)^{\frac{1}{n}}$$

In fact, the exponent can be any real number. In general, the following rules for exponents should be used for any numbers a, b, m, and n.

$a^1 = a.$

$1^a = 1.$

$a^0 = 1.$

$a^m a^n = a^{m+n}.$

$\frac{a^m}{a^n} = a^{m-n}$

$(a^m)^n = a^{m \times n}.$

$(ab)^m = a^m b^m.$

$(\frac{a}{b})^m = \frac{a^m}{b^m}.$

As an example of applying these rules, consider the problem of simplifying the expression:

$$(3x^2y)^3(2xy^4)$$

Start by simplifying the left term using the sixth rule listed. Applying this rule yields the following expression

$$27x^6y^3(2xy^4)$$

The exponents can now be combined with base *x* and the exponents with base *y*. Multiply the coefficients to yield $54x^7y^7$.

In mathematical expressions containing exponents and other operations, the order of operations must be followed. PEMDAS states that exponents are calculated after any parenthesis and grouping symbols but before any multiplication, division, addition, and subtraction.

Here are some of the most important properties of exponents and roots: if *n* is an integer, and if $a^n = b^n$, then $a = b$ if *n* is odd; but $a = \pm b$ if *n* is even. Similarly, if the roots of two things are equal, $\sqrt[n]{a} = \sqrt[n]{b}$, then $a = b$. This means that when starting with a true equation, both sides of that equation can be raised to a given power to obtain another true equation. Beware that when an even-powered root is taken on both sides of the equation, a $\pm$ in the result. For example, given the equation $x^2 = 16$, take the square root of both sides to solve for x. This results in the answer $x = \pm 4$ because $(-4)^2 = 16$ and $(4)^2 = 16$.

Another property is that if $a^n = a^m$, then $n = m$. This is true for any real numbers *n* and *m*.

For solving the equation $\sqrt{x+2} - 1 = 3$, start by moving the -1 over to the right-hand side. This is performed by adding 1 to both sides, which yields $\sqrt{x+2} = 4$. Now, square both sides, but remember that by squaring both sides, the signs are irrelevant. This yields $x + 2 = 16$, which simplifies to give $x = 14$.

Now consider the problem $(x + 1)^4 = 16$. To solve this, take the 4th root of both sides, which means an ambiguity in the sign will be introduced because it is an even root:

$$\sqrt[4]{(x + 1)^4} = \pm\sqrt[4]{16}$$

The right-hand side is 2, since $2^4 = 16$. Therefore:

$$x + 1 = \pm 2 \text{ or } x = -1 \pm 2$$

Thus, the two possible solutions are $x = -3$ and $x = 1$.

Remember that when solving equations, the answer can be checked by plugging the solution back into the problem to make a true statement.

Creating Equivalent Forms of Expressions

Algebraic expressions are made up of numbers, variables, and combinations of the two, using mathematical operations. Expressions can be rewritten based on their factors. For example, the expression $6x + 4$ can be rewritten as $2(3x + 2)$ because 2 is a factor of both $6x$ and 4. More complex expressions can also be rewritten based on their factors. The expression $x^4 - 16$ can be rewritten as $(x^2 - 4)(x^2 + 4)$. This is a different type of factoring, where a difference of squares is factored into a sum and difference of the same two terms. With some expressions, the factoring process is simple and only leads to a different way to represent the expression. With others, factoring and rewriting the expression leads to more information about the given problem.

In the following quadratic equation, factoring the binomial leads to finding the zeros of the function:

$$x^2 - 5x + 6 = y$$

This equation factors into $(x - 3)(x - 2) = y$, where 2 and 3 are found to be the zeros of the function when y is set equal to zero. The zeros of any function are the *x*-values where the graph of the function on the coordinate plane crosses the *x*-axis.

Factoring an equation is a simple way to rewrite the equation and find the zeros, but factoring is not possible for every quadratic. Completing the square is one way to find zeros when factoring is not an option. The following equation cannot be factored: $x^2 + 10x - 9 = 0$. The first step in this method is to move the constant to the right side of the equation, making it $x^2 + 10x = 9$. Then, the coefficient of x is divided by 2 and squared. This number is then added to both sides of the equation, to make the equation still true. For this example, $\left(\frac{10}{2}\right)^2 = 25$ is added to both sides of the equation to obtain:

$$x^2 + 10x + 25 = 9 + 25$$

This expression simplifies to $x^2 + 10x + 25 = 34$, which can then be factored into:

$$(x + 5)^2 = 34$$

Solving for x then involves taking the square root of both sides and subtracting 5. This leads to two zeros of the function:

$$x = \pm\sqrt{34} - 5$$

Depending on the type of answer the question seeks, a calculator may be used to find exact numbers.

Given a quadratic equation in standard form— $ax^2 + bx + c = 0$—the sign of a tells whether the function has a minimum value or a maximum value. If $a > 0$, the graph opens up and has a minimum value. If $a < 0$, the graph opens down and has a maximum value. Depending on the way the quadratic equation is written, multiplication may need to occur before a max/min value is determined.

There are also properties of numbers that are true for certain operations. The **commutative** property allows the order of the terms in an expression to change while keeping the same final answer. Both addition and multiplication can be completed in any order and still obtain the same result. However, order does matter in subtraction and division. The **associative** property allows any terms to be "associated" by parenthesis and retain the same final answer. For example:

$$(4 + 3) + 5 = 4 + (3 + 5)$$

Both addition and multiplication are associative; however, subtraction and division do not hold this property. The **distributive** property states that $a(b + c) = ab + ac$. It is a property that involves both addition and multiplication, and the a is distributed onto each term inside the parentheses.

The expression $4(3 + 2)$ is simplified using the order of operations. Simplifying inside the parenthesis first produces 4×5, which equals 20. The expression $4(3 + 2)$ can also be simplified using the distributive property:

$$4(3 + 2) = 4 \times 3 + 4 \times 2 = 12 + 8 = 20$$

Consider the following example: $4(3x - 2)$. The expression cannot be simplified inside the parenthesis because $3x$ and -2 are not like terms and therefore cannot be combined. However, the expression can be simplified by using the distributive property and multiplying each term inside of the parenthesis by the term outside of the parenthesis: $12x - 8$. The resulting equivalent expression contains no like terms, so it cannot be further simplified.

Consider the expression:

$$(3x + 2y + 1) - (5x - 3) + 2(3y + 4)$$

Again, there are no like terms, but the distributive property is used to simplify the expression. Note there is an implied one in front of the first set of parentheses and an implied -1 in front of the second set of parentheses. Distributing the 1, -1, and 2 produces:

$$1(3x) + 1(2y) + 1(1) - 1(5x) - 1(-3) + 2(3y) + 2(4)$$

$$3x + 2y + 1 - 5x + 3 + 6y + 8$$

This expression contains like terms that are combined to produce the simplified expression:

$$-2x + 8y + 12$$

Algebraic expressions are tested to be equivalent by choosing values for the variables and evaluating both expressions. For example, $4(3x - 2)$ and $12x - 8$ are tested by substituting 3 for the variable *x* and calculating to determine if equivalent values result.

Solving Quadratic Equations

A **quadratic equation** is an equation in the form:

$$ax^2 + bx + c = 0$$

There are several methods to solve such equations. The easiest method will depend on the quadratic equation in question.

Sometimes, it is possible to solve quadratic equations by manually **factoring** them. This means rewriting them in the form $(x + A)(x + B) = 0$. If this is done, then they can be solved by remembering that when $ab = 0$, either *a* or *b* must be equal to zero. Therefore, to have $(x + A)(x + B) = 0$, $(x + A) = 0$ or $(x + B) = 0$ is needed. These equations have the solutions $x = -A$ and $x = -B$, respectively.

In order to factor a quadratic equation, note that:

$$(x + A)(x + B) = x^2 + (A + B)x + AB$$

So, if an equation is in the form $x^2 + bx + c$, two numbers, *A* and *B,* need to be found that will add up to give us *b*, and multiply together to give us *c*.

As an example, consider solving the equation:

$$-3x^2 + 6x + 9 = 0$$

Start by dividing both sides by -3, leaving:

$$x^2 - 2x - 3 = 0$$

Now, notice that $1 - 3 = -2$, and also that:

$$(1)(-3) = -3$$

This means the equation can be factored into:

$$(x + 1)(x - 3) = 0$$

Now, solve $(x + 1) = 0$ and $(x - 3) = 0$ to get $x = -1$ and $x = 3$ as the solutions.

It is useful when trying to factor to remember that:

$$x^2 + 2xy + y^2 = (x + y)^2$$

$$x^2 - 2xy + y^2 = (x - y)^2$$

$$x^2 - y^2 = (x + y)(x - y)$$

However, factoring by hand is often hard to do. If there are no obvious ways to factor the quadratic equation, solutions can still be found by using the **quadratic formula**.

The quadratic formula is:

$$x = \frac{-b \pm \sqrt{b^2 - 4ac}}{2a}$$

This method will always work, although it sometimes can take longer than factoring by hand, if the factors are easy to guess. Using the standard form $ax^2 + bx + c = 0$, plug the values of *a*, *b*, and *c* from the equation into the formula and solve for *x*. There will either be two answers, one answer, or no real answer. No real answer comes when the value of the discriminant, the number under the square root, is a negative number. Since there are no real numbers that square to get a negative, the answer will be no real roots.

Here is an example of solving a quadratic equation using the quadratic formula. Suppose the equation to solve is:

$$-2x^2 + 3x + 1 = 0$$

There is no obvious way to factor this, so the quadratic formula is used, with $a = -2, b = 3, c = 1$. After substituting these values into the quadratic formula, it yields this:

$$x = \frac{-3 \pm \sqrt{3^2 - 4(-2)(1)}}{2(-2)}$$

This can be simplified to obtain:

$$\frac{3 \pm \sqrt{9+8}}{4}$$

or

$$\frac{3 \pm \sqrt{17}}{4}$$

Challenges can be encountered when asked to find a quadratic equation with specific roots. Given roots A and B, a quadratic function can be constructed with those roots by taking $(x - A)(x - B)$. So, in constructing a quadratic equation with roots $x = -2, 3$, it would result in:

$$(x + 2)(x - 3) = x^2 - x - 6$$

Multiplying this by a constant also could be done without changing the roots.

Adding, Subtracting, and Multiplying Polynomial Expressions

An expression of the form ax^n, where n is a non-negative integer, is called a **monomial** because it contains one term. A sum of monomials is called a **polynomial.** For example, $-4x^3 + x$ is a polynomial, while $5x^7$ is a monomial. A function equal to a polynomial is called a **polynomial function**.

The monomials in a polynomial are also called the **terms** of the polynomial.

The constants that precede the variables are called **coefficients**.

The highest value of the exponent of x in a polynomial is called the **degree** of the polynomial. So, $-4x^3 + x$ has a degree of 3, while $-2x^5 + x^3 + 4x + 1$ has a degree of 5. When multiplying polynomials, the degree of the result will be the sum of the degrees of the two polynomials being multiplied.

To add polynomials, add the coefficients of like powers of x. For example:

$$(-2x^5 + x^3 + 4x + 1) + (-4x^3 + x)$$

$$-2x^5 + (1 - 4)x^3 + (4 + 1)x + 1$$

$$-2x^5 - 3x^3 + 5x + 1$$

Likewise, subtraction of polynomials is performed by subtracting coefficients of like powers of x. So:

$$(-2x^5 + x^3 + 4x + 1) - (-4x^3 + x)$$

$$-2x^5 + (1 + 4)x^3 + (4 - 1)x + 1$$

$$-2x^5 + 5x^3 + 3x + 1$$

To multiply two polynomials, multiply each term of the first polynomial by each term of the second polynomial and add the results. For example:

$$(4x^2 + x)(-x^3 + x)$$

$$4x^2(-x^3) + 4x^2(x) + x(-x^3) + x(x)$$

$$-4x^5 + 4x^3 - x^4 + x^2$$

In the case where each polynomial has two terms, like in this example, some students find it helpful to remember this as multiplying the First terms, then the Outer terms, then the Inner terms, and finally the Last terms, with the mnemonic FOIL. For longer polynomials, the multiplication process is the same, but there will be, of course, more terms, and there is no common mnemonic to remember each combination.

Solving Equations with Radicals or Variables in the Denominator

When solving radical and rational equations, extraneous solutions must be accounted for when finding the answers. For example, the equation $\frac{x}{x-5} = \frac{3x}{x+3}$ has two values that create a 0 denominator: $x \neq 5, -3$. When solving for x, these values must be considered because they cannot be solutions. In the given equation, solving for x can be done using cross-multiplication, yielding the equation:

$$x(x + 3) = 3x(x - 5)$$

Distributing results in the quadratic equation $x^2 + 3x = 3x^2 - 15x$; therefore, all terms must be moved to one side of the equals sign. This results in $2x^2 - 18x = 0$, which in factored form is $2x(x - 9) = 0$. Setting each factor equal to zero, the apparent solutions are $x = 0$ and $x = 9$. These two solutions are neither 5 nor -3, so they are viable solutions. Neither 0 nor 9 create a 0 denominator in the original equation.

A similar process exists when solving radical equations. One must check to make sure the solutions are defined in the original equations. Solving an equation containing a square root involves isolating the root and then squaring both sides of the equals sign. Solving a cube root equation involves isolating the radical and then cubing both sides. In either case, the variable can then be solved for because there are no longer radicals in the equation.

For example, the following expression is a radical that can be simplified: $\sqrt{24x^2}$. First, the number must be factored out to the highest perfect square. Any perfect square can be taken out of a radical. Twenty-four can be factored into 4 and 6, and 4 can be taken out of the radical. $\sqrt{4} = 2$ can be taken out, and 6 stays underneath. If $x > 0$, x can be taken out of the radical because it is a perfect square. The simplified radical is $2x\sqrt{6}$. An approximation can be found using a calculator.

Solving a System with One Linear Equation and One Quadratic Equation

A system of equations may also be made up of a linear and a quadratic equation. These systems may have one solution, two solutions, or no solutions. The graph of these systems involves one straight line and one parabola. Algebraically, these systems can be solved by solving the linear equation for one variable and plugging that answer in to the quadratic equation. If possible, the equation can then be solved to find part of the answer. The graphing method is commonly used for these types of systems. On a graph, these two lines can be found to intersect at one point, at two points across the parabola, or at no points.

Solving a system of one linear equation and one quadratic equation algebraically involves using the substitution method. Consider the following system: $y = x^2 + 9x + 11$; $y = 2x - 1$. Substitute the equivalent value of y from the linear equation $(2x - 1)$ into the quadratic equation. The resulting equation would be:

$$2x - 1 = x^2 + 9x + 11$$

Next, solve the resulting quadratic equation using the appropriate method—factoring, taking square roots, or using the quadratic formula. This equation can be solved by factoring:

$$0 = x^2 + 7x + 120$$

$$(x + 3)(x + 4)$$

$$x + 3 = 0 \text{ or } x + 4 = 0$$

$$x = -3 \text{ or } x = -4$$

Next, find the corresponding y-values by substituting the x-values into the original linear equation:

$$y = 2(-4) - 1 = -9$$

$$y = 2(-3) - 1 = -7$$

Write the solutions as ordered pairs: $(-4, -9)$ and $(-3, -7)$. Finally, check the possible solutions by substituting each into both original equations. (In this case, both solutions "check out.")

Rewriting Simple Rational Expressions

A fraction, or ratio, wherein each part is a polynomial, defines **rational expressions**. Some examples include $\frac{2x+6}{x}$, $\frac{1}{x^2-4x+8}$, and $\frac{z^2}{x+5}$. Exponents on the variables are restricted to whole numbers, which means roots and negative exponents are not included in rational expressions.

Rational expressions can be transformed by factoring. For example, the expression $\frac{x^2-5x+6}{(x-3)}$ can be rewritten by factoring the numerator to obtain:

$$\frac{(x-3)(x-2)}{(x-3)}$$

Therefore, the common binomial $(x-3)$ can cancel so that the simplified expression is:

$$\frac{(x-2)}{1} = (x-2)$$

Additionally, other rational expressions can be rewritten to take on different forms. Some may be factorable in themselves, while others can be transformed through arithmetic operations. Rational expressions are closed under addition, subtraction, multiplication, and division by a nonzero expression. **Closed** means that if any one of these operations is performed on a rational expression, the result will still be a rational expression. The set of all real numbers is another example of a set closed under all four operations.

Adding and subtracting rational expressions is based on the same concepts as adding and subtracting simple fractions. For both concepts, the denominators must be the same for the operation to take place. For example, here are two rational expressions:

$$\frac{x^3-4}{(x-3)} + \frac{x+8}{(x-3)}$$

Since the denominators are both $(x-3)$, the numerators can be combined by collecting like terms to form:

$$\frac{x^3+x+4}{(x-3)}$$

If the denominators are different, they need to be made common (the same) by using the **Least Common Denominator** (LCD). Each denominator needs to be factored, and the LCD contains each factor that appears in any one denominator the greatest number of times it appears in any denominator. The original expressions need to be multiplied times a form of 1, which will turn each denominator into the LCD. This process is like adding fractions with unlike denominators. It is also important when working with rational expressions to define what value of the variable makes the denominator zero. For this particular value, the expression is undefined.

Multiplication of rational expressions is performed like multiplication of fractions. The numerators are multiplied; then, the denominators are multiplied. The final fraction is then simplified. The expressions are simplified by factoring and cancelling out common terms. In the following example, the numerator of the second expression can be factored first to simplify the expression before multiplying:

$$\frac{x^2}{(x-4)} \times \frac{x^2 - x - 12}{2}$$

$$\frac{x^2}{(x-4)} \times \frac{(x-4)(x+3)}{2}$$

The $(x-4)$ on the top and bottom cancel out:

$$\frac{x^2}{1} \times \frac{(x+3)}{2}$$

Then multiplication is performed, resulting in:

$$\frac{x^3 + 3x^2}{2}$$

Dividing rational expressions is similar to the division of fractions, where division turns into multiplying by a reciprocal. So, the following expression can be rewritten as a multiplication problem:

$$\frac{x^2 - 3x + 7}{x - 4} \div \frac{x^2 - 5x + 3}{x - 4}$$

$$\frac{x^2 - 3x + 7}{x - 4} \times \frac{x - 4}{x^2 - 5x + 3}$$

The $x - 4$ cancels out, leaving:

$$\frac{x^2 - 3x + 7}{x^2 - 5x + 3}$$

The final answers should always be completely simplified. If a function is composed of a rational expression, the zeros of the graph can be found from setting the polynomial in the numerator as equal to zero and solving. The values that make the denominator equal to zero will either exist on the graph as a hole or a vertical asymptote.

Interpreting Parts of Nonlinear Expressions

When a nonlinear function is used to model a real-life scenario, some aspects of the function may be relevant, while others may not. The context of each scenario will dictate what should be used. In general, x- and y-intercepts will be points of interest. A y-intercept is the value of y when $x = 0$, and an x-intercept is the value of x when $y = 0$. Suppose a nonlinear function models the value of an investment (y) over the course of time (x). It would be relevant to determine the initial value. This initial value would be the y-intercept of the function (where time equals 0). It would also be useful to note any point in time in which the value of the investment would be 0. These would be the x-intercepts of the function.

Another aspect of a function that is typically desired is the **rate of change**. This tells how fast the outputs are growing or decaying with respect to given inputs. The rate of change for a quadratic function in standard form, $y = ax^2 + bx + c$, is determined by the value of a. A positive value indicates growth, and a negative value indicates decay. The rate of change for an exponential function in standard form, $y = (a)(b^x)$, is determined by the value of b. If b is greater than 1, the function describes exponential growth, and if b is less than 1, the function describes exponential decay.

For polynomial functions, the rate of change can be estimated by the highest power of the function. Polynomial functions also include absolute and/or relative minimums and maximums. Consider functions modeling production or expenses. Maximum and minimum values would be relevant aspects of these models.

Finally, the domain and range for a function should be considered for relevance. The domain consists of all input values, and the range consists of all output values. Suppose a function models the volume of a container to be produced in relation to its height. Although the function that models the scenario may include negative values for inputs and outputs, these parts of the function would obviously not be relevant.

Understanding the Relationship Between Zeros and Factors of Polynomials

Finding the zeros of polynomial functions is the same process as finding the solutions of polynomial equations. These are the points at which the graph of the function crosses the x-axis. As stated previously, factors can be used to find the zeros of a polynomial function. The degree of the function shows the number of possible zeros. If the highest exponent on the independent variable is 4, then the degree is 4, and the number of possible zeros is 4. If there are complex solutions, the number of roots is less than the degree.

Given the function $y = x^2 + 7x + 6$, y can be set equal to zero, and the polynomial can be factored. The equation turns into $0 = (x + 1)(x + 6)$, where $x = -1$ and $x = -6$ are the zeros. Since this is a quadratic equation, the shape of the graph will be a parabola. Knowing that zeros represent the points where the parabola crosses the x-axis, the maximum or minimum point is the only other piece needed to sketch a rough graph of the function. By looking at the function in standard form, the coefficient of x is positive; therefore, the parabola opens *up*.

Using the zeros and the minimum, the following rough sketch of the graph can be constructed:

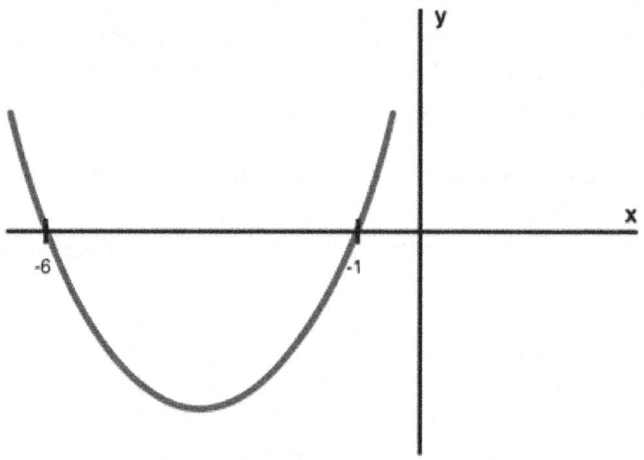

Factors for polynomials are similar to factors for integers—they are numbers, variables, or polynomials that, when multiplied together, give a product equal to the polynomial in question. One polynomial is a factor of a second polynomial if the second polynomial can be obtained from the first by multiplying by a third polynomial.

$6x^6 + 13x^4 + 6x^2$ can be obtained by multiplying together $(3x^4 + 2x^2)(2x^2 + 3)$. This means $2x^2 + 3$ and $3x^4 + 2x^2$ are factors of $6x^6 + 13x^4 + 6x^2$.

In general, finding the factors of a polynomial can be tricky. However, there are a few types of polynomials that can be factored in a straightforward way.

If a certain monomial is in each term of a polynomial, it can be factored out. There are several common forms polynomials take, which if you recognize, you can solve. The first example is a perfect square trinomial. To factor this polynomial, first expand the middle term of the expression:

$$x^2 + 2xy + y^2$$

$$x^2 + xy + xy + y^2$$

Factor out a common term in each half of the expression (in this case x from the left and y from the right):

$$x(x + y) + y(x + y)$$

Then the same can be done again, treating $(x + y)$ as the common factor:

$$(x + y)(x + y) = (x + y)^2$$

Therefore, the formula for this polynomial is:

$$x^2 + 2xy + y^2 = (x + y)^2$$

Next is another example of a perfect square trinomial. The process is the similar, but notice the difference in sign:

$$x^2 - 2xy + y^2$$

$$x^2 - xy - xy + y^2$$

Factor out the common term on each side:

$$x(x - y) - y(x - y)$$

Factoring out the common term again:

$$(x - y)(x - y) = (x - y)^2$$

Thus:

$$x^2 - 2xy + y^2 = (x - y)^2$$

The next is known as a difference of squares. This process is effectively the reverse of binomial multiplication:

$$x^2 - y^2$$

$$x^2 - xy + xy - y^2$$

$$x(x - y) + y(x - y)$$

$$(x + y)(x - y)$$

Therefore:

$$x^2 - y^2 = (x + y)(x - y)$$

The following two polynomials are known as the sum or difference of cubes. These are special polynomials that take the form of $x^3 + y^3$ or $x^3 - y^3$. The following formula factors the sum of cubes:

$$x^3 + y^3 = (x + y)(x^2 - xy + y^2)$$

Next is the difference of cubes, but note the change in sign. The formulas for both are similar, but the order of signs for factoring the sum or difference of cubes can be remembered by using the acronym SOAP, which stands for "same, opposite, always positive." The first sign is the same as the sign in the first expression, the second is opposite, and the third is always positive. The next formula factors the difference of cubes:

$$x^3 - y^3 = (x - y)(x^2 + xy + y^2)$$

The following two examples are expansions of cubed binomials. Similarly, these polynomials always follow a pattern:

$$x^3 + 3x^2y + 3xy^2 + y^3 = (x + y)^3$$

$$x^3 - 3x^2y + 3xy^2 - y^3 = (x - y)^3$$

These rules can be used in many combinations with one another. For example, the expression $3x^3 - 24$ has a common factor of 3, which becomes:

$$3(x^3 - 8)$$

A difference of cubes still remains which can then be factored out:

$$3(x - 2)(x^2 + 2x + 4)$$

There are no other terms to be pulled out, so this expression is completely factored.

When factoring polynomials, a good strategy is to multiply the factors to check the result. Let's try another example:

$$4x^3 + 16x^2$$

Both sides of the expression can be divided by 4, and both contain x^2, because $4x^3$ can be thought of as $4x^2(x)$, so the common term can simply be factored out:

$$4x^2(x + 4)$$

It sometimes can be necessary to rewrite the polynomial in some clever way before applying the above rules. Consider the problem of factoring $x^4 - 1$. This does not immediately look like any of the previous polynomials. However, it's possible to think of this polynomial as $x^4 - 1 = (x^2)^2 - (1^2)^2$, and now it can be treated as a difference of squares to simplify this:

$$(x^2)^2 - (1^2)^2$$

$$(x^2)^2 - x^2 1^2 + x^2 1^2 - (1^2)^2$$

$$x^2(x^2 - 1^2) + 1^2(x^2 - 1^2)$$

$$(x^2 + 1^2)(x^2 - 1^2)$$

$$(x^2 + 1)(x^2 - 1)$$

Understanding Nonlinear Relationships

A polynomial function consists of a monomial or sum of monomials arranged in descending exponential order. The graph of a polynomial function is a smooth continuous curve that extends infinitely on both ends.

The end behavior of the graph of a polynomial function can be determined by the **degree of the function** (largest exponent) and the **leading coefficient** (coefficient of the term with the largest exponent). If the degree is odd and the coefficient is positive, the graph falls to the left and rises to the right. If the degree is odd and the coefficient is negative, the graph rises to the left and falls to the right. If the degree is even and the coefficient is positive, the graph rises to the left and rises to the right. If the degree is even and the coefficient is negative, the graph falls to the left and falls to the right.

The y-intercept for any function is the point at which the graph crosses the y-axis. At this point, $x = 0$; therefore, to determine the y-intercept, substitute $x = 0$ into the function, and solve for y. Likewise, the x-intercepts, also called **zeros**, can be found by substituting $y = 0$ into the function and finding all solutions for x. For a given zero of a function, the graph can either pass through that point or simply touch that point (the graph turns at that zero). This is determined by the multiplicity of that zero. The multiplicity of a zero is the number of times its corresponding factor is multiplied to obtain the function in standard form. For example, $y = x^3 - 4x^2 - 3x + 18$ can be written in factored form as:

$$y = (x + 2)(x - 3)(x - 3) \text{ or } y = (x + 2)(x - 3)^2$$

The zeros of the function would be -2 and 3. The zero at -2 would have a multiplicity of 1, and the zero at 3 would have a multiplicity of 2. If a zero has an even multiplicity, then the graph touches the x-axis at that zero and turns around. If a zero has an odd multiplicity, then the graph crosses the x-axis at that zero.

The graph of a polynomial function can have several **turning points** (where the curve changes from rising to falling or vice versa) equal to one less than the degree of the function. For example, the function $y = 3x^5 + 2x^2 - 3x$ could have no more than four turning points.

Using Function Notation

A **function** is defined as a relationship between inputs and outputs where there is only one output value for a given input. As an example, the following function is in **function notation**:

$$f(x) = 3x - 4$$

The $f(x)$ represents the output value for an input of x. If $x = 2$, the equation becomes:

$$f(2) = 3(2) - 4 = 6 - 4 = 2$$

The input of 2 yields an output of 2, forming the ordered pair $(2, 2)$. The following set of ordered pairs corresponds to the given function: $(2, 2)$, $(0, -4)$, $(-2, -10)$. The set of all possible inputs of a function is its **domain**, and all possible outputs is called the **range**. By definition, each member of the domain is paired with only one member of the range.

Functions can also be defined recursively. In this form, they are not defined explicitly in terms of variables. Instead, they are defined using previously-evaluated function outputs, starting with either $f(0)$ or $f(1)$. An example of a recursively-defined function is:

$$f(1) = 2, f(n) = 2f(n - 1) + 2n, n > 1$$

The domain of this function is the set of all integers.

In many cases, a function can be defined by giving an equation. For instance, $f(x) = x^2$ indicates that given a value for x, the output of f is found by squaring x.

Not all equations in x and y can be written in the form $y = f(x)$. An equation can be written in such a form if it satisfies the **vertical line test**: no vertical line meets the graph of the equation at more than a single point. In this case, y is said to be a **function of x**. If a vertical line meets the graph in two places, then this equation cannot be written in the form $y = f(x)$.

The graph of a function $f(x)$ is the graph of the equation $y = f(x)$. Thus, it is the set of all pairs (x, y) where $y = f(x)$. In other words, it is all pairs $(x, f(x))$. The x-intercepts are called the **zeros** of the function. The y-intercept is given by $f(0)$.

If, for a given function f, the only way to get $f(a) = f(b)$ is for $a = b$, then f is **one-to-one**. Often, even if a function is not one-to-one on its entire domain, it is one-to-one by considering a restricted portion of the domain.

A function $f(x) = k$ for some number k is called a **constant function**. The graph of a constant function is a horizontal line.

The function $f(x) = x$ is called the **identity function**. The graph of the identity function is the diagonal line pointing to the upper right at 45 degrees, $y = x$.

Given two functions, $f(x)$ and $g(x)$, new functions can be formed by adding, subtracting, multiplying, or dividing the functions. Any algebraic combination of the two functions can be performed, including one function being the exponent of the other. If there are expressions for f and g, then the result can be found by performing the desired operation between the expressions. So, if $f(x) = x^2$ and $g(x) = 3x$, then:

$$f \cdot g(x) = x^2 \cdot 3x = 3x^3$$

Given two functions, $f(x)$ and $g(x)$, where the domain of g contains the range of f, the two functions can be combined together in a process called **composition**. The function — "g composed of f" — is written:

$$(g \circ f)(x) = g(f(x))$$

This requires the input of x into f, then taking that result and plugging it in to the function g.

If f is one-to-one, then there is also the option to find the function $f^{-1}(x)$, called the **inverse** of f. Algebraically, the inverse function can be found by writing y in place of $f(x)$, and then solving for x. The inverse function also makes this statement true:

$$f^{-1}(f(x)) = x$$

Computing the inverse of a function f entails the following procedure:

Given $f(x) = x^2$, with a domain of $x \geq 0$.

$x = y^2$is written down o find the inverse.

The square root of both sides is determined to solve for y.

Normally, this would mean $\pm\sqrt{x} = y$. However, the domain of f does not include the negative numbers, so the negative option needs to be eliminated.

The result is $y = \sqrt{x}$, so $f^{-1}(x) = \sqrt{x}$, with a domain of $x \geq 0$.

A function is called **monotone** if it is either always increasing or always decreasing. For example, the functions $f(x) = 3x$ and $f(x) = -x^5$ are monotone.

An **even function** looks the same when flipped over the y-axis:

$$f(x) = f(-x)$$

The following image shows a graphic representation of an even function.

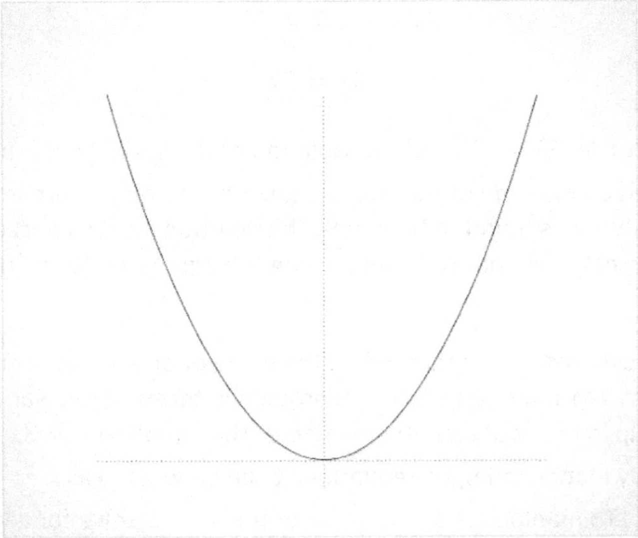

An **odd function** looks the same when flipped over the y-axis and then flipped over the x-axis:

$$f(x) = -f(-x)$$

The following image shows an example of an odd function.

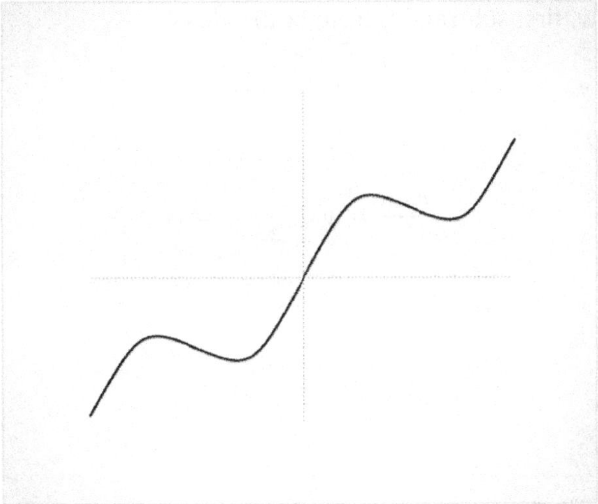

Using Structure to Isolate a Quantity of Interest

Solving equations with one variable is the process of isolating a variable on one side of the equation. For example, in $3x - 7 = 20$, the variable x needs to be isolated. Using opposite operations, the -7 is moved to the right side of the equation by adding seven to both sides:

$$3x - 7 + 7 = 20 + 7$$

$$3x = 27$$

Dividing by three on each side, $\frac{3x}{3} = \frac{27}{3}$, results in isolation of the variable. It is important to note that if an operation is performed on one side of the equals sign, it has to be performed on the other side to maintain equality. The solution is found to be $x = 9$. This solution can be checked for accuracy by plugging $x = 9$ in the original equation. After simplifying the equation, $20 = 20$ is found, which is a true statement.

Formulas are mathematical expressions that define the value of one quantity given the value of one or more different quantities. A formula or equation expressed in terms of one variable can be manipulated to express the relationship in terms of any other variable. The equation $y = 3x + 2$ is expressed in terms of the variable y. By manipulating the equation, it can be written as $x = \frac{y-2}{3}$, which is expressed in terms of the variable x. To manipulate an equation or formula to solve for a variable of interest, consider how the equation would be solved if all other variables were numbers. Follow the same steps for solving, leaving operations in terms of the variables instead of calculating numerical values.

The formula $P = 2l + 2w$ expresses how to calculate the perimeter of a rectangle given its length and width. To write a formula to calculate the width of a rectangle given its length and perimeter, use the previous formula relating the three variables, and solve for the variable w. If P and l were numerical values, this would be a two-step linear equation solved by subtraction and division. To solve the equation $P = 2l + 2w$ for w, first subtract $2l$ from both sides:

$$P - 2l = 2w$$

Then, divide both sides by 2:

$$\frac{P-2l}{2} = w \text{ or } \frac{P}{2} - l = w$$

Additional Topics in Math

Solving Problems Using Volume Formulas

Geometry in three dimensions is similar to geometry in two dimensions. The main new feature is that three points now define a unique **plane** that passes through each of them. Below, some of the possible three-dimensional figures will be provided, along with formulas for their volumes.

A **rectangular prism** is a box whose sides are all rectangles meeting at 90° angles. Such a box has three dimensions: length, width, and height. If the length is x, the width is y, and the height is z, then the volume is given by $V = xyz$.

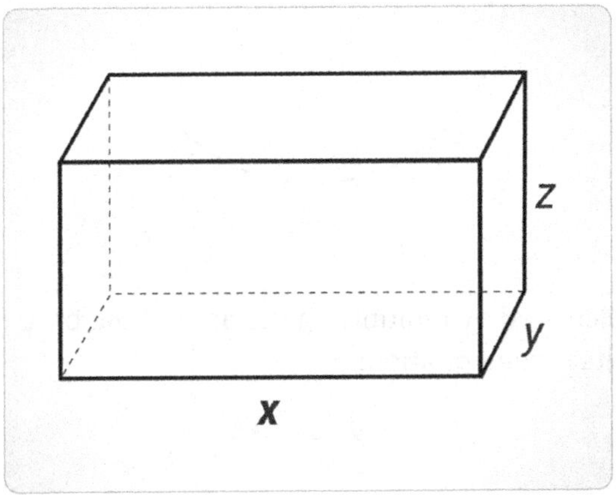

A **rectangular pyramid** is a figure with a rectangular base and four triangular sides that meet at a single vertex. If the rectangle has sides of length x and y, then the volume will be given by:

$$V = \frac{1}{3}xyh$$

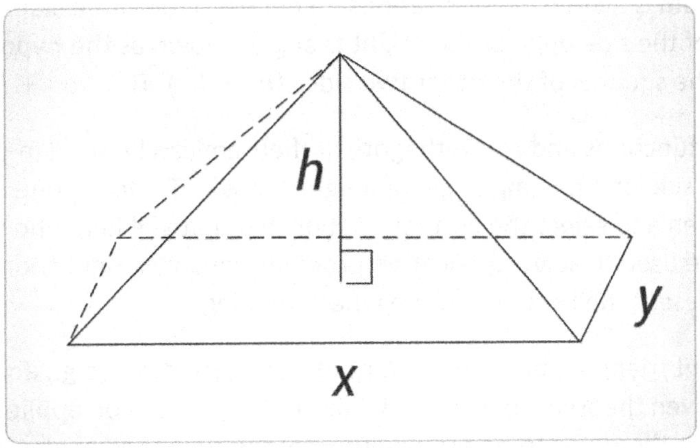

A **sphere** is a set of points all of which are equidistant from some central point. It is like a circle, but in three dimensions. The volume of a sphere of radius r is given by:

$$V = \frac{4}{3}\pi r^3$$

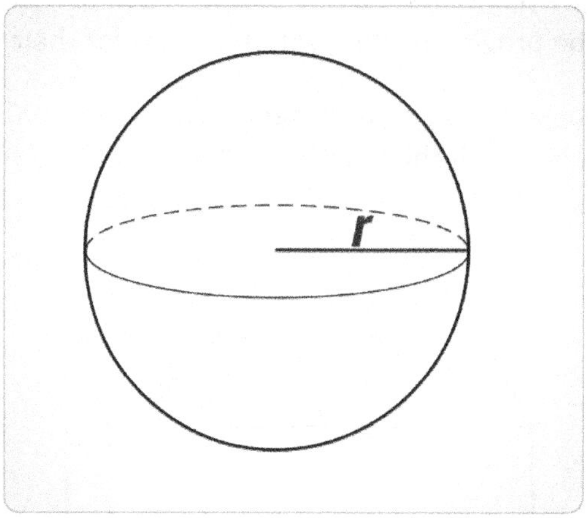

The volume of a **cylinder** is calculated by multiplying the area of the base (which is a circle) by the height of the cylinder. Doing so results in the equation:

$$V = \pi r^2 h$$

The volume of a cone is $\frac{1}{3}$ of the volume of a cylinder. Therefore, the formula for the volume of a cone is:

$$\frac{1}{3}\pi r^2 h$$

Using Trigonometric Ratios and the Pythagorean Theorem

The **Pythagorean theorem** is an important relationship between the three sides of a right triangle. It states that the square of the side opposite the right triangle, known as the **hypotenuse** (denoted as c^2), is equal to the sum of the squares of the other two sides ($a^2 + b^2$). Thus, $a^2 + b^2 = c^2$.

Both the trigonometric functions and the Pythagorean theorem can be used in problems that involve finding either a missing side or a missing angle of a right triangle. To do so, one must look to see what sides and angles are given and select the correct relationship that will help find the missing value. These relationships can also be used to solve application problems involving right triangles. Often, it's helpful to draw a figure to represent the problem to see what's missing.

To prove theorems about triangles, basic definitions involving triangles (e.g., equilateral, isosceles, etc.) need to be realized. Proven theorems concerning lines and angles can be applied to prove theorems about triangles. Common theorems to be proved include: the sum of all angles in a triangle equals 180 degrees; the sum of the lengths of two sides of a triangle is greater than the length of the third side; the base angles of an isosceles triangle are congruent; the line segment connecting the midpoint of two sides of a triangle is parallel to the third side and its length is half the length of the third side; and the medians of a triangle all meet at a single point.

An **isosceles triangle** contains at least two equal sides. Therefore, it must also contain two equal angles and, subsequently, contain two medians of the same length. An isosceles triangle can also be labelled as an **equilateral triangle** (which contains three equal sides and three equal angles) when it meets these conditions. In an equilateral triangle, the measure of each angle is always 60 degrees. Also, within an equilateral triangle, the medians are of the same length. A **scalene triangle** can never be an equilateral or an isosceles triangle because it contains no equal sides and no equal angles. Also, medians in a scalene triangle can't have the same length. However, a **right triangle**, which is a triangle containing a 90-degree angle, can be a scalene triangle.

There are two types of special right triangles. The **30-60-90 right triangle** has angle measurements of 30 degrees, 60 degrees, and 90 degrees. Because of the nature of this triangle, and through the use of the Pythagorean theorem, the side lengths have a special relationship. If x is the length opposite the 30-degree angle, the length opposite the 60-degree angle is $\sqrt{3}x$, and the hypotenuse has length $2x$. The **45-45-90 right triangle** is also special as it contains two angle measurements of 45 degrees. It can be proven that, if x is the length of the two equal sides, the hypotenuse is $x\sqrt{2}$. The properties of all of these special triangles are extremely useful in determining both side lengths and angle measurements in problems where some of these quantities are given and some are not.

Trigonometric functions are also used to describe behavior in mathematics. **Trigonometry** is the relationship between the angles and sides of a triangle. **Trigonometric functions** include sine, cosine, tangent, secant, cosecant, and cotangent. The functions are defined through ratios in a right triangle. SOHCAHTOA is a common acronym used to remember these ratios, which are defined by the relationships of the sides and angles relative to the right angle. **Sine** is opposite over hypotenuse, **cosine** is adjacent over hypotenuse, and **tangent** is opposite over adjacent. These ratios are the reciprocals of secant, cosecant, and cotangent, respectively. Angles can be measured in degrees or radians. Here is a diagram of SOHCAHTOA:

SOH $\sin\theta = \frac{\text{opposite}}{\text{hypotenuse}}$

CAH $\cos\theta = \frac{\text{adjacent}}{\text{hypotenuse}}$

TOA $\tan\theta = \frac{\text{opposite}}{\text{adjacent}}$

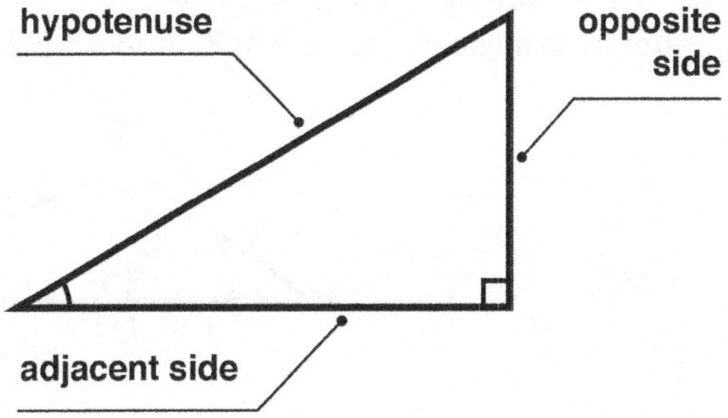

Consider the right triangle shown in this figure:

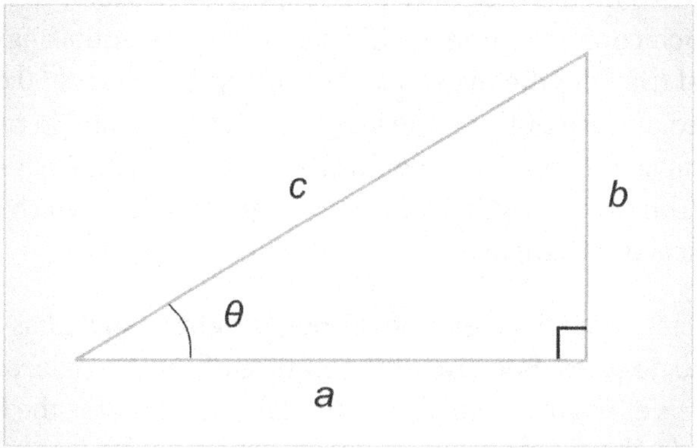

The following hold true:

- $c \sin\theta = b$
- $c \cos\theta = a$
- $\tan\theta = \frac{b}{a}$
- $b \csc\theta = c$
- $a \sec\theta = c$
- $\cot\theta = \frac{a}{b}$

A triangle that isn't a right triangle is known as an **oblique triangle**. It should be noted that even if the triangle consists of three acute angles, it is still referred to as an oblique triangle. *Oblique*, in this case, does not refer to an angle measurement. Consider the following oblique triangle:

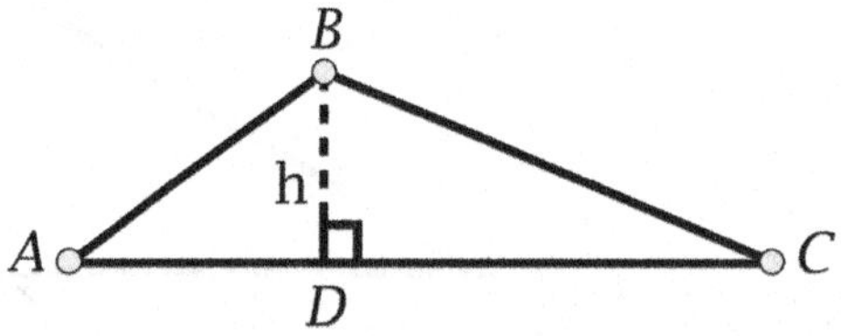

For this triangle:

$$Area = \frac{1}{2} \times base \times height = \frac{1}{2} \times AC \times BD$$

The auxiliary line drawn from the vertex B perpendicular to the opposite side AC represents the height of the triangle. This line splits the larger triangle into two smaller right triangles, which allows for the use of the trigonometric functions (specifically that $\sin A = \frac{h}{AB}$). Therefore:

$$Area = \frac{1}{2} \times AC \times AB \times \sin A$$

Typically, the sides are labelled as the lowercase letter of the vertex that's opposite. Therefore, the formula can be written as $Area = \frac{1}{2}ab \sin A$. This area formula can be used to find areas of triangles when given side lengths and angle measurements, or it can be used to find side lengths or angle measurements based on a specific area and other characteristics of the triangle.

The **law of sines** and **law of cosines** are two more relationships that exist within oblique triangles. Consider a triangle with sides a, b, and c, and angles A, B, and C opposite the corresponding sides.

The law of cosines states that:

$$c^2 = a^2 + b^2 - 2ab\ \cos C$$

The law of sines states that:

$$\frac{\sin A}{a} = \frac{\sin B}{b} = \frac{\sin C}{c}$$

In addition to the area formula, these two relationships can help find unknown angle and side measurements in oblique triangles.

Complex Numbers

Complex numbers are made up of the sum of a real number and an imaginary number. **Imaginary numbers** are the result of taking the square root of -1, and $\sqrt{-1} = i$.

Some examples of complex numbers include $6 + 2i$, $5 - 7i$, and $-3 + 12i$. Adding and subtracting complex numbers is similar to collecting like terms. The real numbers are added together, and the imaginary numbers are added together. For example, if the problem asks to simplify the expression $6 + 2i - 3 + 7i$, the 6 and (-3) are combined to make 3, and the $2i$ and $7i$ combine to make $9i$. Multiplying and dividing complex numbers is similar to working with exponents. One rule to remember when multiplying is that $i \times i = -1$.

For example, if a problem asks to simplify the expression $4i(3 + 7i)$, the $4i$ should be distributed throughout the 3 and the $7i$. This leaves the final expression $12i - 28$. The 28 is negative because $i * i$ results in a negative number. The last type of operation to consider with complex numbers is the conjugate. The **conjugate** of a complex number is a technique used to change the complex number into a real number. For example, the conjugate of $4 - 3i$ is $4 + 3i$. Multiplying $(4 - 3i)(4 + 3i)$ results in $16 + 12i - 12i + 9$, which has a final answer of:

$$16 + 9 = 25$$

Complex numbers may result from solving polynomial equations using the quadratic equation. Since complex numbers result from taking the square root of a negative number, the number found under the radical in the quadratic formula—called the **determinant**—tells whether or not the answer will be real or complex. If the determinant is negative, the roots are complex. Even though the coefficients of the polynomial may be real numbers, the roots are complex.

Solving polynomials by factoring is an alternative to using the quadratic formula. For example, in order to solve $x^2 - b^2 = 0$ for x, it needs to be factored. It factors into:

$$(x + b)(x - b) = 0$$

The solution set can be found by setting each factor equal to zero, resulting in $x = \pm b$. When b^2 is negative, the factors are complex numbers. For example, $x^2 + 64 = 0$ can be factored into:

$$(x + 8i)(x - 8i) = 0$$

The two roots are then found to be $x = \pm 8i$.

When dealing with polynomials and solving polynomial equations, it is important to remember the **fundamental theorem of algebra**. When given a polynomial with a degree of n, the theorem states that there will be n roots. These roots may or may not be complex. For example, the following polynomial equation of degree 2 has two complex roots: $x^2 + 1 = 0$. The factors of this polynomial are $(x + i)$ and $(x - i)$, resulting in the roots $x = i, -i$. As seen on the graph below, imaginary roots occur when the graph does not touch the x-axis.

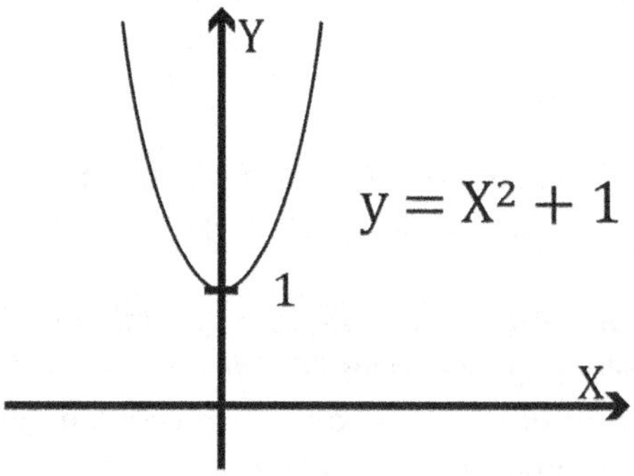

When a graphing calculator is permitted, the graph can always confirm the number and types of roots of the polynomial.

A polynomial identity is a true equation involving polynomials. For example:

$$x^2 - 5x + 6 = (x - 3)(x - 2)$$

This can be proved through multiplication by the FOIL method and factoring. This idea can be extended to involve complex numbers. For example:

$$i^2 = -1$$

$$x^3 + 9x = x(x^2 + 9) = x(x + \sqrt{3}i)(x - \sqrt{3}i)$$

This identity can also be proven through FOIL and factoring.

Converting Between Degrees and Radians

A **radian** is equal to the angle that subtends the arc with the same length as the radius of the circle. It is another unit for measuring angles, in addition to degrees. The unit circle is used to describe different radian measurements and the trigonometric ratios for special angles. The circle has a center at the origin, $(0, 0)$, and a radius of 1, which can be seen below. The points where the circle crosses an axis are labeled.

The Unit Circle

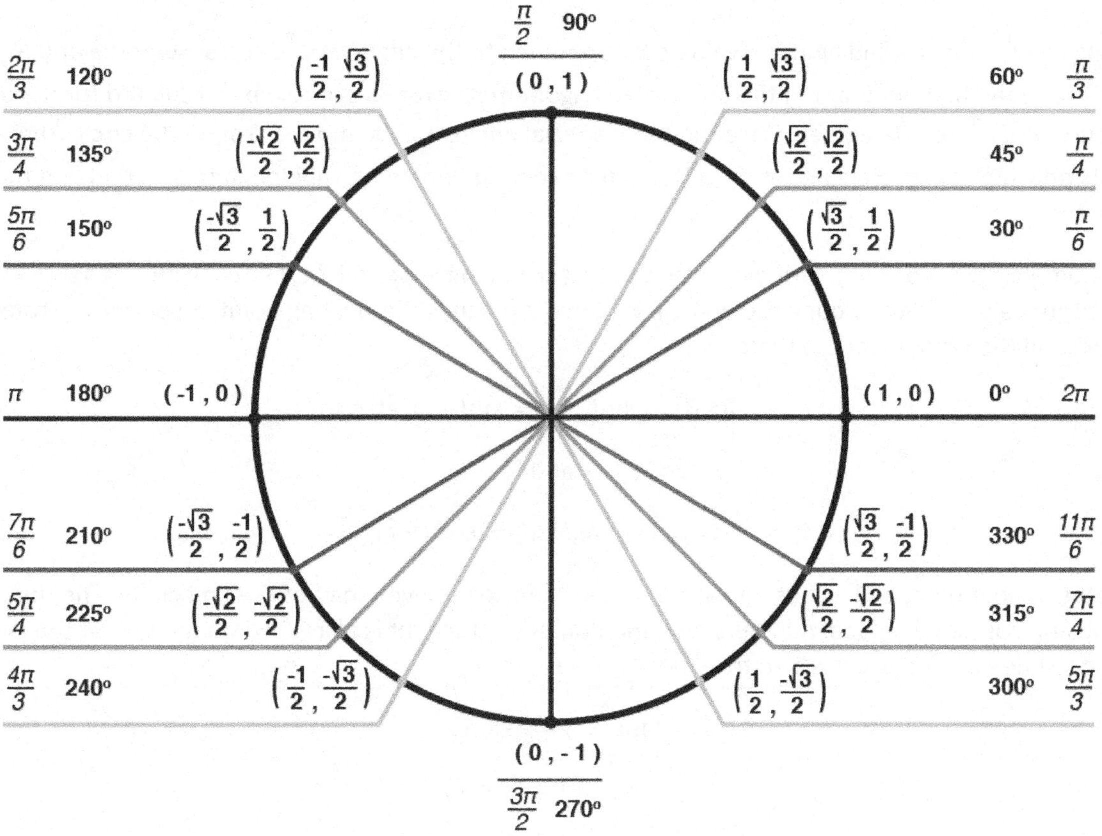

The circle begins on the right-hand side of the x-axis at 0 radians. Since the circumference of a circle is $2\pi r$ and the radius $r = 1$, the circumference is 2π. Zero and 2π are labeled as radian measurements at the point $(1, 0)$ on the graph. The radian measures around the rest of the circle are labeled also in relation to π; π is at the point $(-1, 0)$, also known as 180 degrees. Since these two measurements are equal, $\pi = 180$ degrees written as a ratio can be used to convert degrees to radians or vice versa. For example, to convert 30 degrees to radians, 30 degrees $\times \frac{\pi}{180 \text{ degrees}}$ can be used to obtain $\frac{1}{6}\pi$ or $\frac{\pi}{6}$. This radian measure is a point the unit circle

The coordinates labeled on the unit circle are found based on two common right triangles. The ratios formed in the coordinates can be found using these triangles. Each of these triangles can be inserted into the circle to correspond 30, 45, and 60 degrees or $\frac{\pi}{6}$, $\frac{\pi}{4}$, and $\frac{\pi}{3}$ radians.

By letting the hypotenuse length of these triangles equal 1, these triangles can be placed inside the unit circle. These coordinates can be used to find the trigonometric ratio for any of the radian measurements on the circle.

Given any (x, y) on the unit circle, $\sin(\theta) = y$, $\cos(\theta) = x$, and $\tan(\theta) = \frac{y}{x}$. The value θ is the angle that spans the arc around the unit circle. For example, finding $\sin\left(\frac{\pi}{4}\right)$ means finding the y-value corresponding to the angle $\theta = \frac{\pi}{4}$. The answer is $\frac{\sqrt{2}}{2}$.

Finding $\cos\left(\frac{\pi}{3}\right)$ means finding the x-value corresponding to the angle $\theta = \frac{\pi}{3}$. The answer is $\frac{1}{2}$ or 0.5. Both angles lie in the first quadrant of the unit circle. Trigonometric ratios can also be calculated for radian measures past $\frac{\pi}{2}$, or 90 degrees. Since the same special angles can be moved around the circle, the results only differ with a change in sign. This can be seen at two points labeled in the second and third quadrant.

Trigonometric functions are periodic. Both sine and cosine have period 2π. For each input angle value, the output value follows around the unit circle. Once it reaches the starting point, it continues around and around the circle. It is true that:

$$\sin(0) = \sin(2\pi) = \sin(4\pi), \text{ etc.}$$

and

$$\cos(0) = \cos(2\pi) = \cos(4\pi)$$

Tangent has period π, and its output values repeat themselves every half of the unit circle. The domain of sine and cosine are all real numbers, and the domain of tangent is all real numbers, except the points where cosine equals zero. It is also true that

$$\sin(-x) = -\sin x$$

$$\cos(-x) = \cos(x)$$

$$\tan(-x) = -\tan(x)$$

So, sine and tangent are odd functions, while cosine is an even function. Sine and tangent are symmetric with respect the origin, and cosine is symmetric with respect to the y-axis.

Applying Theorems About Circles

The distance from the middle of a circle to any other point on the circle is known as the **radius**. A **chord** of a circle is a straight line formed when its endpoints are allowed to be any two points on the circle. Many angles exist within a circle. A **central angle** is formed by using two radii as its rays and the center of the circle as its vertex. An **inscribed angle** is formed by using two chords as its rays, and its vertex is a point on the circle itself. Finally, a **circumscribed angle** has a vertex that is a point outside the circle and rays that intersect with the circle.

Some relationships exist between these types of angles, and, in order to define these relationships, arc measure must be understood. An **arc** of a circle is a portion of the circumference. Finding the **arc**

measure is the same as finding the degree measure of the central angle that intersects the circle to form the arc. The measure of an inscribed angle is half the measure of its intercepted arc. It's also true that the measure of a circumscribed angle is equal to 180 degrees minus the measure of the central angle that forms the arc in the angle.

A **tangent line** is a line that touches a curve at a single point without going through it. A **compass** and a **straight edge** are the tools necessary to construct a tangent line from a point *P* outside the circle to the circle. A tangent line is constructed by drawing a line segment from the center of the circle *O* to the point *P*, and then finding its midpoint *M* by bisecting the line segment. By using *M* as the center, a compass is used to draw a circle through points *O* and *P*. *N* is defined as the intersection of the two circles. Finally, a line segment is drawn through *P* and *N*. This is the tangent line. Each point on a circle has only one tangent line, which is perpendicular to the radius at that point. A line similar to a tangent line is a **secant line.** Instead of intersecting the circle at one point, a secant line intersects the circle at two points. A **chord** is a smaller portion of a secant line.

Here's an example:

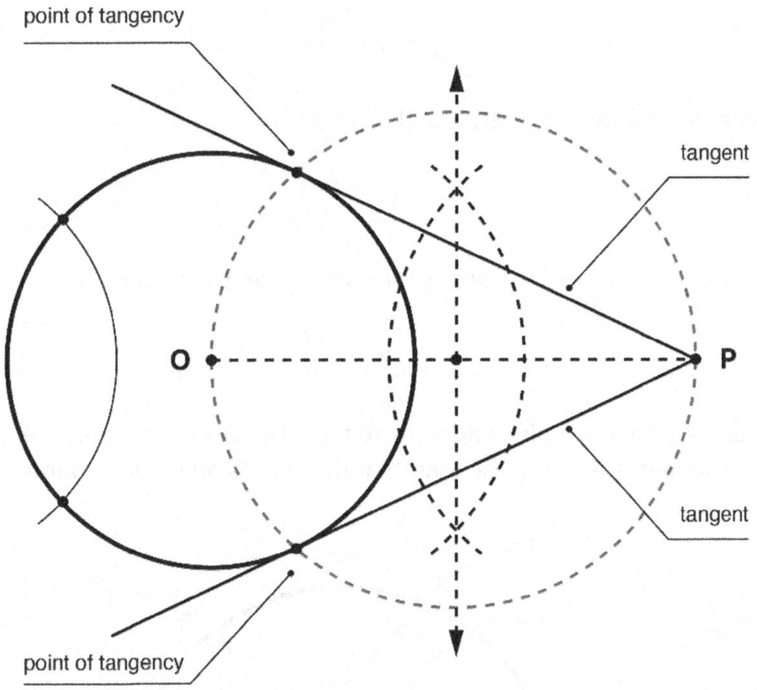

As previously mentioned, angles can be measured in radians, and 180 degrees equals π radians. Therefore, the measure of a complete circle is 2π radians. In addition to arc measure, **arc length** can also be found because the length of an arc is a portion of the circle's circumference. The following proportion is true:

$$\frac{Arc\ measure}{360°} = \frac{arc\ length}{arc\ circumference}$$

Arc measure is the same as the measure of the central angle, and this proportion can be rewritten as:

$$arc\ length = \frac{central\ angle}{360°} \times circumference$$

In addition, the degree measure can be replaced with radians to allow the use of both units. The arc length of a circle in radians is:

$$arc\ length = central\ angle\ \times\ radius$$

Note that arc length is a fractional part of circumference because $\frac{central\ angle}{360°} < 1$.

A **sector** of a circle is a portion of the circle that's enclosed by two radii and an arc. It resembles a piece of a pie, and the area of a sector can be derived using known definitions. The area of a circle can be calculated using the formula $A = \pi r^2$, where r is the radius of the circle. The area of a sector of a circle is a fraction of that calculation. For example, if the central angle θ is known in radians, the area of a sector is defined as:

$$A_s = \pi r^2 \frac{\theta}{2\pi} = \frac{\theta r^2}{2}$$

If the angle θ in degrees is known, the area of the sector is:

$$A_s = \frac{\theta \pi r^2}{360}$$

Finally, if the arc length L is known, the area of the sector can be reduced to:

$$A_s = \frac{rL}{2}$$

A chord is a line segment that contains endpoints on a circle. Given the radius of the circle and the central angle that inscribes the chord, the length of the chord can be determined.

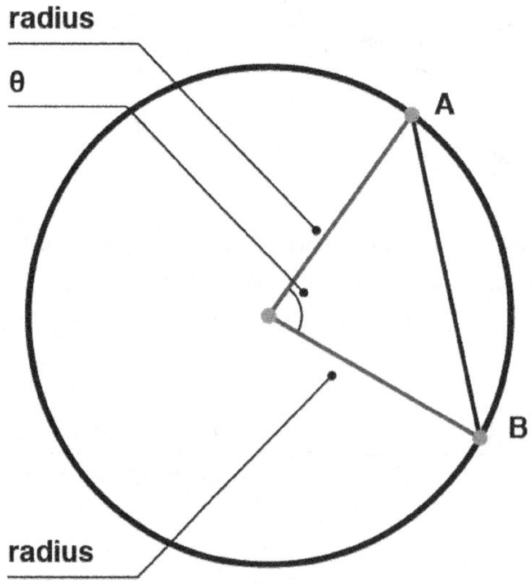

In the above figure, $\overline{AB}$ is a chord inscribed by $\angle\,\theta$. By constructing an angle bisector, the chord is also bisected at a 90-degree angle.

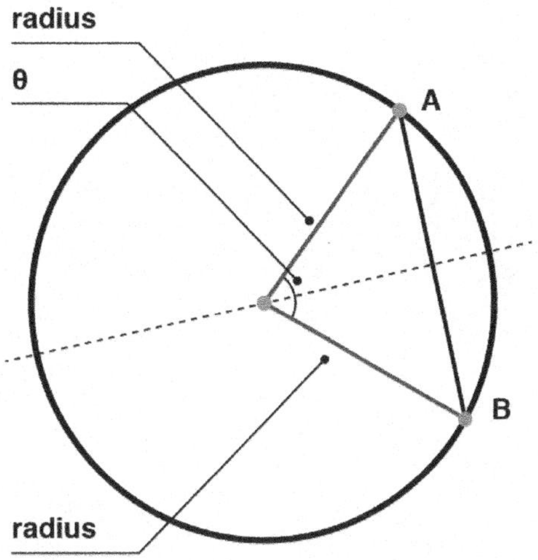

A right triangle is formed consisting of the radius as the hypotenuse, an angle equal to half the measure of θ, and a side opposite to that angle with a length half the length of the chord. Given an angle and the hypotenuse, the sin function can be used to determine the length of the side opposite the angle. Therefore, the formula $n\frac{\theta}{2} = \frac{c}{r}$, where c is the side of the triangle equal to half of the chord, can be used. Manipulating this formula results in:

$$c = r \times \sin\frac{\theta}{2}$$

(Remember that in this formula, c represents half the length of the chord, so double this length to determine the length of the chord.)

Congruence and Similarity

Sometimes, two figures are **similar**, meaning they have the same basic shape and the same interior angles, but they have different dimensions. If the ratio of two corresponding sides is known, then that ratio, or **scale factor**, holds true for all of the dimensions of the new figure.

Here is an example of applying this principle. Suppose that Lara is 5 feet tall and is standing 30 feet from the base of a light pole, and her shadow is 6 feet long. How high is the light on the pole? To figure this, it helps to make a sketch of the situation:

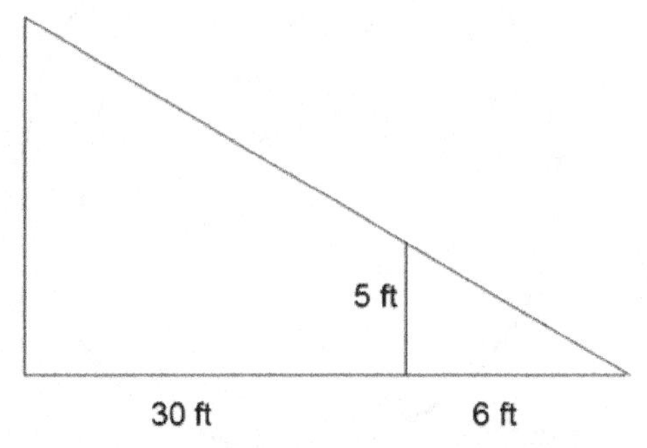

The light pole is the left side of the triangle. Lara is the 5-foot vertical line. Notice that there are two right triangles here, and that they have all the same angles as one another. Therefore, they form similar triangles. So, the ratio of proportionality between them must be determined.

The bases of these triangles are known. The small triangle, formed by Lara and her shadow, has a base of 6 feet. The large triangle formed by the light pole along with the line from the base of the pole out to the end of Lara's shadow is $30 + 6 = 36$ feet long. So, the ratio of the big triangle to the little triangle will be $\frac{36}{6} = 6$. The height of the little triangle is 5 feet. Therefore, the height of the big triangle will be $6 \times 5 = 30$ feet, meaning that the light is 30 feet up the pole.

Notice that the perimeter of a figure changes by the ratio of proportionality between two similar figures, but the area changes by the square of the ratio. This is because if the length of one side is doubled, the area is quadrupled.

As an example, suppose two rectangles are similar, but the edges of the second rectangle are three times longer than the edges of the first rectangle. The area of the first rectangle is 10 square inches. How much more area does the second rectangle have than the first?

To answer this, note that the area of the second rectangle is $3^2 = 9$ times the area of the first rectangle, which is 10 square inches. Therefore, the area of the second rectangle is going to be $9 \times 10 = 90$ square inches. This means it has $90 - 10 = 80$ square inches more area than the first rectangle.

As a second example, suppose X and Y are similar right triangles. The hypotenuse of X is 4 inches. The area of Y is $\frac{1}{4}$ the area of X. What is the hypotenuse of Y?

First, realize the area has changed by a factor of $\frac{1}{4}$. The area changes by a factor that is the square of the ratio of changes in lengths, so the ratio of the lengths is the square root of the ratio of areas. That means that the ratio of lengths must be is $\sqrt{\frac{1}{4}} = \frac{1}{2}$, and the hypotenuse of Y must be $\frac{1}{2} \times 4 = 2$ inches.

Volumes between similar solids change like the cube of the change in the lengths of their edges. Likewise, if the ratio of the volumes between similar solids is known, the ratio between their lengths is known by finding the cube root of the ratio of their volumes.

For example, suppose there are two similar rectangular pyramids X and Y. The base of X is 1 inch by 2 inches, and the volume of X is 8 inches. The volume of Y is 64 inches. What are the dimensions of the base of Y?

To answer this, first find the ratio of the volume of Y to the volume of X. This will be given by $\frac{64}{8} = 8$. Now the ratio of lengths is the cube root of the ratio of volumes, or $\sqrt[3]{8} = 2$. So, the dimensions of the base of Y must be 2 inches by 4 inches.

A **rigid motion** is a transformation that preserves distance and length. Every line segment in the resulting image is congruent to the corresponding line segment in the pre-image. **Congruence** between two figures means a series of transformations (or a rigid motion) can be defined that maps one of the figures onto the other. Basically, two figures are congruent if they have the same shape and size.

A shape is dilated, or a **dilation** occurs, when each side of the original image is multiplied by a given scale factor. If the scale factor is less than 1 and greater than 0, the dilation contracts the shape, and the resulting shape is smaller. If the scale factor equals 1, the resulting shape is the same size, and the dilation is a rigid motion. Finally, if the scale factor is greater than 1, the resulting shape is larger and the dilation expands the shape. The **center of dilation** is the point where the distance from it to any point on the new shape equals the scale factor times the distance from the center to the corresponding point in the pre-image. Dilation isn't an isometric transformation because distance isn't preserved. However, angle measure, parallel lines, and points on a line all remain unchanged.

Two figures are congruent if there is a rigid motion that can map one figure onto the other. Therefore, all pairs of sides and angles within the image and pre-image must be congruent. For example, in triangles, each pair of the three sides and three angles must be congruent. Similarly, in two four-sided figures, each pair of the four sides and four angles must be congruent.

Two figures are **similar** if there is a combination of translations, reflections, rotations, and dilations, which maps one figure onto the other. The difference between congruence and similarity is that dilation can be used in similarity. Therefore, side lengths between each shape can differ. However, angle measure must be preserved within this definition. If two polygons differ in size so that the lengths of corresponding line segments differ by the same factor, but corresponding angles have the same measurement, they are similar.

There are five theorems to show that triangles are congruent when it's unknown whether each pair of angles and sides are congruent. Each theorem is a shortcut that involves different combinations of sides and angles that must be true for the two triangles to be congruent. For example, **side-side-side (SSS)** states that if all sides are equal, the triangles are congruent. **Side-angle-side (SAS)** states that if two pairs of sides are equal and the included angles are congruent, then the triangles are congruent.

Similarly, **angle-side-angle (ASA)** states that if two pairs of angles are congruent and the included side lengths are equal, the triangles are similar.

Angle-angle-side (AAS) states that two triangles are congruent if they have two pairs of congruent angles and a pair of corresponding equal side lengths that aren't included. Finally, **hypotenuse-leg (HL)** states that if two right triangles have equal hypotenuses and an equal pair of shorter sides, then the triangles are congruent. An important item to note is that angle-angle-angle *(AAA)* is not enough information to have congruence. It's important to understand why these rules work by using rigid motions to show congruence between the triangles with the given properties. For example, three reflections are needed to show why *SAS* follows from the definition of congruence.

If two angles of one triangle are congruent with two angles of a second triangle, the triangles are similar. This is because, within any triangle, the sum of the angle measurements is 180 degrees. Therefore, if two are congruent, the third angle must also be congruent because their measurements are equal. Three congruent pairs of angles mean that the triangles are similar.

The criteria needed to prove triangles are congruent involves both angle and side congruence. Both pairs of related angles and sides need to be of the same measurement to use congruence in a proof. The criteria to prove similarity in triangles involves proportionality of side lengths. Angles must be congruent in similar triangles; however, corresponding side lengths only need to be a constant multiple of each other. Once similarity is established, it can be used in proofs as well. Relationships in geometric figures other than triangles can be proven using triangle congruence and similarity. If a similar or congruent triangle can be found within another type of geometric figure, their criteria can be used to prove a relationship about a given formula. For instance, a rectangle can be broken up into two congruent triangles.

Similarity, Triangles, and Trigonometric Ratios

Within similar triangles, corresponding sides are proportional, and angles are congruent. In addition, within similar triangles, the ratio of the side lengths is the same. This property is true even if side lengths are different. Within right triangles, trigonometric ratios can be defined for the acute angle within the triangle. The functions are defined through ratios in a right triangle. Sine of acute angle, *A*, is opposite over hypotenuse, cosine is adjacent over hypotenuse, and tangent is opposite over adjacent. Note that expanding or shrinking the triangle won't change the ratios. However, changing the angle measurements will alter the calculations.

Angles that add up to 90 degrees are **complementary**. Within a right triangle, two complementary angles exist because the third angle is always 90 degrees. In this scenario, the **sine** of one of the complementary angles is equal to the **cosine** of the other angle. The opposite is also true. This relationship exists because sine and cosine will be calculated as the ratios of the same side lengths.

Two lines can be parallel, perpendicular, or neither. If two lines are **parallel**, they have the same slope. This is proven using the idea of similar triangles. Consider the following diagram with two parallel lines, L1 and L2:

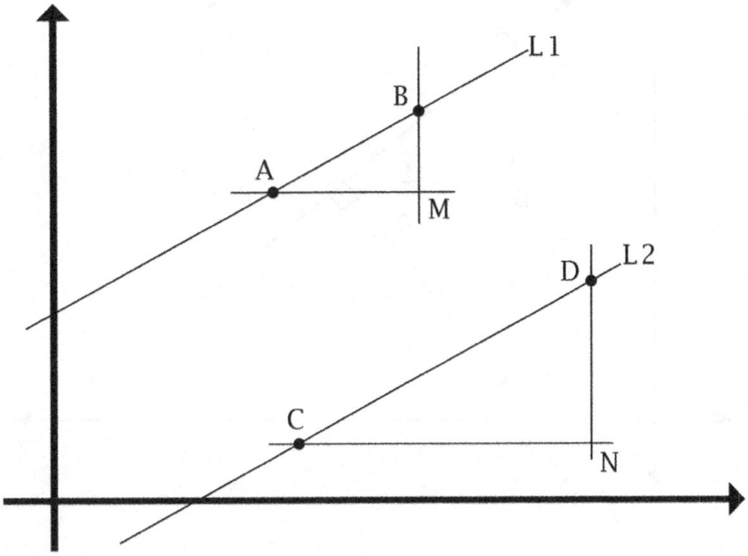

A and B are points on L1, and C and D are points on L2. Right triangles are formed with vertex M and N where lines BM and DN are parallel to the y-axis and AM and CN are parallel to the x-axis. Because all three sets of lines are parallel, the triangles are similar. Therefore, $\frac{\text{BM}}{\text{DN}} = \frac{\text{MA}}{\text{NC}}$. This shows that the rise/run is equal for lines L1 and L2. Hence, their slopes are equal.

Another similar theorem states that if there is a line parallel to one side of a triangle, and it intersects the other sides of the triangle, then the sides that are intersected are divided proportionally.

Secondly, if two lines are perpendicular, the product of their slopes equals -1. This means that their slopes are negative reciprocals of each other. Consider two perpendicular lines, *l* and *n*:

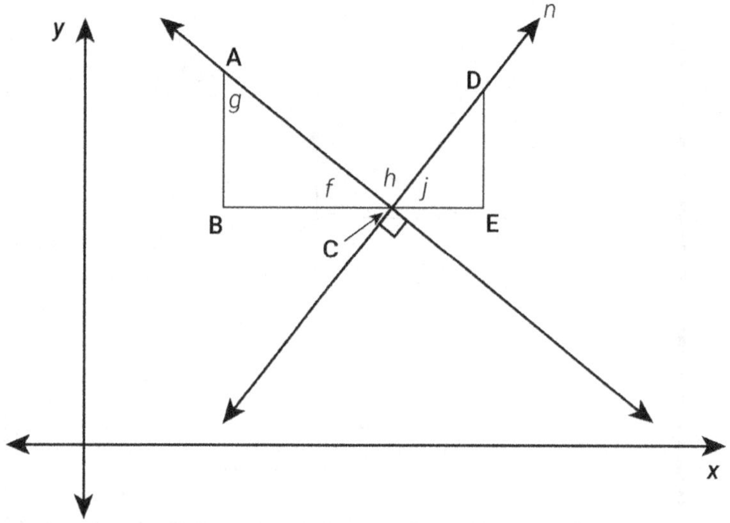

Right triangles ABC and CDE are formed so that lines BC and CE are parallel to the x-axis, and AB and DE are parallel to the y-axis. Because line BE is a straight line, angles $f + h + i = 180$ degrees. However, angle h is a right angle, so $f + j = 90$ degrees. By construction, $f + g = 90$, which means that $g = j$. Therefore, because angles $B = E$ and $g = j$, the triangles are similar and $\frac{\text{AB}}{\text{BC}} = \frac{\text{CE}}{\text{DE}}$. Because slope is equal to rise/run, the slope of line l is $-\frac{AB}{BC}$ and the slope of line *n* is $\frac{DE}{CE}$. Multiplying the slopes together gives:

$$-\frac{AB}{BC} \times \frac{DE}{CE} = -\frac{CE}{DE} \times \frac{DE}{CE} = -1$$

This proves that the product of the slopes of two perpendicular lines equals -1. Both parallel and perpendicular lines can be integral in many geometric proofs, so knowing and understanding their properties is crucial for problem-solving.

Creating Equations to Solve Problems Involving Circles

A **circle** can be defined as the set of all points that are the same distance (known as the radius, r) from a single point *C* (known as the center of the circle). The center has coordinates (h, k), and any point on the circle can be labelled with coordinates (x, y).

As shown below, a **right triangle** is formed with these two points:

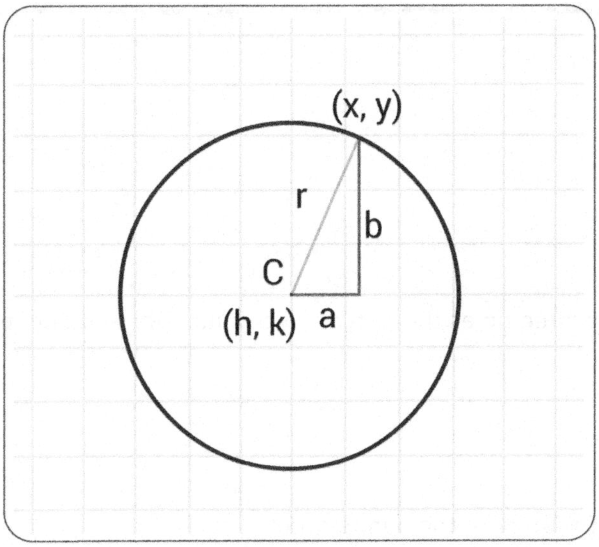

The Pythagorean theorem states that:

$$a^2 + b^2 = r^2$$

However, a can be replaced by $|x - h|$ and b can be replaced by $|y - k|$ by using the **distance formula** which is:

$$d = \sqrt{(x_2 - x_1)^2 + (y_2 - y_1)^2}$$

That substitution results in:

$$(x - h)^2 + (y - k)^2 = r^2$$

This is the formula for finding the equation of any circle with a center (h, k) and a radius r. Note that sometimes c is used instead of r.

Circles aren't always given in the form of the circle equation where the center and radius can be seen so easily. Oftentimes, they're given in the more general format of:

$$ax^2 + by^2 + cx + dy + e = 0$$

This can be converted to the center-radius form using the algebra technique of completing the square in both variables. First, the constant term is moved over to the other side of the equals sign, and then the x- and y-variable terms are grouped together. Then the equation is divided through by a and, because this is the equation of a circle, $a = b$. At this point, the x-term coefficient is divided by 2, squared, and then added to both sides of the equation. This value is grouped with the x terms. The same steps then need to be completed with the y-term coefficient. The trinomial in both x and y can now be factored into a square of a binomial, which gives both $(x - h)^2$ and $(y - k)^2$.

Practice Quiz

1. Solve for x, if $x^2 - 2x - 8 = 0$.
   - a. $2 \pm \frac{\sqrt{30}}{2}$
   - b. $2 \pm 4\sqrt{2}$
   - c. 1 ± 3
   - d. $4 \pm \sqrt{2}$

2. Write the expression for three times the sum of twice a number and one minus 6.
   - a. $2x + 1 - 6$
   - b. $3x + 1 - 6$
   - c. $3(x + 1) - 6$
   - d. $3(2x + 1) - 6$

3. What is the definition of a factor of the number 36?
   - a. A number that can be divided by 36 and have no remainder
   - b. A number that 36 can be divided by and have no remainder
   - c. A prime number that is multiplied by 36
   - d. An even number that is multiplied by 36

4. What are the coordinates of the focus of the parabola $y = -9x^2$?
   - a. $(-3, 0)$
   - b. $\left(-\frac{1}{36}, 0\right)$
   - c. $(0, -3)$
   - d. $\left(0, -\frac{1}{36}\right)$

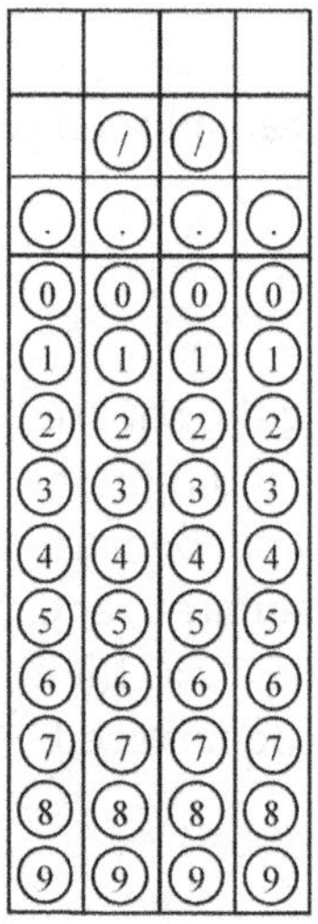

5. The total perimeter of a rectangle is 36 cm. If the length is 12 cm, what is the width?

See answers on next page.

Answer Explanations

1. C: The quadratic formula can be used to solve this problem. Given the equation, use the values $a = 1$, $b = -2$, and $c = -8$.

$$x = \frac{-b \pm \sqrt{b^2 - 4ac}}{2a} = \frac{-(-2) \pm \sqrt{(-2)^2 - 4(1)(-8)}}{2(1)}$$

From here, simplify to solve for x.

$$x = \frac{2 \pm \sqrt{4 + 32}}{2} = \frac{2 \pm \sqrt{36}}{2} = \frac{2 \pm 6}{2} = 1 \pm 3$$

2. D: "Sum" means the result of adding, so "the sum of twice a number and one" can be written as $2x + 1$. Next, "three times the sum of twice a number and one" would be $3(2x + 1)$. Finally, "six less than three times the sum of twice a number and one" would be $3(2x + 1) - 6$.

3. B: A factor of 36 is any number that can be divided into 36 and have no remainder.

$$36 = 36 \times 1, 18 \times 2, 9 \times 4, \text{and } 6 \times 6$$

Therefore, it has 7 unique factors: 36, 18, 9, 6, 4, 2, and 1.

4. D: A parabola of the form $y = \frac{1}{4f}x^2$ has a focus $(0, f)$.

Because $y = -9x^2$, set $-9 = \frac{1}{4f}$.

Solving this equation for f results in $f = -\frac{1}{36}$. Therefore, the coordinates of the focus are $\left(0, -\frac{1}{36}\right)$.

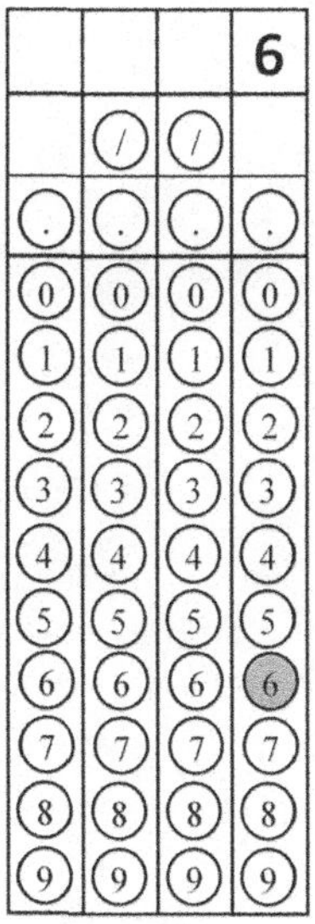

5. The formula for the perimeter of a rectangle is $P = 2L + 2W$, where P is the perimeter, L is the length, and W is the width. The first step is to substitute all of the data into the formula:

$$36 = 2(12) + 2W$$

Simplify by multiplying 2×12:

$$36 = 24 + 2W$$

Simplifying this further by subtracting 24 on each side gives:

$$36 - 24 = 24 - 24 + 2W$$

$$12 = 2W$$

Divide by 2:

$$6 = W$$

The width is 6 cm. Remember to test this answer by substituting this value into the original formula:

$$36 = 2(12) + 2(6)$$

Essay

Introduction to the SAT Essay

The essay on the SAT is now optional, although some schools do require that you write the essay for application. Test takers will have fifty minutes to write their essay. In the SAT Essay section of the exam, you will be given an essay to read and analyze. Keep in mind that you will not be asked to agree or disagree on the topic of the essay or even write about the topic of the essay. You will be asked to write about how the author built that essay and which rhetorical devices they used throughout the essay. Viewers of your essay will be looking for ways in which you explain how the author creates their argument in order to persuade an audience, and you will be expected to support your ideas with evidence from the passage.

Analyzing the Essay

In the prompt of the SAT essay, you will be asked to consider the following three characteristics of an essay: the author's evidence, reasoning, and stylistic elements. The sections below give a description of what to look for in each of these.

Evidence

It's important to evaluate the author's supporting details to be sure that the details are credible, provide evidence of the author's point, and directly support the main idea. Though shocking statistics grab readers' attention, their use could be ineffective information in the piece. Details like this are crucial to understanding the passage and evaluating how well the author presents their argument and evidence.

Fact and Opinion

It is important to distinguish between fact and opinion when reading a piece of writing. When an author presents **facts**, such as statistics or data, readers must make sure they are accurate. When authors use **opinion**, they are sharing their own thoughts and feelings about a subject.

Textual evidence within the details helps readers draw a conclusion about a passage. **Textual evidence** refers to information—facts and examples that support the main point. Textual evidence will likely come from outside sources and can be in the form of quoted or paraphrased material. In order to draw a conclusion from evidence, it's important to examine the credibility and validity of that evidence as well as how (and if) it relates to the main idea.

Credibility

Critical readers examine the facts used to support an author's argument. They check the facts against other sources to be sure those facts are correct. They also check the validity of the sources used to be sure those sources are credible, academic, and/or peer-reviewed. Consider that when an author uses another person's opinion to support their argument, even if it is an expert's opinion, it is still only an opinion and should not be taken as fact. A strong argument uses valid, measurable facts to support ideas. Even then, the reader may disagree with the argument as it may be rooted in their personal beliefs.

An authoritative argument may use the facts to sway the reader. Because of this, a writer may choose to only use the information and expert opinion that supports their viewpoint.

Reasoning

Reasoning has to do with the way the author develops ideas and connects claims and evidence. For this, it's importance to pay attention to the overall structure of the passage. If the passage is sound, the author will use effective transition words that guide the logical progression of the points. A term like *however* alerts the reader that the author is about to present information that contrasts the information presented before. Likewise, if the author were presenting cause/effect, some transition words used might be *because, since, for,* or *due to*. If these transition words are absent, then logical progression of the text is lacking and the author is using an ineffective structure to present their argument.

Counter-Arguments

If an author presents a differing opinion or a **counter-argument** in order to refute it, the reader should consider how and why this information is being presented. It is meant to strengthen the original argument and shouldn't be confused with the author's intended conclusion, but it should also be considered in the reader's final evaluation. On the contrary, sometimes authors will concede to an opposing argument by recognizing the validity the other side has to offer. A concession will allow readers to see both sides of the argument in an unbiased light, thereby increasing the credibility of the author.

Authors can also reflect bias if they ignore an opposing viewpoint or present their side in an unbalanced way. A strong argument considers the opposition and finds a way to refute it. Critical readers should look for an unfair or one-sided presentation of the argument and be skeptical, as a bias may be present. Even if this bias is unintentional, if it exists in the writing, the reader should be wary of the validity of the argument.

Stylistic Elements

Stylistic elements are elements an author uses in order to convey meaning to the text in unique ways. Some of these different ways are appealing to the audience's emotion, the author's word choice, and figurative language.

Appeal to Emotion

The audience is what determines the **rhetorical appeal** the author will use—ethos, pathos, or logos. **Ethos** is a rhetorical appeal to an audience's ethics and/or morals. Ethos is most often used in argumentative and informative writing modes. **Pathos** is an appeal to the audience's emotions and sympathies, and it is found in argumentative, descriptive, and narrative writing modes. **Logos** is an appeal to the audience's logic and reason and is used primarily in informative texts as well as in supporting details for argumentative pieces.

Word Choice

An author's choice of words—also referred to as **diction**—helps to convey their meaning in a particular way. Through diction, an author can convey a particular tone—e.g., a humorous tone, a serious tone—in order to support the thesis in a meaningful way to the reader.

Connotation refers to the implied meaning of a word or phrase. Connotations are the ideas or feelings that words or phrases invoke other than their literal meaning. An example of the use of connotation is in people's use of the word *cheap*. While the literal meaning is something of low cost, people use the word to suggest something is poor in value or to negatively describe a person as reluctant to spend money. When something or someone is described this way, the reader is more inclined to have a particular image or feeling about it or him/her. Thus, connotation can be a very effective language tool in creating emotion and swaying opinion. However, connotations are sometimes hard to pin down because varying emotions can be associated with a word. Generally, though, connotative meanings tend to be fairly consistent within a specific cultural group.

Test takers and critical readers alike should be very aware of technical language used within informational text. **Technical language** refers to terminology that is specific to a particular industry and is best understood by those specializing in that industry. This language is fairly easy to differentiate, since it will most likely be unfamiliar to readers. It's critical to be able to define technical language either by the author's written definition, through the use of an included glossary—if offered—or through context clues that help readers clarify word meaning.

Figurative Language

Literary texts also employ rhetorical devices. Figurative language like simile and metaphor is a type of rhetorical device commonly found in literature. In addition to rhetorical devices that play on the *meanings* of words, there are also rhetorical devices that use the *sounds* of words. These devices are most often found in poetry but may also be found in other types of literature and in non-fiction writing like speech texts.

Alliteration and **assonance** are both varieties of sound repetition. Other types of sound repetition include: **anaphora**, repetition that occurs at the beginning of the sentences; **epiphora**, repetition occurring at the end of phrases; **antimetabole**, repetition of words in reverse order; and **antiphrasis**, a form of denial of an assertion in a text.

Alliteration refers to the repetition of the first sound of each word. Recall Robert Burns' opening line:

> My love is like a red, red rose

This line includes two instances of alliteration: "love" and "like" (repeated *L* sound), as well as "red" and "rose" (repeated *R* sound). Next, assonance refers to the repetition of vowel sounds, and can occur anywhere within a word (not just the opening sound). Here is the opening of a poem by John Keats:

> When I have fears that I may cease to be
> Before my pen has glean'd my teeming brain

Assonance can be found in the words "fears," "cease," "be," "glean'd," and "teeming," all of which stress the long *E* sound. Both alliteration and assonance create a harmony that unifies the writer's language.

Another sound device is **onomatopoeia**, or words whose spelling mimics the sound they describe. Words such as "crash," "bang," and "sizzle" are all examples of onomatopoeia. Use of onomatopoetic language adds auditory imagery to the text.

Readers are probably most familiar with the technique of **pun**. A pun is a play on words, taking advantage of two words that have the same or similar pronunciation. Puns can be found throughout Shakespeare's plays, for instance:

> Now is the winter of our discontent
> Made glorious summer by this son of York

These lines from *Richard III* contain a play on words. Richard III refers to his brother, the newly crowned King Edward IV, as the "son of York," referencing their family heritage from the house of York. However, while drawing a comparison between the political climate and the weather (times of political trouble were the "winter," but now the new king brings "glorious summer"), Richard's use of the word "son" also implies another word with the same pronunciation, "sun"—so Edward IV is also like the sun, bringing light, warmth, and hope to England. Puns are a clever way for writers to suggest two meanings at once.

Writing the Essay

Brainstorming

One of the most important steps in writing an essay is prewriting. Before drafting an essay, it's helpful to think about the topic for a moment or two, in order to gain a more solid understanding of what the task is. Then, spending about five minutes jotting down the immediate ideas that could work for the essay is recommended. This serves as a way to get some words on the page and offer a reference for ideas when drafting. Scratch paper is provided for writers to use any prewriting techniques such as webbing, free writing, or listing. The goal is to get ideas out of the mind and onto the page.

Moving from Brainstorming to Planning

Once the ideas are on the page, it's time to turn them into a solid plan for the essay. The best ideas from the brainstorming results can then be developed into a more formal outline. An outline typically has one main point (the thesis) and at least three sub-points that support the main point.

Here's an example:

Main Idea

- Point #1
- Point #2
- Point #3

Of course, there will be details under each point, but this approach is the best for dealing with timed writing.

Time Management

It is important to manage your time effectively. It is recommended that you allocate time at the beginning of your writing to review the prompt and instructions multiple times and then outline your basic thoughts, either on paper or in your head. This initial thinking process will give you a clear plan of action before you put pen to paper and will result in a more concise and effective argument.

Similarly, it is recommended that you leave a few minutes at the end of your writing to review your piece and ensure it is coherent, includes examples that support each of your key argument points, and specifically addresses the instructions that were provided. Clarity of thought and staying focused on the topic that you were asked to write about are more important than citing every example you can think of that supports your argument in excruciating detail.

Parts of the Essay

The **introduction** has to do a few important things:

- Establish the topic of the essay in original wording (i.e., not just repeating the prompt)
- Clarify the significance/importance of the topic or purpose for writing (not too many details, a brief overview)
- Offer a **thesis statement** that identifies the writer's own viewpoint on the topic (typically one or two brief sentences as a clear, concise explanation of the main point on the topic)

Body paragraphs reflect the ideas developed in the outline. Three or four points is probably sufficient for a short essay, and they should include the following:

- A **topic sentence** that identifies the sub-point (e.g., a reason why, a way how, a cause or effect)
- A detailed explanation of the point, explaining why the writer thinks this point is valid
- Illustrative examples, such as personal examples or real-world examples, that support and validate the point (i.e., "prove" the point)
- A concluding sentence that connects the examples, reasoning, and analysis to the point being made

The **conclusion**, or final paragraph, should be brief and should reiterate the focus, clarifying why the discussion is significant or important. It is important to avoid adding specific details or new ideas to this paragraph. The purpose of the conclusion is to sum up what has been said to bring the discussion to a close.

Don't Panic!

Writing an essay can be overwhelming, and performance panic is a natural response. The outline serves as a basis for the writing and help writers stay focused. Getting stuck can also happen, and it's helpful to remember that brainstorming can be done at any time during the writing process. Following the steps of the writing process is the best defense against writer's block.

Timed essays can be particularly stressful, but assessors are trained to recognize the necessary planning and thinking for these timed efforts. Using the plan above, and sticking to it, helps with time management. Timing each part of the process helps writers stay on track. Sometimes writers try to cover too much in their essays. If time seems to be running out, writers should take the opportunity to determine whether all of the ideas in the outline are necessary. Three body paragraphs are sufficient, and more than that is probably too much to cover in a short essay.

More isn't always *better* in writing. A strong essay will be clear and concise. It will avoid unnecessary or repetitive details. It is better to have a concise, five-paragraph essay that makes a clear point, than a ten-paragraph essay that doesn't. The goal is to write one to two pages of quality writing. Paragraphs should also reflect balance; if the introduction goes to the bottom of the first page, the writing may be going off-track or be repetitive. It's best to fall into the one-to-two-page range, but a complete, well-developed essay is the ultimate goal.

The Final Steps

Leaving a few minutes at the end to revise and proofread offers an opportunity for writers to polish things up. Putting oneself in the reader's shoes and focusing on what the essay actually says helps writers identify problems—it's a movement from the mindset of the writer to the mindset of the editor. The goal is to have a clean, clear copy of the essay. The following areas should be considered when proofreading:

- Sentence fragments
- Awkward sentence structure
- Run-on sentences
- Incorrect word choice
- Grammatical agreement errors
- Spelling errors
- Punctuation errors
- Capitalization errors

The Short Overview

The essay may seem challenging, but following these steps can help writers focus:

- Take one-two minutes to think about the topic.
- Generate some ideas through brainstorming (three-four minutes).
- Organize ideas into a brief outline, selecting just three-four main points to cover in the essay
- Develop essay in parts:
- Introduction paragraph, with intro to topic and main points
- Viewpoint on the subject at the end of the introduction
- Body paragraphs, based on outline
- Each paragraph: makes a main point, explains the viewpoint, uses examples to support the point
- Brief conclusion highlighting the main points and closing
- Read over the essay (last five minutes).
- Look for any obvious errors, making sure that the writing makes sense.

Essay Prompt

As you read the essay below, consider how the author uses these following things:

Evidence to support claims, like facts or examples
Reasoning to develop ideas and connect claims to evidence
Stylistic elements, such as word choice or appeals to emotion, to express ideas

Dana Gioia argues in his article that poetry is dying, now little more than a limited art form confined to academic and college settings. Of course, poetry remains healthy in the academic setting, but the idea of poetry being limited to this academic subculture is a stretch. New technology and social networking alone have contributed to poets and other writers' work being shared across the world. YouTube has emerged to be a major asset to poets, allowing live performances to be streamed to billions of users. Even now, poetry continues to grow and voice topics that are relevant to the culture of our time. Poetry is not in the spotlight as it may have been in earlier times, but it's still a relevant art form that continues to expand in scope and appeal.

Furthermore, Gioia's argument does not account for live performances of poetry. Not everyone has taken a poetry class or enrolled in university—but most everyone is online. The Internet is a perfect launching point to get all creative work out there. An example of this was the performance of Buddy Wakefield's *Hurling Crowbirds at Mockingbars*. Wakefield is a well-known poet who has published several collections of contemporary poetry. One of my favorite works by Wakefield is *Crowbirds*, specifically his performance at New York University in 2009. Although his reading was a campus event, views of his performance online number in the thousands. His poetry attracted people outside of the university setting.

Naturally, the poem's popularity can be attributed both to Wakefield's performance and the quality of his writing. *Crowbirds* touches on themes of core human concepts such as faith, personal loss, and growth. These are not ideas that only poets or students of literature understand, but all human beings: "You acted like I was hurling crowbirds at mockingbars / and abandoned me for not making sense. / Evidently, I don't experience things as rationally as you do." Wakefield weaves together a complex description of the perplexed and hurt emotions of the speaker undergoing a separation from a romantic interest. The line "You acted like I was hurling crowbirds at mockingbars" conjures up an image of someone confused, seemingly out of their mind ... or in the case of the speaker, passionately trying to grasp at a relationship that is fading. The speaker is looking back and finding the words that described how he wasn't making sense. This poem is particularly human and gripping in its message, but the entire effect of the poem is enhanced through the physical performance.

At its core, poetry is about addressing issues/ideas in the world. Part of this is also addressing the perspectives that are exiguously considered. Although the platform may look different, poetry continues to have a steady audience due to the emotional connection the poet shares with the audience.

Write an essay in which you explain how the author builds an argument to persuade the audience that poetry is not dying. In your essay, analyze how the author uses one or more of the features listed in the bullet points above (or features of your own choice) to strengthen the logic and persuasiveness of their argument. Focus on the most relevant features of the passage.

Reading Test

Fiction

Questions 1–10 are based on the following passage:

We made it. We created it. We brought it forth from the night of the ages. We alone. Our hands. Our mind. Ours alone and only.

We know not what we are saying. Our head is reeling. We look upon the light which we have made. We shall be forgiven for anything we say tonight...

Tonight, after more days and trials than we can count, we finished building a strange thing, from the remains of the Unmentionable Times, a box of glass, devised to give forth the power of the sky of greater strength than we had ever achieved before. And when we put our wires to this box, when we closed the current—the wire glowed! It came to life, it turned red, and a circle of light lay on the stone before us.

We stood, and we held our head in our hands. We could not conceive of that which we had created. We had touched no flint, made no fire. Yet here was light, light that came from nowhere, light from the heart of metal.

We blew out the candle. Darkness swallowed us. There was nothing left around us, nothing save night and a thin thread of flame in it, as a crack in the wall of a prison. We stretched our hands to the wire, and we saw our fingers in the red glow. We could not see our body nor feel it, and in that moment nothing existed save our two hands over a wire glowing in a black abyss.

Then we thought of the meaning of that which lay before us. We can light our tunnel, and the City, and all the Cities of the world with nothing save metal and wires. We can give our brothers a new light, cleaner and brighter than any they have ever known. The power of the sky can be made to do men's bidding. There are no limits to its secrets and its might, and it can be made to grant us anything if we but choose to ask.

Then we knew what we must do. Our discovery is too great for us to waste our time in sweeping the streets. We must not keep our secret to ourselves, nor buried under the ground. We must bring it into the sight of all men. We need all our time, we need the work rooms of the Home of the Scholars, we want the help of our brother Scholars and their wisdom joined to ours. There is so much work ahead for all of us, for all the Scholars of the world.

In a month, the World Council of Scholars is to meet in our City. It is a great Council, to which the wisest of all lands are elected, and it meets once a year in the different Cities of the earth. We shall go to this Council and we shall lay before them, as our gift, this glass box with the power of the sky. We shall confess everything to them. They will see, understand and forgive. For our gift is greater than our transgression. They will explain it to the Council of Vocations, and we shall be assigned to the Home of the Scholars. This has never been done before, but neither has a gift such as ours ever been offered to men.

We must wait. We must guard our tunnel as we had never guarded it before. For should any men save the Scholars learn of our secret, they would not understand it, nor would they believe us. They would see nothing, save our crime of working alone, and they would destroy us and our light. We care not about our body, but our light is...

Yes, we do care. For the first time do we care about our body. For this wire is as a part of our body, as a vein torn from us, glowing with our blood. Are we proud of this thread of metal, or of our hands which made it, or is there a line to divide these two?

Excerpt from *Anthem* by Ayn Rand

1. What is the overall tone of this passage?
   a. Dreary
   b. Unnerving
   c. Excited
   d. Humorous

2. Why must the invention be kept a secret?
   a. It is illegal to work alone.
   b. The Home of the Scholars will try to take credit.
   c. They were supposed to be sweeping streets.
   d. Remains from the Unmentionable Times are off limits.

3. Which literary device is used in the following sentence from paragraph five?

   Darkness swallowed us.

   a. Metaphor
   b. Synecdoche
   c. Flashback
   d. Personification

4. What does the narrator compare their discovery to?
   a. The sun
   b. A candle
   c. Prison
   d. Blood

5. Why does the narrator expect to be forgiven?
   a. Their invention will save the City money.
   b. The possibilities of the invention outweigh their crime.
   c. They will apologize to the World Council of Scholars.
   d. Their invention is part of their body.

6. What is the meaning of the word *transgression* mean in paragraph eight?
   a. Obedience
   b. Disruption
   c. Confession
   d. Offense

7. Which quote is an example of personification?
   a. "Our head is reeling."
   b. "Darkness swallowed us."
   c. "We stood, and we held our head in our hands."
   d. "We care not about our body, but our light is..."

8. What will NOT help advance the narrator's discovery?
   a. Using the work rooms of the Home of the Scholars
   b. Gaining wisdom from the brother Scholars
   c. Keeping the discovery a secret from the World Council of Scholars
   d. Stopping the sweeping of the streets

9. How does the narrator feel their status will change as a result of their invention?
   a. They will advance from street sweeper to the Home of the Scholars.
   b. Their status will remain the same after their confession.
   c. They will rise in status from tunnel worker to the Council of Vocations.
   d. They are not sure how their status will change due to the crime they committed.

10. Which transformation has happened by the end of the passage?
   a. The narrator has been forgiven for their transgression.
   b. The gift of electricity has been shared with all the cities of the world.
   c. The discovery has made it easier to sweep streets and light tunnels.
   d. The narrator recognizes the significance of their body.

History/Social Studies

Questions 11–20 are based upon the following passage:

> Our people are losing that faith, not only in government itself but in the ability as citizens to serve as the ultimate rulers and shapers of our democracy. As a people we know our past and we are proud of it. Our progress has been part of the living history of America, even the world. We always believed that we were part of a great movement of humanity itself called democracy, involved in the search for freedom, and that belief has always strengthened us in our purpose. But just as we are losing our confidence in the future, we are also beginning to close the door on our past.
>
> In a nation that was proud of hard work, strong families, close-knit communities, and our faith in God, too many of us now tend to worship self-indulgence and consumption. Human identity is no longer defined by what one does, but by what one owns. But we've discovered that owning things and consuming things does not satisfy our longing for meaning. We've learned that piling up material goods cannot fill the emptiness of lives which have no confidence or purpose.

The symptoms of this crisis of the American spirit are all around us. For the first time in the history of our country a majority of our people believe that the next five years will be worse than the past five years. Two-thirds of our people do not even vote. The productivity of American workers is actually dropping, and the willingness of Americans to save for the future has fallen below that of all other people in the Western world.

As you know, there is a growing disrespect for government and for churches and for schools, the news media, and other institutions. This is not a message of happiness or reassurance, but it is the truth and it is a warning.

These changes did not happen overnight. They've come upon us gradually over the last generation, years that were filled with shocks and tragedy.

We were sure that ours was a nation of the ballot, not the bullet, until the murders of John Kennedy and Robert Kennedy and Martin Luther King, Jr. We were taught that our armies were always invincible and our causes were always just, only to suffer the agony of Vietnam. We respected the Presidency as a place of honor until the shock of Watergate.

We remember when the phrase "sound as a dollar" was an expression of absolute dependability, until ten years of inflation began to shrink our dollar and our savings. We believed that our Nation's resources were limitless until 1973, when we had to face a growing dependence on foreign oil.

These wounds are still very deep. They have never been healed. Looking for a way out of this crisis, our people have turned to the Federal Government and found it isolated from the mainstream of our Nation's life. Washington, D.C., has become an island. The gap between our citizens and our Government has never been so wide. The people are looking for honest answers, not easy answers; clear leadership, not false claims and evasiveness and politics as usual.

What you see too often in Washington and elsewhere around the country is a system of government that seems incapable of action. You see a Congress twisted and pulled in every direction by hundreds of well-financed and powerful special interests. You see every extreme position defended to the last vote, almost to the last breath by one unyielding group or another. You often see a balanced and a fair approach that demands sacrifice, a little sacrifice from everyone, abandoned like an orphan without support and without friends.

Often you see paralysis and stagnation and drift. You don't like it, and neither do I. What can we do?

First of all, we must face the truth, and then we can change our course. We simply must have faith in each other, faith in our ability to govern ourselves, and faith in the future of this Nation. Restoring that faith and that confidence to America is now the most important task we face. It is a true challenge of this generation of Americans.

Excerpt from "The Crisis of Confidence" by Jimmy Carter

11. What is the underlying message of Jimmy Carter's speech?
    a. There is no hope for the future of the United States.
    b. The American people have lost faith in their government.
    c. Finding the way again as a nation will be hard and will require facing the truth.
    d. America is not as great as other Western countries.

12. What is NOT a symptom of the crisis of the American spirit?
    a. Too many people tend to worship self-indulgence and consumption.
    b. Respect for government, churches and schools is growing.
    c. Two-thirds of American people do not vote.
    d. The willingness to save for the future has fallen.

13. Which phrase could replace "sound as a dollar" in paragraph seven?
    a. Hands down
    b. Solid as a rock
    c. Piece of cake
    d. Fair and square

14. Pointing out the shortcomings of government makes President Carter sound like he is:
    a. Unreliable as a leader
    b. Desperate for acceptance
    c. Relatable and empathetic
    d. Condescending toward citizens

15. What does Carter mean, metaphorically, when he says that "Washington, D.C. has become an island"?
    a. Members of Congress are relaxing on vacation while the people suffer.
    b. The government is using limited resources unwisely.
    c. The White House is an oasis for Americans in need.
    d. The government has isolated itself from its citizens.

16. What is the purpose of paragraphs six and seven?
    a. To point out that previous presidents have made mistakes
    b. To provide examples of why people are losing respect for government and other institutions
    c. To prove that our past is full of tragedy and our future is full of hope
    d. To suggest Americans' expectations are too high

17. According to President Carter, what is "politics as usual"?
    a. Decisions that do not benefit the executive branch
    b. Jargon that does not make sense to the average American
    c. A way of proceeding that is full of false claims, evasiveness, and inactivity
    d. A balanced and fair approach that demands sacrifice

18. In the second-to-last paragraph, the word *stagnation* means a lack of:
    a. Progress
    b. Understanding
    c. Knowledge
    d. Empathy

19. How does the tone shift from the beginning to the end of the passage?
    a. The tone starts informally but ends seriously.
    b. The tone starts elevated but ends unremarkably.
    c. The tone starts bleakly but ends optimistically.
    d. The tone starts preachy but ends humbly.

20. What is Carter's proposed solution to the crisis of confidence in America?
    a. Healing the wounds, shocks, and tragedies of the past
    b. Removing special interest groups from the government
    c. Restoring faith in ourselves, democracy, and our nation
    d. Reverting back to strong families and close-knit communities

History/Social Studies

Questions 21–30 is based on the following passage:

The peoples of a number of countries of the world have recently had totalitarian regimes forced upon them against their will. The Government of the United States has made frequent protests against coercion and intimidation, in violation of the Yalta agreement, in Poland, Rumania, and Bulgaria. I must also state that in a number of other countries there have been similar developments.

At the present moment in world history nearly every nation must choose between alternative ways of life. The choice is too often not a free one.

One way of life is based upon the will of the majority, and is distinguished by free institutions, representative government, free elections, guarantees of individual liberty, freedom of speech and religion, and freedom from political oppression.

The second way of life is based upon the will of a minority forcibly imposed upon the majority. It relies upon terror and oppression, a controlled press and radio; fixed elections, and the suppression of personal freedoms.

I believe that it must be the policy of the United States to support free peoples who are resisting attempted subjugation by armed minorities or by outside pressures.

I believe that we must assist free peoples to work out their own destinies in their own way.

I believe that our help should be primarily through economic and financial aid which is essential to economic stability and orderly political processes.

The world is not static, and the status quo is not sacred. But we cannot allow changes in the status quo in violation of the Charter of the United Nations by such methods as coercion, or by such subterfuges as political infiltration. In helping free and independent nations to maintain their freedom, the United States will be giving effect to the principles of the Charter of the United Nations.

It is necessary only to glance at a map to realize that the survival and integrity of the Greek nation are of grave importance in a much wider situation. If Greece should fall under the control of an armed minority, the effect upon its neighbor, Turkey, would be immediate and serious. Confusion and disorder might well spread throughout the entire Middle East.

Moreover, the disappearance of Greece as an independent state would have a profound effect upon those countries in Europe whose peoples are struggling against great difficulties to maintain their freedoms and their independence while they repair the damages of war.

It would be an unspeakable tragedy if these countries, which have struggled so long against overwhelming odds, should lose that victory for which they sacrificed so much. Collapse of free institutions and loss of independence would be disastrous not only for them but for the world. Discouragement and possibly failure would quickly be the lot of neighboring peoples striving to maintain their freedom and independence.

Should we fail to aid Greece and Turkey in this fateful hour, the effect will be far reaching to the West as well as to the East.

We must take immediate and resolute action.

I therefore ask the Congress to provide authority for assistance to Greece and Turkey in the amount of $400,000,000 for the period ending June 30, 1948. In requesting these funds, I have taken into consideration the maximum amount of relief assistance which would be furnished to Greece out of the $350,000,000 which I recently requested that the Congress authorize for the prevention of starvation and suffering in countries devastated by the war.

In addition to funds, I ask the Congress to authorize the detail of American civilian and military personnel to Greece and Turkey, at the request of those countries, to assist in the tasks of reconstruction, and for the purpose of supervising the use of such financial and material assistance as may be furnished. I recommend that authority also be provided for the instruction and training of selected Greek and Turkish personnel.

Finally, I ask that the Congress provide authority which will permit the speediest and most effective use, in terms of needed commodities, supplies, and equipment, of such funds as may be authorized.

If further funds, or further authority, should be needed for purposes indicated in this message, I shall not hesitate to bring the situation before the Congress. On this subject the Executive and Legislative branches of the Government must work together.

This is a serious course upon which we embark.

Excerpt from "The Truman Doctrine" by Harry S. Truman

21. What is the primary purpose of this speech?
   a. To persuade
   b. To describe
   c. To entertain
   d. To analyze

22. After hearing this speech, one could infer Truman believes that the United States is _________ and Greece and Turkey are _________.
    a. A developed nation; third-world countries
    b. Part of the United Nations; not part of the United Nations
    c. A free democracy; under dictatorships
    d. An altruistic hero; potential victims of oppression

23. President Truman describes two ways of life. Which statement corresponds to his description?
    a. The first way of life is distinguished by free institutions; the second is marked by freedom of religion.
    b. The first way of life relies on terror and oppression; the second controls the press and radio.
    c. The first way of life guarantees individual liberties; the second suppresses personal freedoms.
    d. The first way of life suppresses individual liberties; the second guarantees personal freedoms.

24. What does the underlined word mean in the following sentence?

> "But we cannot allow changes in the status quo in violation of the Charter of the United Nations by such methods as coercion, or by such <u>subterfuges</u> as political infiltration."

    a. Helpful pieces of intel
    b. Tricky deceptions
    c. Time-consuming activities
    d. Underground routes

25. Based on the speech, what would be an immediate effect of Greece falling under the control of an armed minority?
    a. Turkey and the entire Middle East might experience unprecedented turmoil.
    b. The Charter of the United Nations would prevent any negative repercussions.
    c. Greece would receive hundreds of millions of dollars from the United States.
    d. Greece might become absorbed into another country and disappear off the map completely.

26. Truman states, "Should we fail to aid Greece and Turkey in this fateful hour, the effect will be far reaching to the West as well as to the East." What emotion might members of Congress feel at this moment?
    a. Disgust
    b. Astonishment
    c. Concern
    d. Eagerness

27. What is NOT one of Truman's requests to Congress?
    a. Send four million dollars in relief funds to Greece and Turkey.
    b. Overhaul the governments of Greece and Turkey.
    c. Deploy civil personnel to Greece and Turkey.
    d. Authorize the fastest and most effective use of supplies and equipment.

28. If Congress does not agree to Truman's plea, what is likely to happen?
   a. Another country will step up and offer similar relief aid.
   b. Greece and Turkey will rely on each other to avoid suppression.
   c. Most Eastern countries will experience the collapse of institutions and freedom.
   d. The United Nations will force the U.S. Congress to accept Truman's terms.

29. Which quote indicates that time is of the essence?
   a. "The choice is too often not a free one."
   b. "The world is not static, and the status quo is not sacred."
   c. "This is a serious course upon which we embark."
   d. "We must take immediate and resolute action."

30. How is this speech organized?
   a. Problem and solution
   b. Chronological order
   c. Compare and contrast
   d. Categorical

Science

Questions 31–42 are based on the following two passages:

Passage 1

"Insects are the flower's auxiliaries. Flies, wasps, honeybees, bumblebees, beetles, butterflies, all vie with one another in rendering aid by carrying the pollen of the stamens to the stigmas. They dive into the flower, enticed by a honeyed drop expressly prepared at the bottom of the corolla. In their efforts to obtain it they shake the stamens and daub themselves with pollen, which they carry from one flower to another. Who has not seen bumblebees coming out of the bosom of the flowers all covered with pollen? Their hairy stomachs, powdered with pollen, have only to touch a stigma in passing to communicate life to it. When in the spring you see on a blooming pear-tree, a whole swarm of flies, bees, and butterflies, hurrying, humming, and fluttering, it is a triple feast, my friends: a feast for the insect that pilfers in the depth of the flowers; a feast for the tree whose ovaries are quickened by all these merry little people; and a feast for man, to whom abundant harvest is promised. The insect is the best distributor of pollen. All the flowers it visits receive their share of quickening dust."

[...]

"To attract the insect that it needs, every flower has at the bottom of its corolla a drop of sweet liquor called nectar. From this liquor bees make their honey. To draw it from corollas shaped like a deep funnel, butterflies have a long trumpet, curled in a spiral when at rest, but which they unroll and plunge into the flower like a bore when they wish to obtain the delicious drink. The insect does not see this drop of nectar; however, it knows that it is there and finds it without hesitation. But in some flowers a grave difficulty presents itself: these flowers are closed tight everywhere. How is the treasure to be got

at, how find the entrance that leads to the nectar? Well, these closed flowers have a signboard, a mark that says clearly: Enter here."

"You won't make us believe that!" cried Claire.

"I am not going to make you believe anything, my dear child; I am going to show you. Look at this snapdragon blossom. It is shut tight, its two closed lips leave no passage between. Its color is a uniform purplish red; but there, just in the middle of the lower lip, is a large spot of bright yellow. This spot, so appropriate for catching the eye, is the mark, the signboard I told you of. By its brightness it says: Here is the keyhole.

"Press your little finger on the spot. You see. The flower yawns immediately, the secret lock works. And you think the bumblebee does not know these things? Watch it in the garden and you will see how it can read the signs of the flowers. When it visits a snapdragon, it always alights on the yellow spot and nowhere else. The door opens, it enters. It twists and turns in the corolla and covers itself with pollen, with which it daubs the stigma. Having drunk the drop, it goes off to other flowers, forcing the opening of which it knows the secret thoroughly.

"All closed flowers have, like the snapdragon, a conspicuous point, a spot of bright color, a sign that shows the insect the entrance to the corolla and says to it: Here it is. Finally, insects whose trade it is to visit flowers and make the pollen fall from the stamens on to the stigma, have a wonderful knowledge of the significance of this spot. It is on it they use their strength to make the flower open.

"Let us recapitulate. Insects are necessary to flowers to bring pollen to the stigmas. A drop of nectar, distilled on purpose for this, attracts them to the bottom of the corolla; a bright spot shows them the road to follow. Either I am a triple idiot or we have here an admirable chain of facts. Later, my children, you will find only too many people saying: This world is the product of chance, no intelligence rules it, no Providence guides it. To those people, my friends, show the snapdragon's yellow spot. If, less clear-sighted than the burly bumblebee, they do not understand it, pity them: they have diseased brains."

Excerpt from *The Storybook of Science* by Jean-Henri Fabre

Passage 2

A very complete knowledge of the pollen-gathering behavior of the worker honeybee may be obtained by a study of the actions of bees which are working upon a plant which yields pollen in abundance. Sweet corn is an ideal plant for this purpose, and it will be used as a basis for the description which follows.

The movements of the legs and of the mouthparts are so rapid and so many members are in action at once that it is impossible for the eye to follow all at the same time. However, long-continued observation, assisted by the study of instantaneous photographs, gives confidence that the statements recorded are accurate, although some movements may have escaped notice.

To obtain pollen from corn the bee must find a tassel in the right stage of ripeness, with flowers open and stamens hanging from them. The bee alights upon a spike and crawls along it, clinging to the pendent anthers. It crawls over the anthers, going from one flower to another along the spike, being all the while busily engaged in the task of obtaining pollen. This reaches its body in several ways.

As the bee moves over the anthers it uses its mandibles and tongue, biting the anthers and licking them and securing a considerable amount of pollen upon these parts. This pollen becomes moist and sticky, since it is mingled with fluid from the mouth. A considerable amount of pollen is dislodged from the anthers as the bee moves over them. All of the legs receive a supply of this free pollen and much adheres to the hairs which cover the body, more particularly to those upon the ventral surface. This free pollen is dry and powdery and is very different in appearance from the moist pollen masses with which the bee returns to the hive. Before the return journey this pollen must be transferred to the baskets and securely packed in them.

After the bee has traversed a few flowers along the spike and has become well supplied with free pollen it begins to collect it from its body, head, and forward appendages and to transfer it to the posterior pair of legs. This may be accomplished while the bee is resting upon the flower or while it is hovering in the air before seeking additional pollen. It is probably more thoroughly and rapidly accomplished while the bee is in the air, since all of the legs are then free to function in the gathering process.

If the collecting bee is seized with forceps and examined after it has crawled over the stamens of a few flowers of the corn, its legs and the ventral surface of its body are found to be thickly powdered over with pollen. If the bee hovers in the air for a few moments and is then examined very little pollen is found upon the body or upon the legs, except the masses within the pollen baskets. While in the air it has accomplished the work of collecting some of the scattered grains and of storing them in the baskets, while others have been brushed from the body.

In attempting to describe the movements by which this result is accomplished it will be best first to sketch briefly the roles of the three pairs of legs. They are as follows:

(a) The first pair of legs remove scattered pollen from the head and the region of the neck, and the pollen that has been moistened by fluid substances from the mouth.

(b) The second pair of legs remove scattered pollen from the thorax, more particularly from the ventral region, and they receive the pollen that has been collected by the first pair of legs.

(c) The third pair of legs collect a little of the scattered pollen from the abdomen and they receive pollen that has been collected by the second pair. Nearly all of this pollen is collected by the pollen combs of the hind legs, and is transferred from the combs to the pollen baskets or corbiculae in a manner to be described later.

It will thus be seen that the manipulation of pollen is a successive process, and that most of the pollen at least passes backward from the point where it happens to touch the bee until it finally reaches the corbiculae or is accidentally dislodged and falls from the rapidly moving limbs.

Excerpt from *The Behavior of the Honey Bee in Pollen Collection* by Dana Brackenridge Casteel

31. What do these two articles have in common?
    a. Both articles describe the roles of the bee's three different sets of legs.
    b. Both articles articulate the important role insects play in pollination.
    c. Both articles present their findings in a formal and scientific manner.
    d. Both articles discuss the methods that flowers use to attract pollinators.

32. The diction Jean-Henri Fabre uses in the first passage is:
    a. Pedantic
    b. Emotional
    c. Whimsical
    d. Ambiguous

33. What does the underlined word mean in the following sentence?

    "After the bee has traversed a few flowers along the spike and has become well supplied with free pollen it begins to collect it from its body, head, and forward appendages and to transfer it to the posterior pair of legs."

    a. Strongest
    b. Anterior
    c. Ambulatory
    d. Rear

34. Which type of evidence is used by the author of the second passage, Dana Brackenridge?
    a. Anecdotal
    b. Hypothetical
    c. Experimental
    d. Observational

35. In the first passage, what conclusion can be drawn about this character's feeling toward nature from the following sentence?

    "To those people, my friends, show the snapdragon's yellow spot."

    a. The character believes nature is designed with purpose and intent.
    b. The character believes nature is vibrant yet random.
    c. The character believes nature's most beautiful plant is the snapdragon.
    d. The character believes nature is difficult to predict and understand.

36. Which entity does NOT benefit from the "triple feast?"
    a. Trees
    b. Insects
    c. Pollen
    d. Humans

37. Pollen manipulation by the honeybee is a successive process that:
   a. Starts in the pollen basket and moves toward the legs
   b. Starts on the body, moves to the legs, and eventually ends at the corbiculae
   c. Starts on the thorax and moves toward the tongue and mandibles
   d. Starts on the antennae, moves to the wings, and eventually ends at the pollen basket

38. Which two terms are synonyms?
   a. Nectar; honey
   b. Stamen; stigma
   c. Pollen baskets; corbiculae
   d. Thorax; abdomen

39. Which kind of logical fallacy is presented in the following sentence?

   "Either I am a triple idiot or we have here an admirable chain of facts."

   a. Slippery slope
   b. Ad hominem
   c. Red herring
   d. False dichotomy

40. In paragraph five of the first passage, what speaker imply when he says the "flower yawns"?
   a. The petals of the flower are opening up slowly.
   b. The flower is worn out from pollination and needs rest.
   c. The flower is expanding its surface area to absorb more carbon dioxide.
   d. The flower is having a difficult time regulating night and day.

41. Why does the study in the second passage use sweet corn?
   a. Honeybees are attracted to the natural sweetness of the plant.
   b. The region has an abundance of sweet corn available for study.
   c. Sweet corn does not attract any other species of pollinator, making it easier to focus on bees.
   d. Sweet corn yields a generous amount of pollen.

42. What conclusion can be drawn after reading both of these passages?
   a. To date, science has had very to say little about bees, flowers, and pollination.
   b. Honeybees and flowers have a mutually beneficial relationship.
   c. Bees are the most advanced pollinator.
   d. The process of pollination is more accidental than intentional.

Science

Questions 43–52 are based upon the following passage:

How does soap make your hands clean?

Why will gasoline take a grease spot out of your clothes?

If we were to go back to our convenient imaginary switchboard to turn off another law, we should find near the heat switches, and not far from the chemistry ones, a switch labeled Solution. Suppose we turned it off:

The fishes in the sea are among the first creatures to be surprised by our action. For instantly all the salt in the ocean drops to the bottom like so much sand, and most saltwater fishes soon perish in the freshwater.

[...]

Probably we had better let the Solution switch alone, after all. Instead, here are a couple of experiments that will help to make clear what happens when anything dissolves to make a solution.

Experiment 80. Fill a test tube one fourth full of cold water. Slowly stir in salt until no more will dissolve. Add half a teaspoonful more of salt than will dissolve. Dry the outside of the test tube and heat the salty water over the Bunsen burner. Will hot water dissolve things more readily or less readily than cold? Why do you wash dishes in hot water?

Experiment 81. Fill a test tube one fourth full of any kind of oil, and one fourth full of water. Hold your thumb over the top of the test tube and shake it hard for a minute or two. Now look at it. Pour it out, and shake some prepared cleanser into the test tube, adding a little more water. Shake the test tube thoroughly and rinse. Put it away clean.

When you shake the oil with the water, the oil breaks up into tiny droplets. These droplets are so small that they reflect the light that strikes them and so look white, or pale yellow. This milky mixture is called an emulsion. Milk is an emulsion; there are tiny droplets of butter fat and other substances scattered all through the milk. The butter fat is not dissolved in the rest of the milk, and the oil is not dissolved in the water. But the droplets may be so small that an emulsion acts almost exactly like a solution.

But when you shake or stir salt or sugar in water, the particles divide up into smaller and smaller pieces, until probably each piece is just a single molecule of the salt or sugar. And these molecules get into the spaces between the water molecules and bounce around among them. They therefore act like the water and let the light through. This is a solution. The salt or sugar is dissolved in the water. Any liquid mixture which remains clear is a solution, no matter what the color. Most red ink, most blueing, clear coffee, tea, and ocean water are solutions. If a liquid is clear, no matter what the color, you can be sure that whatever things may be in it are dissolved.

Experiment 82. Pour alcohol into a test tube (square-bottomed test tubes are best for this experiment), standing the tube up beside a ruler. When the alcohol is just one inch high in the tube, stop pouring. Put exactly the same amount of water in another test tube of the same size. When you pour them together, how many inches high do you think the mixture will be? Pour the water into the alcohol, shake the mixture a little, and measure to see how high it comes in the test tube. Did you notice the warmth when you shook the tube?

If you use denatured alcohol, you are likely to have an emulsion as a result of the mixing. The alcohol part of the denatured alcohol dissolves in the water well enough, but the denaturing substance in the alcohol will not dissolve in water; so it forms tiny droplets that make the mixture of alcohol and water cloudy.

The purpose of this experiment is to show that the molecules of water get into the spaces between the molecules of alcohol. It is as if you were to add a pail of pebbles to a pail of apples. The pebbles would fill in between the apples, and the mixture would not nearly fill two pails.

Excerpt from "Common Science" by Carleton W. Washburne

43. Which title best suits this chapter?
    a. Cleaning with Science
    b. Experiments You Can Do at Home
    c. Solutions and Emulsions
    d. Solution Switchboard

44. What effect does the author achieve by presenting the scenario of the imaginary?
    a. Humor through a hypothetical situation
    b. Shock through a surprise twist
    c. Deception through misleading information
    d. Curiosity through growing suspense

45. Why does the author ask rhetorical questions?
    a. To reveal their opinion on the topic
    b. To encourage the reader to draw their own conclusions
    c. To ensure the reader is following along
    d. To convince the reader to conduct the experiments at home

46. How are emulsions different from solutions?
    a. Emulsions are clear; solutions are cloudy.
    b. Emulsions are non-potable; solutions are potable.
    c. Emulsions have a low temperature; solutions have a high temperature.
    d. Emulsions have tiny, suspended droplets; solutions are completely dissolved.

47. What is the most likely result of Experiment 80?
    a. The heat was unable to dissolve the additional salt.
    b. Once heated, the additional salt dissolved completely.
    c. The additional salt prevented the water from heating up more than room temperature.
    d. The heated salt and water solution could be used to wash dishes.

48. When might an emulsion pass as a solution?
    a. When the scattered droplets cannot be detected because they are so small.
    b. When the substance is heated to its boiling point.
    c. When the emulsion has been stirred or shaken thoroughly.
    d. Emulsions cannot pass as solutions.

49. Which analogy makes the correct comparison?
    a. Pebbles are to apples as alcohol is to water.
    b. Water is to pebbles as alcohol is to apples.
    c. Apples are to water as pebbles are to alcohol.
    d. Alcohol and water are to emulsion as apples and pebbles are to solution.

50. What can be inferred about denatured alcohol?
    a. It can be dangerous to work with in a laboratory.
    b. It has the same basic properties as regular alcohol.
    c. It needs to be heated in order to completely dissolve.
    d. There are better alternatives to form true solutions.

51. Using deductive reasoning, how high will the mixture measure at the end of Experiment 82?
    a. Exactly two inches
    b. More than two inches
    c. Less than two inches
    d. There is no way to tell unless you conduct the experiment.

52. Which idiom could be explained using evidence from this passage?
    a. That is like comparing apples to oranges.
    b. She is going to be in hot water.
    c. They are like oil and water.
    d. No use crying over spilled milk.

Writing and Language Test

Questions 1–9 are based on the following passage:

While all dogs (1) descend through gray wolves, it's easy to notice that dog breeds come in a variety of shapes and sizes. With such a (2) drastic range of traits, appearances and body types, dogs are one of the most variable and adaptable species on the planet. (3) But why so many differences. The answer is that humans have actually played a major role in altering the biology of dogs. (4) This was done through a process called selective breeding.

(5) Selective breeding which is also called artificial selection is the process in which animals with desired traits are bred in order to produce offspring that share the same traits. In natural evolution, (6) animals must adapt to their environments increase their chance of survival. Over time, certain traits develop in animals that enable them to thrive in these environments. Those animals with more of these traits, or better versions of these traits, gain an (7) advantage over others of their species. Therefore, the animal's chances to mate are increased and these useful (8) genes are passed into their offspring. With dog breeding, humans select traits that are desired and encourage more of these desired traits in other dogs by breeding dogs that already have them.

The reason for different breeds of dogs is that there were specific needs that humans wanted to fill with their animals. For example, scent hounds are known for their extraordinary ability to track game through scent. These breeds are also known for their endurance in seeking deer and other prey. Therefore, early hunters took dogs that displayed these abilities and bred them to encourage these traits. Later generations took on characteristics that aided these desired traits. (9) For example, Bloodhounds have broad snouts and droopy ears that fall to the ground when they smell. These physical qualities not only define the look of the bloodhound, but also contribute to their amazing tracking ability. The broad snout is able to define and hold onto scents longer than many other breeds. The long, floppy ears serve to collect and hold the scents the earth holds so that the smells are clearer and able to be distinguished.

1. Which of the following would be the best choice for this sentence (reproduced below)?

While all dogs (1) descend through gray wolves, it's easy to notice that dog breeds come in a variety of shapes and sizes.

a. NO CHANGE
b. descend by gray wolves
c. descend from gray wolves
d. descended through gray wolves

2. Which of the following would be the best choice for this sentence (reproduced below)?

With such a (2) drastic range of traits, appearances and body types, dogs are one of the most variable and adaptable species on the planet.

a. NO CHANGE
b. drastic range of traits, appearances, and body types,
c. drastic range of traits and appearances and body types,
d. drastic range of traits, appearances, as well as body types,

3. Which of the following would be the best choice for this sentence (reproduced below)?

(3) But why so many differences.

a. NO CHANGE
b. But are there so many differences?
c. But why so many differences are there.
d. But why are there so many differences?

4. Which of the following would be the best choice for this sentence (reproduced below)?

(4) This was done through a process called selective breeding.

a. NO CHANGE
b. This was done, through a process called selective breeding.
c. This was done, through a process, called selective breeding.
d. This was done through selective breeding, a process.

5. Which of the following would be the best choice for this sentence (reproduced below)?

(5) Selective breeding which is also called artificial selection is the process in which animals with desired traits are bred in order to produce offspring that share the same traits.

a. NO CHANGE
b. Selective breeding, which is also called artificial selection is the process
c. Selective breeding which is also called, artificial selection, is the process
d. Selective breeding, which is also called artificial selection, is the process

6. Which of the following would be the best choice for this sentence (reproduced below)?

In natural evolution, (6) animals must adapt to their environments increase their chance of survival.

a. NO CHANGE
b. animals must adapt to their environments to increase their chance of survival.
c. animals must adapt to their environments, increase their chance of survival.
d. animals must adapt to their environments, increasing their chance of survival.

7. Which of the following would be the best choice for this sentence (reproduced below)?

Those animals with more of these traits, or better versions of these traits, gain an (7) advantage over others of their species.

a. NO CHANGE
b. advantage over others, of their species.
c. advantages over others of their species.
d. advantage over others.

8. Which of the following would be the best choice for this sentence (reproduced below)?

Therefore, the animal's chances to mate are increased and these useful (8) genes are passed into their offspring.

a. NO CHANGE
b. genes are passed onto their offspring.
c. genes are passed on to their offspring.
d. genes are passed within their offspring.

9. Which of the following would be the best choice for this sentence (reproduced below)?

(9) For example, Bloodhounds have broad snouts and droopy ears that fall to the ground when they smell.

a. NO CHANGE
b. For example, Bloodhounds,
c. For example Bloodhounds
d. For example, bloodhounds

Questions 10–18 are based on the following passage:

I'm not alone when I say that it's hard to pay attention sometimes. I can't count how many times I've sat in a classroom, lecture, speech, or workshop and (10) been bored to tears or rather sleep. (11) Usually I turn to doodling in order to keep awake. This never really helps; I'm not much of an artist. Therefore, after giving up on drawing a masterpiece, I would just concentrate on keeping my eyes open and trying to be attentive. This didn't always work because I wasn't engaged in what was going on.

(12) Sometimes in particularly dull seminars, I'd imagine comical things going on in the room or with the people trapped in the room with me. Why? (13) Because I wasn't invested in what was going on I wasn't motivated to listen. I'm not going to write about how I conquered the difficult task of actually paying attention in a difficult or unappealing class—it can be done, sure. I have sat through the very epitome of boredom (in my view at least) several times and come away learning something. (14) Everyone probably has had to at one time or another do this. What I want to talk about is that profound moment when curiosity is sparked (15) in another person drawing them to pay attention to what is before them and expand their knowledge.

What really makes people pay attention? (16) Easy it's interest. This doesn't necessarily mean (17) embellishing subject matter drawing people's attention. This won't always work. However, an individual can present material in a way that is clear to understand and actually engages the audience. Asking questions to the audience or class will make them a part of the topic at hand. Discussions that make people think about the content and (18) how it applies to there lives world and future are key. If math is being discussed, an instructor can explain the purpose behind the equations or perhaps use real-world applications to show how relevant the topic is. When discussing history, a lecturer can prompt students to imagine themselves in the place of key figures and ask how they might respond. The bottom line is to explore the ideas rather than just lecture. Give people the chance to explore material from multiple angles, and they'll be hungry to keep paying attention for more information.

10. Which of the following would be the best choice for this sentence (reproduced below)?

I can't count how many times I've sat in a classroom, lecture, speech, or workshop and (10) been bored to tears or rather sleep.

a. NO CHANGE
b. been bored to, tears, or rather sleep.
c. been bored, to tears or rather sleep.
d. been bored to tears or, rather, sleep.

11. Which of the following would be the best choice for this sentence (reproduced below)?

(11) Usually I turn to doodling in order to keep awake.

a. NO CHANGE
b. Usually I turn to doodling in order to keep awakened.
c. Usually I turn to doodling, in order, to keep awake.
d. Usually I turns to doodling in order to keep awake.

12. Which of the following would be the best choice for this sentence (reproduced below)?

> (12) Sometimes in particularly dull seminars, I'd imagine comical things going on in the room or with the people trapped in the room with me.

a. NO CHANGE
b. Sometimes, in particularly, dull seminars,
c. Sometimes in particularly dull seminars
d. Sometimes in particularly, dull seminars,

13. Which of the following would be the best choice for this sentence (reproduced below)?

> (13) Because I wasn't invested in what was going on I wasn't motivated to listen.

a. NO CHANGE
b. Because I wasn't invested, in what was going on, I wasn't motivated to listen.
c. Because I wasn't invested in what was going on. I wasn't motivated to listen.
d. I wasn't motivated to listen because I wasn't invested in what was going on.

14. Which of the following would be the best choice for this sentence (reproduced below)?

> (14) Everyone probably has had to at one time or another do this.

a. NO CHANGE
b. Everyone probably has had to, at one time or another. Do this.
c. Everyone's probably had to do this at one time.
d. At one time or another everyone probably has had to do this.

15. Which of the following would be the best choice for this sentence (reproduced below)?

> What I want to talk about is that profound moment when curiosity is sparked (15) in another person drawing them to pay attention to what is before them and expand their knowledge.

a. NO CHANGE
b. in another person, drawing them to pay attention to what is before them
c. in another person; drawing them to pay attention to what is before them
d. in another person, drawing them to pay attention to what is before them.

16. Which of the following would be the best choice for this sentence (reproduced below)?

> (16) Easy it's interest.

a. NO CHANGE
b. Easy it is interest.
c. Easy its interest.
d. Easy—it's interest.

17. Which of the following would be the best choice for this sentence (reproduced below)?

> This doesn't necessarily mean (17) embellishing subject matter drawing people's attention.

a. NO CHANGE
b. embellishing subject matter which draws people's attention.
c. embellishing subject matter to draw people's attention.
d. embellishing subject matter for the purpose of drawing people's attention.

18. Which of the following would be the best choice for this sentence (reproduced below)?

> Discussions that make people think about the content and (18) how it applies to there lives world and future are key.

a. NO CHANGE
b. how it applies to their lives, world, and future are key.
c. how it applied to there lives world and future are key.
d. how it applies to their lives, world, and future, are key.

Questions 19–27 are based on the following passage:

> Since the first discovery of dinosaur bones, (19) scientists has made strides in technological development and methodologies used to investigate these extinct animals. We know more about dinosaurs than ever before and are still learning fascinating new things about how they looked and lived. However, one has to ask, (20) how if earlier perceptions of dinosaurs continue to influence people's understanding of these creatures? Can these perceptions inhibit progress towards further understanding of dinosaurs?
>
> (21) The biggest problem with studying dinosaurs is simply that there are no living dinosaurs to observe. All discoveries associated with these animals are based on physical remains. To gauge behavioral characteristics, scientists cross-examine these (22) finds with living animals that seem similar in order to gain understanding. While this method is effective, these are still deductions. Some ideas about dinosaurs can't be tested and confirmed simply because humans can't replicate a living dinosaur. For example, a Spinosaurus has a large sail, or a finlike structure that grows from its back. Paleontologists know this sail exists and have ideas for the function of (23) the sail however they are uncertain of which idea is the true function. Some scientists believe (24) the sail serves to regulate the Spinosaurus' body temperature and yet others believe its used to attract mates. Still, other scientists think the sail is used to intimidate other predatory dinosaurs for self-defense. These are all viable explanations, but they are also influenced by what scientists know about modern animals. (25) Yet, it's quite possible that the sail could hold a completely unique function.
>
> While it's (26) plausible, even likely that dinosaurs share many traits with modern animals, there is the danger of overattributing these qualities to a unique, extinct species. For much of the early nineteenth century, when people first started studying dinosaur bones, the assumption was that they were simply giant lizards. (27) For the longest time this image was the prevailing view on dinosaurs, until evidence indicated

that they were more likely warm blooded. Scientists have also discovered that many dinosaurs had feathers and actually share many traits with modern birds.

19. Which of the following would be the best choice for this sentence (reproduced below)?

Since the first discovery of dinosaur bones, (19) scientists has made strides in technological development and methodologies used to investigate these extinct animals.

a. NO CHANGE
b. scientists has made strides in technological development, and methodologies, used to investigate
c. scientists have made strides in technological development and methodologies used to investigate
d. scientists, have made strides in technological development and methodologies used, to investigate

20. Which of the following would be the best choice for this sentence (reproduced below)?

However, one has to ask, (20) how if earlier perceptions of dinosaurs continue to influence people's understanding of these creatures?

a. NO CHANGE
b. how perceptions of dinosaurs
c. how, if, earlier perceptions of dinosaurs
d. do earlier perceptions of dinosaurs

21. Which of the following would be the best choice for this sentence (reproduced below)?

(21) The biggest problem with studying dinosaurs is simply that there are no living dinosaurs to observe.

a. NO CHANGE
b. The biggest problem with studying dinosaurs is simple, that there are no living dinosaurs to observe.
c. The biggest problem with studying dinosaurs is simple, there are no living dinosaurs to observe.
d. The biggest problem with studying dinosaurs, is simply that there are no living dinosaurs to observe.

22. Which of the following would be the best choice for this sentence (reproduced below)?

To gauge behavioral characteristics, scientists cross-examine these (22) finds with living animals that seem similar in order to gain understanding.

a. NO CHANGE
b. finds with living animals to explore potential similarities.
c. finds with living animals to gain understanding of similarities.
d. finds with living animals that seem similar, in order, to gain understanding.

23. Which of the following would be the best choice for this sentence (reproduced below)?

> Paleontologists know this sail exists and have ideas for the function of (23) the sail however they are uncertain of which idea is the true function.

a. NO CHANGE
b. the sail however, they are uncertain of which idea is the true function.
c. the sail however they are, uncertain, of which idea is the true function.
d. the sail; however, they are uncertain of which idea is the true function.

24. Which of the following would be the best choice for this sentence (reproduced below)?

> Some scientists believe (24) the sail serves to regulate the Spinosaurus' body temperature and yet others believe its used to attract mates.

a. NO CHANGE
b. the sail serves to regulate the Spinosaurus' body temperature, yet others believe it's used to attract mates.
c. the sail serves to regulate the Spinosaurus' body temperature and yet others believe it's used to attract mates.
d. the sail serves to regulate the Spinosaurus' body temperature however others believe it's used to attract mates.

25. Which of the following would be the best choice for this sentence (reproduced below)?

> (25) Yet, it's quite possible that the sail could hold a completely unique function.

a. NO CHANGE
b. Yet, it's quite possible,
c. It's quite possible,
d. Its quite possible

26. Which of the following would be the best choice for this sentence (reproduced below)?

> While it's (26) plausible, even likely that dinosaurs share many traits with modern animals, there is the danger of over attributing these qualities to a unique, extinct species.

a. NO CHANGE
b. plausible, even likely that, dinosaurs share many
c. plausible, even likely, that dinosaurs share many
d. plausible even likely that dinosaurs share many

27. Which of the following would be the best choice for this sentence (reproduced below)?

> (27) For the longest time this image was the prevailing view on dinosaurs, until evidence indicated that they were more likely warm blooded.

a. NO CHANGE
b. For the longest time this was the prevailing view on dinosaurs
c. For the longest time, this image, was the prevailing view on dinosaurs
d. This was the prevailing view of dinosaurs

Questions 28–36 are based on the following passage written about Perelandra *by C.S. Lewis:*

> Everyone has heard the (28) idea of the end justifying the means; that would be Weston's philosophy. Weston is willing to cross any line, commit any act no matter how heinous, to achieve success in his goal. (29) Ransom is repulsed by this fact, seeing total evil in Weston's plan. To do an evil act in order (30) to gain a result that's supposedly good would ultimately warp the final act. (31) This opposing viewpoints immediately distinguishes Ransom as the hero. In the conflict with Un-man, Ransom remains true to his moral principles, someone who refuses to be compromised by power. Instead, Ransom makes it clear that by allowing such processes as murder and lying to dictate how one attains a positive outcome, (32) the righteous goal becomes corrupted. The good end would not be truly good, but a twisted end that conceals corrupt deeds.
>
> (33) This idea of allowing necessary evils to happen, is very tempting, it is what Weston fell prey to. (34) The temptation of the evil spirit Un-man ultimately takes over Weston and he is possessed. However, Ransom does not give into temptation. He remains faithful to the truth of what is right and incorrect. This leads him to directly face Un-man for the fate of Perelandra and its inhabitants.
>
> Just as Weston was corrupted by the Un-man, (35) Un-man after this seeks to tempt the Queen of Perelandra to darkness. Ransom must literally (36) show her the right path, to accomplish this, he does this based on the same principle as the "means to an end" argument—that good follows good, and evil follows evil. Later in the plot, Weston/Un-man seeks to use deceptive reasoning to turn the queen to sin, pushing the queen to essentially ignore Maleldil's rule to satisfy her own curiosity. In this sense, Un-man takes on the role of a false prophet, a tempter. Ransom must shed light on the truth, but this is difficult; his adversary is very clever and uses brilliant language. Ransom's lack of refinement heightens the weight of Un-man's corrupted logic, and so the Queen herself is intrigued by his logic.

28. Which of the following would be the best choice for this sentence (reproduced below)?

> Everyone has heard the (28) idea of the end justifying the means; that would be Weston's philosophy.

a. NO CHANGE
b. idea of the end justifying the means; this is Weston's philosophy.
c. idea of the end justifying the means, this is the philosophy of Weston.
d. idea of the end justifying the means. That would be Weston's philosophy.

29. Which of the following would be the best choice for this sentence (reproduced below)?

(29) Ransom is reviled by this fact, seeing total evil in Weston's plan.

a. NO CHANGE
b. Ransom is reviled by this fact; seeing total evil in Weston's plan.
c. Ransom, is reviled by this fact, seeing total evil in Weston's plan.
d. Ransom reviled by this, sees total evil in Weston's plan.

30. Which of the following would be the best choice for this sentence (reproduced below)?

To do an evil act in order (30) to gain a result that's supposedly good would ultimately warp the final act.

a. NO CHANGE
b. for an outcome that's for a greater good would ultimately warp the final act.
c. to gain a final act would warp its goodness.
d. to achieve something that's supposedly good would ultimately warp the final result.

31. Which of the following would be the best choice for this sentence (reproduced below)?

(31) This opposing viewpoints immediately distinguishes Ransom as the hero.

a. NO CHANGE
b. This opposing viewpoints immediately distinguishes Ransom, as the hero.
c. This opposing viewpoint immediately distinguishes Ransom as the hero.
d. Those opposing viewpoints immediately distinguishes Ransom as the hero.

32. Which of the following would be the best choice for this sentence (reproduced below)?

Instead, Ransom makes it clear that by allowing such processes as murder and lying to dictate how one attains a positive outcome, (32) the righteous goal becomes corrupted.

a. NO CHANGE
b. the goal becomes corrupted and no longer righteous.
c. the righteous goal becomes, corrupted.
d. the goal becomes corrupted, when once it was righteous.

33. Which of the following would be the best choice for this sentence (reproduced below)?

(33) This idea of allowing necessary evils to happen, is very tempting, it is what Weston fell prey to.

a. NO CHANGE
b. This idea of allowing necessary evils to happen, is very tempting. This is what Weston fell prey to.
c. This idea, allowing necessary evils to happen, is very tempting, it is what Weston fell prey to.
d. This tempting idea of allowing necessary evils to happen is what Weston fell prey to.

34. Which of the following would be the best choice for this sentence (reproduced below)?

(34) The temptation of the evil spirit Un-man ultimately takes over Weston and he is possessed.

a. NO CHANGE
b. Weston gives into the temptation of the evil spirit Un-man and becomes possessed.
c. Weston is possessed as a result of the temptation of the evil spirit Un-man ultimately, who takes over.
d. The temptation of the evil spirit Un-man takes over Weston and he is possessed ultimately.

35. Which of the following would be the best choice for this sentence (reproduced below)?

Just as Weston was corrupted by the Un-man, (35) Un-man after this seeks to tempt the Queen of Perelandra to darkness.

a. NO CHANGE
b. Un-man, after this, would tempt the Queen of Perelandra
c. Un-man, after this, seeks to tempt the Queen of Perelandra
d. Un-man then seeks to tempt the Queen of Perelandra

36. Which of the following would be the best choice for this sentence (reproduced below)?

Ransom must literally (36) show her the right path, to accomplish this, he does this based on the same principle as the "means to an end" argument—that good follows good, and evil follows evil.

a. NO CHANGE
b. show her the right path. To accomplish this, he uses the same principle as the "means to an end" argument
c. show her the right path; to accomplish this he uses the same principle as the "means to an end" argument
d. show her the right path, to accomplish this, the same principle as the "means to an end" argument is applied

Questions 37–45 are based on the following passage:

(37) What's clear about the news today is that the broader the media the more ways there are to tell a story. Even if different news groups cover the same story, individual newsrooms can interpret or depict the story differently than other counterparts. Stories can also change depending on the type of (38) media in question incorporating different styles and unique ways to approach the news. (39) It is because of these respective media types that ethical and news-related subject matter can sometimes seem different or altered. But how does this affect the narrative of the new story?

I began by investigating a written newspaper article from the Baltimore Sun. Instantly striking are the bolded headlines. (40) These are clearly meant for direct the viewer to the most exciting and important stories the paper has to offer. What was particularly noteworthy about this edition was that the first page dealt with two major ethical issues. (41) On a national level there was a story on the evolving Petraeus scandal involving his supposed affair. The other article was focused locally in Baltimore, a piece questioning the city's Ethics Board and their current director. Just as a television newscaster communicates the story through camera and dialogue, the printed article applies intentional and targeted written narrative style. More so than any of the mediums, a news article seems to be focused specifically on a given story without need to jump to another. Finer details are usually expanded on (42) in written articles, usually people who read newspapers or go online for web articles want more than a quick blurb. The diction of the story is also more precise and can be either straightforward or suggestive (43) depending in earnest on the goal of the writer. However, there's still plenty of room for opinions to be inserted into the text.

Usually, all news (44) outlets have some sort of bias, it's just a question of how much bias clouds the reporting. As long as this bias doesn't withhold information from the reader, it can be considered credible. (45) However an over use of bias, opinion, and suggestive language can rob readers of the chance to interpret the news events for themselves.

37. Which of the following would be the best choice for this sentence (reproduced below)?

(37) What's clear about the news today is that the broader the media the more ways there are to tell a story.

a. NO CHANGE
b. What's clear, about the news today, is that the broader the media
c. What's clear about the news today is that, the broader the media
d. The news today is broader than earlier media

38. Which of the following would be the best choice for this sentence (reproduced below)?

Stories can also change depending on the type of (38) media in question incorporating different styles and unique ways to approach the news.

a. NO CHANGE
b. media in question; each incorporates different styles and unique
c. media in question. To incorporate different styles and unique
d. media in question, incorporating different styles and unique

39. Which of the following would be the best choice for this sentence (reproduced below)?

(39) It is because of these respective media types that ethical and news-related subject matter can sometimes seem different or altered.

a. NO CHANGE
b. It is because of these respective media types, that ethical and news-related subject matter, can sometimes seem different or altered.
c. It is because of these respective media types, that ethical and news-related subject matter can sometimes seem different or altered.
d. It is because of these respective media types that ethical and news-related subject matter can sometimes seem different. Or altered.

40. Which of the following would be the best choice for this sentence (reproduced below)?

> (40) These are clearly meant for direct the viewer to the most exciting and important stories the paper has to offer.

a. NO CHANGE
b. These are clearly meant for the purpose of giving direction to the viewer
c. These are clearly meant to direct the viewer
d. These are clearly meant for the viewer to be directed

41. Which of the following would be the best choice for this sentence (reproduced below)?

> (41) On a national level there was a story on the evolving Petraeus scandal involving his supposed affair.

a. NO CHANGE
b. On a national level a story was there
c. On a national level; there was a story
d. On a national level, there was a story

42. Which of the following would be the best choice for this sentence (reproduced below)?

> Finer details are usually expanded on (42) in written articles, usually people who read newspapers or go online for web articles want more than a quick blurb.

a. NO CHANGE
b. in written articles. People who usually
c. in written articles, usually, people who
d. in written articles usually people who

43. Which of the following would be the best choice for this sentence (reproduced below)?

> The diction of the story is also more precise and can be either straightforward or suggestive (43) depending in earnest on the goal of the writer.

a. NO CHANGE
b. depending; in earnest on the goal of the writer.
c. depending, in earnest, on the goal of the writer.
d. the goal of the writer, in earnest, depends on the goal of the writer.

44. Which of the following would be the best choice for this sentence (reproduced below)?

> Usually, all news (44) outlets have some sort of bias, it's just a question of how much bias clouds the reporting.

a. NO CHANGE
b. outlets have some sort of bias; it's just a question of how much
c. outlets have some sort of bias it can just be a question of how much
d. outlets have some sort of bias, its just a question of how much

45. Which of the following would be the best choice for this sentence (reproduced below)?

> (45) However an over use of bias, opinion, and suggestive language can rob readers of the chance to interpret the news events for themselves.

a. NO CHANGE
b. However, an over use of bias,
c. However, with too much bias,
d. However, an overuse of bias,

Math Test

Calculator Questions

1. Which of the following inequalities is equivalent to $3 - \frac{1}{2}x \geq 2$?
   a. $x \geq 2$
   b. $x \leq 2$
   c. $x \geq 1$
   d. $x \leq 1$

2. If $g(x) = x^3 - 3x^2 - 2x + 6$ and $f(x) = 2$, then what is $g(f(x))$?
   a. -26
   b. 6
   c. $2x^3 - 6x^2 - 4x + 12$
   d. -2

3. What is the definition of a factor of the number 36?
   a. A number that can be divided by 36 and have no remainder
   b. A number that 36 can be divided by and have no remainder
   c. A prime number that is multiplied times 36
   d. An even number that is multiplied times 36

4. What are the coordinates of the focus of the parabola $y = -9x^2$?
   a. $(-3, 0)$
   b. $\left(-\frac{1}{36}, 0\right)$
   c. $(0, -3)$
   d. $\left(0, -\frac{1}{36}\right)$

5. What is the volume of a cube with the side equal to 3 inches?
   a. 6 in^3
   b. 27 in^3
   c. 9 in^3
   d. 3 in^3

6. What is the volume of a rectangular prism with the height of 3 centimeters, a width of 5 centimeters, and a depth of 11 centimeters?

a. 19 cm^3
b. 165 cm^3
c. 225 cm^3
d. 150 cm^3

7. What is the volume of a cylinder, in terms of π, with a radius of 5 inches and a height of 10 inches?

a. $250\,\pi \text{ in}^3$
b. $50\,\pi \text{ in}^3$
c. $100\,\pi \text{ in}^3$
d. $200\,\pi \text{ in}^3$

8. What is the solution to the following system of equations?

$$x^2 - 2x + y = 8$$

$$x - y = -2$$

a. $(-2, 3)$
b. There is no solution.
c. $(-2, 0)\ (1, 3)$
d. $(-2, 0)\ (3, 5)$

9. What is the equation for the line passing through the origin and the point $(2, 1)$?

a. $y = 2x$
b. $y = \frac{1}{2}x$
c. $y = x - 2$
d. $2y = x + 1$

10. A rectangle was formed out of pipe cleaner. Its length was $\frac{1}{2}$ of a foot and its width was $\frac{11}{2}$ inches. What is its area in square inches?

a. $\frac{11}{4} \text{ in}^2$
b. $\frac{11}{2} \text{ in}^2$
c. 22 in^2
d. 33 in^2

11. What type of function is modeled by the values in the following table?

x	$f(x)$
1	2
2	4
3	8
4	16
5	32

a. Linear
b. Exponential
c. Quadratic
d. Cubic

12. A shuffled deck of 52 cards contains 4 kings. One card is drawn, and is not put back in the deck. Then a second card is drawn. What's the probability that both cards are kings?

a. $\frac{1}{169}$

b. $\frac{1}{221}$

c. $\frac{1}{13}$

d. $\frac{4}{13}$

13. In the image below, what is demonstrated by the two triangles?

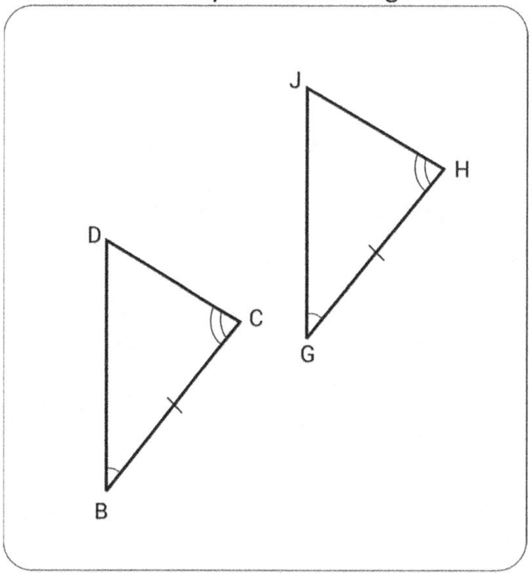

a. According to Side-Side-Side, the triangles are congruent.
b. According to Angle-Angle-Angle, the triangles are congruent.
c. According to Angle-Side-Angle, the triangles are congruent.
d. There is not enough information to prove the two triangles are congruent.

14. On Monday, Robert mopped the floor in 4 hours. On Tuesday, he did it in 3 hours. If on Monday, his average rate of mopping was p sq. ft. per hour, what was his average rate on Tuesday?

a. $\frac{4}{3}p$ sq. ft. per hour

b. $\frac{3}{4}p$ sq. ft. per hour

c. $\frac{5}{4}p$ sq. ft. per hour

d. $p + 1$ sq. ft. per hour

15. If $\sqrt{5+x} = 5$, what is x?

a. 10
b. 15
c. 20
d. 25

16. Which of the following polynomials is equal to $(2x - 4y)^2$?

a. $4x^2 - 16xy + 16y^2$
b. $4x^2 - 8xy + 16y^2$
c. $4x^2 - 16xy - 16y^2$
d. $2x^2 - 8xy + 8y^2$

17. What are the zeros of $f(x) = x^2 + 4$?

a. $x = -4$
b. $x = \pm 2i$
c. $x = \pm 2$
d. $x = \pm 4i$

18. What is the simplified form of the expression $(7n + 3n^3 + 3) + (8n + 5n^3 + 2n^4)$?

a. $9n^4 + 15n - 2$
b. $2n^4 + 5n^3 + 15n - 2$
c. $9n^4 + 8n^3 + 15n$
d. $2n^4 + 8n^3 + 15n + 3$

19. What is the simplified result of $\frac{15}{23} \times \frac{54}{127}$?

a. $\frac{810}{2{,}921}$

b. $\frac{81}{292}$

c. $\frac{69}{150}$

d. $\frac{810}{2929}$

20. What is the product of the following expression?

$$(4x - 8)(5x^2 + x + 6)$$

a. $20x^3 - 36x^2 + 16x - 48$
b. $6x^3 - 41x^2 + 12x + 15$
c. $20x^3 + 11x^2 - 37x - 12$
d. $2x^3 - 11x^2 - 32x + 20$

21. What is the solution for the following equation?

$$\frac{x^2 + x - 30}{x - 5} = 11$$

a. $x = -6$
b. There is no solution.
c. $x = 16$
d. $x = 5$

22. If x is not zero, then $\frac{3}{x} + \frac{5u}{2x} - \frac{u}{4} =$
a. $\frac{12+10u-ux}{4x}$
b. $\frac{3+5u-ux}{x}$
c. $\frac{12x+10u+ux}{4x}$
d. $\frac{12+10u-u}{4x}$

23. What are the zeros of the function: $f(x) = x^3 + 4x^2 + 4x$?
a. -2
b. 0, -2
c. 2
d. 0, 2

24. Is the following function even, odd, neither, or both?

$$y = \frac{1}{2}x^4 + 2x^2 - 6$$

a. Even
b. Odd
c. Neither
d. Both

25. Which of the following formulas would correctly calculate the perimeter of a legal-sized piece of paper that is 14 inches long and $8\frac{1}{2}$ inches wide?

a. $P = 14 + 8\frac{1}{2}$

b. $P = 14 + 8\frac{1}{2} + 14 + 8\frac{1}{2}$

c. $P = 14 \times 8\frac{1}{2}$

d. $P = 14 \times \frac{17}{2}$

26. A grocery store is selling individual bottles of water, and each bottle contains 750 milliliters of water. If 12 bottles are purchased, what conversion will correctly determine how many liters that customer will take home?

a. 100 milliliters equals 1 liter
b. 1,000 milliliters equals 1 liter
c. 1,000 liters equals 1 milliliter
d. 10 liters equals 1 milliliter

27. Given the following triangle, what's the length of the missing side? Round the answer to the nearest tenth.

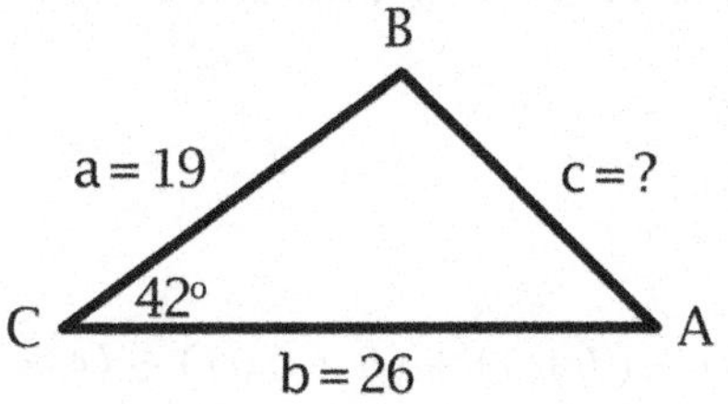

a. 17.0
b. 17.4
c. 18.0
d. 18.4

28. For the following similar triangles, what are the values of x and y (rounded to one decimal place)?

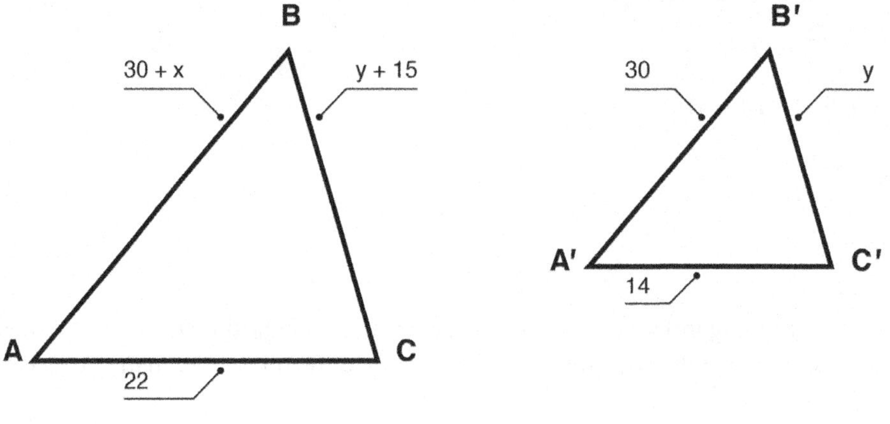

a. $x = 16.5, y = 25.1$
b. $x = 19.5, y = 24.1$
c. $x = 17.1, y = 26.3$
d. $x = 26.3, y = 17.1$

29. What are the center and radius of a circle with equation $4x^2 + 4y^2 - 16x - 24y + 51 = 0$?
a. Center $(3, 2)$ and radius $1/2$
b. Center $(2, 3)$ and radius $1/2$
c. Center $(3, 2)$ and radius $1/4$
d. Center $(2, 3)$ and radius $1/4$

30. What is the solution to $(2 \times 20) \div (7 + 1) + (6 \times 0.01) + (4 \times 0.001)$?
a. 5.064
b. 5.64
c. 5.0064
d. 48.064

31. A piggy bank contains 12 dollars' worth of nickels. A nickel weighs 5 grams, and the empty piggy bank weighs 1,050 grams. What is the total weight of the full piggy bank?
a. 1,110 grams
b. 1,200 grams
c. 2,250 grams
d. 2,200 grams

32. Last year, the New York City area received approximately $27\frac{3}{4}$ inches of snow. The Denver area received approximately 3 times as much snow as New York City. How much snow fell in Denver?
a. 60 inches
b. $27\frac{1}{4}$ inches
c. $9\frac{1}{4}$ inches
d. $83\frac{1}{4}$ inches

33. If $-3(x+4) \geq x+8$, what is the value of x?
   a. $x = 4$
   b. $x \geq 2$
   c. $x \geq -5$
   d. $x \leq -5$

34. Karen gets paid a weekly salary and a commission for every sale that she makes. The table below shows the number of sales and her pay for different weeks.

Sales	2	7	4	8
Pay	\$380	\$580	\$460	\$620

Which of the following equations represents Karen's weekly pay?
   a. $y = 90x + 200$
   b. $y = 90x - 200$
   c. $y = 40x + 300$
   d. $y = 40x - 300$

35. The square and circle have the same center. The circle has a radius of r. What is the area of the shaded region?

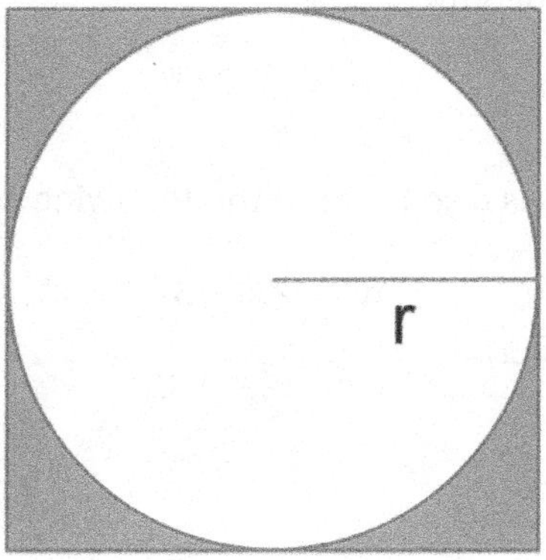

   a. $r^2 - \pi r^2$
   b. $4r^2 - 2\pi r$
   c. $(4-\pi)r^2$
   d. $(\pi - 1)r^2$

36. The graph shows the position of a car over a 10-second time interval. Which of the following is the correct interpretation of the graph for the interval 1 to 3 seconds?

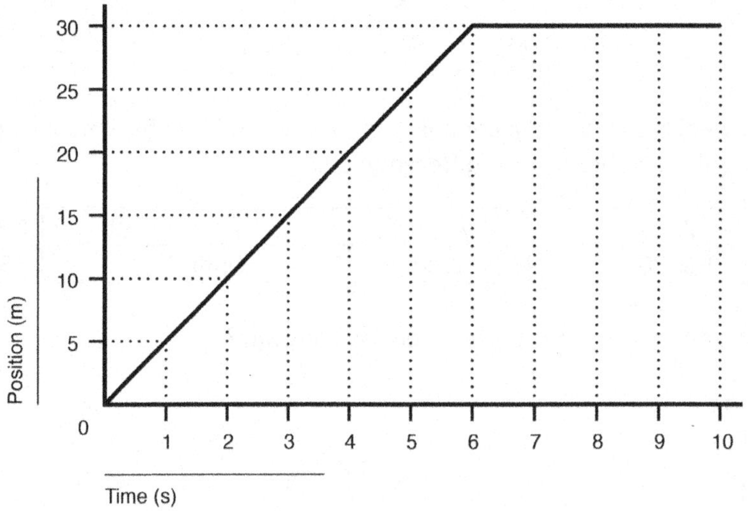

a. The car remains in the same position.
b. The car is traveling at a speed of 5 m/s.
c. The car is traveling up a hill.
d. The car is traveling at 5 mph.

37. Which of the ordered pairs below is a solution to the following system of inequalities?

$$y > 2x - 3$$

$$y < -4x + 8$$

a. $(4,5)$
b. $(-3,-2)$
c. $(3,-1)$
d. $(5,2)$

38. Which equation best represents the scatter plot below?

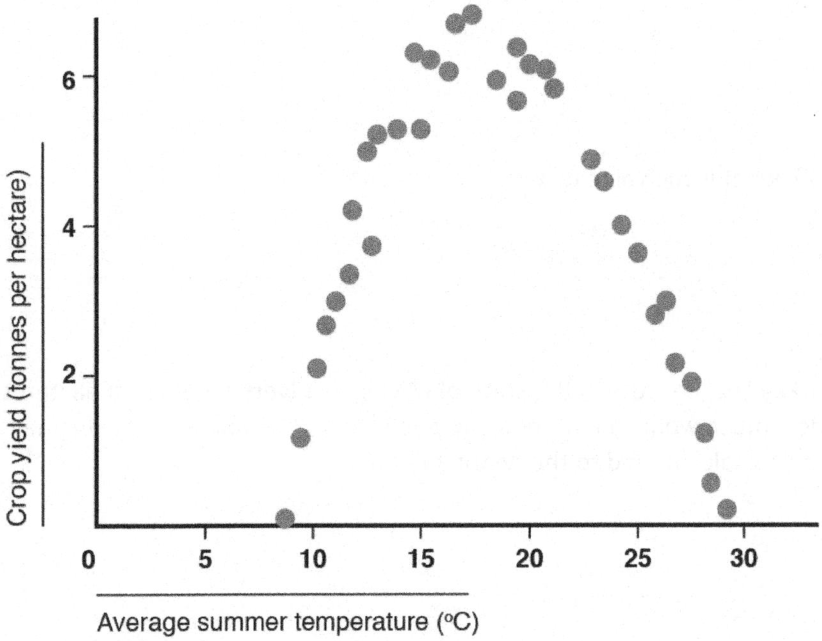

a. $y = 3x - 4$
b. $y = 2x^2 + 7x - 9$
c. $y = (3)(4^x)$
d. $y = -\frac{1}{14}x^2 + 2x - 8$

39. What is the solution to $9 \times 9 \div 9 + 9 - 9 \div 9$?
a. 0
b. 17
c. 81
d. 9

40. What is the solution to the radical equation $\sqrt[3]{2x + 11} + 9 = 12$?
a. −8
b. 8
c. 0
d. 12

41. The hospital has a nurse-to-patient ratio of 1: 25. If there is a maximum of 325 patients admitted at a time, how many nurses are there?
a. 13 nurses
b. 25 nurses
c. 325 nurses
d. 12 nurses

42. A hospital has a bed to room ratio of 2 to 1. If there are 145 rooms, how many beds are there?
   a. 145 beds
   b. 2 beds
   c. 90 beds
   d. 290 beds

43. If $\frac{2x}{5} - 1 = 59$, what is the value of x?
   a. 60
   b. 145
   c. 150
   d. 115

44. A National Hockey League store in the state of Michigan advertises 50% off all items. Sales tax in Michigan is 6%. How much would a hat originally priced at $32.99 and a jersey originally priced at $64.99 cost during this sale? Round to the nearest penny.
   a. $97.98
   b. $103.86
   c. $51.93
   d. $48.99

45. Store brand coffee beans cost $1.23 per pound. A local coffee bean roaster charges $1.98 per $1\frac{1}{2}$ pounds. How much more would 5 pounds from the local roaster cost than 5 pounds of the store brand?
   a. $0.55
   b. $1.55
   c. $1.45
   d. $0.45

46. Paint Inc. charges $2,000 for painting the first 1,800 feet of trim on a house and $1.00 per foot for each foot after. How much would it cost to paint a house with 3125 feet of trim?
   a. $3,125
   b. $2,000
   c. $5,125
   d. $3,325

No Calculator Questions

47. A bucket can hold 11.4 liters of water. A kiddie pool needs 35 gallons of water to be full. How many times will the bucket need to be filled to fill the kiddie pool?
   a. 12
   b. 35
   c. 11
   d. 45

48. In Jim's school, there are 3 girls for every 2 boys. There are 650 students in total. Using this information, how many students are girls?

a. 260
b. 130
c. 65
d. 390

49. What is the volume of a pyramid, with a square base whose side is 6 inches, and the height is 9 inches?

a. 324 in^3
b. 72 in^3
c. 108 in^3
d. 18 in^3

50. Convert $\frac{2}{9}$ to a percentage.

a. 22%
b. 4.5%
c. 450%
d. 0.22%

51. What is the volume of a cone, in terms of π, with a radius of 10 centimeters and height of 12 centimeters?

a. 400 cm^3
b. 200 cm^3
c. 120 cm^3
d. 140 cm^3

52. What is 3 out of 8 expressed as a percent?

a. 37.5%
b. 37%
c. 26.7%
d. 2.67%

53. The area of a given rectangle is 24 square centimeters. If the measure of each side is multiplied by 3, what is the area of the new figure?

a. 48 cm^2
b. 72 cm^2
c. 216 cm^2
d. $13{,}824 \text{ cm}^2$

54. If $4x - 3 = 5$, what is the value of x?

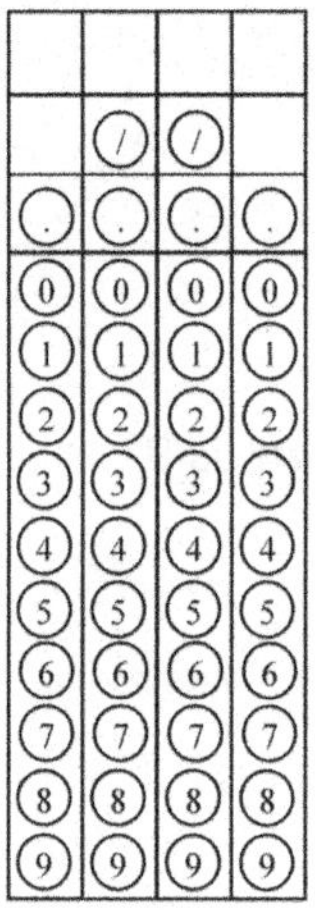

55. What is $4 \times 7 + (25 - 21)^2 \div 2$?

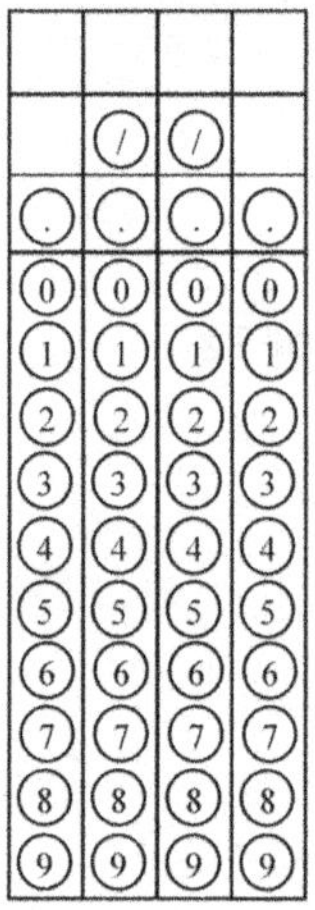

56. What is the solution to the following expression?

$$\left(\sqrt{36} \times \sqrt{16}\right) - 3^2$$

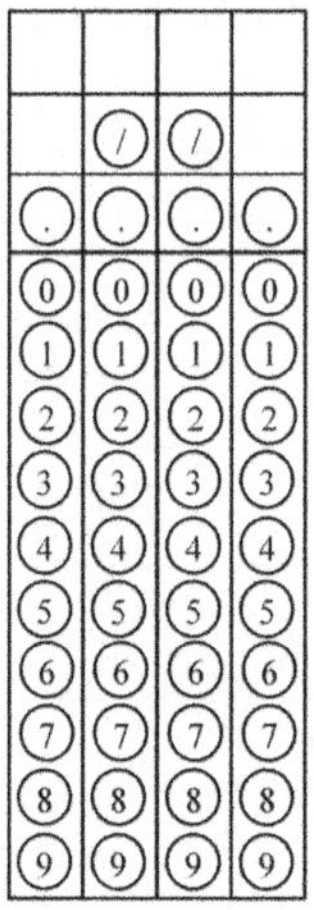

57. What is the overall median of Dwayne's current test scores: 78, 92, 83, 97?

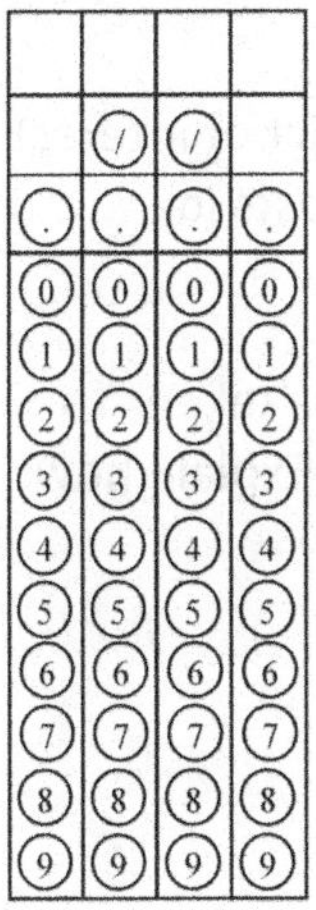

58. The total perimeter of a rectangle is 36 cm. If the length is 12 cm, what is the width?

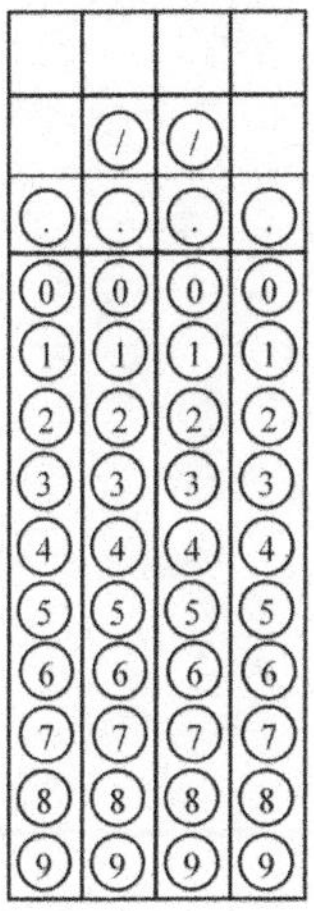

Essay Prompt

> For-profit institutions of learning should be illegal because they suffer from a conflict of interest between the student receiving the best education and the institution minimizing costs in providing instruction and other services to remain profitable.

Write a response in support or nonsupport of the statement in regard to the position that is taken. To support your stance, evaluate how your position may or may not be true to the argument. Explain how you've come to your position and provide examples in support of your argument.

The following pages are provided for writing your essay.

Answer Explanations #1

Reading Test

1. C: There is a tone of excitement throughout the passage; this tone is conveyed through the narrator's account of the life-changing discovery of electricity. Mentions of tunnels and darkness could evoke a tone of dreariness, but that represents the past. This passage is looking forward to what the future will hold with this new form of light, making Choice *A* incorrect. Choice *B* is incorrect because the narrator does not feel unnerved when about the idea of confessing their crime to the Council. This passage does not use humor or lightheartedness, making Choice *D* incorrect.

2. A: Evidence for the correct answer can be found here: "They would see nothing, save our crime of working alone, and they would destroy us and our light." In this society, things must be done as a collective, not individually. The narrator hopes to join the Home of the Scholars, and wants their input and work space, which makes Choice *B* incorrect. Street sweeping is the narrator's role but it's not what makes their discovery a crime. That is why Choice *C* is incorrect. Besides the word *Unmentionable*, nothing indicates that remainders from former times are off-limits, making Choice *D* incorrect.

3. D: The sentence uses personification, whereby darkness is given a human quality—being able to swallow. There are no comparison being made, making metaphor, Choice *A,* incorrect. Synecdoche, which is a device that uses a part to represent a whole or vice versa is not present, making Choice *B* incorrect. The sentence has no interjected scenes from a previous point in the narrative, making flashback, Choice *C,* incorrect.

4. A: Multiple times the narrator calls their discovery "the power of the sky" which is an allusion to the sun. For example, in the third paragraph, the narrator reports, "we finished building a strange thing...a box of glass, devised to give forth the power of the sky of greater strength than we had ever achieved before." Candles were a source of light before this discovery, making Choice *B* incorrect. Prison represents the darkness, not the light, making Choice *C* incorrect. The narrator does feel that their invention is a part of their body, the way blood runs through their veins, but does not directly equate to their overall invention of electricity. This makes Choice *D* incorrect.

5. B: The narrator is confident their crime will be forgiven by the World Council of Scholars, because their "gift is greater than [their] transgression." The passage does not address the money their invention will save the City, making Choice *A* incorrect. It is not the apology alone that will grant the narrator forgiveness, making Choice *C* incorrect. By the end, the narrator does feel a strong connection to their invention, but the wires are only metaphorically part of their body, and the wires are not the reason the narrator believes they'll be forgiven. This makes Choice *D* incorrect.

6. D: *Transgression* most closely means *offense* in paragraph eight. Obedience, or following the rules, is the opposite of transgression, making Choice *A* incorrect. The word *transgression* has a moral or legal connotation that is lacking in the more abstract word *disruption*, making Choice *B* incorrect. Confession, or admitting to an offense, is what the narrator is going to do as a result of their transgression, making Choice *D* incorrect.

7. B: Personification is a literary device in which human characteristics are attributed to something nonhuman. So, when the narrator says "darkness swallowed us," they give a human characteristic (swallowing) to something nonhuman (darkness). Choice *A* is incorrect because it is just an expression used to indicate there are a lot of thoughts swirling around in the narrator's head. Choice *C* is refers to the human narrator's head and hands; since the narrator is a person, they cannot be personified. Choice *D* is incorrect because it is a thought that trails off using ellipsis, not personification, to indicate that the narrator has changed their opinion on the value of their body.

8. C: The narrator wants to keep their invention a secret until they are able to confess everything to the World Council of Scholars. Paragraph seven lists the resources that are necessary to advance the discovery. Those include work rooms, which makes Choice *A* incorrect. The narrator also wants help and wisdom from the brother Scholars, making Choice *B* incorrect. The narrator feels that they will need to focus all their time on their discovery, which means they will need to stop sweeping the streets, leaving Choice *D* incorrect.

9. A: Moving from street sweeper to the Home of the Scholars will be an advancement in society. This is apparent because the narrator currently lives in a tunnel with no electricity, while the wisest in all the lands are elected to the World Council of Scholars. Choice *B* is incorrect because the text indicates that being a Scholar is more desirable than being a street sweeper, so their status will not remain the same. The Council of Vocations decides what jobs people will have, and would be the group to assign the narrator to the House of Scholars. This makes Choice *C* incorrect. The narrator is not concerned with the negative consequences of their confession and is confident they will be propelled to Scholar status. This is why Choice *D* is incorrect.

10. D: The last paragraph reveals the shift in how the narrator suddenly cares about their body for the first time after they discover electricity. The passage cuts off before the author shares whether the transgression is forgiven, making Choice *A* incorrect. The plan is to share the gift of electricity with all the Cities, but the reader does not know if that plan will come to fruition. This makes Choice *B* incorrect. It's likely that electricity will make all tasks, especially those that happen at night, easier. But Choice *C* is incorrect because those benefits are not discussed in this passage.

11. C: Jimmy Carter talks about how Americans are losing confidence in their government, their ability to self-govern, and democracy. He basically says America has lost its way and must find it again. That will be hard and will require facing the truth. In the last paragraph, he says that we need to change course and restore confidence and faith. Choice *A* is incorrect because Carter believes that faith can be restored, meaning there is hope for the future. Choice *B* only addresses part of the speech, so it is not the best answer. While Carter does reference other people in the Western world, that is irrelevant to the underlying message, making Choice *D* incorrect.

12. B: Worshiping self-indulgence and consumption is cited as a symptom of the crisis of the American spirit. Additionally, Choices *C* and *D* are both listed in the third paragraph as examples of symptoms of the crisis of the American spirit, which makes them incorrect answers. Another symptom is that the majority of people believe the next five years will be worse than the last five. However, Choice *B* is wrong. Carter says, "there is a growing disrespect for government and for churches and for schools, the news media, and other institutions." Therefore, respect isn't growing, *disrespect* is,

13. B: Using context clues from the passage, a reader can infer that the saying *sound as a dollar* means something is dependable and reliable. *Solid as a rock* is another phrase that means dependability and reliability. *Hands down* refers to intensity or completeness; something that is "the best value, hands down," is absolutely the best value. The phrase *hands down* does not speak to dependability, making

Choice *A* incorrect. Ease, not reliability, is the meaning behind the phrase *piece of cake*. This makes Choice *C* incorrect. Choice *D* is incorrect because getting something fair and square means it was earned honestly.

14. C: The goal of Carter's speech is to sound relatable and capable of understanding of Americans' frustration with government. Carter emphasizes his empathy when he says, "Often you see paralysis and stagnation and drift. You don't like it, and neither do I. What can we do?" Nothing in his speech would indicate he is unqualified for the role of president, making Choice *A* incorrect. Carter may be desperate to restore faith and confidence in Americans, but not desperate for their acceptance. This makes Choice *B* incorrect. Choice *D* is incorrect because Jimmy Carter fully believes in democracy and is encouraging Americans to believe in it.

15. D: Out of context, Washington, D.C. being an island could mean many things. The meaning of the metaphor can be found in the sentences that precede and follow it, which mention isolation and a wide gap between the government and its citizens. Choice *A* is wrong because Carter is not mentioning an island to describe a vacation. This metaphor does not allude to resource, so Choice *B* is incorrect. Choice *C* implies that Americans have access to the "island" of government, but the real meaning is the opposite, that government has become unresponsive to citizens. Therefore, Choice *C* is incorrect.

16. B: According to Carter, these examples are the shocks and tragedies that have gradually caused Americans to lose their faith and confidence in government and other institutions such as schools and media. While there are references to previous presidents, it is not Carter's intention to grade their time in office, making Choice *A* incorrect. The future is not mentioned in paragraphs six and seven, rendering Choice *C* incorrect. President Carter believes Americans have very reasonable expectations, even when they're not being met. For that reason, Choice *D* is incorrect.

17. C: It is in paragraph eight that Carter mentions *politics as usual,* and then describes it in detail in paragraph nine. He does it at the same time he is describing the negative aspects of politics, like false claims, evasiveness, inactivity, and a lack of support. Carter does not mention how decisions affect any of the branches of government, making Choice *A* wrong. Choice *B* is incorrect because there is no textual evidence to support Carter's concern with how political language reads to the average American. According to Carter, a balanced and fair approach that demands sacrifice is what politics should look like, but is rarely, if ever, the case. This is what makes Choice *D* incorrect.

18. A: Stagnation is a lack of movement; in this context, it is a lack of forward movement or progress toward ideals. Context clues like "incapable of action" and "paralysis" help define stagnation. *Confusion* would be a better word for lack of understanding, which makes Choice *B* incorrect. *Ignorance* would be a better word for lack of knowledge, making Choice *C* incorrect. A lack of empathy would be apathy, not stagnation, making Choice *D* wrong as well.

19. C: President Carter begins by addressing the events that have led to the crisis of confidence in America, such as the murder of Martin Luther King Jr. and the inflation and collapse of the American dollar. The last paragraph offers a message of hope for the future, ending in an optimistic tone. Since this is a presidential speech, the entire speech will be formal, making Choice *A* incorrect. The speech remains elevated and the last paragraph offers hope for the future, the opposite of unremarkable. This makes Choice *B* incorrect. Since President Carter wants to be relatable and empathetic, he avoids sounding preachy, which is why Choice *D* is wrong.

20. C: In the final paragraph, Carter answers the question of what to do; he gives a plan to face the truth and restore faith. There are wounds from the past, but Carter does not suggest healing them as a solution to the crisis. This makes Choice *A* incorrect. Choice *B* is incorrect because Carter admits special interest groups are detrimental to running a smooth government but does not propose removing them to mend the crisis. Close-knit communities are a healthy side effect of, not the solution to, restoring faith and confidence in America. This is why Choice *D* is incorrect.

21. A: Truman presented his argument to Congress in order to persuade it to take action to support Greece and Turkey. Truman does not rely on descriptive language, so Choice *B* is not accurate. This speech did not intend to entertain listeners, since there are no attempts at humor or amusement, making Choice *C* incorrect. This speech does analyze a situation, but analysis is not the main purpose of the speech, making Choice *D* wrong.

22. D: When Truman says, "I believe...I believe...I believe...," he means the United States is obligated to take care of other countries in need. Truman is concerned Greece and Turkey will fall under the sway of a small number of armed insurgents. Choice *A* is wrong because there is not any information in the passage that deals with the economic status of Greece and Turkey Choice *B* is incorrect because Truman doesn't list the countries that are in the United Nations. The passage does not describe anything about whether Greece nor Turkey is under a dictatorship, so we cannot infer this information from what is provided. This makes Choice *C* incorrect.

23. C: In the first way of life, countries ruled by a majority, with representative government, free elections, and freedom of speech. In the second way of life, the will of a small number of people is forcibly imposed upon the majority. These countries are characterized by terror and oppression. Choice *A* is wrong because both parts of the sentence describe the first way of life. Choice *B* is wrong because both qualities describe the second way of life. Choice *D* is incorrect because it is the opposite of what Truman describes; the first part describes the second way of life, and vice versa.

24. B: The word *subterfuges* could be replaced with *tricky deceptions* and the sentence would retain the same meaning. This can be gathered from nearby words like *violation*, *coercion*, and *infiltration*. *Helpful pieces of intel* would be information of military or political value, not deceit, which makes Choice *A* wrong. Political infiltration may be a time-consuming activity, but it does not address the deception of subterfuge. This leaves Choice *C* incorrect. The prefix "sub-" in the word *subterfuge* does mean "under," but it would only mean underground in a word like *subterranean*. This makes Choice *D* wrong.

25. A: President Truman argues that without interference from the United States, Greece will inevitably be oppressed by a small number of people who take up arms against the majority of the people. That will cause a ripple through Turkey, the entire Middle East, and beyond. Nothing indicates that the United Nations would step in, nor is it the responsibility of the UN to provide relief funds. This makes Choice *B* incorrect. The Truman Doctrine is a plan of preventative measures, to help Greece and Turkey recover from war. There is not a logical timeline where Truman's plan is not approved by Congress, Greece falls under the control of an armed minority, and then the United States retracts and sends hundreds of millions of dollars to Greece. This makes Choice *C* invalid. Choice *D* is incorrect because the only mention of Greece disappearing was in reference to its status as a free state.

26. C: Truman's warning about what will happen if the United States fails to help Greece and Turkey should leave his listeners with a sense of concern. Congress would feel disgusted if Truman described something revolting. This is why Choice *A* is incorrect. Choice *B* is incorrect because an audience would feel astonishment if Truman shared surprising new information. Choice *D* is not the best option because there are other sentences from the speech that would be more likely to evoke an eagerness to help (e.g., "This is a serious course upon which we embark.").

27. B: Nowhere does Truman mention overhauling the governments of Greece and Turkey. He actually believes Greece and Turkey can help themselves when they are provided with ample funds and resources. Choices *A, C,* and *D* can all be found directly in paragraphs fourteen, fifteen, and sixteen, which is what makes them incorrect answers.

28. C: President Truman felt the United States was the sole entity responsible for helping free people resisting a takeover from armed aggressors or outside threats. Truman does not allude to the possibility of another country stepping in, which is why Choice *A* is doubtful and incorrect. Since Greece and Turkey will both be in similar states of turmoil it is unlikely they will be of any help to one another. This makes Choice *B* wrong. It is not the responsibility of the United Nations to intervene in these matters, and cannot force the United States to send funds to foreign countries, which renders Choice *D* incorrect.

29. D: The use of the phrase "immediate and resolute action" conveys a sense of urgency. Choice *A* is about the cost of safeguarding freedom; it does not refer to time, which makes it incorrect. Choice *B* focuses on how the world is always changing, but it does not mention time, making it wrong as well. Choice *C* is incorrect because while it does speak to the gravity of the situation, it does not attest to the time-sensitive nature of the matter.

30. A: The vulnerability Greece and Turkey is the problem, and the proposed three-step process that involves sharing funds and resources is the solution. Since there is only one date listed and events are not structured in a timeline, this speech is not organized chronologically. That makes Choice *B* incorrect. Other than a quick comparison between two ways of life, Truman's speech does not rely on comparing and contrasting, making Choice *C* incorrect. Categorical structure usually involves the classification of equally important groups or subgroups, which is not observed here, making Choice *D* incorrect.

31. B: Although these passages are written in completely different styles, they're both centered around the role insects play in pollination. Choice *A* is incorrect because only the second article breaks down the role of the three different sets of legs. The first article is not written scientifically, making Choice *C* wrong. Only the first passage goes into depth about nectar and the signals plants use to communicate to bees. This is why Choice *D* is not the best answer.

32. C: The passage by Jean-Henri Fabre was written for a children's storybook, which is why he uses whimsical language. Personifying both the bee and the flower and using terms like "signboard," "enter here," and "keyhole" evoke the mood of a fairytale or fable. Pedantic word choice suggests a pompous scholarly paper. This passage is anything but pompous and scholarly, making Choice *A* incorrect. This passage is light-hearted, while something emotional usually plays on deep or dark emotions. This is why Choice *B* is incorrect. Choice *D* is incorrect because, despite whimsical storytelling, the message and information are clear, not ambiguous.

33. D: The best substitution for the word *posterior* is *rear*. This answer can be drawn from realizing posterior legs means the opposite of "forward appendages." Also the prefix *post-* means behind or after. While the word *strongest* fits in the sentence nicely, nothing implies that that particular set of legs is the strongest. This makes Choice *A* incorrect. *Anterior*, meaning front, is actually the antonym for the word *posterior*, so Choice *B* is wrong. *Ambulatory* is a word that could describe any pair of functioning legs and does not differentiate the hind legs from the front or middle, which makes Choice *C* incorrect.

34. D: The scientists in the second passage use observation to conduct research on honeybees. This is set up at the beginning of the passage when the author mentions continuous observation and instantaneous photos. The author does not use the art of storytelling to reinforce their research, making the word *anecdotal*, Choice *A,* wrong. The researcher collected data by observing the pollination process between bees and sweet corn, none of which was hypothetical. This makes Choice *B* incorrect. Choice *C* is incorrect because the researchers did not conduct tests or introduce variables, meaning the evidence was merely observational, not experimental.

35. A: The character believes that the snapdragon's yellow spot is evidence that Providence or some higher power has designed nature. When a bee lands on the yellow spot of a closed snapdragon, the flower opens up so the bee can access the nectar and pollen. The preceding sentence confirms that the character does not believe that nature happens by chance, making Choice *B* incorrect. The character makes no claim that snapdragons are more beautiful than any other plant. This makes Choice *C* wrong. This character's speech continuously highlights the intentional behaviors between flowers and bees, so Choice *D* is incorrect.

36. C: The triple feast, introduced in the first paragraph of the first passage, has three beneficiaries: trees, insects, and humans. Pollen is part of the transaction between these three, but pollen not directly benefit, which is why Choices *A, B,* and *D* are incorrect.

37. B: When bees interact with the anthers of the flowers, the hairs of their bodies get covered in pollen. The bee's legs collect the pollen from all over the body and transfer it back toward the pollen baskets, also known as the corbiculae. Choice *B* best explains the order of the pollen manipulation process. Choices *A, C,* and *D* incorrectly describe (either by order or parts) the way bees move pollen across their bodies.

38. C: Synonyms are two words that have the same meaning. The second-to-last paragraph is where the reader learns that *corbiculae* is another term for pollen baskets. Nectar is what bees find inside the flowers, and honey is a result of what bees do with the nectar. This is why Choice *A* is incorrect. Stamen and stigma are both parts of the anatomy of a flower but serve different purposes, which makes Choice *B* incorrect. Choice *D* is wrong because the thorax is adjacent to the abdomen; it is not the same part of the bee's body.

39. D: In a false dichotomy, also known as an either-or fallacy, only two alternative points are presented, even though other alternative points are available. The author is indirectly saying that if someone does not understand the relationship between the bee and the snapdragon, they are an idiot. That is a rather harsh two-option opinion. A slippery slope fallacy is when someone claims that a series of small events will necessarily result in one major bad event, which is not presented here, making Choice *A* incorrect. Choice *B,* ad hominem, is incorrect because the author does not attack another person's character. There are no distractions or misleading clues that would indicate a red herring fallacy, making Choice *C* wrong.

40. A: The author means the flower's petals open up slowly like a person yawning. "To open" or "to gape" is one of the meanings of the verb "yawn." Choice *B* is incorrect because it focuses on the sleepiness of yawning, not the motion. Choice *C* is wrong because it inaccurately parallels how yawning allows people to receive more oxygen to their brains. There is no evidence to indicate the flower is having issues with regulation or time of day, making Choice *D* erroneous.

41. D: The researchers chose sweet corn because sweet corn produces an abundance of pollen, making it easier to observe. The passage does not mention that bees are more attracted to sweeter flowers or that sweet corn is particularly sweet to bees. This makes Choice *A* incorrect. Sweet corn was used because of its abundance of pollen, not its abundance of itself, making Choice *B* incorrect. While the article does focus on bees, it does not address other pollinators, leaving Choice *C* incorrect.

42. B: Although written in very different ways, both passages describe a mutually beneficial relationship between bees and flowers when it comes to pollination. Based on the level of detail provided, it is safe to say that the behavior of honeybees and pollen collection is well studied, making Choice *A* incorrect. Even though both passages focus their attention on honeybees, neither one states that bees are superior pollinators, making Choice *C* wrong. Both authors feel very strongly that the act of pollination is purposeful and intentional, and they feel that nothing can be attributed to randomness. This is what makes Choice *D* incorrect.

43. C: *Solution and Emulsions* is not just the correct answer, it is the exact title of the passage from *Common Science*. The title *Solutions and Emulsions* fully covers what this excerpt is about. Choice *A* is incorrect because it too narrowly focuses on the aspect of cleaning when that is only a side benefit to learning about solutions and emulsions. Choice *B* is wrong because this passage did not contain experiments about any topic other than solutions and emulsions. Choice *D* is overly focused on the opening and doesn't account for the rest of the passage, making it incorrect.

44. A: The author conjures up a world where there is an imaginary switchboard that can turn off the law of solutions, runs through an example where all saltwater fish die, and then decides the switchboard should be left alone. This is a comedic hypothetical to open the topic of solutions and emulsions. There is not an element of shock or surprise, making Choice *B* incorrect. Despite the fiction, all the information presented was logical and complete, which leaves Choice *C* incorrect. Since the author tells the reader exactly what happens when the Solutions switch is turned off, there is no element of suspense, making Choice *D* incorrect.

45. B: All of the rhetorical questions are designed to make the reader think about the results and effects of the different experiments, eventually leading them to draw their own conclusions. Science is made up of facts, not opinions, so Choice *A* is incorrect. These rhetorical questions have a greater purpose than to just ensure the readers are following along. This makes Choice *C* incorrect. There is an assumption the reader is already invested in doing the experiments and would not need prodding from rhetorical questions, which is why Choice *D* is wrong.

46. D: Evidence for this answer can be derived from the example of milk and its emulsion tendencies. Little droplets of butter and fat are suspended in milk and are not completely dissolved like sugar would be in water when making simple syrup. Since sugar can completely dissolve into water, simple syrup is a solution. Choice *A* is incorrect because solutions are actually more likely to be clear. Both emulsions and solutions can be drinkable or non-drinkable, just depends on what components are being used. This makes Choice *B* incorrect. Choice *C* is erroneous because emulsions and solutions do not naturally have lower or higher temperatures.

47. B: After the experimenter is asked to add more salt than can be dissolved and then to use a Bunsen burner to heat the test tube, a logical result would be that the heat is an agent to dissolve the salt more readily. Choice *A* is the opposite of what result should be expected. The rhetorical question that follows the instructions implies that the salt will not impede the heating element, making Choice *C* incorrect. While the author does mention washing dishes, using the saltwater solution as soap is an inaccurate connection, leaving Choice *D* incorrect.

48. A: The passage mentions briefly that emulsions can act as solutions if their suspended droplets are so small they can't be identified. Heating can help dissolve more solute into solvent but is not the reason emulsions can act like solutions, making Choice *B* incorrect. Shaking and stirring does not change the smallest size droplets can be inside an emulsion, rendering Choice *C* incorrect. Because the passage directly says "But the droplets may be so small that an emulsion acts almost exactly like a solution," Choice *D* cannot be correct.

49. B: The last paragraph offers an analogy to better explain the results of Experiment 82. When a pail of pebbles is poured into a pail of apples, the pebbles will fill in the empty spaces between the apples. Likewise, when water is poured into alcohol, the water molecules will rest between the molecules of alcohol, meaning the combined liquids of equal measure do not quite double in size. Choice *A* and *C* both get the analogy backwards. "Pebbles are to apples" is a statement of how they relate; the pebbles fill the spaces between the apples. The second half should therefore be "as water is to alcohol." Therefore Choice *A* is incorrect. Choice *C* also incorrectly equates the apples to water molecules and the pebbles to alcohol molecules. Choice *D* is incorrect because the scenario of the pebbles and the apples is meant to explain emulsion; the apples and pebbles are not in solution, and neither are the alcohol and the water.

50. D: Even if you do not know that denatured means the alcohol has been altered in some fashion, there are context clues that imply the solution will not be pure due to the denatured substances. There is no evidence to indicate denatured alcohol is dangerous or unfit for a laboratory, making Choice *A* wrong. Choice *B* is incorrect because the author wrote an entire paragraph differentiating denatured alcohol from regular alcohol. And there is no amount of heating that will cause the denatured components to dissolve, which is what makes Choice *C* incorrect.

51. C: The apple and pebble analogy in the last paragraph explains the purpose of Experiment 82. Because the water molecules will fill the gaps between the larger alcohol molecules, it can be deduced that the mixture will measure less than two inches, which is the combined separate measurements of water and alcohol. The experiment would not prove anything if the total height measured exactly two inches, making Choice *A* incorrect. Nothing in the passage indicates the alcohol or water would expand when combined, leaving Choice *B* incorrect. There is enough surrounding evidence to make a reasonable prediction about the result of Experiment 82, which makes Choice *D* wrong.

52. C: When two people are described as oil and water it means they do not mix well or they are incompatible. This passage explains that oil and water can only be an emulsion because the two substances can never fully combine into a homogenous solution. The idiom *comparing apples to oranges* means you are comparing two unlike things, which is not explained in this passage. That makes Choice *A* incorrect. When someone is *in hot water* it means they are in trouble, which is not described in this passage, making Choice *B* wrong. When someone says *do not cry over spilled milk*, they mean advising someone not be upset over something that happened in the past and cannot be change. Choice *D* is incorrect because we learned that milk is an emulsion, but there was no advice about what to do when it is spilled.

Writing and Language Test

1. C: Choice *C* correctly uses *from* to describe the fact that dogs are related to wolves. The word *through* is incorrectly used here, so Choice *A* is incorrect. Choice *B* does not make sense. Choice *D* unnecessarily changes the verb tense in addition to incorrectly using *through*.

2. B: Choice *B* is correct because the Oxford comma is applied, clearly separating the specific terms. Choice *A* lacks this clarity. Choice *C* is correct but too wordy since commas can be easily applied. Choice *D* doesn't flow with the sentence's structure.

3. D: Choice *D* correctly uses the question mark and includes the verb, fixing the sentence's main issues. Thus, Choice *A* is incorrect because questions do not end with periods. Choice *B,* although correctly written, changes the meaning of the original sentence. Choice *C* is incorrect because it completely changes the direction of the sentence, disrupts the flow of the paragraph, and lacks the crucial question mark.

4. A: Choice *A* is correct since there are no errors in the sentence. Choices *B* and *C* both have extraneous commas, disrupting the flow of the sentence. Choice *D* unnecessarily rearranges the sentence.

5. D: Choice *D* is correct because the commas serve to distinguish that *artificial selection* is just another term for *selective breeding* before the sentence continues. The structure is preserved, and the sentence can flow with more clarity. Choice *A* is incorrect because the sentence needs commas to avoid being a run-on. Choice *B* is close but still lacks the required comma after *selection*, so this is incorrect. Choice *C* is incorrect because the comma to set off the aside should be placed after *breeding* instead of *called*.

6. B: Choice *B* is correct because the sentence is talking about a continuing process. Therefore, the best modification is to add the word *to* in front of *increase*. Choice *A* is incorrect because this modifier is missing. Choice *C* is incorrect because, with the additional comma, the present tense of *increase* is inappropriate. Choice *D* makes more sense, but the tense is still not the best to use.

7. A: Choice *B* is incorrect because it adds an unnecessary comma. Choice *C* is incorrect because *advantage* should not be plural in this sentence unless the singular article *an* is removed. Choice *D* is very tempting. Although this would make the sentence more concise, it leaves out critical information, which makes it incorrect.

8. C: Choice *C* correctly uses *on to*, describing the way genes are passed generationally. The use of *into* is inappropriate for this context, which makes Choice *A* incorrect. Choice *B* is close, but *onto* refers to something being placed on a surface. Choice *D* doesn't make logical sense.

9. D: Choice *D* is correct, since only proper names should be capitalized. Because "bloodhound" is not a proper name, Choice *A* is incorrect. Only the proper nouns within breed names need to be capitalized, such as a German shepherd. In terms of punctuation, only one comma after example is needed, so Choices *B* and *C* are incorrect.

10. D: Choice *D* is the correct answer because *rather* acts as an interrupting word here and thus should be separated by commas. Choices *B* and *C* use commas incorrectly, breaking the flow of the sentence.

11. A: Choice *B* incorrectly changes *awake* to *awakened*. Choice *C* adds unnecessary commas. Choice *D* incorrectly changes *turn* to *turns*.

12. A: In Choice *A,* the dependent clause "Sometimes in particularly dull seminars" is seamlessly attached with a single comma after *seminars*. Choice *B* contains too many commas. Choice *C* does not correctly combine the dependent clause with the independent clause. Choice *D* introduces too many unnecessary commas.

13. D: Choice *D* rearranges the sentence to be more direct and straightforward, so it is correct. Choice *A* needs a comma after *on*. Choice *B* introduces unnecessary commas. Choice *C* creates an incomplete sentence, since "Because I wasn't invested in what was going on" is a dependent clause.

14. C: This revision improves the awkward wording of the original. Choice *B* adds an unnecessary comma and period. Choice *D* leaves out the required comma after the word another.

15. B: Choice *B* correctly adds a comma after the word person. Choice *C* inserts a semicolon where a comma is needed. Choice *D* adds a period to the middle of the sentence.

16. D: This sentence, though short, is a complete sentence. The only thing the sentence needs is an em dash after *easy*. In this sentence, the em dash works to add emphasis to the word *easy* and also acts in place of a colon, but in a less formal way. Therefore, Choice *D* is correct. Choices *A* and *B* lack the crucial comma, while Choice *C* unnecessarily breaks the sentence apart.

17. C: Choice *C* successfully fixes the construction of the sentence, changing *drawing* into *to draw*. Keeping the original sentence disrupts the flow, so Choice *A* is incorrect. Choice *B*'s use of *which* offsets the whole sentence. Choice *D* is incorrect because it unnecessarily expands the sentence content and makes it more confusing.

18. B: Choice *B* fixes the homophone issue. Because the author is talking about people, *their* must be used instead of *there*. This revision also appropriately uses the Oxford comma, separating and distinguishing *lives, world, and future*. Choice *A* uses the wrong homophone and is missing commas. Choice *C* incorrectly changes applies to applied, fails to change there to their, and fails to add the necessary punctuation. Choice *D* incorrectly adds a comma between the subject (Discussions that make people think about the content and how it applies to their lives, world, and future) and the predicate (are key).

19. C: Choice *C* is correct because it fixes the core issue with this sentence: the singular has does not agree with the plural *scientists*. Choices *B* and *D* add unnecessary commas.

20. D: Choice *D* correctly conveys the writer's intention of asking if early perceptions of dinosaurs still influence people. Choice *A* does not make sense the way it is worded. Choice *B* is better, but *how* doesn't make sense in context, because the author doesn't specifically explore how early perceptions influence understanding. Choice *C* adds unnecessary commas.

21. A: Choice *B* incorrectly replaces simply with simple and adds an unnecessary comma. Choice *C* uses a comma where a semicolon is needed. Choice *D* adds an unnecessary comma.

22. B: Choice *B* is the strongest revision, as adding *to explore* is very effective in both shortening the sentence and maintaining, even enhancing, the point of the writer. Choice *A* is not technically incorrect, but it is overcomplicated. Choice *C* is a decent revision, but the sentence could still be more condensed and sharpened. Choice *D* fails to make the sentence more concise and inserts unnecessary commas.

23. D: Choice *D* correctly applies a semicolon to introduce a new line of thought while remaining in a single sentence. The comma after *however* is also appropriately placed. Choice *A* is a run-on sentence. Choice *B* is incorrect because the single comma is not enough to fix the sentence. Choice *C* adds commas around *uncertain* which are unnecessary.

24. B: Choice *B* changes *its,* which is possessive, to *it's,* which is a contraction of "it is." It also separates the two independent clauses with a comma and streamlines the sentence by eliminating *and*. Choices *C* and *D* are run-on sentences.

25. A: Choices *B* and *C* add unnecessary commas, while Choice *D* uses the possessive *its* instead of the contraction *it's*.

26. C: Choice *C* is correct because the phrase even likely is a parenthetical element, which must be set off by commas. Choice *D* does not set off the phrase with commas. Choice *A* omits the second required comma, and Choice *B* misplaces it.

27. D: Choice *D* strengthens the overall sentence structure while condensing the words. This makes the subject of the sentence, and the emphasis of the writer, much clearer to the reader. In Choice *A*, the language is choppy and over-complicated. Choice *B* is better but lacks the reference to a specific image of dinosaurs. Choice *C* introduces unnecessary commas.

28. B: Choices *A* and *D* use the wrong verb tense in the second clause. Choice *C* uses a comma where a semicolon is needed and rephrases the second clause awkwardly.

29. A: Choices *B* and *C* employ unnecessary semicolons and commas. Choice *D* would be an ideal revision, but it lacks the comma that would be needed after Ransom.

30. D: By reorganizing the sentence, the context becomes clearer with Choice *D*. Choice *A* has an awkward sentence structure and is less direct than Choice *D.* Choice *B* offers a revision that doesn't correspond well with the original sentence's intent. Choice *C* cuts out too much of the original content, losing the full meaning.

31. C: Choice *C* fixes the disagreement between the singular *this* and the plural *viewpoints*. Choice *A,* therefore, is incorrect. Choice *B* additionally introduces an unnecessary comma. In Choice *D, those* agrees with *viewpoints,* but neither agrees with *distinguishes*.

32. A: Choice *A* is direct and clear, without any punctuation errors. Choice *B* is well written but too wordy. Choice *C* adds an unnecessary comma. Choice *D* is also well written but much less concise than Choice *A.*

33. D: Choice *D* rearranges the sentence to improve clarity and impact, with *tempting* directly describing *idea*. On its own, Choice *A* has an unnecessary comma and a comma splice between two independent clauses. Choice *B* is better because it separates the clauses, but it keeps an unnecessary comma. Choice *C* is also an improvement but still has a comma splice.

34. B: Choice *B* is the best answer because it brings more clarity to the message of the sentence. Choice *A*, the original sentence, unnecessarily includes the word ultimately and leaves out a comma before the independent clause at the end. Choices *C* and *D* are awkward and wordy; therefore, neither is the best answer.

35. D: Changing the phrase *after this* to *then* makes the sentence less complicated and captures the writer's intent, making Choice *D* correct. Choice *A* is awkwardly constructed. Choices *B* and *C* misuse their commas and do not adequately improve the clarity.

36. B: By starting a new sentence, the run-on issue is eliminated, and a new line of reasoning can be seamlessly introduced, making Choice *B* correct. While Choice *C* fixes the run-on via a semicolon, a comma is still needed after *this*. Choice *D* contains a comma splice. The independent clauses must be separated by more than just a comma, even with the rearrangement of the second half of the sentence.

37. C: Choice *C* condenses the original sentence while being more active in communicating the emphasis on the changing times and media that the author is going for, so it is correct. Choice *A* is clunky because it lacks a comma after *today* to successfully transition into the second half of the sentence. Choice *B* inserts unnecessary commas. Choice *D* is a good revision of the underlined section, but not only does it not fully capture the original meaning, it also does not flow into the rest of the sentence.

38. B: Choice *B* makes it clear that "incorporating different styles and unique ways to approach the news" refers to the different types of media rather than to the stories. Choice *D* adds the missing comma before incorporating but doesn't clarify the meaning the way Choice *B* does. Choice *C* is incorrect because the period inserted after question makes the following sentence incomplete.

39. A: Choice *A* is correct: while the sentence seems long, it actually doesn't require any commas. The conjunction "that" successfully combines the two parts of the sentence without the need for additional punctuation. Choices *B* and *C* insert commas unnecessarily. Choice *D* alters the meaning of the original text by creating a new sentence, which is only a fragment.

40. C: Choice *C* correctly replaces for with to. Choice *B* is unnecessarily long and disrupts the original sentence structure. Choice *D* is also too wordy and lacks parallel structure.

41. D: Choice *D* correctly inserts a comma between the dependent and independent clauses. Choice *B* is grammatically incorrect, and Choice *C* adds a semicolon instead of a comma.

42. B: Choice *B* correctly separates the section into two sentences and changes the word order to make the second part clearer. Choice *A* is incorrect because it is a run-on. Choice *C* adds an extraneous comma, while Choice *D* makes the run-on worse and does not coincide with the overall structure of the sentence.

43. C: Choice *C* is the best answer because of how the commas are used to flank *in earnest*. This distinguishes the side thought (*in earnest*) from the rest of the sentence. Choice *A* needs punctuation. Choice *B* inserts a semicolon in a spot that doesn't make sense, resulting in a fragmented sentence and lost meaning. Choice *D* is unnecessarily repetitive and creates a run-on.

44. A: Choice *A* is correct because the sentence contains no errors. The comma after *bias* successfully links the two halves of the sentence, and the use of *it's* is correct as a contraction of *it is*. Choice *B* creates a sentence fragment, while Choice *C* creates a run-on. Choice *D* incorrectly changes *it's* to the possessive *its*.

45. D: Choice *D* correctly inserts a comma after However and makes over use one word. Choice *C* would create a grammatically incorrect sentence.

Math Test

Calculator Questions

1. B: To simplify this inequality, subtract 3 from both sides to get $-\frac{1}{2}x \geq -1$. Then, multiply both sides by -2 (remembering this flips the direction of the inequality) to get $x \leq 2$.

2. D: This problem involves a composition function, where one function is plugged into the other function. In this case, the $f(x)$ function is plugged into the $g(x)$ function for each x value. Since $f(x) = 2$, the composition equation becomes:

$$g(f(x)) = g(2) = (2)^3 - 3(2)^2 - 2(2) + 6$$

Simplifying the equation gives the answer:

$$g(f(x)) = 8 - 3(4) - 2(2) + 6$$

$$g(f(x)) = 8 - 12 - 4 + 6$$

$$g(f(x)) = -2$$

3. B: A factor of 36 is any number that can be divided into 36 and have no remainder.

$$36 = 36 \times 1, 18 \times 2, 9 \times 4, \text{and } 6 \times 6$$

Therefore, it has 7 unique factors: 36, 18, 9, 6, 4, 2, and 1.

4. D: A parabola of the form $y = \frac{1}{4f}x^2$ has a focus $(0, f)$.

Because $y = -9x^2$, set $-9 = \frac{1}{4f}$.

Solving this equation for f results in $f = -\frac{1}{36}$. Therefore, the coordinates of the focus are $\left(0, -\frac{1}{36}\right)$.

5. B: The volume of a cube is the length of the side cubed, and 3 inches cubed is 27 in^3.

Choice *A* is not the correct answer because that is 2×3 inches.

Choice *C* is not the correct answer because that is 3×3 inches, and Choice *D* is not the correct answer because there was no operation performed.

6. B: The volume of a rectangular prism is the $length \times width \times height$, and $3\ cm \times 5\ cm \times 11\ cm$ is 165 cm^3.

Choice *A* is not the correct answer because that is $3 \text{ cm} + 5 \text{ cm} + 11 \text{ cm}$. Choice *C* is not the correct answer because that is 15^2. Choice *D* is not the correct answer because that is $3 \text{ cm} \times 5 \text{ cm} \times 10 \text{ cm}$.

7. A: The volume of a cylinder is $\pi r^2 h$, and $\pi \times 5^2 \times 10$ is $250\,\pi\text{ in}^3$.

Choice *B* is not the correct answer because that is $5^2 \times 2\pi$. Choice *C* is not the correct answer since that is $5\text{ in} \times 10\pi$. Choice *D* is not the correct answer because that is $10^2 \times 2\text{ in}$.

8. D: This system of equations involves one quadratic function and one linear function, as seen from the degree of each equation. One way to solve this is through substitution.

Solving for y in the second equation yields:

$$y = x + 2$$

Plugging this equation in for the y of the quadratic equation yields:

$$x^2 - 2x + x + 2 = 8$$

Simplifying the equation, it becomes:

$$x^2 - x + 2 = 8$$

Setting this equal to zero and factoring, it becomes:

$$x^2 - x - 6 = 0 = (x - 3)(x + 2)$$

Solving these two factors for x gives the zeros:

$$x = 3, -2$$

To find the y-value for the point, each number can be plugged in to either original equation. Solving each one for y yields the points $(3, 5)$ and $(-2, 0)$.

9. B: The slope will be given by $\frac{1-0}{2-0} = \frac{1}{2}$.

The y-intercept will be 0, since it passes through the origin. Using slope-intercept form, the equation for this line is $y = \frac{1}{2}x$.

10. D: Recall the formula for area of a rectangle, area $=$ length $\times$ width. The answer must be in square inches, so all values must be converted to inches. Half of a foot is equal to 6 inches. Therefore, the area of the rectangle is equal to:

$$6\text{ in} \times \frac{11}{2}\text{in} = \frac{66}{2}\text{in}^2 = 33\text{ in}^2$$

11. B: The table shows values that are increasing exponentially. The differences between the inputs are the same, while the differences in the outputs are changing by a factor of 2. The values in the table can be modeled by the equation $f(x) = 2^x$.

12. B: For the first card drawn, the probability of a king being pulled is $\frac{4}{52}$. Since this card isn't replaced, if a king is drawn first, the probability of a king being drawn second is $\frac{3}{51}$. The probability of a king being drawn in both the first and second draw is the product of the two probabilities:

$$\frac{4}{52} \times \frac{3}{51} = \frac{12}{2,652}$$

To reduce this fraction, divide the top and bottom by 12 to get $\frac{1}{221}$.

13. C: The picture demonstrates Angle-Side-Angle congruence. Choice *A* and *B* are incorrect because the picture does not show Side-Side-Side congruence and angles alone cannot prove congruence. Choice *D* is not the correct answer because there is already enough information to prove congruence.

14. A: If s is the size of the floor in square feet and r is the rate on Tuesday, then, based on the information given, $p = \frac{s}{4}$ and $r = \frac{s}{3}$. Solve the Monday rate for s, $s = 4p$, and then substitute that in the expression for Tuesday.

15. C: To solve this equation, square both sides to eliminate the radical, resulting in $x + 5 = 25$. Subtracting 5 from both sides to solve for x gives $x = 20$.

16. A: To expand a squared binomial, it's necessary to use the FOIL (First, Outer, Inner, Last) method:

$$(2x - 4y)^2$$

$$2x \times 2x + 2x(-4y) + (-4y)(2x) + (-4y)(-4y)$$

$$4x^2 - 8xy - 8xy + 16y^2$$

$$4x^2 - 16xy + 16y^2$$

17. B: The zeros of this function can be found by setting $f(x)$ equal to 0 and solving for x.

$$0 = x^2 + 4$$

$$-4 = x^2$$

$$\sqrt{-4} = x$$

Taking the square root of a negative number results in an imaginary number, so the solution is $x = \pm 2i$.

18. D: The expression is simplified by collecting like terms. Terms with the same variable and exponent are like terms, and their coefficients can be added.

19. A: To simplify this expression, first line up the fractions:

$$\frac{15}{23} \times \frac{54}{127}$$

Multiply across the top and across the bottom to find the numerator and denominator:

$$\frac{15 \times 54}{23 \times 127} = \frac{810}{2921}$$

Because the numerator and denominator do not share any common factors, the resulting fraction cannot be reduced.

20. A: Finding the product means distributing one polynomial to the other so that each term in the first is multiplied by each term in the second. Then, like terms can be collected. Multiplying the factors yields the expression:

$$20x^3 + 4x^2 + 24x - 40x^2 - 8x - 48$$

Collecting like terms means adding the x^2 terms and adding the x terms. The final answer after simplifying the expression is:

$$20x^3 - 36x^2 + 16x - 48$$

21. B: The equation can be solved by factoring the numerator into $(x + 6)(x - 5)$. Since $(x - 5)$ exists on top and bottom, that factor cancels. This leaves the equation $x + 6 = 11$. Solving the equation gives the answer $x = 5$. When this value is plugged into the equation, it yields a zero in the denominator of the fraction. Since this is undefined, there is no solution.

22. A: The common denominator here will be $4x$. Rewrite these fractions as:

$$\frac{3}{x} + \frac{5u}{2x} - \frac{u}{4}$$

$$\frac{12}{4x} + \frac{10u}{4x} - \frac{ux}{4x}$$

$$\frac{12 + 10u - ux}{4x}$$

23. B: There are two zeros for the given function. They are $x = 0, -2$. The zeros can be found a number of ways, but this particular equation can be factored into:

$$f(x) = x(x^2 + 4x + 4) = x(x + 2)(x + 2)$$

By setting each factor equal to zero and solving for x, there are two solutions: $x = 0$ and $x = -2$. On a graph, these zeros can be seen where the line crosses the x-axis.

24. A: The equation is *even* because $f(-x) = f(x)$. Plugging in a negative value will result in the same answer as when plugging in the positive of that same value. The function:

$$f(-2) = \frac{1}{2}(-2)^4 + 2(-2)^2 - 6$$

$$8 + 8 - 6 = 10$$

This function yields the same value as:

$$f(2) = \frac{1}{2}(2)^4 + 2(2)^2 - 6$$

$$8 + 8 - 6 = 10$$

25. B: The perimeter of a rectangle is the sum of all four sides. Therefore, the answer is:

$$P = 14 + 8\frac{1}{2} + 14 + 8\frac{1}{2}$$

$$14 + 14 + 8 + \frac{1}{2} + 8 + \frac{1}{2} = 45 \text{ square inches}$$

26. B: The amount of water in one bottle is measured in milliliters but the question asks for an amount in liters. Therefore, the conversion from milliliters to liters is needed. There are 1,000 milliliters in 1 liter.

27. B: Because this isn't a right triangle, the SOHCAHTOA mnemonic can't be used. However, the law of cosines can be used:

$$c^2 = a^2 + b^2 - 2ab\cos C$$

$$c^2 = 19^2 + 26^2 - 2 \times 19 \times 26 \times \cos 42° = 302.773$$

Taking the square root and rounding to the nearest tenth results in $c = 17.4$.

28. C: Because the triangles are similar, the lengths of the corresponding sides are proportional. Therefore:

$$\frac{30 + x}{30} = \frac{22}{14} = \frac{y + 15}{y}$$

Using cross multiplication on the first two terms results in the equation:

$$14(30 + x) = 22 \times 30$$

When solved, this gives:

$$x \approx 17.1$$

Using cross multiplication on the last two terms results in the equation:

$$14(y + 15) = 22y$$

When solved, this gives:

$$y \approx 26.3$$

29. B: The technique of completing the square must be used to change the equation below into the standard equation of a circle:

$$4x^2 + 4y^2 - 16x - 24y + 51 = 0$$

First, the constant must be moved to the right-hand side of the equals sign and each term must be divided by the coefficient of the x^2-term (which is 4). The x- and y-terms must be grouped together to obtain:

$$x^2 - 4x + y^2 - 6y = -\frac{51}{4}$$

Then, the process of completing the square must be completed for each variable. This gives:

$$(x^2 - 4x + 4) + (y^2 - 6y + 9) = -\frac{51}{4} + 4 + 9$$

The equation can be written as:

$$(x - 2)^2 + (y - 3)^2 = \frac{1}{4}$$

Therefore, the center of the circle is $(2, 3)$ and the radius is:

$$\sqrt{\frac{1}{4}} = \frac{1}{2}$$

30. A: Operations within the parentheses must be completed first. Then, division is completed. Finally, addition is the last operation to complete. When adding decimals, digits within each place value are added together. Therefore, the expression is evaluated as:

$$(2 \times 20) \div (7 + 1) + (6 \times 0.01) + (4 \times 0.001)$$

$$40 \div 8 + 0.06 + 0.004 = 5 + 0.06 + 0.004 = 5.064$$

31. C: A dollar contains 20 nickels. Therefore, if there are 12 dollars' worth of nickels, there are $12 \times 20 = 240$ nickels. Each nickel weighs 5 grams. Therefore, the weight of the nickels is $240 \times 5 = 1{,}200$ grams. Adding in the weight of the empty piggy bank, the filled bank weighs 2,250 grams.

32. D: To find Denver's total snowfall, 3 must be multiplied times $27\frac{3}{4}$. In order to easily do this, the mixed number should be converted into an improper fraction.

$$27\frac{3}{4} = \frac{27 \times 4 + 3}{4} = \frac{111}{4}$$

Therefore, Denver had approximately $\frac{3 \times 111}{4} = \frac{333}{4}$ inches of snow. The improper fraction can be converted back into a mixed number through division.

$$\frac{333}{4} = 83\frac{1}{4} \text{inches}$$

33. D: Solve a linear inequality in a similar way to solving a linear equation. First, start by distributing the -3 on the left side of the inequality.

$$-3x - 12 \geq x + 8$$

Then, add 12 to both sides.

$$-3x \geq x + 20$$

Next, subtract x from both sides.

$$-4x \geq 20$$

Finally, divide both sides of the inequality by -4. Don't forget to flip the inequality sign because you are dividing by a negative.

$$x \leq -5$$

34. C: $y = 40x + 300$. In this scenario, the variables are the number of sales and Karen's weekly pay. The weekly pay depends on the number of sales. Therefore, weekly pay is the dependent variable (y), and the number of sales is the independent variable (x). Each pair of values from the table can be written as an ordered pair (x, y): $(2, 380)$, $(7, 580)$, $(4, 460)$, $(8, 620)$. The ordered pairs can be substituted into the equations to see which create true statements (both sides equal) for each pair. Even if one ordered pair produces equal values for a given equation, the other three ordered pairs must be checked. The only equation which is true for all four ordered pairs is $y = 40x + 300$:

$$380 = 40(2) + 300 \rightarrow 380 = 380$$

$$580 = 40(7) + 300 \rightarrow 580 = 580$$

$$460 = 40(4) + 300 \rightarrow 460 = 460$$

$$620 = 40(8) + 300 \rightarrow 620 = 620$$

35. C: The area of the shaded region is the area of the square minus the area of the circle. The area of the circle is πr^2. The side of the square will be $2r$, so the area of the square will be $4r^2$. Therefore, the difference is:

$$4r^2 - \pi r^2 = (4 - \pi)r^2$$

36. B: The car is traveling at a speed of 5 meters per second. On the interval from 1 to 3 seconds, the position changes by 10 meters. This is 10 meters in 2 seconds, or 5 meters in each second.

37. B: For an ordered pair to be a solution to a system of inequalities, it must make a true statement for BOTH inequalities when substituting its values for x and y. Substituting $(-3, -2)$ into the inequalities produces $(-2) > 2(-3) - 3$, which is $-2 > -9$, and $(-2) < -4(-3) + 8$, or $-2 < 20$. Both are true statements.

38. D: The shape of the scatter plot is a parabola (U-shaped). This eliminates Choices *A* (a linear equation that produces a straight line) and *C* (an exponential equation that produces a smooth curve upward or downward). The value of a for a quadratic function in standard form ($y = ax^2 + bx + c$) indicates whether the parabola opens up (U-shaped) or opens down (upside-down U). A negative value for a produces a parabola that opens down; therefore, Choice *B* can also be eliminated.

39. B: According to the order of operations, multiplication and division must be completed first from left to right. Then, addition and subtraction are completed from left to right. Therefore:

$$9 \times 9 \div 9 + 9 - 9 \div 9$$

$$81 \div 9 + 9 - 9 \div 9$$

$$9 + 9 - 9 \div 9$$

$$9 + 9 - 1$$

$$18 - 1$$

$$17$$

40. B: First, subtract 9 from both sides to isolate the radical. Then, cube each side of the equation to obtain:

$$\sqrt[3]{2x + 11} + 9 = 12$$

$$\sqrt[3]{2x + 11} = 3$$

$$2x + 11 = 27$$

Subtract 11 from both sides, and then divide by 2.

$$2x = 16$$

The result is $x = 8$.

Plug 8 back into the original equation to check the answer:

$$\sqrt[3]{16 + 11} + 9 = 12$$

$$\sqrt[3]{27} + 9 = 12$$

$$3 + 9 = 12$$

41. A: 13 nurses. Using the given information of 1 nurse to 25 patients and 325 patients, set up an equation to solve for number of nurses (N):

$$\frac{N}{325} = \frac{1}{25}$$

Multiply both sides by 325 to get N by itself on one side:

$$\frac{N}{1} = \frac{325}{25} = 13 \text{ nurses}$$

42. D: 290 beds. Using the given information of 2 beds to 1 room and 145 rooms, set up an equation to solve for number of beds (B):

$$\frac{B}{145} = \frac{2}{1}$$

Multiply both sides by 145 to get B by itself on one side.

$$\frac{B}{1} = \frac{290}{1} = 290 \text{ beds}$$

43. C: $x = 150$. Set up the initial equation:

$$\frac{2x}{5} - 1 = 59$$

Add 1 to both sides:

$$\frac{2x}{5} - 1 + 1 = 59 + 1$$

Multiply both sides by $\frac{5}{2}$:

$$\frac{2x}{5} \times \frac{5}{2} = 60 \times \frac{5}{2} = 150$$

$$x = 150$$

44. C: First, list the givens:

$$Tax = 6.0\% = 0.06$$

$$Sale = 50\% = 0.5$$

$$Hat = \$32.99$$

$$Jersey = \$64.99$$

Calculate the sale prices for hats and jerseys:

$$Hat\ sale = 0.5\ (32.99) = 16.495$$

$$Jersey\ sale = 0.5\ (64.99) = 32.495$$

Total the sale prices:

$$Hat\ sale + jersey\ sale = 16.495 + 32.495 = 48.99$$

Finally, calculate the sales tax and add it to the total sale prices:

$$Total\ after\ tax = 48.99 + (48.99 \times 0.06) = \$51.93$$

45. D: First, list the givens:

$$Store\ coffee = \$1.23/\text{lb}$$

$$Local\ roaster\ coffee = \frac{\$1.98}{1.5\ \text{lb}}$$

Calculate the cost for 5 pounds of store brand coffee.

$$\frac{\$1.23}{1\text{ lb}} \times 5\text{ lb} = \$6.15$$

Calculate the cost for 5 pounds of the local roaster's coffee:

$$\frac{\$1.98}{1.5\text{ lb}} \times 5\text{ lb} = \$6.60$$

Subtract to find the difference in price for 5 pounds of coffee:

$$\$6.60 - \$6.15 = \$0.45$$

46. D: First, list the givens:

$$1{,}800\, ft \ = \ \$2{,}000$$

$$Cost\ after\ 1{,}800\, ft \ = \ \$1.00/\text{ft}$$

Find how many feet left after the first 1,800 ft:

$$3125\text{ ft} - 1{,}800\text{ ft} = 1325\text{ ft}$$

Calculate the cost for the feet over 1,800 ft:

$$1{,}325\, ft \times \frac{\$1.00}{1\, ft} = \$1{,}325$$

Total for entire cost:

$$\$2{,}000 + \$1{,}325 = \$3{,}325$$

No Calculator Questions

47. A: 12. Calculate how many gallons the bucket holds:

$$11.4\, L \times \frac{1\, gal}{3.8\, L} = 3\, gal$$

Now how many buckets to fill the pool which needs 35 gallons:

$$\frac{35\, gal}{3\, gal} = 11.67$$

Since the amount is more than 11 but less than 12, we must fill the bucket 12 times.

48. D: Three girls for every two boys can be expressed as a ratio: $3:2$. This can be visualized as splitting the school into 5 groups: 3 girl groups and 2 boy groups. The number of students that are in each group can be found by dividing the total number of students by 5:

$$\frac{650 \text{ students}}{5 \text{ groups}} = \frac{130 \text{ students}}{\text{group}}$$

To find the total number of girls, multiply the number of students per group (130) by the number of girl groups in the school (3). This equals 390, Choice *D*.

49. C: The volume of a pyramid is $length \times width \times height$, divided by 3, and $6 \times 6 \times 9$, divided by 3 is 108 in^3. Choice *A* is incorrect because 324 in^3 is $length \times width \times height$ without dividing by 3. Choice *B* is incorrect because 6 is used for height instead of 9 $(6 \times 6 \times 6)$ and divided by 3 to get 72 in^3. Choice *D* is incorrect because 18 in^3 is 6×9, divided by 3, and leaving out a 6.

50. A: 22%. Converting from a fraction to a percentage generally involves two steps. First, the fraction needs to be converted to a decimal:

$$\frac{2}{9} = 0.\overline{22}$$

The top line indicates that the decimal actually goes on forever with an endless amount of 2's.

Second, the decimal needs to be moved two places to the right to convert to a percent:

$$22\%$$

51. A: The volume of a cone is $\pi r^2 h$, divided by 3, and $\pi \times 10^2 \times 12$, divided by 3, is 400 cm^3. Choice *B* is $10^2 \times 2$. Choice *C* is incorrect because it is 10×12. Choice *D* is also incorrect because that is $10^2 + 40$.

52. A: 37.5%. Solve this by setting up the percent formula:

$$\frac{3}{8} = \frac{\%}{100}$$

Multiply 3 by 100 to get 300. Then divide 300 by 8:

$$\frac{300}{8} = 37.5\%$$

Note that with the percent formula, 37.5 is automatically a percentage and does not need to have any further conversions.

53. C: Because area is a two-dimensional measurement, the dimensions are multiplied by a scale factor that is squared to determine the scale factor of the corresponding areas. The dimensions of the rectangle are multiplied by a scale factor of 3. Therefore, the area is multiplied by a scale factor of 3^2 (which is equal to 9):

$$24 \text{ cm}^2 \times 9 = 216 \text{ cm}^2$$

54. Add 3 to both sides to get $4x = 8$. Then, divide both sides by 4 to get $x = 2$.

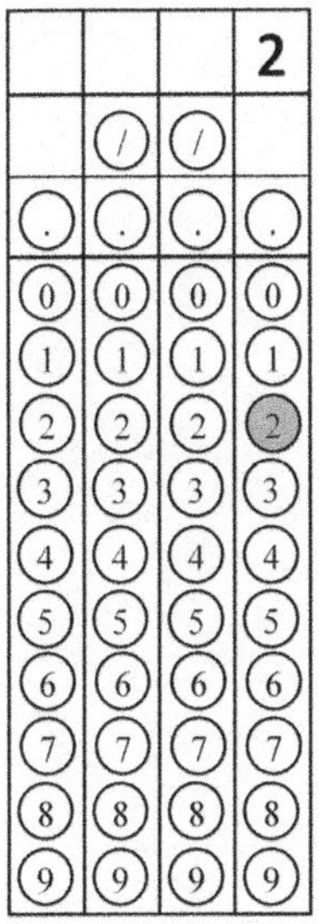

55. To solve this correctly, keep in mind the order of operations with the mnemonic PEMDAS (Please Excuse My Dear Aunt Sally). This stands for Parentheses, Exponents, Multiplication, Division, Addition, Subtraction. Taking it step by step, solve inside the parentheses first:

$$4 \times 7 + (4)^2 \div 2$$

Then, apply the exponent:

$$4 \times 7 + 16 \div 2$$

Multiplication and division are both performed next:

$$28 + 8$$

Addition and subtraction are done last.

$$28 + 8 = 36$$

The solution is 36.

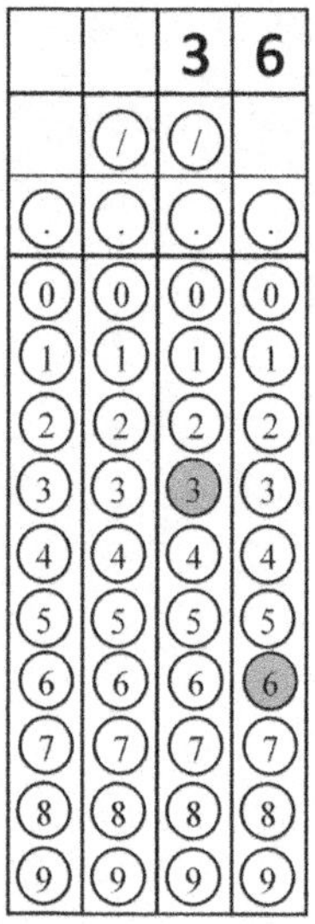

56. Follow the order of operations in order to solve this problem. Solve the parentheses first, being sure to follow the order of operations inside the parentheses as well. First, simplify the square roots:

$$(6 \times 4) - 3^2$$

Then, multiply inside the parentheses:

$$24 - 3^2$$

Next, simplify the exponent:

$$24 - 9$$

Finally, subtract to get 15.

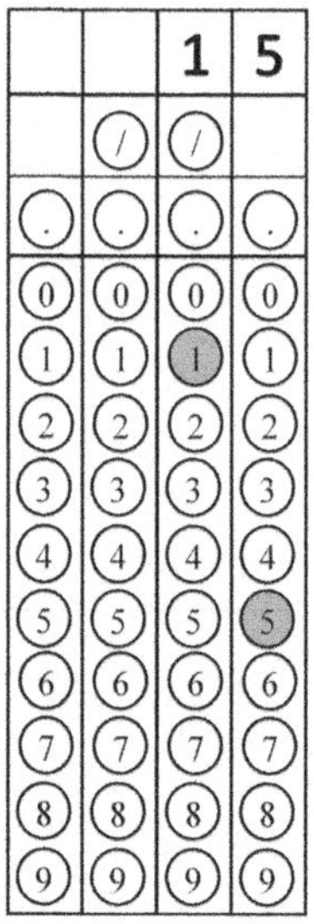

57. For an even number of total values, the *median* is calculated by finding the *mean,* or average, of the two middle values once all values have been arranged in ascending order from least to greatest. In this case, $(92 + 83) \div 2$ would equal the median 87.5.

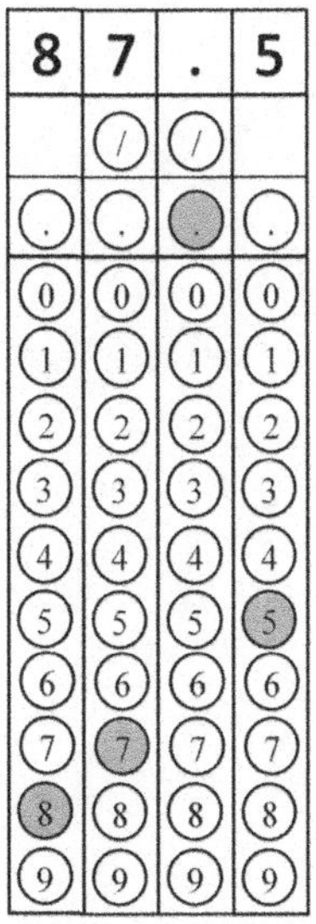

58. The formula for the perimeter of a rectangle is $P = 2L + 2W$, where P is the perimeter, L is the length, and W is the width. The first step is to substitute all of the data into the formula:

$$36 = 2(12) + 2W$$

Simplify by multiplying 2×12:

$$36 = 24 + 2W$$

Simplifying this further by subtracting 24 on each side gives:

$$36 - 24 = 24 - 24 + 2W$$

$$12 = 2W$$

Divide by 2:

$$6 = W$$

The width is 6 cm. Remember to test this answer by substituting this value into the original formula:

$$36 = 2(12) + 2(6)$$

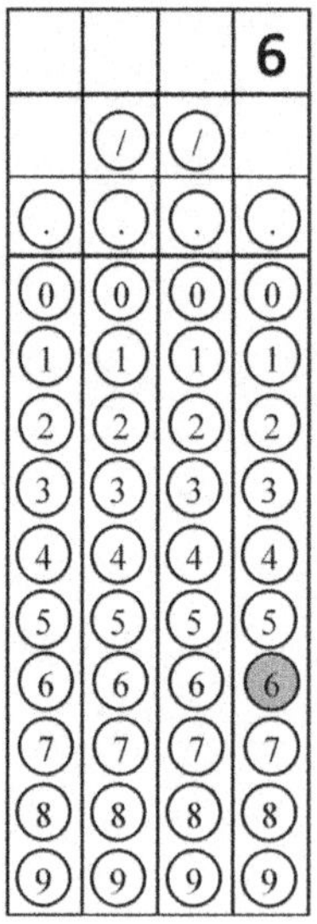

SAT Practice Test #2

Reading Test

Fiction

Questions 1–10 are based on the following passage:

A lane was forthwith opened through the crowd of spectators. Preceded by the beadle, and attended by an irregular procession of stern-browed men and unkindly visaged women, Hester Prynne set forth towards the place appointed for her punishment. A crowd of eager and curious school-boys, understanding little of the matter in hand, except that it gave them a half-holiday, ran before her progress, turning their heads continually to stare into her face, and at the winking baby in her arms, and at the ignominious letter on her breast. It was no great distance, in those days, from the prison-door to the market-place. Measured by the prisoner's experience, however, it might be reckoned a journey of some length; for, haughty as her demeanor was, she perchance underwent an agony from every footstep of those that thronged to see her, as if her heart had been flung into the street for them all to spurn and trample upon. In our nature, however, there is a provision, alike marvelous and merciful, that the sufferer should never know the intensity of what he endures by its present torture, but chiefly by the pang that rankles after it. With almost a serene deportment, therefore, Hester Prynne passed through this portion of her ordeal, and came to a sort of scaffold, at the western extremity of the market-place. It stood nearly beneath the eaves of Boston's earliest church, and appeared to be a fixture there.

In fact, this scaffold constituted a portion of a penal machine, which now, for two or three generations past, has been merely historical and traditionary among us, but was held, in the old time, to be as effectual an agent, in the promotion of good citizenship, as ever was the guillotine among the terrorists of France. It was, in short, the platform of the pillory; and above it rose the framework of that instrument of discipline, so fashioned as to confine the human head in its tight grasp, and thus hold it up to the public gaze. The very ideal of ignominy was embodied and made manifest in this contrivance of wood and iron. There can be no outrage, methinks, against our common nature,—whatever be the delinquencies of the individual,—no outrage more flagrant than to forbid the culprit to hide his face for shame; as it was the essence of this punishment to do. In Hester Prynne's instance, however, as not unfrequently in other cases, her sentence bore, that she should stand a certain time upon the platform, but without undergoing that gripe about the neck and confinement of the head, the proneness to which was the most devilish characteristic of this ugly engine. Knowing well her part, she ascended a flight of wooden steps, and was thus displayed to the surrounding multitude, at about the height of a man's shoulders above the street.

The scene was not without a mixture of awe, such as must always invest the spectacle of guilt and shame in a fellow-creature, before society shall have grown corrupt enough to smile, instead of shuddering, at it. The witnesses of Hester Prynne's disgrace had not yet passed beyond their simplicity. They were stern enough to look upon her death, had that been the sentence, without a murmur at its severity, but had none of the heartlessness of another social state, which would find only a theme for jest in an exhibition like the present. Even had there been a disposition to turn the matter into ridicule, it must have been repressed and overpowered by the solemn presence of men no less dignified than the Governor, and several of his counsellors, a judge, a general, and the ministers of the town; all of whom sat or stood in a balcony of the meeting-house, looking down upon the platform. When such personages could constitute a part of the spectacle, without risking the majesty or reverence of rank and office, it was safely to be inferred that the infliction of a legal sentence would have an earnest and effectual meaning. Accordingly, the crowd was sombre and grave. The unhappy culprit sustained herself as best a woman might, under the heavy weight of a thousand unrelenting eyes, all fastened upon her, and concentrated at her bosom. It was almost intolerable to be borne. Of an impulsive and passionate nature, she had fortified herself to encounter the stings and venomous stabs of public contumely, wreaking itself in every variety of insult; but there was a quality so much more terrible in the solemn mood of the popular mind, that she longed rather to behold all those rigid countenances contorted with scornful merriment, and herself the object. Had a roar of laughter burst from the multitude,—each man, each woman, each little shrill-voiced child, contributing their individual parts,—Hester Prynne might have repaid them all with a bitter and disdainful smile. But, under the leaden infliction which it was her doom to endure, she felt, at moments, as if she must needs shriek out with the full power of her lungs, and cast herself from the scaffold down upon the ground, or else go mad at once.

Excerpt from *The Scarlet Letter*, Nathaniel Hawthorne, 1878

1. Based on the first paragraph, what might Hester Prynne feel on her walk from prison to marketplace?
   a. Anger
   b. Fear
   c. Agony
   d. Proud

2. Based on the passage, what is the spectators' mood?
   a. Grave
   b. Amused
   c. Vengeful
   d. Outraged

3. The passage includes a description of the stockade but states it was not part of Hester's punishment. What can we infer from its inclusion?
   a. They didn't use it because she was a woman.
   b. The townspeople would have preferred its use.
   c. The threat of it was often a deterrent.
   d. The punishment could have been harsher.

4. Based on paragraph 3 of the passage, why was Prynne not mocked or ridiculed?
    a. Others had also committed crimes.
    b. She appeared too proud.
    c. Dignitaries were present.
    d. The crowd wanted to see her hanged.

5. In the final paragraph, what does the word "disdainful" mean?
    a. Admiring
    b. Contemptuous
    c. Sympathetic
    d. Mournful

6. In the first paragraph, why might a prisoner find the walk from prison to marketplace longer than the actual distance?
    a. The spectators watching cause the prisoner an emotional burden.
    b. The prisoner's ankles were shackled.
    c. Prisoners are forced to walk slowly.
    d. Kids keep running in front, taunting.

7. How did the crowd's reaction defy Prynne's expectations?
    a. She expected silence, but they cheered.
    b. She expected cheering, but they mocked her.
    c. She expected physical attacks, but they laughed.
    d. She expected verbal attacks but got none.

8. What can we conclude about Prynne's need to shriek and throw herself down or go mad?
    a. The weight of the punishment has finally hit her.
    b. Someone has attacked her.
    c. She has finally been placed in the stockade.
    d. She wants to respond to the crowd.

9. Over the course of the passage, the main point of view shifts among...
    a. A witness, the judge, and Hester Prynne
    b. Hester Prynne's experience, the crowd's experience, and Prynne's husband
    c. The narrator's viewpoint, Hester Prynne, and the crowd
    d. Hester Prynne, members of the crowd, and the town historian

10. Based on the passage, Hester's character can best be described as:
    a. Tenacious
    b. Ashamed
    c. Bashful
    d. Enraged

History/Social Studies

Questions 11–20 are based on the following passage:

> The basic problem confronting the world today, as I said in the beginning, is the preservation of human freedom for the individual and consequently for the society of

which he is a part. We are fighting this battle again today as it was fought at the time of the French Revolution and as the time of the American Revolution. The issue of human liberty is as decisive now as it was then. I want to give you my conception of what is meant in my country by freedom of the individual.

Long ago in London during a discussion with Mr. Vyshinsky, he told me there was no such thing as freedom for the individual in the world. All freedom of the individual was conditioned by the rights of other individuals. That of course, I granted. I said: "We approach the question from a different point of view: we here in the United Nations are trying to develop ideals which will be broader in outlook, which will consider first the rights of man, which will consider what makes man more free; not governments, but man."

The totalitarian state typically places the will of the people second to decrees promulgated by a few men at the top.

Naturally there must always be consideration of the rights of others; but in a democracy this is not a restriction. Indeed, in our democracies we make our freedoms secure because each of us is expected to respect the rights of others and we are free to make our own laws. Freedom for our peoples is not only a right, but also a tool. Freedom of speech, freedom of the press, freedom of information, freedom of assembly—these are not just abstract ideals to us; they are tools with which we create a way of life, a way of life in which we can enjoy freedom.

Sometimes the processes of democracy are slow, and I have known some of our leaders to say that a benevolent dictatorship would accomplish the ends desired in a much shorter time than it takes to go through the democratic processes of discussion and the slow formation of public opinion. But there is no way of insuring that a dictatorship will remain benevolent or that power once in the hands of a few will be returned to the people without struggle or revolution. This we have learned by experience and we accept the slow processes of democracy because we know that shortcuts compromise principles on which no compromise is possible.

The final expression of the opinion of the people with us is through free and honest elections, with valid choices on basic issues and candidates. The secret ballot is an essential to free elections but you must have a choice before you. I have heard my husband say many times that a people need never lose their freedom if they kept their right to a secret ballot and if they used that secret ballot to the full. Basic decisions of our society are made through the expressed will of the people. That is why when we see these liberties threatened, instead of falling apart, our nation becomes unified and our democracies come together as a unified group in spite of our varied backgrounds and many racial strains.

In the United States we have a capitalistic economy. That is because public opinion favors that type of economy under the conditions in which we live. But we have imposed certain restraints; for instance, we have antitrust laws. These are the legal evidence of the determination of the American people to maintain an economy of free competition and not to allow monopolies to take away the people's freedom.

Excerpt from Eleanor Roosevelt's "The Struggle for Human Rights," September 28, 1948

11. What does the writer say about freedom as a tool?
    a. Dictators can use it to manipulate populations.
    b. It's not just a concept; it can help achieve a desired lifestyle.
    c. It can be abused and misused by people.
    d. Only skilled individuals should be able to wield such a powerful tool.

12. According to Roosevelt, why do some people argue in favor of dictatorship?
    a. Dictatorships need not be tyrannical.
    b. Dictators come to power for a reason.
    c. Some dictators have been quite successful and popular.
    d. They believe that a dictator could achieve goals could more quickly.

13. According to the passage, what is the goal of antitrust laws?
    a. To establish trust between governments and populations
    b. To force businesses to be fair to consumers
    c. To foster economic competition
    d. To allow businesses to compete with the government

14. In the final sentence of the second paragraph, what does the word "promulgated" mean?
    a. Stifled
    b. Whispered
    c. Promoted
    d. Attacked

15. What is the main idea of this passage?
    a. We need democracy to maintain and protect individual freedom.
    b. Dictatorships can be benevolent and should be considered viable.
    c. Elections guarantee democracy and require secret ballots.
    d. Capitalism directly supports democracy and so should be encouraged.

16. Why does Roosevelt refer to both the French and American Revolutions?
    a. To demonstrate her understanding of history
    b. To draw a comparison to successful fights for freedom and democracy
    c. To highlight the fact that she is speaking to both American and French citizens
    d. To emphasize that she is speaking on the anniversary of both events

17. The tone of the passage is:
    a. Earnest
    b. Satirical
    c. Accusatory
    d. Conciliatory

18. Based on the passage, we can conclude that Roosevelt values:
    a. The relationship between France and America
    b. Capitalistic economy
    c. Knowledge of history
    d. Freedom and democracy

19. What is Roosevelt's concern about a "benevolent dictator"?
    a. The US has never had a dictator, so she is unfamiliar with them.
    b. The world is still recovering from World War II.
    c. There is no guarantee that a dictator will remain benevolent.
    d. There is no way a dictator will be benevolent.

20. Why does Roosevelt assert that a "secret" ballot is important?
    a. Public votes were too raucous an event.
    b. It decreases the chance for bribery.
    c. Privacy secures freedom of choice.
    d. It ensures physical safety.

History/Social Studies

Questions 21–31 are based on the following passage:

> At times history and fate meet at a single time in a single place to shape a turning point in man's unending search for freedom. So it was at Lexington and Concord. So it was a century ago at Appomattox. So it was last week in Selma, Alabama. There, long-suffering men and women peacefully protested the denial of their rights as Americans. Many were brutally assaulted. One good man, a man of God, was killed.
>
> There is no cause for pride in what has happened in Selma. There is no cause for self-satisfaction in the long denial of equal rights of millions of Americans. But there is cause for hope and for faith in our democracy in what is happening here tonight. For the cries of pain and the hymns and protests of oppressed people have summoned into convocation all the majesty of this great government—the government of the greatest nation on earth. Our mission is at once the oldest and the most basic of this country: to right wrong, to do justice, to serve man.
>
> In our time we have come to live with the moments of great crisis. Our lives have been marked with debate about great issues—issues of war and peace, issues of prosperity and depression. But rarely in any time does an issue lay bare the secret heart of America itself. Rarely are we met with a challenge, not to our growth or abundance, or our welfare or our security, but rather to the values, and the purposes, and the meaning of our beloved nation.
>
> The issue of equal rights for American Negroes is such an issue.
>
> And should we defeat every enemy, and should we double our wealth and conquer the stars, and still be unequal to this issue, then we will have failed as a people and as a nation. For with a country as with a person, "What is a man profited, if he shall gain the whole world, and lose his own soul?"

There is no Negro problem. There is no Southern problem. There is no Northern problem. There is only an American problem. And we are met here tonight as Americans—not as Democrats or Republicans. We are met here as Americans to solve that problem.

This was the first nation in the history of the world to be founded with a purpose. The great phrases of that purpose still sound in every American heart, North and South: "All men are created equal," "government by consent of the governed," "give me liberty or give me death." Well, those are not just clever words, or those are not just empty theories. In their name Americans have fought and died for two centuries, and tonight around the world they stand there as guardians of our liberty, risking their lives.

Those words are a promise to every citizen that he shall share in the dignity of man. This dignity cannot be found in a man's possessions; it cannot be found in his power, or in his position. It really rests on his right to be treated as a man equal in opportunity to all others. It says that he shall share in freedom, he shall choose his leaders, educate his children, provide for his family according to his ability and his merits as a human being. To apply any other test—to deny a man his hopes because of his color, or race, or his religion, or the place of his birth is not only to do injustice, it is to deny America and to dishonor the dead who gave their lives for American freedom.

Except from Lyndon Johnson's "Address to Joint Session of Congress," March 15, 1965

21. What was being protested in Selma?
    a. The closing of a bridge
    b. Denial of rights
    c. A murder
    d. Loss of wealth

22. Based on this passage, why does Johnson suggest there is hope in the events of Selma?
    a. Police responded immediately to the situation.
    b. Lots of citizens showed up to protest.
    c. It forced attention on the issue and sparked conversations about it.
    d. Despite the violence, only one life was lost.

23. How does Johnson suggest this issue is different from other debates?
    a. Other debates haven't led to protests.
    b. It is easier to solve.
    c. It is more difficult to solve.
    d. It concerns our values.

24. Based on Johnson's words, where does dignity lie?
    a. In equality
    b. In freedom to protest
    c. In American might
    d. In American abundance

25. What best describes the tone of Johnson's speech?
    a. Righteous
    b. Saccharine
    c. Scathing
    d. Vindictive

26. What does Johnson suggest will indicate failure, even among amazing successes?
    a. Failure to reach the Moon
    b. A loss of wealth
    c. Military defeat
    d. Moral or spiritual decay

27. In the second paragraph of this passage, what does the word "convocation" mean?
    a. A vocal duet
    b. A second career
    c. A gathering or assembly
    d. Closure

28. Based on the examples Johnson provides in the next to last paragraph of the passage, what can we conclude about the purpose for which America was founded?
    a. To fight wars and protect nations
    b. To lead the world
    c. To foster equality, democracy, and freedom
    d. To establish a country that others envy

29. Based on context, who are the "guardians of liberty" Johnson refers to?
    a. American citizens
    b. American troops
    c. American government
    d. Selma protestors

30. Which of the following best encapsulates the purpose of this speech?
    a. To entertain
    b. To describe
    c. To teach
    d. To persuade

31. What does the phrase "government by consent of the governed" mean?
    a. The governed people must like their government.
    b. The governed people must choose their government.
    c. The government must treat the governed people fairly.
    d. The government is not required to hold elections.

Science

Questions 32–42 are based on the following passage:

These community assessments conducted during the Zika outbreak, hurricane responses, and hurricane recovery in U.S. Virgin Islands (USVI) found that households were more concerned about contracting mosquito-borne diseases shortly after the Zika outbreak than during the hurricane response and hurricane recovery, even though reported mosquito biting activity increased, and environmental conditions were more favorable for mosquito breeding and exposure to bites following the hurricanes. In addition, although mosquito-borne diseases are endemic in USVI, and the population might be aware of the risk, households had concerns after the hurricanes that did not exist during the Zika outbreak, such as lack of shelter, clean water, and electricity. These differing levels of concern did not, however, change the community's support for mosquito spraying, although support for specific spray methods varied.

VIDOH used the Community Assessments for Public Health Emergency Response (CASPERs) data to make real-time outbreak and hurricane response decisions to improve mosquito bite prevention, mosquito control, and community education. For example, because the percentage of households concerned about contracting mosquito-borne diseases declined after the hurricanes compared with during the Zika outbreak response, VIDOH hurricane response education campaigns prioritized household-level mosquito bite prevention. The differing levels of support for various spray methods were also recognized and considered during decision making. For example, these data, along with unique environmental considerations, were used by the administration in place during the responses and recovery to determine backpack spraying to be the only acceptable option.

The CASPER is a useful tool for assessing mosquito-borne disease risk factors and creating immediately useable data to guide vector-related public health campaigns. According to CDC's internal CASPER database, a limited number of CASPERs have been conducted that assess mosquito bite prevention- and control-related factors, such as knowledge of mosquito-borne diseases; ways to protect against mosquito bites; and how to identify, quantify, and manage potential mosquito breeding sites. Even fewer CASPERs have focused solely on mosquitoes. A CASPER in Long Beach, California, during a Zika outbreak identified the need for increased mosquito abatement. In two areas of Texas, CASPERs successfully assessed the prevalence of vector-borne disease risk factors and the communities' knowledge of mosquito bite prevention and Zika virus. A CASPER conducted in American Samoa identified increased vector problems and the need for vector control after a tsunami.

Not only is CASPER an important tool for emergency response and recovery, it is also useful for collecting community public health information unrelated to an emergency. Vector control programs can use CASPERs during nonemergency situations to enhance and increase operation efficacy by evaluating the effectiveness of community campaigns and understanding community knowledge, attitudes, and practices.

Seger KR, Roth J Jr., Schnall AH, Ellis BR, Ellis EM. Community Assessments for Mosquito Prevention and Control Experiences, Attitudes, and Practices — U.S. Virgin Islands, 2017 and 2018. MMWR Morb Mortal Wkly Rep 2019;68:500–504.
DOI: http://dx.doi.org/10.15585/mmwr.mm6822a3external icon.

32. Based on the passage, how did residents' self-assessment of their risk differ from the actual risk?
   a. Residents rated risk higher during the Zika outbreak than after the hurricane.
   b. Residents saw no risk at all from Zika.
   c. Residents saw no risk after the hurricane.
   d. Residents believed the risks to be equivalent.

33. The research in the first paragraph attempts to draw a correlation between which two things?
   a. Zika and hurricanes
   b. Resident concerns and Zika spread
   c. Hurricanes and mosquito spraying
   d. Basic necessities and mosquito-borne diseases

34. Which factor of Zika response have CASPERs in the U.S. Virgin Islands assessed?
   a. Hurricane response
   b. Swamp size
   c. Bite prevention
   d. Backpack spraying

35. Based on the passage, what does the term "vector-related" mean?
   a. Related to a region of a country
   b. Concerning avenues or pathways through which disease is spread
   c. Concerning a treatment area
   d. Related to lines in space

36. Based on context, what does the word "abatement" mean?
   a. Increase
   b. Sterilization
   c. Reduction
   d. Intensification

37. Based on information provided, why might other types of spraying plans be less desirable than backpack spraying?
   a. Human exposure to harmful chemicals
   b. The inability to target specific areas of mosquito proliferation
   c. Lack of community support for other methods
   d. Lack of household participation

38. In non-emergency situations, which factors of disease vector control can CASPERs be helpful in understanding?
   a. Community knowledge
   b. Lack of shelter
   c. Spraying support
   d. Risk assessment

39. Based on the passage, we can conclude that:
    a. Backpack spraying will become the primary disease control mechanism.
    b. The risks associated with mosquito-borne diseases can increase with hurricanes.
    c. CASPERs will become a primary tool used by government organizations.
    d. Disease vector problems will remain isolated to island nations and the developing world.

40. What is main takeaway of the final paragraph?
    a. Mosquito-borne diseases are a serious risk for most of the developing world.
    b. Community knowledge of mosquito abatement is well below where it should be.
    c. Community action on mosquito bite prevention needs to be supported by governments.
    d. CASPERs are a vital tool for assessing the public health of communities in emergency and non-emergency situations.

41. Based on the passage, what can we say about why mosquito-borne diseases are more prevalent post-hurricane?
    a. Environmental conditions are favorable.
    b. Mosquitoes don't bite during storms.
    c. Fewer preventative drugs are available.
    d. Residents have raised awareness.

42. Based on the passage, which statement would researchers most agree with?
    a. CASPERs are best used in emergency situations.
    b. Aerial spraying is most effective to combat Zika.
    c. Hurricanes greatly increase the negative risks associated with mosquitos in the US Virgin Islands.
    d. Bite prevention is the best strategy for fighting mosquito-borne diseases.

Science

Questions 43–52 are based on the following two passages:

Passage 1

In 1992, the City of Madison, Wisconsin, found concentrations of lead in their drinking water exceeding the 90th percentile action level of 0.015 mg/L set by EPA. Lead (Pb) is a naturally occurring metal that was commonly used in household plumbing materials, such as lead service lines and leaded solder joints, before limits were set on its use in 1986.

However, in houses built before 1986, lead pipes can still be in use. Lead is rarely found in source water, but it can enter tap water as the water enters pipes with lead in older systems. Since some homes have lead service lines, the water coming into the house may be transported via lead pipes even though there are no lead pipes inside the home. Brass plumbing fixtures can also contain small amounts of lead.

The Madison Water Utility chose to implement full lead service line replacement from 2001 through 2011 to eliminate the most significant source of lead in its water system. In 2003, sixty home taps were monitored after full lead service line replacement. They found that lead levels in the first liter of water were still high at some sites where the lead service line pipes had mostly been replaced within the previous four years. This phenomenon had been seen in other water systems, which had puzzled drinking water practitioners as to why elevated lead levels could persist for so long.

Coincident to the Madison Water Utility studies before and after the lead service line replacement program, lead service lines had been harvested from the water system and sent to EPA scientists. The EPA had the instrumentation and unique expertise to search for clues of lead release in pipe scales. That is, the materials that build up on the inside of pipes display chemical characteristics that reflect the chemical processes occurring in the water system, including the release of lead. The EPA conducted detailed analyses—color, texture, mineralogical and elemental composition—on five lead service pipe samples excavated between 2001 and 2006 from two different Madison neighborhoods.

Before the lead service line replacement program, Madison's water was delivered by an estimated 8000 lead service lines, which had been in service for 75 years or longer. The city's drinking water originated from numerous wells. The first set of lead service lines studied by EPA revealed that a highly insoluble and protective lead oxide compound had formed on the pipe walls. If all lead pipe walls had this formation, high lead releases would not be expected in the water system.

However, the second set of lead service lines came from a different neighborhood in the city. This neighborhood was fed by wells that were rich in manganese and iron. Both manganese and iron can form scales and accumulate metals, such as lead, from upstream sources, especially from upstream corroded lead pipes. EPA's results revealed that the accumulation of manganese and iron from the well water onto pipe walls had adsorbed lead and had the potential to crumble from the pipe walls and carry the lead to consumers' taps by means of the scale particulate matter entrained in the water. This finding corroborated with the results of the 2003 study where the higher lead concentration found at consumers' taps was mostly in particulate form. The presence of the manganese and iron scale on the pipe walls was the reason for high lead release in parts of the Madison water system, before and even after the lead pipes were removed.

As the 2003 residential study had shown, once the principal lead source was removed, it took more than four years in some cases for the accumulated lead to be released, which explains why lead levels remained high after the lead pipes had been replaced. Eventually, removing the source of lead did eliminate the significant lead concentration and achieved compliance with EPA's regulations.

Overall, this research showed that controlling lead exposure from water is more complicated than simply adding corrosion control chemicals to reduce the solubility of lead minerals. Buildup of manganese and iron scale in water pipes should also be considered as a source for accumulating and releasing lead, and other contaminants of concern, into water. What happened in Madison highlights the importance of analyzing pipe scales to understand how lead accumulates and releases into the water over time.

From: "Revealing the Complicated Nature of Tap Water Lead Contamination: A Madison, Wisconsin Case Study," July 30, 2018. EPA. https://www.epa.gov/sciencematters/revealing-complicated-nature-tap-water-lead-contamination-madison-wisconsin-case

Passage 2

An estimated six to ten million older homes across the country have lead service lines. Service lines connect individual houses to the water main in the street; this means that water coming into a house may be transported via a lead service line even if no lead pipes are visible inside the home. Lead can be transferred from the lead pipe into the drinking water when the pipe materials corrode, when there are physical disturbances to the pipe, or when there are changes to the quality of water entering the home.

Given that there are many lead service lines in use across the country, limiting corrosion is a necessary step to reduce potential lead exposure from drinking water. Public water systems can control corrosion through a variety of methods including strict control of key water quality parameters and proper addition of a phosphate or silicate corrosion control inhibitor. Public water systems sometimes use modeling to inform corrosion control. EPA researchers recently looked at how well these models were predicting what is happening in the real world.

Water systems in EPA's Region 5—comprised of Minnesota, Wisconsin, Michigan, Illinois, Indiana, and Ohio—shared lead service line pipes and water quality data with EPA researchers. Actual pieces of pipe were taken out of the water systems and sent to EPA where scientists examined the pipe scales, the materials that build up on the inside of pipes. These pipe scales reveal chemical characteristics that reflect the chemical and physical processes occurring within the water system including the release of lead into drinking water.

Once EPA researchers cut open the pipes and took the scales apart, they examined each layer of scale and the minerals that were present. Different minerals have different inherent solubilities which clued researchers in to which minerals may be dissolving into the water. EPA researchers looked at which minerals were predicted to form based on the modeling, and then looked at pipe scales found on the lead service lines from those systems to see which minerals really were forming.

EPA and other outside organizations have applied predictive solubility models to try and help systems pick the right corrosion control treatment that fits their system's individual needs. These models provide guidance regarding which mineral phases are predicted to control lead release in a given environment. EPA's model uses parameters like alkalinity and pH to predict which mineral would be expected to form in the lead service lines of a water system and how much dissolved lead you would expect to find in the water.

The researchers, including EPA's Jennifer Tully, Mike DeSantis, and Mike Schock, found various lead minerals, and other non-crystalline materials forming on the inside of the pipes. They discovered that there was almost always a mix of different lead minerals present in the scale. A little more than half of the lead service lines they looked at showed that the minerals present were not the same minerals that the models were predicting would be present.

Next, EPA researchers looked at water quality data from several systems that had supplied lead service lines for analysis. Since the pipe scales showed that the models were not always predicting the right mineral composition, the scientists wanted to see how well the corrosion control was working. What they found in limited sampling was that the models often have difficulty predicting real world scenarios due to the complexity of corrosion control, and this study shows the need for further evaluation and water sampling beyond just modeling to ensure that systems are using the correct treatment to keep lead out of drinking water.

From "EPA Researchers Help Water Systems Keep Lead out of Drinking Water," March 3, 2020.

43. Based on Passage 1, what complicates efforts to address lead exposure via household taps?
   a. Lack of reporting on the issue
   b. Lack of testing in many regions of the United States
   c. Inability to identify and track the sources of lead
   d. Multiple ways that lead accumulates and is released

44. Based on Passage 2, what is the public water system's role in lead contamination control?
   a. Informing residents of lead levels in their tap water
   b. Monitoring quality and corrosion control additives
   c. Replacing lead pipes in homes with safer plumbing systems
   d. Providing researchers the opportunity to track lead contamination sources

45. According to the findings in Passage 1, even if there are no lead pipes in the home, why is lead present?
   a. Some lead levels are present in all water
   b. Lead is present in the city's water source
   c. Testing is sometimes unreliable
   d. Lead service lines and accumulation leading to the home

46. According to the findings in Passage 2, why is modeling sometimes ineffective?
   a. Real-world scenarios don't always match the models.
   b. Researchers rarely have all the data to predict source points.
   c. Models are not updated to reflect new mineral presence.
   d. Changes in service lines change the outcome.

47. Based on the two passages, what would the authors most agree on?
   a. Low lead levels in water after line changes are not as concerning.
   b. Corrosion inhibitors in water source points are the most effective option.
   c. Lead is leaching from scaling in older pipes in homes.
   d. Well water is safer than municipal water.

48. In Passage 1, why were lead levels still present even after the primary lead source had been removed?
   a. Accumulated lead and minerals in the system took four years to resolve.
   b. The lead was determined to be coming from the water source itself.
   c. Corrosion inhibitors had not yet been introduced.
   d. False positive tests were reported due to other minerals.

49. In the fourth paragraph of Passage 2, what does the word "solubilities" mean?
    a. Concentration levels
    b. Bonding strengths
    c. Levels of condensation
    d. Abilities to dissolve

50. Based on both passages, in older homes, what initial mitigation strategy would the researchers agree on?
    a. High-end water filtration systems
    b. Replacing lead service lines
    c. Switching water sources
    d. Corrosion additives in municipal water

51. Which statement would both research groups agree with?
    a. Replacing lead lines in homes will resolve lead levels.
    b. Addressing scaling and mineral accumulation is crucial.
    c. Scientific modeling will continue to be a fundamental tool.
    d. Source point lead pollution is the biggest concern.

52. Which statement would researchers from both passages most DISAGREE with?
    a. Low lead levels can be handled by sink filtration.
    b. Lead eradication is easier with well water.
    c. Corrosion control at water sources is our best weapon.
    d. In five years, we can control lead levels in water.

Writing and Language Test

Read the essay entitled "Education is Essential to Civilization" and answer Questions 1–15.

Early in my career, (1) a master's teacher shared this thought with me "Education is the last bastion of civility." While I did not completely understand the scope of those words at the time, I have since come to realize the depth, breadth, truth, and significance of what he said. (2) Education provides society with a vehicle for (3) raising it's children to be civil, decent, human beings with something valuable to contribute to the world. It is really what makes us human and what (4) distinguishes us as civilised creatures.

Being "civilized" humans means being "whole" humans. Education must address the mind, body, and soul of students. (5) It would be detrimental to society, only meeting the needs of the mind, if our schools were myopic in their focus. As humans, we are multi-dimensional, multi-faceted beings who need more than head knowledge to survive. (6) The human heart and psyche have to be fed in order for the mind to develop properly, and the body must be maintained and exercised to help fuel the working of the brain. Education is a basic human right, and it allows us to sustain a democratic society in which participation is fundamental to its success. It should inspire students to seek better solutions to world problems and to dream of a more equitable society. Education should never discriminate on any basis, and it should create individuals who are self-sufficient, patriotic, and tolerant of (7) others' ideas.

(8) All children can learn. Although not all children learn in the same manner. All children learn best, however, when their basic physical needs are met and they feel safe, secure, and loved. Students are much more responsive to a teacher who values them and shows them respect as individual people. Teachers must model at all times the way they expect students to treat them and their peers. If teachers set high expectations for (9) there students, the students will rise to that high level. Teachers must make the well-being of students their primary focus and must not be afraid to let students learn from their own mistakes.

In the modern age of technology, a teacher's focus is no longer the "what" of the content, (10) but more importantly, the 'why.' Students are bombarded with information and have access to ANY information they need right at their fingertips. Teachers have to work harder than ever before to help students identify salient information (11) so to think critically about the information they encounter. Students have to (12) read between the lines, identify bias, and determine who they can trust in the milieu of ads, data, and texts presented to them.

Schools must work in concert with families in this important mission. While children spend most of their time in school, they are dramatically and indelibly shaped (13) with the influences of their family and culture. Teachers must not only respect this fact, (14) but must strive to include parents in the education of their children and must work to keep parents informed of progress and problems. Communication between classroom and home is essential for a child's success.

Humans have always aspired to be more, do more, and to better ourselves and our communities. This is where education lies, right at the heart of humanity's desire to be all that we can be. Education helps us strive for higher goals and better treatment of ourselves and others. I shudder to think what would become of us if education ceased to be the "last bastion of civility." (15) We must be unapologetic about expecting excellence from our students? Our very existence depends upon it.

1. What edit is needed to correct sentence 1 (reproduced below)?

Early in my career, (1) a master's teacher shared this thought with me "Education is the last bastion of civility."

a. NO CHANGE
b. a master's teacher shared this thought with me: "Education is the last bastion of civility."
c. a master's teacher shared this thought with me: "Education is the last bastion of civility".
d. a master's teacher shared this thought with me. "Education is the last bastion of civility."

2. What edit is needed to correct sentence 2 (reproduced below)?

(2) Education provides society with a vehicle for raising it's children to be civil, decent, human beings with something valuable to contribute to the world.

a. NO CHANGE
b. Education provide
c. Education will provide
d. Education providing

3. What edit is needed to correct sentence 3 (reproduced below)?

Education provides society with a vehicle for (3) raising it's children to be civil, decent, human beings with something valuable to contribute to the world.

a. NO CHANGE
b. raises its children to be
c. raising its' children to be
d. raising its children to be

4. Which word, if any, is misspelled?
a. None of these are misspelled.
b. Distinguishes
c. Civilised
d. Creatures

5. What edit is needed to correct sentence 5 (reproduced below)?

(5) It would be detrimental to society, only meeting the needs of the mind, if our schools were myopic in their focus.

a. NO CHANGE
b. It would be detrimental to society if our schools were myopic in their focus, only meeting the needs of the mind.
c. Only meeting the needs of our mind, our schools were myopic in their focus, detrimental to society.
d. Myopic is the focus of our schools, being detrimental to society for only meeting the needs of the mind.

6. Which of these sentences, if any, should begin a new paragraph?
a. NO CHANGE
b. The human heart and psyche have to be fed in order for the mind to develop properly, and the body must be maintained and exercised to help fuel the working of the brain.
c. Education is a basic human right, and it allows us to sustain a democratic society in which participation is fundamental to its success.
d. It should inspire students to seek better solutions to world problems and to dream of a more equitable society.

7. What edit is needed to correct sentence 7 (reproduced below)?

Education should never discriminate on any basis, and it should create individuals who are self-sufficient, patriotic, and tolerant of (7) others' ideas.

a. NO CHANGE
b. other's ideas
c. others ideas
d. others's ideas

8. What edit is needed to correct sentence 8 (reproduced below)?

(8) All children can learn. Although not all children learn in the same manner.

a. NO CHANGE
b. All children can learn although not all children learn in the same manner.
c. All children can learn although, not all children learn in the same manner.
d. All children can learn, although not all children learn in the same manner.

9. What edit is needed to correct sentence 9 (reproduced below)?

If teachers set high expectations for (9) there students, the students will rise to that high level.

a. NO CHANGE
b. they're students
c. their students
d. thare students

10. What edit is needed to correct sentence 10 (reproduced below)?

In the modern age of technology, a teacher's focus is no longer the "what" of the content, (10) but more importantly, the 'why.'

a. NO CHANGE
b. but more importantly, the "why."
c. but more importantly, the 'why'.
d. but more importantly, the "why".

11. What edit is needed to correct sentence 11 (reproduced below)?

Teachers have to work harder than ever before to help students identify salient information (11) so to think critically about the information they encounter.

a. NO CHANGE
b. and to think critically
c. but to think critically
d. nor to think critically

12. What edit is needed to correct sentence 12 (reproduced below)?

Students have to (12) read between the lines, identify bias, and determine who they can trust in the milieu of ads, data, and texts presented to them.

a. NO CHANGE
b. read between the lines, identify bias, and determining
c. read between the lines, identifying bias, and determining
d. reads between the lines, identifies bias, and determines

13. What edit is needed to correct sentence 13 (reproduced below)?

While children spend most of their time in school, they are dramatically and indelibly shaped (13) with the influences of their family and culture.

a. NO CHANGE
b. for the influences
c. to the influences
d. by the influences

14. What edit is needed to correct sentence 14 (reproduced below)?

Teachers must not only respect this fact, (14) but must strive to include parents in the education of their children and must work to keep parents informed of progress and problems.

a. NO CHANGE
b. but to strive
c. but striving
d. but strived

15. What edit is needed to correct sentence 15 (reproduced below)?

(15) We must be unapologetic about expecting excellence from our students? Our very existence depends upon it.

a. NO CHANGE
b. We must be unapologetic about expecting excellence from our students, our very existence depends upon it.
c. We must be unapologetic about expecting excellence from our students—our very existence depends upon it.
d. We must be unapologetic about expecting excellence from our students our very existence depends upon it.

Questions 16–24 are based on the following passage about Frankenstein *by Mary Shelley:*

(16) One of the icon's of romantic and science fiction literature remains Mary Shelley's classic, *Frankenstein, or The Modern Prometheus*. Schools throughout the world still teach the book in literature and philosophy courses. Scientific communities also engage in discussion on the novel. But why? Besides the novel's engaging (17) writing style the story's central theme remains highly relevant in a world of constant discovery and moral

dilemmas. Central to the core narrative is the (18) struggle between enlightenment and the cost of overusing power.

The subtitle, *The Modern Prometheus*, encapsulates the inner theme of the story more than the main title of *Frankenstein*. As with many romantic writers, Shelley invokes the classical myths and (19) symbolism of Ancient Greece and Rome to high light core ideas. Looking deeper into the myth of Prometheus sheds light not only on the character of Frankenstein (20) but also poses a psychological dilemma to the audience. Prometheus is the titan who gave fire to mankind. (21) However, more than just fire he gave people knowledge and power. The power of fire advanced civilization. Yet, for giving fire to man, Prometheus is (22) punished by the gods bound to a rock and tormented for his act. This is clearly a parallel to Frankenstein—he is the modern Prometheus.

Frankenstein's quest for knowledge becomes an obsession. It leads him to literally create new life, breaking the bounds of conceivable science to illustrate that man can create life out of nothing. (23) Yet he ultimately faltered as a creator, abandoning his progeny in horror of what he created. Frankenstein then suffers his creature's wrath, (24) the result of his pride, obsession for power and lack of responsibility.

Shelley isn't condemning scientific achievement. Rather, her writing reflects that science and discovery are good things, but, like all power, it must be used wisely. The text alludes to the message that one must have reverence for nature and be mindful of the potential consequences. Frankenstein did not take responsibility or even consider how his actions would affect others. His scientific brilliance ultimately led to suffering.

16. Which of the following would be the best choice for this sentence (reproduced below)?

(16) One of the icon's of romantic and science fiction literature remains Mary Shelley's classic, *Frankenstein, or The Modern Prometheus*.

a. NO CHANGE
b. One of the icons of romantic and science fiction literature
c. One of the icon's of romantic, and science fiction literature,
d. The icon of romantic and science fiction literature

17. Which of the following would be the best choice for this sentence (reproduced below)?

Besides the novel's engaging (17) writing style the story's central theme remains highly relevant in a world of constant discovery and moral dilemmas.

a. NO CHANGE
b. writing style the central theme of the story
c. writing style, the story's central theme
d. the story's central theme's writing style

18. Which of the following would be the best choice for this sentence (reproduced below)?

> Central to the core narrative is the (18) <u>struggle between enlightenment and the cost of overusing power.</u>

a. NO CHANGE
b. struggle between enlighten and the cost of overusing power.
c. struggle between enlightenment's cost of overusing power.
d. struggle between enlightening and the cost of overusing power.

19. Which of the following would be the best choice for this sentence (reproduced below)?

> As with many romantic writers, Shelley invokes the classical myths and (19) <u>symbolism of Ancient Greece and Rome to high light core ideas.</u>

a. NO CHANGE
b. symbolism of Ancient Greece and Rome to highlight core ideas.
c. symbolism of ancient Greece and Rome to highlight core ideas.
d. symbolism of Ancient Greece and Rome highlighting core ideas.

20. Which of the following would be the best choice for this sentence (reproduced below)?

> Looking deeper into the myth of Prometheus sheds light not only on the character of Frankenstein (20) <u>but also poses a psychological dilemma to the audience.</u>

a. NO CHANGE
b. but also poses a psychological dilemma with the audience.
c. but also poses a psychological dilemma for the audience.
d. but also poses a psychological dilemma there before the audience.

21. Which of the following would be the best choice for this sentence (reproduced below)?

> (21) <u>However, more than just fire he gave people knowledge and power.</u>

a. NO CHANGE
b. However, more than just fire he gave people, knowledge, and power.
c. However, more than just fire, he gave people knowledge and power.
d. In addition to fire, Prometheus gave people knowledge and power.

22. Which of the following would be the best choice for this sentence (reproduced below)?

> Yet, for giving fire to man, Prometheus is (22) <u>punished by the gods bound to a rock and tormented for his act.</u>

a. NO CHANGE
b. punished by the gods, bound to a rock and tormented for his act.
c. bound to a rock and tormented by the gods as punishment.
d. punished for his act by being bound to a rock and tormented as punishment from the gods.

23. Which of the following would be the best choice for this sentence (reproduced below)?

> (23) Yet he ultimately faltered as a creator, abandoning his progeny in horror of what he created.

a. NO CHANGE
b. Yet, he ultimately falters as a creator by
c. Yet, he ultimately faltered as a creator,
d. Yet he ultimately falters as a creator by

24. Which of the following would be the best choice for this sentence (reproduced below)?

> Frankenstein then suffers his creature's wrath, (24) the result of his pride, obsession for power and lack of responsibility.

a. NO CHANGE
b. the result of his pride, obsession for power and lacking of responsibility.
c. the result of his pride, obsession for power, and lack of responsibility.
d. the result of his pride and also his obsession for power and lack of responsibility.

Questions 25–33 are based on the following passage:

> The power of legends continues to enthrall our imagination, provoking us both to wonder and explore. (25) Who doesnt love a good legend? Some say legends never (26) die and this is certainly the case for the most legendary creature of all, Bigfoot. To this day, people still claim sightings of the illusive cryptid. Many think of Bigfoot as America's monster, yet many nations have legends of a similar creature. In my own research I have found that Australia has the Yowie, China has the Yerin, and Russia has the Almas. (27) Their all over the world, the bigfoots and the legends tied to them. Does this mean they could exist?
>
> There are many things to consider when addressing (28) this question but the chief factor is whether there is credible evidence. (29) For science to formally recognize that such a species exists, there needs to be physical proof. While people have found supposed footprints and even (30) captured photos and film of the creature, this validity of such evidence is up for debate. There is room for uncertainty. Most visual evidence is out of focus, thus (31) there is often skepticism whether such images are real. Some researchers have even claimed to have hair and blood samples, but still there is doubt in the scientific community. The reason is simple: there needs to be a body or living specimen found and actively studied in order to prove the Bigfoots' existence.
>
> Yet, one cannot ignore the fact that (32) hundreds of witnesses continuing to describe a creature with uniform features all over the world. These bigfoot sightings aren't a modern occurrence either. Ancient civilizations have reported (33) seeing Bigfoot as well including Native Americans. It is from Native Americans that we gained the popular term Sasquatch, which is the primary name for the North American bigfoot. How does their testimony factor in? If indigenous people saw these animals, could they not have existed at some point? After all, when Europeans first arrived in Africa, they disbelieved the

native accounts of the gorilla. But sure enough, Europeans eventually found gorillas and collected a body.

25. Which of the following would be the best choice for this sentence (reproduced below)?

(25) Who doesnt love a good legend?

a. NO CHANGE
b. Who does not love a good legend?
c. A good legend, who doesn't love one?
d. Who doesn't love a good legend?

26. Which of the following would be the best choice for this sentence (reproduced below)?

Some say legends never (26) die and this is certainly the case for the most legendary creature of all, Bigfoot.

a. NO CHANGE
b. die, and this is certainly the case
c. die; this is certainly the case
d. die. This is certainly the case

27. Which of the following would be the best choice for this sentence (reproduced below)?

(27) Their all over the world, the bigfoots and the legends tied to them.

a. NO CHANGE
b. There all over the world, the
c. They're all over the world, the
d. All over the world they are, the

28. Which of the following would be the best choice for this sentence (reproduced below)?

There are many things to consider when addressing (28) this question but the chief factor is whether there is credible evidence.

a. NO CHANGE
b. this question, but the chief factor
c. this question however the chief factor
d. this question; but the chief factor

29. Which of the following would be the best choice for this sentence (reproduced below)?

(29) For science to formally recognize that such a species exists, there needs to be physical proof.

a. NO CHANGE
b. Physical proof are needed in order for science to formally recognize that such a species exists.
c. For science to formally recognize that such a species exists there needs to be physical proof.
d. For science, to formally recognize that such a species exists, there needs to be physical proof.

30. Which of the following would be the best choice for this sentence (reproduced below)?

> While people have found supposed footprints and even (30) captured photos and film of the creature, this validity of such evidence is up for debate.

a. NO CHANGE
b. captured photos and film of the creature. This validity of such evidence is up for debate.
c. captured photos and film of the creature, the validities of such evidence is up for debate.
d. captured photos and film of the creature, the validity of such evidence is up for debate.

31. Which of the following would be the best choice for this sentence (reproduced below)?

> Most visual evidence is out of focus, thus (31) there is often skepticism whether such images are real.

a. NO CHANGE
b. often skepticism whether such images are real.
c. there is often skepticism, whether such images are real.
d. there is often skepticism weather such images are real.

32. Which of the following would be the best choice for this sentence (reproduced below)?

> Yet, one cannot ignore the fact that (32) hundreds of witnesses continuing to describe a creature with uniform features all over the world.

a. NO CHANGE
b. hundreds of witnesses continuing to describing a creature
c. hundreds of witnesses continue to describe a creature
d. hundreds of the witnesses continue to described a creature

33. Which of the following would be the best choice for this sentence (reproduced below)?

> Ancient civilizations have reported (33) seeing Bigfoot as well including Native Americans.

a. NO CHANGE
b. seeing Bigfoot, Native Americans as well.
c. seeing Bigfoot also the Native Americans.
d. seeing Bigfoot, including Native Americans.

Questions 34–40 are based on the following passage:

> I have to admit that when my father bought a recreational vehicle (RV), I thought he was making a huge mistake. I didn't really know anything about RVs, but I knew that my dad was as big a "city slicker" as there was. (34) In fact, I even thought he might have gone a little bit crazy. On trips to the beach, he preferred to swim at the pool, and whenever he went hiking, he avoided touching any plants for fear that they might be poison ivy. Why would this man, with an almost irrational fear of the outdoors, want a 40-foot camping behemoth?

(35) The RV was a great purchase for our family and brought us all closer together. Every morning (36) we would wake up, eat breakfast, and broke camp. We laughed at our own comical attempts to back The Beast into spaces that seemed impossibly small. (37) We rejoiced as "hackers." When things inevitably went wrong and we couldn't solve the problems on our own, we discovered the incredible helpfulness and friendliness of the RV community. (38) We even made some new friends in the process.

(39) Above all, it allowed us to share adventures. While traveling across America, which we could not have experienced in cars and hotels. Enjoying a campfire on a chilly summer evening with the mountains of Glacier National Park in the background or waking up early in the morning to see the sun rising over the distant spires of Arches National Park are memories that will always stay with me and our entire family. (40) Those are also memories that my siblings and me have now shared with our own children.

34. Which of the following would be the best choice for this sentence (reproduced below)?

(34) In fact, I even thought he might have gone a little bit crazy.

a. NO CHANGE
b. Move the sentence so that it comes before the preceding sentence.
c. Move the sentence to the end of the first paragraph.
d. Omit the sentence.

35. In context, which is the best version of the underlined portion of this sentence (reproduced below)?

(35) The RV was a great purchase for our family and brought us all closer together.

a. NO CHANGE
b. Not surprisingly, the RV
c. Furthermore, the RV
d. As it turns out, the RV

36. Which is the best version of the underlined portion of this sentence (reproduced below)?

Every morning (36) we would wake up, eat breakfast, and broke camp.

a. NO CHANGE
b. we would wake up, eat breakfast, and break camp.
c. would we wake up, eat breakfast, and break camp?
d. we are waking up, eating breakfast, and breaking camp.

37. Which is the best version of the underlined portion of this sentence (reproduced below)?

(37) We rejoiced as "hackers."

a. NO CHANGE
b. To a nagging problem of technology, we rejoiced as "hackers."
c. We rejoiced when we figured out how to "hack" a solution to a nagging technological problem.
d. To "hack" our way to a solution, we had to rejoice.

38. Which is the best version of the underlined portion of this sentence (reproduced below)?

> (38) We even made some new friends in the process.

a. NO CHANGE
b. In the process was the friends we were making.
c. We are even making some new friends in the process.
d. We will make new friends in the process.

39. Which is the best version of the underlined portion of this sentence (reproduced below)?

> (39) Above all, it allowed us to share adventures. While traveling across America, which we could not have experienced in cars and hotels.

a. NO CHANGE
b. Above all, it allowed us to share adventures while traveling across America
c. Above all, it allowed us to share adventures; while traveling across America
d. Above all, it allowed us to share adventures—while traveling across America

40. Which is the best version of the underlined portion of this sentence (reproduced below)?

> (40) Those are also memories that my siblings and me have now shared with our own children.

a. NO CHANGE
b. Those are also memories that me and my siblings
c. Those are also memories that my siblings and I
d. Those are also memories that I and my siblings

Questions 41–45 are based on the following passage:

> We live in a savage world; that's just a simple fact. It is a time of violence, when the need for self-defense is imperative. (41) Martial arts, like Jiu-Jitsu, still play a vital role in ones survival. (42) Jiu-Jitsu, however doesn't justify kicking people around, even when being harassed or attacked. Today, laws prohibit the (43) use of unnecessary force in self-defense; these serve to eliminate beating someone to a pulp once they have been neutralized. Such laws are needed. Apart from being unnecessary to continually strike a person when (44) their down, its immoral. Such over-aggressive retaliation turns the innocent into the aggressor. Jiu-Jitsu provides a way for defending oneself while maintaining the philosophy of restraint and self-discipline. (45) Integrated into its core philosophy, jiujitsu tempers the potential to do great physical harm with respect for that power and for life.

41. Which of the following would be the best choice for this sentence (reproduced below)?

> (41) Martial arts, like Jiu-Jitsu, still play a vital role in ones survival.

a. NO CHANGE
b. Martial arts, like Jiu-Jitsu, still play a vital role in one's survival.
c. Martial arts, like Jiu-Jitsu still play a vital role in ones survival.
d. Martial arts, like Jiu-Jitsu, still plays a vital role in one's survival.

42. Which of the following would be the best choice for this sentence (reproduced below)?

(42) Jiu-Jitsu, however doesn't justify kicking people around, even when being harassed or attacked.

a. NO CHANGE
b. Jiu-Jitsu, however, isn't justified by kicking people around,
c. However, Jiu-Jitsu doesn't justify kicking people around,
d. Jiu-Jitsu however doesn't justify kicking people around,

43. Which of the following would be the best choice for this sentence (reproduced below)?

Today, laws prohibit the (43) use of unnecessary force in self-defense; these serve to eliminate beating someone to a pulp once they have been neutralized.

a. NO CHANGE
b. use of unnecessary force in self-defense serving to eliminate
c. use of unnecessary force, in self-defense, these serve to eliminate
d. use of unnecessary force. In self-defense, these serve to eliminate

44. Which of the following would be the best choice for this sentence (reproduced below)?

Apart from being unnecessary to continually strike a person when (44) their down, its immoral.

a. NO CHANGE
b. their down, it's immoral.
c. they're down, its immoral.
d. they're down, it's immoral.

45. Which of the following would be the best choice for this sentence (reproduced below)?

(45) Integrated into its core philosophy, Jiu-Jitsu tempers the potential to do great physical harm with respect for that power, and for life.

a. NO CHANGE
b. Integrated into its core philosophy
c. Integrated into it's core philosophy
d. Integrated into its' core philosophy,

Math Test

Calculator Questions

1. If a car can travel 300 miles in 4 hours, how far can it go in an hour and a half?
   a. 100 miles
   b. 112.5 miles
   c. 135.5 miles
   d. 150 miles

2. At the store, Jan spends $90 on apples and oranges. Apples cost $1 each and oranges cost $2 each. If Jan buys the same number of apples as oranges, how many oranges did she buy?
    a. 20
    b. 25
    c. 30
    d. 35

3. What is the volume of a box with rectangular sides 5 feet long, 6 feet wide, and 3 feet high?
    a. 60 cubic feet
    b. 75 cubic feet
    c. 90 cubic feet
    d. 14 cubic feet

4. A train traveling 50 miles per hour takes a trip lasting 3 hours. If a map has a scale of 1 inch per 10 miles, how many inches apart are the train's starting point and ending point on the map if it traveled in a straight line?
    a. 14
    b. 12
    c. 13
    d. 15

5. A traveler takes an hour to drive to a museum, spends 3 hours and 30 minutes there, and takes half an hour to drive home. What percentage of their time was spent driving?
    a. 15%
    b. 30%
    c. 40%
    d. 60%

6. A truck is carrying three cylindrical barrels. Their bases have a diameter of 2 feet, and they have a height of 3 feet. What is the total volume of the three barrels in cubic feet?
    a. 3π
    b. 9π
    c. 12π
    d. 15π

7. Greg buys a $10 lunch with 5% sales tax. He leaves a $2 tip after his bill. How much money does he spend?
    a. $12.50
    b. $12
    c. $13
    d. $13.25

8. Marty wishes to save $150 over a 4-day period. How much must Marty save each day on average?
    a. $37.50
    b. $35
    c. $45.50
    d. $41

9. Bernard can make $80 per day. If he needs to make $300 and only works full days, how many days will this take?

a. 6
b. 3
c. 5
d. 4

10. A couple buys a house for $150,000. They sell it for $165,000. By what percentage did the house's value increase?

a. 10%
b. 13%
c. 15%
d. 17%

11. A school has 15 teachers and 20 teaching assistants. They have 200 students. What is the ratio of faculty to students?

a. $3 : 20$
b. $4 : 17$
c. $5 : 54$
d. $7 : 40$

12. A map has a scale of 1 inch per 5 miles. A car can travel 60 miles per hour. If the distance from the start to the destination is 3 inches on the map, how long will it take the car to make the trip?

a. 12 minutes
b. 15 minutes
c. 17 minutes
d. 20 minutes

13. Taylor works two jobs. The first pays $20,000 per year. The second pays $10,000 per year. She donates 15% of her income to charity. How much does she donate each year?

a. $4,500
b. $5,000
c. $5,500
d. $6,000

14. A box with rectangular sides is 24 inches wide, 18 inches deep, and 12 inches high. What is the volume of the box in cubic feet?

a. 2
b. 3
c. 4
d. 5

15. Kristen purchases $100 worth of CDs and DVDs. The CDs cost $10 each and the DVDs cost $15. If she bought four DVDs, how many CDs did she buy?

a. 5
b. 6
c. 3
d. 4

16. If Sarah reads at an average rate of 21 pages in four nights, how long will it take her to read 140 pages?

a. 6 nights
b. 26 nights
c. 8 nights
d. 27 nights

17. Mom's car drove 72 miles in 90 minutes. There are 5,280 feet per mile. How fast did she drive in feet per second?

a. 0.8 feet per second
b. 48.9 feet per second
c. 0.009 feet per second
d. 70.4 feet per second

18. This chart indicates how many sales of CDs, vinyl records, and MP3 downloads occurred over the last year. Approximately what percentage of the total sales was from CDs?

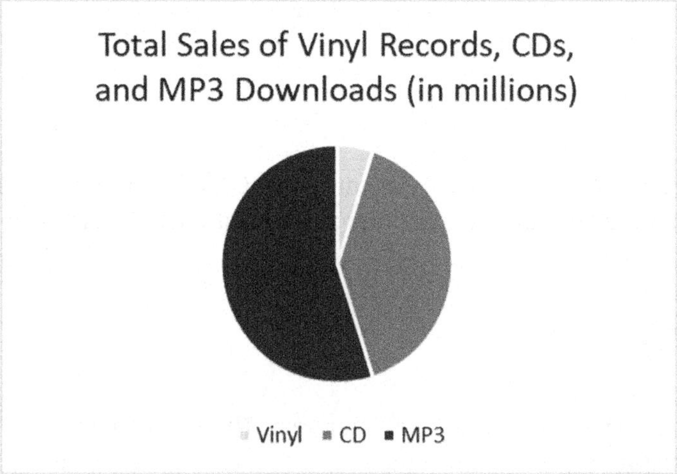

a. 55%
b. 25%
c. 40%
d. 5%

19. After a 20% sale discount, Frank purchased a new refrigerator for $850. How much did he save from the original price?

a. $170
b. $212.50
c. $105.75
d. $200

20. Which of the following is NOT a way to write 40 percent of N?
   a. $(0.4)N$
   b. $\frac{2}{5}N$
   c. $40N$
   d. $\frac{4N}{10}$

21. The graph of which function has an x-intercept of -2?
   a. $y = 2x - 3$
   b. $y = 4x + 2$
   c. $y = x^2 + 5x + 6$
   d. $y = 2x^2 + 3x - 1$

22. The table below displays the number of three-year-olds at Kids First Daycare who are potty-trained and those who still wear diapers.

	Potty-trained	**Wear diapers**	**Sum**
Boys	26	22	48
Girls	34	18	52
Total	60	40	

What is the probability of a three-year-old girl from the school being potty-trained?
   a. 52%
   b. 34%
   c. 65%
   d. 57%

23. A clothing company with a target market of U.S. boys surveys 2,000 twelve-year-old boys to find their height. The average height of the boys is 61 inches. For the above scenario, 61 inches represents which of the following?
   a. Sample statistic
   b. Population parameter
   c. Confidence interval
   d. Measurement error

24. A government agency is researching the average consumer cost of gasoline throughout the United States. Which data collection method would produce the most valid results?
   a. Randomly choosing one hundred gas stations in the state of New York
   b. Randomly choosing ten gas stations from each of the fifty states
   c. Randomly choosing five hundred gas stations from across all fifty states with the number chosen proportional to the population of the state
   d. All three methods would each produce equally valid results.

25. Suppose an investor deposits $1,200 into a bank account that accrues 1 percent interest per month. Assuming x represents the number of months since the deposit and y represents the money in the account, which of the following exponential functions models the scenario?

a. $y = (0.01)(1200^x)$
b. $y = (1200)(0.01^x)$
c. $y = (1.01)(1200^x)$
d. $y = (1200)(1.01^x)$

26. A student gets an 85% on a test with 20 questions. How many answers did the student solve correctly?

a. 15
b. 16
c. 17
d. 18

27. Four people split a bill. The first person pays for $\frac{1}{5}$, the second person pays for $\frac{1}{4}$, and the third person pays for $\frac{1}{3}$. What fraction of the bill does the fourth person pay?

a. $\frac{13}{60}$
b. $\frac{47}{60}$
c. $\frac{1}{4}$
d. $\frac{4}{15}$

28. Which of the following fractions is equal to 9.3?

a. $9\frac{3}{7}$
b. $\frac{903}{1,000}$
c. $\frac{9.03}{100}$
d. $9\frac{3}{10}$

29. What is the solution to $3\frac{2}{3} - 1\frac{4}{5}$?

a. $1\frac{13}{15}$
b. $\frac{14}{15}$
c. $2\frac{2}{3}$
d. $\frac{4}{5}$

30. What is $\frac{420}{98}$ rounded to the nearest integer?
a. 4
b. 3
c. 5
d. 6

31. What is the solution to $4\frac{1}{3} + 3\frac{3}{4}$?
a. $6\frac{5}{12}$
b. $8\frac{1}{12}$
c. $8\frac{2}{3}$
d. $7\frac{7}{12}$

32. Five of six numbers have a sum of 25. The average of all six numbers is 6. What is the sixth number?
a. 8
b. 10
c. 11
d. 12

33. Suppose the function $y = \frac{1}{8}x^3 + 2x - 21$ approximates the population of a given city between the years 1900 and 2000 with x representing the year (where 1900 is $x = 0$) and y representing the population (in thousands). Which of the following domains are relevant for the scenario?
a. $(-\infty, \infty)$
b. [1900, 2000]
c. [0, 100]
d. [0, 0]

34. What is the equation of a circle whose center is (0, 0) and whole radius is 5?
a. $(x - 5)^2 + (y - 5)^2 = 25$
b. $(x)^2 + (y)^2 = 5$
c. $(x)^2 + (y)^2 = 25$
d. $(x + 5)^2 + (y + 5)^2 = 25$

35. What is the equation of a circle whose center is (1, 5) and whole radius is 4?
a. $(x - 1)^2 + (y - 25)^2 = 4$
b. $(x - 1)^2 + (y - 25)^2 = 16$
c. $(x + 1)^2 + (y + 5)^2 = 16$
d. $(x - 1)^2 + (y - 5)^2 = 16$

36. Where does the point $(-3, -4)$ lie on the circle with the equation $(x)^2 + (y)^2 = 25$?
a. Inside of the circle
b. Outside of the circle
c. On the circle
d. There is not enough information to tell

37. A drug needs to be stored at room temperature (68 °F). What is the equivalent temperature in degrees Celsius?

a. 36 °C
b. 72 °C
c. 68 °C
d. 20 °C

38. What is the slope of this line?

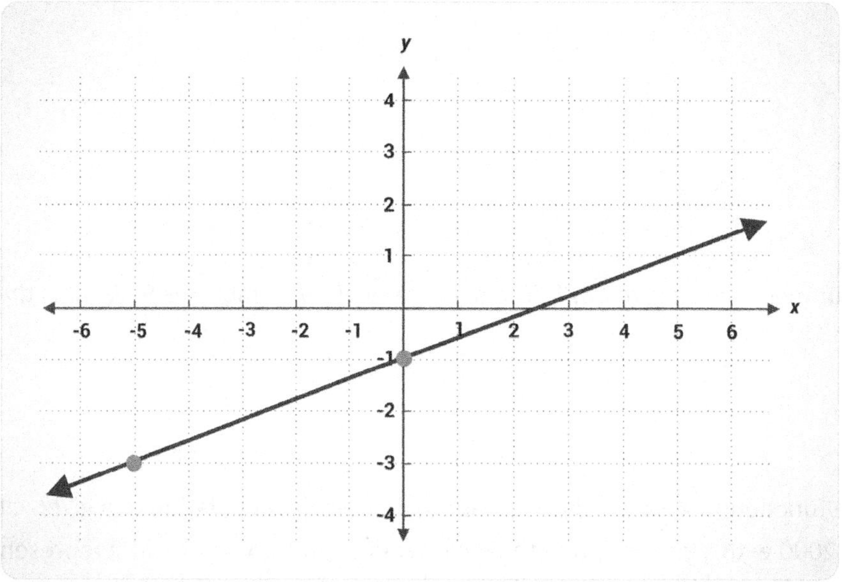

a. 2
b. $\frac{5}{2}$
c. $\frac{1}{2}$
d. $\frac{2}{5}$

39. What is the perimeter of the figure below? Note that the solid outer line is the perimeter.

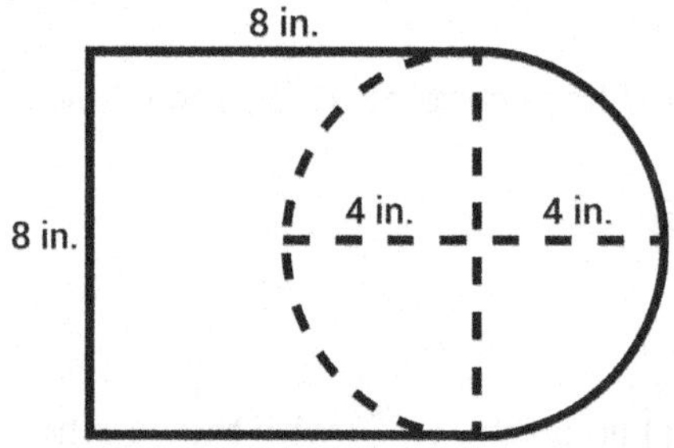

a. 48.566 ft
b. 36.566 ft
c. 19.78 ft
d. 30.566 ft

40. Which of the following equations best represents the problem below?

The width of a rectangle is 2 centimeters less than the length. If the perimeter of the rectangle is 44 centimeters, then what are the dimensions of the rectangle?

a. $2l + 2(l - 2) = 44$
b. $(l + 2) + (l + 2) + l = 48$
c. $l \times (l - 2) = 44$
d. $(l + 2) + (l + 2) + l = 44$

41. How will the following algebraic expression be simplified: $(5x^2 - 3x + 4) - (2x^2 - 7)$?
a. x^5
b. $3x^2 - 3x + 11$
c. $3x^2 - 3x - 3$
d. $x - 3$

42. What is 39% of 164?
a. 63.96
b. 23.78
c. 6,396
d. 2.38

43. Kimberley earns $10 an hour babysitting, and after 10 p.m., she earns $12 an hour. The time she works is rounded to the nearest hour for pay purposes. On her last job, she worked from 5:30 p.m. to 11 p.m. In total, how much did Kimberley earn for that job?
a. $45
b. $57
c. $62
d. $42

44. Keith's bakery had 252 customers go through its doors last week. This week, that number increased to 378. By what percentage did his customer volume increase?
a. 26%
b. 50%
c. 35%
d. 12%

No Calculator Questions

45. A family purchases a vehicle in 2005 for $20,000. In 2010, they decide to sell it for a newer model. They are able to sell the car for $8,000. By what percentage did the value of the family's car drop?
a. 40%
b. 68%
c. 60%
d. 33%

46. In May of 2010, a couple purchased a house for $100,000. In September of 2016, the couple sold the house for $93,000 so they could purchase a bigger one to start a family. How many months did they own the house?

a. 76
b. 54
c. 85
d. 93

47. At the beginning of the day, Xavier has 20 apples. At lunch, he meets his sister Emma and gives her half of his apples. After lunch, he stops by his neighbor Jim's house and gives him 6 of his apples. He then uses 3/4 of his remaining apples to make an apple pie for dessert at dinner. At the end of the day, how many apples does Xavier have left?

a. 4
b. 6
c. 2
d. 1

48. If $\frac{5}{2} \div \frac{1}{3} = n$, then n is between:

a. 5 and 7
b. 7 and 9
c. 9 and 11
d. 3 and 5

49. A closet is filled with red, blue, and green shirts. If $\frac{1}{3}$ of the shirts are green and $\frac{2}{5}$ are red, what fraction of the shirts are blue?

a. $\frac{4}{15}$
b. $\frac{1}{5}$
c. $\frac{7}{15}$
d. $\frac{1}{2}$

50. Shawna buys $2\frac{1}{2}$ gallons of paint. If she uses $\frac{1}{3}$ of it on the first day, how much does she have left?

a. $1\frac{5}{6}$ gallons
b. $1\frac{1}{2}$ gallons
c. $1\frac{2}{3}$ gallons
d. 2 gallons

51. What is the volume of a cylinder, in terms of π, with a radius of 6 centimeters and a height of 2 centimeters?

a. $36\,\pi\ \text{cm}^3$
b. $24\,\pi\ \text{cm}^3$
c. $72\,\pi\ \text{cm}^3$
d. $48\,\pi\ \text{cm}^3$

52. What is the length of the hypotenuse of a right triangle with one leg equal to 3 centimeters and the other leg equal to 4 centimeters?

a. 7 cm
b. 5 cm
c. 25 cm
d. 12 cm

53. 20 is 40% of what number?

a. 50
b. 8
c. 200
d. 5,000

54. If Danny takes 48 minutes to walk 3 miles, how many minutes should it take him to walk 5 miles maintaining the same speed?

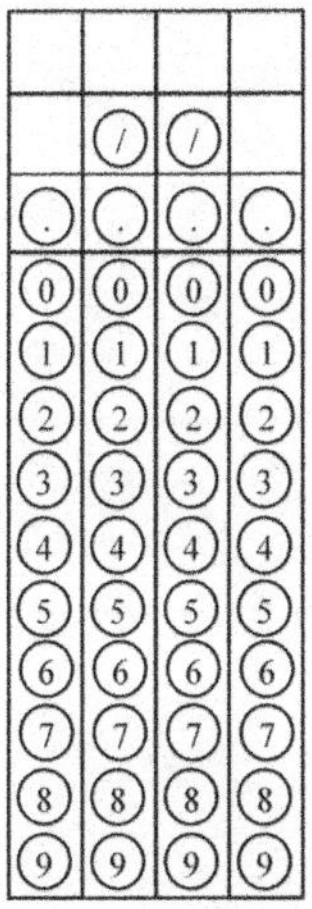

55. The perimeter of a 6-sided polygon is 56 cm. The lengths of three sides are 9 cm each. The lengths of two other sides are 8 cm each. What is the length of the missing side?

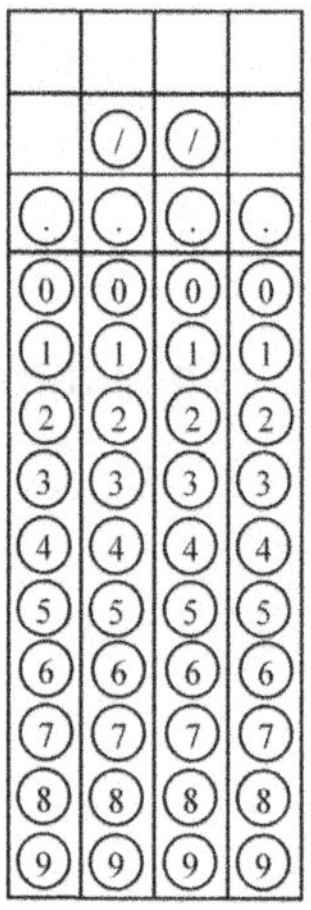

56. If the sine of $30° = x$, the cosine of what angle, in degrees, also equals x?

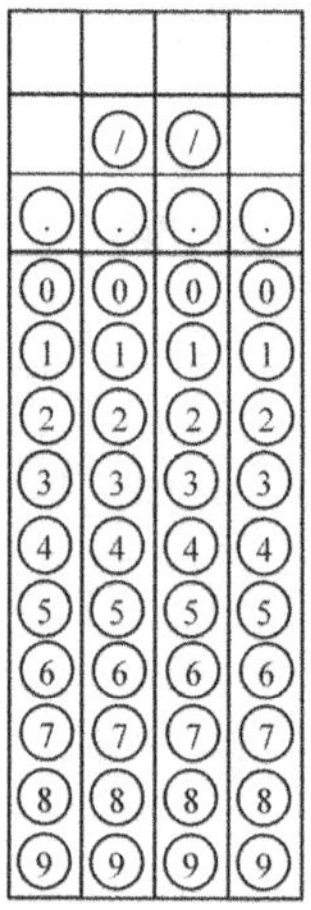

57. What is the value of $x^2 - 2xy + 2y^2$ when $x = 2$ and $y = 3$?

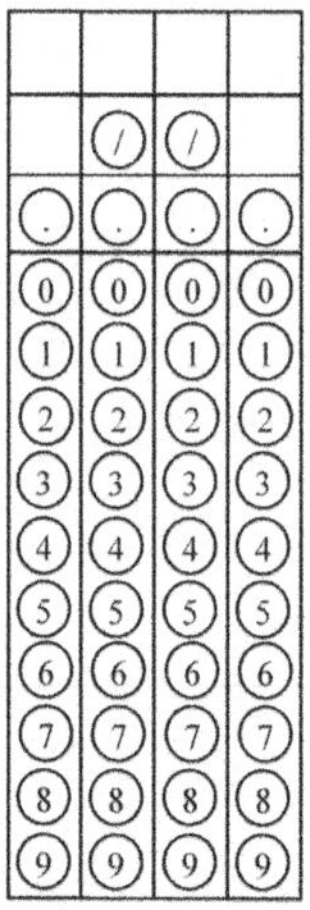

58. What is the value of x if $4x - 3 = 5$?

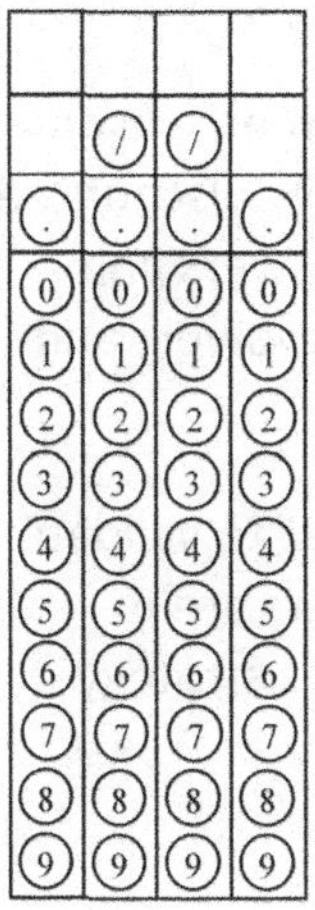

Essay Prompt

Bob's lawnmower shop has an excess supply of lawnmowers at the end of the summer season for the first time in years. Bob's son reasons that this excess supply should be heavily discounted and sold as quickly as possible to make room for winter equipment such as snowblowers and snowmobiles to maximize profits and revenue. Bob wants to keep the unsold lawnmowers and attempt to sell them again next year when demand returns.

Write a response in which you discuss what questions should be asked and resolved in order to validate Bob's strategy as a valid one versus his son's idea. Be sure to explain how easy those answers are to obtain, what assumptions they involve, and how the answers to the questions support Bob's strategy and confirm that it has a high probability of success.

The following pages are provided for writing your essay.

Answer Explanations #2

Reading Test

1. C: Choice *C* is the correct answer. It is easy to imagine that she may have felt either anger, Choice *A*, or fear, Choice *B*, but those are not expressed in the text. Instead, while the passage mentions that her appearance was haughty, Choice *D*, it goes on to say that she likely felt agony, Choice *C*.

2. A: Choice *A* is correct. The passage does not mention feeling vengeful, Choice *C*. Further, the passage mentions that the crowd may have been tempted to ridicule and therefore be amused, Choice *B*, but they were not. Nor are they outraged, Choice *D*, as the passage notes that the nature of the punishment wouldn't lend itself to that feeling.

3. D: Choice *D* is correct. The passage states that Prynne was only required to stand on the scaffold, not be in the stockade, though the stockade was still in use. There is no mention of the stockade's not being used because she is a woman, Choice *A*, nor that the townspeople wanted her to be in it, Choice *B*. Finally, Choice *C* is incorrect because the passage does not discuss the stockade's use as a deterrent.

4. C: Choice *C* is correct. The passage clearly mentions that if the crowd had any inclination to ridicule, it would be suppressed by the presence of the governor, a judge, and other dignitaries. There is no mention in the passage of crimes committed by others, Choice *A*. Though her demeanor was proud, this was not the reason given for the lack of ridicule, so Choice *B* is not correct. Though there is mention of a death sentence, the passage does not say that the crowd wanted to see her put to death, so Choice *D* is also not correct.

5. B: Choice *B* is correct. Based on the context of the sentence and the paired adjective in the passage ("bitter"), a reader can infer that the meaning is not a positive one; therefore, Choice *A* is incorrect. Further, Choice *C* is incorrect as there is no logical reason why Prynne would be sympathetic. Finally, the text does not say that Prynne is mourning, so Choice *D* is incorrect.

6. A: Choice *A* is correct. The passage notes the agony felt by a prisoner who is exposed to spectators and laid bare for all to see. There is no mention of shackled ankles or walking speed, so Choice *B* and Choice *C* are incorrect. While there is mention of children later in the passage, it is not connected to the walk from prison to marketplace, so Choice *D* is incorrect.

7. D: Choice *D* is correct. The final paragraph of the passage notes that she expected venomous attacks, but the event was quiet instead. Therefore, Choice *A* which suggests cheering, Choice *B*, which suggests mocking, and Choice *C*, which suggests laughter, are all incorrect.

8. A: Choice *A* is correct. The passage's final sentences suggest the weight of her sentence and its looming duration as the reason for her need for emotional release. No one attacks her, so Choice *B* is incorrect. She is never placed in the stockade, so Choice *C* is incorrect. The crowd has been solemn and does not mock or ridicule her; while she might want to respond to the silence, that is not suggested by the passage. Choice *D* is, therefore, incorrect.

9. C: Choice *C* is correct. The passage opens with the third person narrator describing the scene, then moves to Prynne's experience, then that of the crowd and moves between those over the course of the paragraphs. While the judge is mentioned, an entire crowd acts as witness so Choice *A* is incorrect.

Prynne's husband is not present in this passage, so Choice *B* is incorrect. The town historian is not identified or discussed, though we do get town history, so Choice *D* is incorrect

10. A: Choice *A* is correct. The passage describes her at times as serene, strong, sustained, and fortified, so tenacious is the best fit. She walks almost proudly so Choice *B* and Choice *C* are incorrect. At the end of the passage, it notes that she wanted to yell, but it does not note that the desire is out of anger, Choice *D*, at the crowd or herself, but rather out of a need for release from the heaviness of the moment.

11. B: Choice *B* is correct. The writer notes specifically that they are tools to create a way of life we can enjoy. As such, while dictators do limit freedoms, but no in a way that populations typically enjoy, so Choice *A* is not correct. The passage does note that laws, but freedom ensures we can make our own, but not abuse or misuse so Choice *C* is incorrect. Finally, Choice *D* is incorrect because there is no mention of how we limit who uses the tool.

12. D: Choice *D* is correct. Roosevelt notes that without the processes and discussions that democracy requires, a dictatorship can achieve the same result much more quickly. While it is true that dictatorships may be benevolent, this is not the argument Roosevelt offers, so Choice *A* is incorrect. It is true that multiple factors enable dictators to rise to power, but this is not the reason Roosevelt offers, so Choice *B* is incorrect. Finally, Choice *C* suggests that dictators have been successful and popular, and though that might be true in some instances, it is also not what the passage discusses.

13. C: Choice *C* is correct. The passage states that antitrust laws maintain economic competition and prevent monopolies from limiting people's freedoms. Choice *A* is incorrect as antitrust laws are intended to protect consumers, and while they contribute to a relationship between governments and populations, that's not their primary goal. Choice *B* is incorrect as there are still ways in which businesses can manipulate markets, and so fairness isn't the ultimate outcome. Finally, businesses do compete with the government in certain industries, and that is not the purpose of antitrust laws, so Choice *D* is incorrect.

14. C: Choice *C* is correct. "Promulgated" means to promoted or spread. Therefore, Choices *A, B*, and *D* are incorrect as they are opposites and do not suggest spreading or championing an idea.

15. A: Choice *A* is correct. Multiple supporting points throughout the passage support Choice *A,* and paragraph 3 clarifies this main idea clearly. While Choice *B, Choice C,* and Choice *D* are all mentioned in the paragraph, they are mentioned as supporting points rather than the main idea.

16. B: Choice *B* is correct. While Choice *A* is true, that's not the reason to include it. The goal of mentioning the two is to compare the current situation to two major movements for democracy and their successful campaigns thereby highlighting the importance of such fights. While his audience might include both American and French citizens, he is speaking to a much larger audience, and that is not the primary reason, so Choice *C* is not the best answer. Finally, Choice *D* is incorrect as the date of the speech does not commemorate both events.

17. A: Choice *A* is correct. The speech highlights the ideals of human freedom and democracy, and altogether it implies that Roosevelt feels very strongly about these ideals. A satirical speech, Choice *B*, is one that scorns or ridicules, and that is incorrect. Choice *C* suggests someone is being attacked, and that's not accurate either. Finally, Choice *D* suggest she is appeasing someone, and that isn't correct either.

18. D: Choice *D* is correct. Because freedom and democracy are the main focus of each of the points Roosevelt brings up, it's clear that she values them above other ideals. While Choice *A, Choice B,* and Choice *C* might be true, they are not reflected as clearly in the passage as Choice *D* is. Those values are brought up in the passage, but only in support of freedom and democracy.

19. C: Choice *C* is correct. Roosevelt clearly states that her concern is that there is no guarantee a dictator will remain benevolent and no guarantee that power would be returned to the populace. While Choice *A* is true, it is not Roosevelt's concern. Choice *B* is also correct, but not discussed in the passage. Choice *D* is too extreme; Roosevelt does not say it's impossible for a dictator to be benevolent, though she does have concerns about them staying that way.

20. C: Choice *C* is correct. Roosevelt notes that secrecy ensures an individual's right to vote as she chooses. Choice *A* and Choice *D* may be true; public votes were known for their carnivalesque atmosphere, and private votes protect voters from violent confrontations with their political foes. However, these ideas are not stated in the passage. Choice *B* is incorrect as the opposite may be true. Privacy might increase the likelihood that, because the vote is secret, an individual can attest to voting one way but actually vote another without any accountability. This would make bribery a risk.

21. B: Choice *B* is correct. Johnson notes that Selma is an opportunity to right wrongs and seek justice as it relates to the denial of equal rights. Though a bridge played prominent in the Selma protest march, it was not the cause, so Choice *A* is incorrect. A man was killed, but that happened during the protest so could not be the cause. Therefore, Choice *C* is not correct. Finally, though Johnson discusses wealth in this passage, he does not say it is the cause of the events in Selma, so Choice *D* is incorrect.

22. C: Choice *C* is correct. Johnson says the cries created conversation and garnered the attention of the government to redress the issues raised. There is no mention of police response, so Choice *A* is incorrect. Similarly, there is no mention of the turnout at the protest, so Choice *B* is also incorrect. Finally, while Johnson does mention that one life was lost at the protest, he does not present this as cause for hope nor does he say it was "only" one life. Therefore, Choice *D* is also incorrect.

23. D: Choice *D* is correct. Johnson says that this challenge speaks "to the values, and the purposes, and the meaning of our beloved nation." There is no mention of other protests, Choice *A*, and there is no mention or whether those issues are easier, Choice *B*, or harder, Choice *C*, to solve, so those are not correct.

24. A: Choice *A* is correct. Johnson writes that a person's dignity "rests on his right to be treated as a man equal in opportunity to all others." Though Johnson discusses the protests, Choice *B*, American might and abundance, Choices *C* and *D*, they are not the defined as the source of a person's dignity.

25. A: Choice *A* is correct. What is righteous is morally just, and that characterizes Johnson's tone, so Choice *A* is the best answer. Choice *B*, "quixotic," means excessively or foolishly idealistic. To call Johnson's speech quixotic would mean that its goals of dignity and equality were foolish ones. Both scathing, Choice *C*, and vindictive, Choice *D*, suggest anger, harsh language, and bitterness. Johnson speaks of hope and progress, and he does not use language that suggests he is trying to chastise his audience, so these answers are incorrect.

26. D: Choice *D* is correct. Johnson says even if we "defeat every enemy", Choice *C*, "double our wealth" (Choice *B*), or conquer the stars, Choice *A*, the greater failure is for a person to lose "his own soul." In this speech, "soul" refers to a person's moral or spiritual core, and to lose one's soul in this context means to lose moral or spiritual integrity.

27. C: Choice *C* is correct. Convocation means a gathering or a formal assembly. In this case, the people are summoning the leaders of government to an assembly. Based on context and conventional definitions of the words, Choices *A, B,* and *D* are incorrect.

28. C: Choice *C* is correct. The three quotations Johnson offers in this paragraph refer to the three ideals listed in Choice *C.* While there is mention of the military in this paragraph, it is not the purpose of the country, so Choice *A* is incorrect. While America is a world leader, it became a world leader some time after it was founded, so Choice *B* is incorrect. Finally, while America has prided itself on much, the goal was not to create envy, so Choice *D* is incorrect.

29. B: Choice *B* is correct. Johnson says these guardians "fought and died," and he says that they stand as guardians "around the world," referring to American troops. While some American citizens live in other parts of the world, they are not guarding liberty, so that answer is incorrect. "American government", Choice *C,* is singular and "guardians" is plural, so that answer doesn't fit. The protestors are located in Selma and not "around the world," so Choice *D* is also incorrect.

30. D: Choice *D* is correct. Johnson is passionately speaking about civil rights and racial equality and is aiming to impart this mindset to all Americans.

31. B: Choice *B* is correct. Consent of the governed means the governed people must give permission to the government to lead them, presumably through elections and the structure of representation. Consent does not imply liking; therefore, Choice *A* is incorrect. Consent of the governed does not mean the governed must be treated fairly, so Choice *B* is incorrect. Consent of the governed requires that the governed have a voice; therefore, Choice *D* is incorrect.

32. A: Choice *A* is correct. According to the research, residents saw the risk of mosquito-borne illnesses as higher during the Zika outbreak despite the risk being higher post hurricane. It does not suggest that they saw no risk from either, so Choice *B* and Choice *C* are incorrect. Choice *D* is also incorrect as they did not see the risks as the same.

33. D: Choice *D* is correct. According to the research, one can infer that concerns about basic necessities like shelter, post-hurricane, may impact rates of mosquito-borne illnesses. There is no connection mentioned between Zika and hurricanes, though the research does compare the two in terms of mosquito problems, so Choice *A* is incorrect. Similarly, Choice *B* is incorrect as though the passage discusses resident concerns of risk and Zika, it does so in connection with mosquito-borne illnesses, not in regard to the spread of Zika specifically. Choice *C* is also incorrect because, again, though discussed together, there's no real correlation discussed in the passage.

34. C: Choice *C* is correct. The passage notes that CASPERs have been used to assess bite prevention and control-related factors, diseases, and breeding areas. CASPERs were used in the US Virgin Islands to mitigate mosquito-borne issues after the hurricane, not as a direct response to the hurricane, so Choice *A* is incorrect. While standing water might be one of the environmental factors included in post-hurricane mosquito proliferation, swamp size specifically was not addressed by CASPERs in the US Virgin Islands, so Choice *B* is incorrect. Backpack spraying was found to be an optimal strategy after evaluating information from CASPERs; the CASPER itself was not about backpack spraying, so Choice *D* is incorrect.

35. B: Choice *B* is correct. In the context of health, and as used in the passage, vector-related refers to the pathway by which a disease or pathogen is spread. For example, a vector-borne illness is transmitted from an insect or other organism (considered the vector) to another organism or plant.

36. C: Choice *C* is correct. In the third paragraph, the passage refers to the need for increased mosquito "abatement." Based on the focus of the paragraph, Choice *A* and Choice *D* would represent the spread of mosquitoes and are therefore incorrect. While sterilization might be an option for abatement, it's not mentioned specifically nor is it the only tactic for abatement, so Choice *B* is incorrect.

37. B: Choice *B* is correct. Based on the information provided, backpack spraying best addresses the need to spray targeted areas with greatest risk. Human exposure to mosquito bites is mentioned, but not to the chemicals used in spraying, so Choice *A* is incorrect. Though the passage mentions community support for spraying, it doesn't specify the type of support, so Choice *C* is incorrect. Finally, while the passage mentions household-level prevention, it doesn't specify how household participation affects spraying, so Choice *D* is also incorrect.

38. A: Choice *A* is correct. According to the passage, CASPERs may help assess community campaigns and reveal community knowledge, attitudes, and practices. Lack of shelter and spraying support are noted directly in reference to post-hurricane concerns, which is an emergency situation, so Choice *B* and Choice *C* are incorrect. While some of the efforts of CASPERs may reveal community risks, particularly as it relates to actual versus perceived risks, it is not listed among the non-emergency applications in the final paragraph and so Choice *D* is incorrect.

39. B: Choice *B* is correct. While backpack spraying is noted as the acceptable option, we cannot determine how communities will move forward with its inclusion in their response without more information, so Choice *A* is incorrect. Similarly, this passaged argues for the inclusion of CASPERs as a tool in emergency and non-emergency situations, but we cannot draw a conclusion regarding future use, so Choice *C* is incorrect. Given the nature of increased storm activity across the world, we cannot be certain that these disease vector problems will remain isolated to island nations, so Choice *D* is incorrect. However, given the increase in severe storms, we can conclude that risks with mosquito-borne illnesses will also increase, meaning Choice *B* is correct.

40. D: Choice *D* is correct. The primary focus of this paragraph is to discuss how CASPER can be used to assist communities and governments in addressing both emergency and non-emergency issues. While Choices *A, B*, and *C* are true, they are supporting details in the paragraph and not the focus of the passage itself.

41. A: Choice *A* is correct. The passage notes, in paragraph 1, that environmental conditions for mosquito breeding and exposure are more favorable after a hurricane. While it might be true that mosquitoes bite less during storms, Choice *B*, or that fewer preventative medications are available, Choice *C*, these are not discussed in the passage. Finally, it is noted that residents seem to be aware of an elevated risk post-hurricane, but awareness does not cause disease, so Choice *D* is incorrect.

42. C: Choice *C* is correct. The passage notes that CASPERs would be incredibly useful in non-emergency situations as well, so Choice *A* is incorrect. Aerial spraying is not mentioned specifically, especially in relation to Zika, so Choice *B* is incorrect. Finally, researchers agree that controlling mosquito-borne diseases involves bite prevention, but also requires control, community knowledge and other factors, so while Choice *D* is part of the solution, it may not be the best option.

43. D: Choice *D* is correct. Both Choice *A* and Choice *B* suggest that researchers and residents are unaware of the lead problem in much of America's water. However, the existence of the research itself contradicts both these answers. Similarly, Choice *C* directly contradicts the research presented in both passages, which not only identify but also track the lead sources.

44. B: Choice *B* is correct. The passage states that public systems can measure water quality and use corrosion inhibitors to improve water quality. While a city may inform residents of high lead levels, that's not noted in this passage regarding the public system's role. Therefore, Choice *A* is incorrect. Similarly, public water systems are not responsible for replacing home piping, Choice *C*. Further, while systems clearly allow and likely encourage research, their objective is to mitigate lead exposure, so Choice *D* is not the best answer.

45. D: Choice *D* is correct. The research suggests that if the lead pipes have been removed from the home, the city's service lines could be a source for lead. Choice *A* and Choice *C* are not discussed in the passage and are, therefore, incorrect. While Choice *B* is possible, it is not presented as the cause nor discussed in the passage.

46. A: Choice *A* is correct. While Choice *B,* Choice *C,* and Choice *D* are all reasonable possibilities, they are not discussed in the article. Though we know researchers do not have all the data, Choice *B*, there is no reference to this being related to source points. We do not get any information about how researchers are adapting the models to new information, Choice *C*, so that is incorrect as well. Finally, there is no data presented regarding how changes in the service lines impact the models being used.

47. C: Choice *C* is correct. There is no data to support Choice *A;* in fact, some of the research suggests that even changes the lines has little initial impact on lead levels. Choice *B* is mentioned as a mitigation and control factor, but it is not suggested that it's the most effective. Choice *D* is not discussed at all. In fact, lead levels are a concern regardless of the water source.

48. A: Choice *A* is correct. There was no mention in passage 1 of lead levels in the water sources themselves, so Choice *B* is incorrect. Similarly, passage 1 discusses corrosion inhibitors, but not as related to their introduction and its impact on the research, so Choice *C* is incorrect. There is no mention of false positives, so Choice *D* is incorrect.

49. D: Choice *D* is correct. Based on the sentence it is used in, one can infer the meaning from the context. Later in the sentence, the writer uses the word "dissolve" in place of "solubility." Choice *B* and Choice *C* are both the opposite of the correct meaning and, therefore, incorrect. Choice *A* is the result of the dissolution and also incorrect.

50. B: Choice *B* is correct. Both passages focus on the need to replace lead service lines in older homes as the first step to addressing lead levels in tap water. High-end water filtration systems are not discussed at all, so Choice *A* is incorrect. Lead levels were found in both types of water sources, so Choice *C* is not the correct answer. While Choice *D* is one of the methods discussed, it is secondary to the replacement of service lines and, therefore, incorrect.

51. B: Choice *B* is correct. In both passages, the researchers focus on the accumulation of minerals and scaling in pipes, problems that must be handled through service line replacement and corrosion inhibitors. While replacing lines in older homes, Choice *A,* is one solution, neither group believes it will resolve the issue. Choice *C* may be true, and though it is discussed in the second passage, it is not discussed in the first passage; nor does either passage discuss its role in future research. Finally, source point pollution is not discussed in either passage though water sources are discussed, so Choice *D* is incorrect.

52. D: Choice *D* is correct. Because of the scope of work, and because of the existence of lead in water up to four years after lead lines have been replaced in the home, one can infer that Choice *D* is the statement researchers would most disagree with. Because they do not discuss tap filtration, we cannot gauge where researchers would stand on how this method would work, so Choice *A* is incorrect. Well water is not without its own issues, particularly in relation to scaling and additional minerals. Researchers would likely agree that the issue is different rather than determining whether it's easier, so Choice *B* is incorrect. Finally, corrosion control, Choice *C*, is a valuable weapon, but researchers would not agree that it's the best option, based on both passages. Instead, they'd likely argue that corrosion control is part of a multi-step process.

Writing and Language Test

1. B: Here, a colon is used to introduce an explanation. Colons either introduce explanations or lists. Additionally, the quote ends with the punctuation inside the quotes, unlike Choice *C*.

2. A: The verb tense in this passage is predominantly in the present tense, so Choice *A* is the correct answer. Choice *B* is incorrect because the subject and verb do not agree. It should be "Education provides," not "Education provide." Choice *C* is incorrect because the passage is in present tense, and "Education will provide" is future tense. Choice *D* doesn't make sense when placed in the sentence.

3. D: The possessive form of the word "it" is "its." The contraction "it's" denotes "it is." Thus, Choice *A* is wrong. The word "raises" in Choice *B* makes the sentence grammatically incorrect. Choice *C* adds an apostrophe at the end of "its." While adding an apostrophe to most words would indicate possession, adding *'s* to the word "it" indicates a contraction.

4. C: The word *civilised* should be spelled *civilized.* The words *distinguishes* and *creatures* are both spelled correctly.

5. B: Choice *B* is correct because it provides clarity by describing what "myopic" means right after the word itself. Choice *A* is incorrect because the explanation of "myopic" comes before the word; thus, the meaning is skewed. It's possible that Choice *C* makes sense within context. However, it's not the *best* way to say this. Choice *D* is confusingly worded. Using "myopic focus" is not detrimental to society; however, the way *D* is worded makes it seem that way.

6. C: Again, we see where the second paragraph can be divided into two parts due to separate topics. The first section's main focus is education addressing the mind, body, and soul. The first section, then, could end with the concluding sentence, "The human heart and psyche ..." The next sentence to start a new paragraph would be "Education is a basic human right." The rest of this paragraph talks about what education is and some of its characteristics.

7. A: Choice *A* is correct because the phrase "others' ideas" is both plural and indicates possession. Choice *B* is incorrect because "other's" indicates only one "other" that's in possession of "ideas," which is incorrect. Choice *C* is incorrect because no possession is indicated. Choice *D* is incorrect because the word *other* does not end in *s*. *Others's* is not a correct form of the word in any situation.

8. D: This sentence must have a comma before *although* because the word *although* is connecting two independent clauses. Thus, Choices *B* and *C* are incorrect. Choice *A* is incorrect because the second sentence in the underlined section is a fragment.

9. C: Choice *C* is the correct choice because the word *their* indicates possession, and the text is talking about "their students," or the students of someone. Choice *A, there*, means at a certain place and is incorrect. Choice *B, they're*, is a contraction and means *they are*. Choice *D* is not a word.

10. B: Choice *B* uses all punctuation correctly in this sentence. In American English, single quotes should only be used if they are quotes within a quote, making Choices *A* and *C* incorrect. Additionally, punctuation here should go inside the quotes, making Choice *D* incorrect.

11. B: Choice *B* is correct because the conjunction *and* is used to connect phrases that are to be used jointly, such as teachers working hard to help students "identify salient information" and to "think critically." The conjunctions *so, but*, and *nor* are incorrect in the context of this sentence.

12. A: Choice *A* has consistent parallel structure with the verbs *read, identify*, and *determine*. Choices *B* and *C* have faulty parallel structure with the words *determining* and *identifying*. Choice *D* has incorrect subject/verb agreement. The sentence should read, "Students have to read ... identify ... and determine."

13. D: The correct choice for this sentence is that "they are ... shaped by the influences." The prepositions "for," "to," and "with" do not make sense in this context. People are *shaped by*, not *shaped for, shaped to,* or *shaped with*.

14. A: To see which answer is correct, it might help to place the subject, teachers, near the verb. Choice *A* is correct: "Teachers ... must strive" makes grammatical sense here. Choice *B* is incorrect because "Teachers ... to strive" does not make grammatical sense. Choice *C* is incorrect because "Teachers must not only respect ... but striving" eschews parallel structure. Choice *D* is incorrect because it is in past tense, and this passage is in present tense.

15. C: Choice *C* is correct because it uses an em-dash. Em-dashes are versatile. They can separate phrases that would otherwise be in parenthesis, or they can stand in for a colon. In this case, a colon would be another decent choice for this punctuation mark because the second sentence expands upon the first sentence. Choice *A* is incorrect because the statement is not a question. Choice *B* is incorrect because adding a comma here would create a comma splice. Choice *D* is incorrect because this creates a run-on sentence since the sentence contains two independent clauses.

16. B: Choice *B* is correct because it removes the apostrophe from *icon's*, since the noun *icon* is not possessing anything. This conveys the author's intent of setting *Frankenstein* apart from other icons of the romantic and science fiction genres. Choices *A* and *C* are therefore incorrect. Choice *D* is a good revision but alters the meaning of the sentence—*Frankenstein* is one of the icons, not the sole icon.

17. C: Choice *C* correctly adds a comma after *style*, successfully joining the dependent and the independent clauses as a single sentence. Choice *A* is incorrect because the dependent and independent clauses remain unsuccessfully combined without the comma. Choices *B* and *D* do nothing to fix this.

18. A: Choice *A* is correct, as the sentence doesn't require changes. Choice *B* incorrectly changes the noun *enlightenment* into the verb *enlighten*. Choices *C* and *D* alter the original meaning of the sentence.

19. B: Choice *B* is correct, fixing the incorrect split of *highlight*. This is a polyseme, a word combined from two unrelated words to make a new word. On their own, *high* and *light* make no sense for the sentence, making Choice *A* incorrect. Choice *C* incorrectly decapitalizes *Ancient*—since it modifies *Greece* and works with the noun to describe a civilization, *Ancient Greece* functions as a proper noun, which should be capitalized. Choice *D* uses *highlighting*, a gerund, but the present tense of *highlight* is what works with the rest of the sentence; to make this change, a comma would be needed after *Rome*.

20. A: Choice *A* is correct, as *not only* and *but also* are correlative pairs. In this sentence, *but* successfully transitions the first part into the second half, making punctuation unnecessary. Additionally, the use of *to* indicates that an idea or challenge is being presented to the reader. Choices *B, C*, and *D* are not as active, meaning these revisions weaken the sentence.

21. D: Choice *D* is correct, adding finer details to help the reader understand exactly what Prometheus did and his impact: fire came with knowledge and power. Choice *A* lacks a comma after *fire*. Choice *B* inserts unnecessary commas since *people* is not part of the list *knowledge and power*. Choice *C* is a strong revision but could be confusing, hinting that the fire was knowledge and power itself, as opposed to being symbolized by the fire.

22. C: Choice *C* reverses the order of the section, making the sentence more direct. Choice *A* lacks a comma after *gods*, and although Choice *B* adds this, the structure is too different from the first half of the sentence to flow correctly. Choice *D* is overly complicated and repetitious in its structure even though it doesn't need any punctuation.

23. B: Choice *B* fixes the two problems of the sentence, changing *faltered* to present tense in agreement with the rest of the passage, and correctly linking the two dependent clauses. Choice *A* is therefore incorrect. Choice *C* does not correct the past tense of *faltered*. Choice *D* correctly adds the conjunction *by*, but it lacks a comma after the conjunction *yet*.

24. C: Choice *C* successfully applies a comma after *power*, distinguishing the causes of Frankenstein's suffering and maintaining parallel structure. Choice *A* is thus incorrect. Choice *B* lacks the necessary punctuation and unnecessarily changes *lack* to a gerund. Choice *D* is unnecessarily wordy, making the sentence more cumbersome.

25. D: Choice *D* correctly inserts an apostrophe into the contraction *doesn't*. Choice *A* is incorrect because of this omission. Choices *B* and *C* are better than the original but do not fit well with the informal tone of the passage.

26. B: Choice *B* is correct, successfully combining the two independent clauses of this compound sentence by adding a comma before *and* to create the effective pause and transition between clauses. Choice *A* does not join the independent clauses correctly. Choices *C* and *D* offer alternate ways of joining these clauses, but since *and* is already part of the sentence, adding the comma is the most logical choice. This also keeps the informal tone set by the rest of the passage.

27. C: Choice *C* correctly fixes the homophone issue of *their* and *they're*. *Their* implies ownership, which is not needed here. The author intends *they're*, a contraction of *they are*. Thus, Choices *A* and *B* are incorrect because they use the homophone *there*. Choice *D* eliminates the homophone issue altogether, but the sentence becomes more clunky because of that.

28. B: Choice *B* correctly joins the two independent clauses with a comma before *but*. Choice *A* is incorrect because, without the comma, it is a run-on sentence. Choice *C* also lacks punctuation and uses *however*, which should be reserved for starting a new sentence or perhaps after a semicolon. Choice *D* is incorrect because the semicolon throws off the sentence structure and is incorrectly used; the correct revision would have also removed *but*.

29. A: Choice *A* is correct because the sentence does not require modification. Choice *B* is incorrect because it uses the faulty subject-verb agreement, "Physical proof are." Choice *C* is incorrect because a comma would need to follow *exists*. Choice *D* is incorrect because the comma after *science* is unnecessary.

30. D: Choice *D* correctly changes *this* to *the* and retains *validity*, making it the right choice. Choices *A* and *B* keep *this*, which is not as specific as *the*. Choice *C* incorrectly pluralizes *validity*.

31. A: Choice *A* is correct because the sentence is fine without revisions. Choice *B* is incorrect, since removing *there is* is unnecessary and confusing. Choice *C* is incorrect since it inserts an unnecessary comma. Choice *D* introduces a homophone issue: *weather* refers to climatic states and atmospheric events, while *whether* expresses doubt, which is the author's intent.

32. C: Choice *C* correctly changes *continuing* to the present tense. Choice *A* is incorrect because of this out-of-place gerund use. Choice *B* not only does not fix this issue but also incorrectly changes *describe* into a gerund. While Choice *D* correctly uses *continue*, *describe* is incorrectly put in the past tense.

33. D: Choice *D* is correct because it moves the modifying clause "including Native Americans" so that it comes after what it describes: "Ancient civilizations." This adds clarity to the sentence and makes it more direct. Choice *A* uses redundant phrases as well and including. It also lacks punctuation. Choice *B* is poorly constructed, taking out the clearer including. Choice *C* also makes little sense.

34. B: For this question, place the underlined sentence in each prospective choice's position. Leaving the sentence in place is incorrect because the father "going crazy" doesn't logically follow the fact that he was a "city slicker." Choice *C* is incorrect because the sentence in question is not a concluding sentence and does not transition smoothly into the second paragraph. Choice *D* is incorrect because the sentence doesn't necessarily need to be omitted since it logically follows the very first sentence in the passage.

35. D: Choice *D* is correct because "As it turns out" indicates a contrast from the previous sentiment, that the RV was a great purchase. Choice *A* is incorrect because the sentence needs an effective transition from the paragraph before. Choice *B* is incorrect because the text indicates it *is* surprising that the RV was a great purchase because the author was skeptical beforehand. Choice *C* is incorrect because the transition "furthermore" does not indicate a contrast.

36. B: This sentence calls for parallel structure. Choice *B* is correct because the verbs "wake," "eat," and "break" are consistent in tense and parts of speech. Choice *A* is incorrect because the words "wake" and "eat" are present tense while the word "broke" is in past tense. Choice *C* is incorrect because this turns the sentence into a question, which doesn't make sense within the context. Choice *D* is incorrect because it breaks tense with the rest of the passage. "Waking," "eating," and "breaking" are all present participles, and the context around the sentence is in past tense.

37. C: Choice *C* is correct because it is clear and fits within the context of the passage. Choice *A* is incorrect because "We rejoiced as 'hackers'" does not explain what was meant by "hackers" or why it was a cause for rejoicing. Choice *B* is incorrect because it does not mention a solution being found and is therefore not specific enough. Choice *D* is incorrect because the meaning is eschewed by the helping verb "had to rejoice," and the sentence suggests that rejoicing was necessary to "hack" a solution.

38. A: The original sentence is correct because the verb tense as well as the order of the sentence makes sense in the given context. Choice *B* is incorrect because the order of the words makes the sentence more confusing than it otherwise would be. Choice *C* is incorrect because "We are even making" is in present tense. Choice *D* is incorrect because "We will make" is future tense. The surrounding text of the sentence is in past tense.

39. B: Choice *B* is correct because there is no punctuation needed if a dependent clause ("while traveling across America") is located behind the independent clause ("it allowed us to share adventures"). Choice *A* is incorrect because there are two dependent clauses connected and no independent clause, and a complete sentence requires at least one independent clause. Choice *C* is incorrect because of the same reason as Choice *A*. Semicolons connect closely related independent clauses on either side of the semicolon. Choice *D* is incorrect because the dash simply interrupts the complete sentence.

40. C: The rule for "me" and "I" is that one should use "I" when it is the subject pronoun of a sentence, and "me" when it is the object pronoun of the sentence. Break the sentence up to see if "I" or "me" should be used. To say "Those are memories that I have now shared" makes more sense than to say "Those are memories that me have now shared." Choice *D* is incorrect because "my siblings" should come before "I."

41. B: Choice *B* is correct because it adds an apostrophe to *ones*, which indicates *one's* possession of *survival*. Choice *A* doesn't do this, so it is incorrect. This is the same for Choice *C*, but that option also takes out the crucial comma after *Jiu-Jitsu*. Choice *D* is incorrect because it changes *play* to *plays*. This disagrees with the plural *martial arts*, which is given by having an example of its many forms, *Jiu-Jitsu*. Therefore, *play* is required.

42. C: Choice *C* is the best answer because it most clearly defines the point that the author is trying to make. The original sentence would need a comma after *however* in order to continue the sentence fluidly—but this option isn't available. Choice *B* is close, but this option changes the meaning of the sentence. Therefore, the best alternative is to begin the sentence with *however* and have a comma follow right after it in order to introduce a new idea. The original context is still maintained, but the flow of the language is more streamlined. Thus, Choice *A* is incorrect. Choice *D* would need a comma before and after *however*, so it is also incorrect.

43. A: Choice *A* is the best answer for several reasons. To begin, the section is grammatically correct in using a semicolon to connect the two independent clauses. This allows the two ideas to be connected without separating them. In this context, the semicolon makes more sense for the overall sentence structure and passage as a whole. Choice *B* is incorrect because it forms a run-on. Choice *C* applies a comma in incorrect positions. Choice *D* separates the sentence in a place that does not make sense for the context.

44. D: Choice *D* is the correct answer because it fixes two key issues. First, *their* is incorrectly used. *Their* is a possessive indefinite pronoun and also an antecedent—neither of these fit the context of the sentence, so Choices *A* and *B* are incorrect. What should be used instead is *they're*, which is the contraction of *they are*, emphasizing action or the result of action in this case. Choice *D* also corrects another contraction-related issue with *its*. Again, *its* indicates possession, while *it's* is the contraction of *it is*. The latter is what's needed for the sentence to make sense and be grammatically correct. Thus, Choice *C* is also incorrect.

45. A: Choice *B* is incorrect because it lacks a comma after philosophy, needed to link the first clause with the second. Choice *C* changes *its* to *it's*; since it is does not make sense in this sentence, this is incorrect. Choice *D* is incorrect because *its* is already a possessive and does not need an apostrophe.

Math Test

Calculator Questions

1. B: 300 miles in 4 hours is $\frac{300}{4} = 75$ miles per hour. In 1.5 hours, the car will go 1.5×75 miles, or 112.5 miles.

2. C: The best way to solve this problem is by using a system of equations. We know that Jan bought $90 worth of apples ($a$) and oranges ($o$) at $1 and $2 respectively. That means our first equation is:

$$1(a) + 2(o) = 90$$

We also know that she bought an equal number of apples and oranges, which gives us our second equation $a = o$. We can then replace a with o in the first equation to give:

$$1(o) + 2(o) = 90 \text{ or } 3(o) = 90$$

Which yields,

$$o = 30$$

Thus, Jan bought 30 oranges (and 30 apples).

3. C: The formula for the volume of a box with rectangular sides is the length times width times height, so $5 \times 6 \times 3 = 90$ cubic feet.

4. D: First, the train's journey in the real word is $3 \times 50 = 150$ miles. On the map, 1 inch corresponds to 10 miles, so that is equivalent to $\frac{150}{10} = 15$ inches on the map.

5. B: The total trip time is $1 + 3.5 + 0.5 = 5$ hours. The total time driving is $1 + 0.5 = 1.5$ hours. So, the fraction of time spent driving is $\frac{1.5}{5}$ or $\frac{3}{10}$.

To get the percentage, convert this to a fraction out of 100. The numerator and denominator are multiplied by 10, with a result of $\frac{30}{100}$. The percentage is the numerator in a fraction out of 100, so 30%.

6. B: The formula for the volume of a cylinder is $\pi r^2 h$, where r is the radius and h is the height. The diameter is twice the radius, so these barrels have a radius of 1 foot. That means each barrel has a volume of:

$$\pi \times 1^2 \times 3 = 3\pi \text{ ft}^3$$

Since there are three of them, the total is:

$$3 \times 3\pi = 9\pi \text{ ft}^3$$

7. A: The tip is not taxed, so he pays 5% tax only on the \$10. The tax is 5% of \$10, or $0.05 \times 10 = \$0.50$. Add up $\$10 + \$2 + \$0.50$ to get \$12.50.

8. A: In order to determine the savings needed per day, divide up \$150 into four equal parts:

$$\frac{\$150}{4\text{ d}} = \frac{\$37.5}{\text{d}}$$

So, she needs to save an average of \$37.50 per day.

9. D: The number of days can be found by taking the total amount Bernard needs to make and dividing it by the amount he earns per day:

$$\frac{300}{80} = \frac{30}{8} = \frac{15}{4} = 3.75$$

But Bernard is only working full days, so he will need to work 4 days since 3 days is not a sufficient amount of time.

10. A: The value went up by $\$165{,}000 - \$150{,}000 = \$15{,}000$.

Out of \$150,000, this is $\frac{15{,}000}{150{,}000} = \frac{1}{10}$ or 0.1. To get the percentage, multiply 0.1 by 100 to get 10%.

11. D: The total faculty is:

$$15 + 20 = 35$$

So, the ratio is 35 : 200. Then, divide both of these numbers by 5, since 5 is a common factor to both, with a result of 7 : 40.

12. B: The journey will be $5 \times 3 = 15$ miles. A car traveling at 60 miles per hour is traveling at 1 mile per minute. The resulting equation would be:

$$\frac{15\text{ mi}}{1\frac{\text{mi}}{\text{min}}} = 15\text{ min}$$

Therefore, it will take 15 minutes to make the journey.

13. A: Taylor's total income is $\$20{,}000 + \$10{,}000 = \$30{,}000$. Fifteen percent as a fraction is $\frac{15}{100} = \frac{3}{20}$. So,

$$\frac{3}{20} \times \$30{,}000 = \frac{\$90{,}000}{20}$$

$$\frac{\$9{,}000}{2} = \$4{,}500$$

14. B: Since the answer will be in cubic feet rather than inches, the first step is to convert from inches to feet for the dimensions of the box. There are 12 inches per foot, so the box is $24 \div 12 = 2$ feet wide, $18 \div 12 = 1.5$ feet deep, and $12 \div 12 = 1$ foot high. The volume is the product of these three together:

$$2 \times 1.5 \times 1 = 3 \text{ cubic feet}$$

15. D: Kristen bought four DVDs, which would cost a total of $4 \times 15 = \$60$. She spent a total of $100, so she spent $\$100 - \$60 = \$40$ on CDs. Since they cost $10 each, she must have purchased $40 \div 10 = 4$ CDs.

16. D: This problem can be solved by setting up a proportion involving the given information and the unknown value. The proportion is:

$$\frac{21 \text{ pages}}{4 \text{ nights}} = \frac{140 \text{ pages}}{x \text{ nights}}$$

We can cross-multiply to get $21x = 4 \times 140$. Solving this, we find $x \approx 26.67$. Since this is not an integer, we round up to 27 nights. 26 nights would not give Sarah enough time.

17. D: This problem can be solved by using unit conversion. The initial units are miles per minute. The final units need to be feet per second. Converting miles to feet uses the equivalence statement $1 \text{ mi} = 5{,}280 \text{ ft}$. Converting minutes to seconds uses the equivalence statement $1 \text{ min} = 60 \text{ s}$. Setting up the ratios to convert the units is shown in the following equation:

$$\frac{72 \text{ mi}}{90 \text{ min}} \times \frac{1 \text{ min}}{60 \text{ s}} \times \frac{5{,}280 \text{ ft}}{1 \text{ mi}} = 70.4 \frac{\text{ft}}{\text{s}}$$

The initial units cancel out, and the new units are left.

18. C: The total percentage of a pie chart equals 100%. We can see that CD sales make up less than half of the chart (50%) and more than a quarter (25%), and the only answer choice that meets these criteria is Choice *C*, 40%.

19. B: Since $850 is the price after a 20% discount, $850 represents 80% of the original price. To determine the original price, set up a proportion with the ratio of the sale price (850) to the original price (unknown) equal to the ratio of the sale percentage (where x represents the unknown original price):

$$\frac{850}{x} = \frac{80}{100}$$

To solve a proportion, cross multiply and set the products equal to each other:

$$(850)(100) = (80)(x)$$

Multiplying each side results in the equation:

$$85{,}000 = 80x$$

To solve for x, divide both sides by 80:

$$\frac{85{,}000}{80} = \frac{80x}{80}$$

$$x = 1{,}062.5$$

Remember that x represents the original price. Subtracting the sale price from the original price ($\$1{,}062.50 - \$850$) indicates that Frank saved \$212.50.

20. C: $40N$ would be 4,000% of N. All of the other coefficients are equivalent to $\frac{40}{100}$ or 40%.

21. C: An x–intercept is the point where the graph crosses the x–axis. At this point, the value of y is 0. To determine if an equation has an x–intercept of –2, substitute –2 for x, and calculate the value of y. If the value of –2 for x corresponds with a y–value of 0, then the equation has an x–intercept of –2. The only answer choice that produces this result is Choice *C.*

$$0 = (-2)^2 + 5(-2) + 6$$

22. C: There are 34 girls who are potty-trained out of a total of 52 girls:

$$34 \div 52 = 0.65 = 65\%$$

23. A: A sample statistic indicates information about the data that was collected (in this case, the heights of those surveyed). A population parameter describes an aspect of the entire population (in this case, all twelve-year-old boys in the United States). A confidence interval would consist of a range of heights likely to include the actual population parameter. Measurement error relates to the validity of the data that was collected.

24. C: To ensure valid results, samples should be taken across the entire scope of the study. Since all states are not equally populated, representing each state proportionately would result in a more accurate statistic.

25. D: Exponential functions can be written in the form: $y = a \times b^x$. The equation for an exponential function can be written given the y-intercept (a) and the growth rate (b).

The y-intercept is the output (y) when the input (x) equals zero. It can be thought of as an "original value," or starting point. The value of b is the rate at which the original value increases ($b > 1$) or decreases ($b < 1$).

In this scenario, the y-intercept, a, would be \$1200, and the growth rate, b, would be 1.01 (100% of the original value combined with 1% interest, or $100\% + 1\% = 101\% = 1.01$).

26. C: To get 85% of a number, multiply it by 0.85.

$$\frac{17}{20} \times \frac{20}{1} = 17$$

27. A: To find the fraction of the bill that the first three people pay, the fractions need to be added, which means finding the common denominator. The common denominator will be 60:

$$\frac{1}{5}+\frac{1}{4}+\frac{1}{3}=\frac{12}{60}+\frac{15}{60}+\frac{20}{60}=\frac{47}{60}$$

The remainder of the bill is:

$$1-\frac{47}{60}=\frac{60}{60}-\frac{47}{60}=\frac{13}{60}$$

28. D: $9\frac{3}{10}$. To convert a decimal to a fraction, remember that any number to the left of the decimal point will be a whole number. Then, sense 0.3 goes to the tenths place, it can be placed over 10.

29. A: Convert the mixed fractions to improper fractions: $\frac{11}{3}-\frac{9}{5}$. Subtract using 15 as a common denominator and rewrite to get rid of the improper fraction:

$$\frac{11}{3}-\frac{9}{5}=\frac{55}{15}-\frac{27}{15}=\frac{28}{15}=1\frac{13}{15}$$

30. A: Dividing by 98 can be approximated by dividing by 100, which would mean shifting the decimal point of the numerator to the left by 2. The result is 4.2 and rounds to 4.

31. B: First, separate out and add the whole numbers from the mixed fractions:

$$4\frac{1}{3}+3\frac{3}{4}$$

$$4+3+\frac{1}{3}+\frac{3}{4}$$

$$7+\frac{1}{3}+\frac{3}{4}$$

Adding the fractions gives:

$$\frac{1}{3}+\frac{3}{4}$$

$$\frac{4}{12}+\frac{9}{12}$$

$$\frac{13}{12}$$

$$1+\frac{1}{12}$$

Thus,

$$7+\frac{1}{3}+\frac{3}{4}=7+1+\frac{1}{12}=8\frac{1}{12}$$

32. C: The average is calculated by adding all six numbers, then dividing by 6. The first five numbers have a sum of 25. This means $\frac{(25+n)}{6} = 6$, where n is the unknown number. Multiplying both sides by 6, we get $25 + n = 36$, which means $n = 11$.

33. C: The domain consists of all possible inputs, or x-values. The scenario states that the function approximates the population between the years 1900 and 2000. It also states that $x = 0$ represents the year 1900 with x representing the year (where 1900 is $x = 0$) and y representing the population (in thousands). Therefore, the year 2000 would be represented by $x = 100$. Only inputs between 0 and 100 are relevant in this case.

34. C: Nothing is added to x and y since the center is 0 and 5^2 is 25. Choice *A* is not the correct answer because you do not subtract the radius from x and y. Choice *B* is not the correct answer because you must square the radius on the right side of the equation. Choice *D* is not the correct answer because you do not add the radius to x and y in the equation.

35. D: Subtract the center from the x- and y-values of the equation and square the radius on the right side of the equation. Choice *A* is not the correct answer because you need to square the radius of the equation. Choice *B* is not the correct answer because you do not square the centers of the equation. Choice *C* is not the correct answer because you need to subtract (not add) the centers of the equation.

36. C: Plug in the values for x and y to discover that the solution works, which is:

$$(-3)^2 + (-4)^2 = 25$$

Choices *A* and *B* are not the correct answers since the solution works. Choice *D* is not the correct answer because there is enough information to tell where the given point lies on the circle.

37. D: The correct answer of 20 °C can be found using the appropriate temperature conversion formula:

$$°C = (°F - 32) \times \frac{5}{9}$$

38. D: The slope is given by the change in y divided by the change in x. Specifically, it's:

$$slope = \frac{y_2 - y_1}{x_2 - x_1}$$

The first point is $(-5, -3)$, and the second point is $(0, -1)$. Work from left to right when identifying coordinates. Thus, the point on the left is point 1 $(-5, -3)$ and the point on the right is point 2 $(0, -1)$.

Now we need to just plug those numbers into the equation:

$$slope = \frac{-1 - (-3)}{0 - (-5)}$$

It can be simplified to:

$$slope = \frac{-1+3}{0+5}$$

$$slope = \frac{2}{5}$$

39. B: The figure is composed of three sides of a square and a semicircle. The sides of the square are simply added:

$$8 \text{ in} + 8 \text{ in} + 8 \text{ in} = 24 \text{ in}$$

The circumference of a circle is found by the equation $C = 2\pi r$. The radius is 4 in, so the circumference of the circle is 25.13 in. Only half of the circle makes up the outer border of the figure (part of the perimeter) so half of 25.13 in is 12.565 in. Therefore, the total perimeter is:

$$24 \text{ in} + 12.565 \text{ in} = 36.565 \text{ in}$$

40. A: The first step is to determine the unknown, which is in terms of the length, l.

The second step is to translate the problem into the equation using the perimeter of a rectangle:

$$P = 2l + 2w$$

The width is the length minus 2 centimeters. The resulting equation is:

$$2l + 2(l-2) = 44$$

The equation can be solved as follows:

$2l + 2l - 4 = 44$	Apply the distributive property on the left side of the equation
$4l - 4 = 44$	Combine like terms on the left side of the equation
$4l = 48$	Add 4 to both sides of the equation
$l = 12$	Divide both sides of the equation by 4

The length of the rectangle is 12 centimeters. The width is the length minus 2 centimeters, which is 10 centimeters. Checking the answers for length and width forms the following equation:

$$44 = 2(12) + 2(10)$$

The equation can be solved using the order of operations to form a true statement: $44 = 44$.

41. B: $3x^2 - 3x + 11$. By distributing the implied one in front of the first set of parentheses and the -1 in front of the second set of parentheses, the parentheses can be eliminated:

$$1(5x^2 - 3x + 4) - 1(2x^2 - 7)$$

$$5x^2 - 3x + 4 - 2x^2 + 7$$

Next, like terms (same variables with same exponents) are combined by adding the coefficients and keeping the variables and their powers the same:

$$5x^2 - 3x + 4 - 2x^2 + 7 = 3x^2 - 3x + 11$$

42. A: This question involves the percent formula. Since we're beginning with a percent, also known as a number over 100, we'll put 39 on the right side of the equation:

$$\frac{x}{164} = \frac{39}{100}$$

Now, multiply 164 and 39 to get 6,396, which then needs to be divided by 100.

$$6{,}396 \div 100 = 63.96$$

43. C: Kimberley worked 4.5 hours at the rate of $\$10$ / h and 1 hour at the rate of $\$12$ / h. The problem states that her time is rounded to the nearest hour, so the 4.5 hours would round up to 5 hours at the rate of $\$10$ / h.

$$(5\text{h}) \times \left(\frac{\$10}{\text{h}}\right) + (1\text{h}) \times \left(\frac{\$12}{\text{h}}\right) = \$50 + \$12 = \$62$$

44. B: The first step is to calculate the difference between the larger value and the smaller value:

$$378 - 252 = 126$$

To calculate this difference as a percentage of the original value, and thus calculate the percentage *increase*, 126 is divided by 252, then this result is multiplied by 100 to find the percentage: 50%, or Choice *B*.

No Calculator Questions

45. C: In order to find the percentage by which the value of the car has been reduced, the current cash value should be subtracted from the initial value and then the difference divided by the initial value. The result should be multiplied by 100 to find the percentage decrease.

$$\frac{20{,}000 - 8{,}000}{20{,}000} = 0.6$$

$$(0.6) \times 100 = 60\%$$

46. A: This problem can be solved by simple multiplication and addition. Since the sale date is over six years apart, 6 can be multiplied by 12 for the number of months in a year, and then the remaining 4 months can be added.

$$(6 \times 12) + 4 = ?$$

$$72 + 4 = 76$$

47. D: This problem can be solved using basic arithmetic. Xavier starts with 20 apples, then gives his sister half, so 20 divided by 2.

$$\frac{20}{2} = 10$$

He then gives his neighbor 6, so 6 is subtracted from 10.

$$10 - 6 = 4$$

Lastly, he uses $\frac{3}{4}$ of his apples to make an apple pie, so to find remaining apples, the first step is to subtract $\frac{3}{4}$ from one and then multiply the difference by 4.

$$\left(1 - \frac{3}{4}\right) \times 4 = ?$$

$$\left(\frac{4}{4} - \frac{3}{4}\right) \times 4 = ?$$

$$\left(\frac{1}{4}\right) \times 4 = 1$$

48. B: To find the value of n, multiply $\frac{5}{2}$ by the reciprocal of $\frac{1}{3}$ and simplify:

$$n = \frac{5}{2} \div \frac{1}{3} = \frac{5}{2} \times \frac{3}{1} = \frac{15}{2} = 7.5$$

49. A: The total fraction taken up by green and red shirts will be:

$$\frac{1}{3} + \frac{2}{5} = \frac{5}{15} + \frac{6}{15} = \frac{11}{15}$$

The remaining fraction is:

$$1 - \frac{11}{15} = \frac{15}{15} - \frac{11}{15} = \frac{4}{15}$$

50. C: If she has used $\frac{1}{3}$ of the paint, she has $\frac{2}{3}$ remaining. The mixed fraction can be converted because $2\frac{1}{2}$ gallons is the same as $\frac{5}{2}$ gallons. The calculation is:

$$\frac{2}{3} \times \frac{5}{2} = \frac{5}{3} = 1\frac{2}{3} \text{ gal}$$

51. C: The volume of a cylinder is $\pi r^2 h$, and $\pi \times 6^2 \times 2$ is $72\,\pi$ cm^3. Choice *A* is not the correct answer because that is only $6^2 \times \pi$. Choice *B* is not the correct answer because that is $2^2 \times 6 \times \pi$. Choice *D* is not the correct answer because that is $2^3 \times 6 \times \pi$.

52. B: This answer is correct because $3^2 + 4^2$ is $9 + 16$, which is 25. Taking the square root of 25 is 5. Choice *A* is not the correct answer because that is $3 + 4$. Choice *C* is not the correct answer because that is stopping at $3^2 + 4^2$ is $9 + 16$, which is 25. Choice *D* is not the correct answer because that is 3×4.

53. A: Setting up a proportion is the easiest way to represent this situation. The proportion is $\frac{20}{x} = \frac{40}{100}$, and cross-multiplication can be used to solve for x. Here, $40x = 2000$, so $x = 50$.

54. To solve the problem, a proportion is written consisting of ratios comparing distance and time. One way to set up the proportion is $\frac{3}{48} = \frac{5}{x}$ or $\left(\frac{distance}{time} = \frac{distance}{time}\right)$, where x represents the unknown value of time. To solve a proportion, the ratios are cross-multiplied:

$$(3)(x) = (5)(48)$$

$$3x = 240$$

The equation is solved by isolating the variable, or dividing by 3 on both sides, to produce $x = 80$.

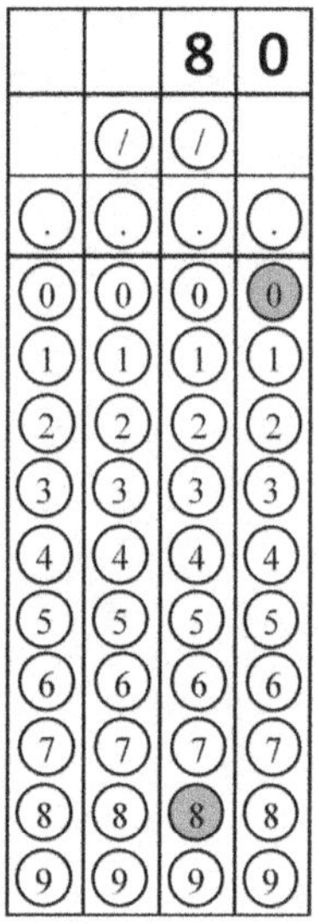

55. The perimeter is found by calculating the sum of all sides of the polygon:

$$9 + 9 + 9 + 8 + 8 + s = 56$$

s is the missing side length. Therefore, $43 + s = 56$. The missing side length is 13 cm.

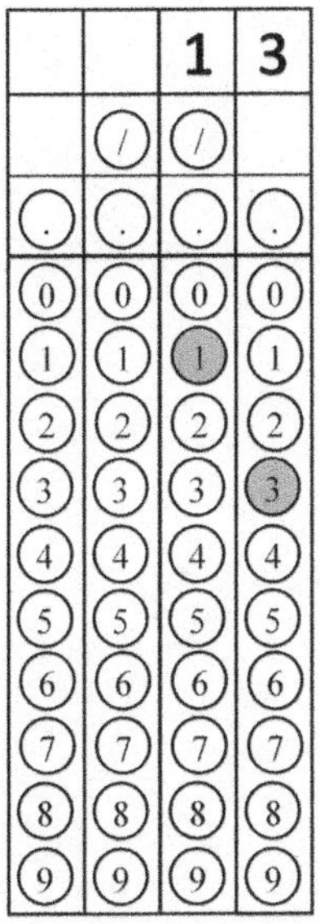

56. When x and y are complementary angles, the sine of x is equal to the cosine of y. The complementary angle of 30 is $90 - 30 = 60$ degrees. Therefore, the answer is 60 degrees.

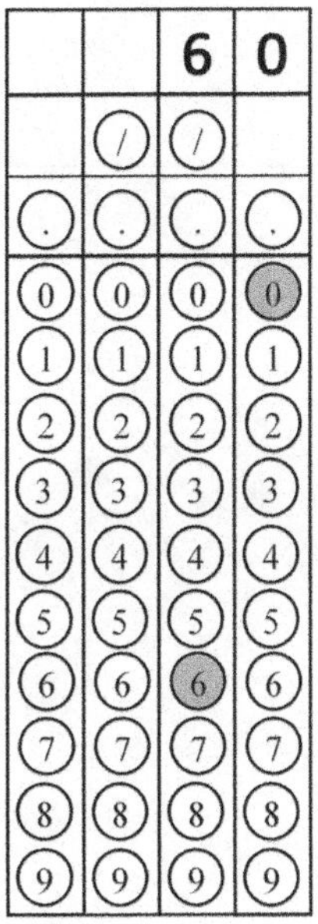

57. Start with the original equation: $x - 2xy + 2y$, then replace each instance of x with a 2, and each instance of y with a 3 to get:

$$2^2 - 2 \times 2 \times 3 + 2 \times 3^2$$

$$4 - 12 + 18 = 10$$

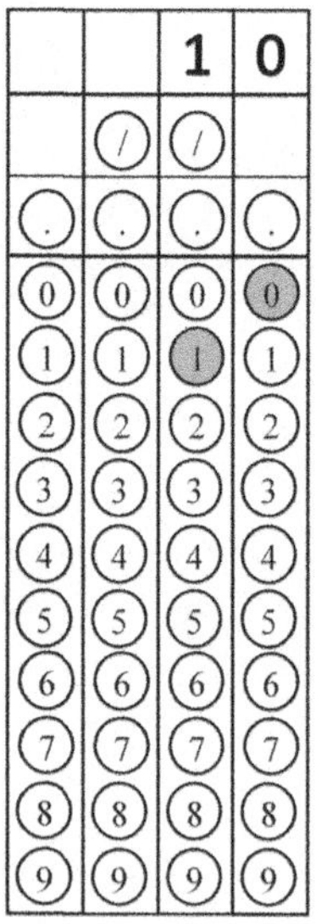

58. Add 3 to both sides to get $4x = 8$. Then divide both sides by 4 to get $x = 2$.

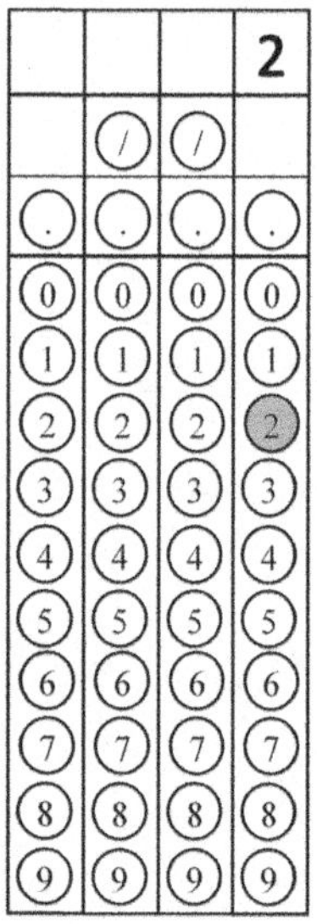

SAT Practice Tests #3, #4, #5, #6, and #7

To keep the size of this book manageable, save paper, and provide a digital test-taking experience, the 3rd - 7th practice tests can be found online. Scan the QR code or go to this link to access it:

testprepbooks.com/bonus/sat

SCAN ME

The first time you access the tests, you will need to register as a "new user" and verify your email address.

If you have any issues, please email support@testprepbooks.com.

Dear SAT Test Taker,

Thank you for purchasing this study guide for your SAT exam. We hope that we exceeded your expectations.

Our goal in creating this study guide was to cover all of the topics that you will see on the test. We also strove to make our practice questions as similar as possible to what you will encounter on test day. With that being said, if you found something that you feel was not up to your standards, please send us an email and let us know.

We would also like to let you know about other books in our catalog that may interest you.

ACCUPLACER

This can be found on Amazon: amazon.com/dp/1637750250

TSI

amazon.com/dp/1637754434

We have study guides in a wide variety of fields. If the one you are looking for isn't listed above, then try searching for it on Amazon or send us an email.

Thanks Again and Happy Testing!
Product Development Team
info@studyguideteam.com

Made in the USA
Monee, IL
05 February 2024

52958240R00168